The Distributional Impact of Taxes and Transfers

DIRECTIONS IN DEVELOPMENT
Poverty

The Distributional Impact of Taxes and Transfers

Evidence from Eight Low- and Middle-Income Countries

Gabriela Inchauste and Nora Lustig, Editors

WORLD BANK GROUP

Contents

Figures

Tables

Foreword

In addition to its impact on economic growth and macroeconomic stability, fiscal policy affects the distribution of income across households and individuals through the use of taxes and expenditures. As a result, policy makers and development partners are likely to be interested in the answers to, among others, the following questions: What is the combined impact of taxes and transfers on poverty and inequality? How progressive or regressive are different fiscal interventions, and what are their contributions to the overall impact? What is the distributive efficiency of the existing fiscal package? What is the distributional impact of a particular policy reform? What are the characteristics of net payers into and net beneficiaries from the fiscal package?

The World Bank has partnered with the Commitment to Equity (CEQ) Institute at Tulane University to answer these questions using the Institute's comprehensive fiscal incidence diagnostic tool. This tool—the CEQ Assessment—is designed to assess how taxation and public expenditures affect the income of different households, individuals, and socioeconomic groups as well as the distribution of income across the entire population.

This volume presents a set of studies for low- and middle-income countries that use the CEQ approach to examine the distributional effects of individual taxes, transfers, and subsidies as well as their combined impact. Most of the case studies were produced with the objective of informing the World Bank in-country dialogue on fiscal policy or fiscal reform. Often the results from the CEQ assessments both influenced the decisions made by the governments that had requested the work and spurred interest in this kind of analysis among a broader set of client countries.

Until recently, evidence on the distributional impacts of taxes and spending in developing countries was relatively scarce, typically partial, and not comparable across countries. In this context, the CEQ approach aims to be as comprehensive as possible by evaluating the distributional impact of both taxes and expenditures. This is important because often those who actually bear the burden of taxes (economic incidence) differ from those who are legally liable to make payments to tax authorities (statutory incidence). Similarly, the benefits of different public spending programs are likely to vary across socioeconomic groups and types of households. Consequently, while conducting incidence analysis for each fiscal intervention helps to determine whether individual interventions are progressive or redistributive, assessing their combined effects can provide important additional insights on the distributional impacts and the redistributive efficiency of the overall fiscal package. In addition, the application of a common analytical framework to all case studies allows for cross-country comparability and benchmarking, both of which have proven to be powerful and influential tools in the context of in-country policy dialogue.

The studies presented in this volume are part of a larger research effort led by Tulane's CEQ Institute in collaboration with the World Bank and other institutions aimed at increasing the information available on fiscal incidence in developing countries. To the extent that these assessments provide an evidence base for and bring an equity lens to the decision-making process surrounding tax and spending policy reforms, we hope they will be valuable to both policy makers and development practitioners.

Carolina Sanchez-Paramo
Senior Director
Poverty and Equity Global Practice
The World Bank

Acknowledgments

This book is a partnership between the Commitment to Equity Institute and the World Bank. We are grateful to the many people in both institutions who supported it throughout its three-year lifespan. We would like to thank Carolina Sanchez-Paramo, Ana Revenga, and Carlos Silva-Jauregui, who supported the project's completion, as well as Jaime Saavedra and Christina Malmberg-Calvo, who supported the birth and initial stages of the project.

We are also very grateful to Francisco Ferreira and David Coady, who commented on various versions of the work, from research proposal to finished papers. The final product has also benefited from useful peer-review comments from Shubham Chaudhuri, Aline Coudouel, Johannes Hoogeveen, Blanca Moreno-Dodson, and Rashmi Shankar.

We are similarly indebted to a number of participants in seminars and workshops that took place throughout the life of this project as well as to those who assisted with earlier versions of the chapters, including James Alm, Gary Burtless, Samuel Freije-Rodriguez, Jorge Martinez-Vasquez, Cormac O'Dea, Ian Preston, David Philipps, Luis Serven, and Sally Wallace.

The book would not have been possible without the research and technical assistance from Sean Higgins, who provided guidance, codes, and in-depth quality control. Sandra Martínez ensured the final consistency of the tables and figures. Ali Enami, Jacob Edelson, Nicole Florack, Xinghao Gong, Catherine Lee, and David Roberts supported the quality control effort.

Our greatest debt, of course, is to the authors of the eight case studies, who really wrote the book and stood by us in the many iterations and consistency checks and throughout the learning process. Their names and affiliations are listed separately in the coming pages. We thank them profoundly for their commitment and endurance during the long process of producing this volume. Finally, the book would not have been possible without the dedication, professionalism, and attention to detail of our editor, Mary A. Anderson.

This book was cofunded by the Poverty and Equity Global Practice and the Poverty and Social Impact Analysis (PSIA) Multi-Donor Trust Fund, and the CEQ Institute at Tulane University, which gratefully acknowledges the support of the Bill & Melinda Gates Foundation and Tulane's Center for Inter-American Policy and Research (CIPR).

About the Authors

Rythia Afkar is an economist in the World Bank's Education Global Practice, based in Jakarta, Indonesia. She has worked on a wide range of economic policy issues in areas including education, poverty, and social protection. She has a master's degree in quantitative economics from Pantheon-Sorbonne University and a doctorate from the University of Bonn.

Shamma Alam is an assistant professor in the Department of International Studies at Dickinson College. His areas of expertise are development economics, health economics, and demography. He has published in top academic journals, such as the *Journal of Health Economics* and *Journal of Agricultural and Resource Economics*. Before working at the World Bank as a consultant, he served as a consultant to the Agriculture Policies team at the Bill & Melinda Gates Foundation. He holds a doctorate in economics from the University of Washington in Seattle.

Nisha Arunatilake is a research fellow and the head of Labor, Employment, and Human Resource Development Policy unit at the Institute of Policy Studies of Sri Lanka (IPS). Since joining the IPS in 1995, her research and publications have covered various dimensions of development, especially in the areas of education, health, labor, employment, and social protection. As a graduate student, she worked at the Center for Health Policy & Inequalities Research at Duke University, where she conducted policy-related research on substance abuse and aging. She has also participated in several professional training courses, including "Labor Market Policies" conducted by the World Bank Institute and "Assessment of the Poverty Impact of Public Programs" conducted by the Canadian government's International Development Research Centre. She was a visiting researcher at the United Nations Educational, Scientific, and Cultural Organization International Institute for Education Planning. She holds a doctorate in economics from Duke University.

Elena Bondarenko is an economist in the World Bank's Macroeconomics and Fiscal Management Global Practice. Her recent work has focused on fiscal policy, economic growth, and distribution issues in Central Asia, the Russian Federation, and the South Caucasus. She has led projects analyzing fiscal accounts and implementation completion results of the Bank's development policy operations.

Before joining the World Bank, she worked at Cushman & Wakefield, conducting in-depth macroeconomic policy impact analysis on real estate market developments. She holds a doctorate and a master's degree in economics from West Virginia University and a bachelor's degree in economics and management from Southern Federal University, Russia.

Cesar Cancho is an economist in the World Bank's Poverty and Equity Global Practice for the Eastern Europe and Central Asia region. His recent work has focused on poverty measurement issues, fiscal incidence analysis, distributional impact of reforms, and analysis of subjective well-being. Before joining the Bank, he worked on poverty and social development issues in the Latin American region for the Inter-American Development Bank, the government of Peru, and local research centers. He received his doctorate in economics from Texas A&M University.

Ruth Hill is a senior economist in the World Bank's Poverty and Equity Global Practice, focusing primarily on Ethiopia and Uganda. Before joining the World Bank in 2013, she worked at the International Food Policy Research Institute as a senior research fellow in the Markets, Trade and Institutions Division. She received a doctorate in economics from the University of Oxford.

Gabriela Inchauste is a lead economist in the Poverty and Equity Global Practice, where she focuses on Eastern Europe and Central Asia. In addition, she is the global lead on Fiscal and Social Policies for Poverty Reduction and Shared Prosperity, and in this role she has been working on the distributional impact of fiscal policy and on ex ante analysis of the distributional impacts of policy reforms. Before joining the Bank, she worked at the Inter-American Development Bank and the International Monetary Fund. She holds a doctorate in economics from the University of Texas at Austin.

Jon Jellema is the Commitment to Equity (CEQ) Institute's associate director for Africa, Asia, and Europe and a World Bank consultant. He is leading the CEQ assessments in the Comoros, Indonesia, Namibia, Uganda, and Vietnam and has participated in the CEQ effort in Ethiopia, Jordan, and South Africa. He previously worked as a poverty economist and social development specialist in the World Bank's Jakarta, Indonesia, office. He received a doctorate in economics from the University of California, Berkeley.

Artsvi Khachatryan has been a World Bank consultant since 1999 and has worked on a wide range of economic issues, primarily macroeconomic research, projections, statistical data processing, and economic analysis. He graduated from Yerevan State University, Armenia, in 1993 and was awarded the qualification of economist-mathematician.

Luis F. López-Calva is practice manager of the Eastern Europe and Central Asia region in the World Bank's Poverty and Equity Global Practice. Previously, he was the codirector of the World Bank's *World Development Report 2017: Governance and the Law*. He also has been the lead economist and regional poverty adviser for the Bank's Europe and Central Asia Region. He served as chief economist for Latin America and the Caribbean at the United Nations Development Programme in New York from 2007 to 2010. In Mexico, he was an associate professor and the chair of the master's degree program in public economies at Tecnológico de Monterrey (Mexico City campus) and professor at El Colegio de México. His publications and research interests focus on labor markets, poverty and inequality, institutions, and development economics. He holds a master's degree in economics from Boston University and a master's degree and doctorate in economics from Cornell University.

Nora Lustig is Samuel Z. Stone Professor of Latin American Economics and director of the CEQ Institute at Tulane University. She is also a nonresident fellow at the Center for Global Development and the Inter-American Dialogue. Her current research focuses on assessing the impact of taxation and social spending on inequality and poverty in developing countries and on the determinants of income distribution in Latin America. She is a founding member and past president of the Latin American and Caribbean Economic Association and was a codirector of the World Bank's *World Development Report 2000/2001: Attacking Poverty*. She is the editor of the *Journal of Economic Inequality's* Forum. In addition, she is a coprincipal investigator of the United Nations University World Institute for Development Economics Research (UNU-WIDER) project, "Inequality in the Giants," and serves on the Atkinson Commission on Global Poverty as well as on the High Level Group on the Measurement of Economic Performance and Social Progress. She received her doctorate in economics from the University of California, Berkeley.

Mashekwa Maboshe is a doctoral candidate in the School of Economics at the University of Cape Town and a nonresident research associate at the CEQ Institute. His doctoral work focuses on the economic effects of corporate taxation in developing countries. His recent research work involves CEQ assessment of the distributional impact of fiscal policy in South Africa. His research interests include the impact of corporate tax policy on firm behavior, labor markets, and poverty and inequality. He has an honor's degree and a master's degree in economics from the University of Cape Town and a bachelor's degree in economics from the University of Zambia.

Mikhail Matytsin is a research analyst in the World Bank's Poverty and Equity Global Practice. He works on the issues of poverty, shared prosperity, and inequality in Belarus, Moldova, the Russian Federation, Ukraine, and other countries in the World Bank's Europe and Central Asia region. He has a doctorate in econometrics from the National Research University Higher School of Economics in Moscow and a master's degree in economics from the New Economic School in Moscow.

Daria Popova is a senior research officer at the Institute for Social and Economic Research at the University of Essex, United Kingdom, and a developer for EUROMOD, the tax-benefit microsimulation model for the European Union. Her research area is the comparative analysis of the welfare states, distributional issues, and family dynamics. She is a research associate at the Higher School of Economics, Moscow, and the CEQ Institute. She received her doctorate in political science from European University Institute and has previously worked as a lecturer at the University of Michigan, Ann Arbor.

Catriona Purfield was recently the World Bank's lead economist for Botswana, Lesotho, Namibia, South Africa, and Swaziland. Before joining the Bank in July 2013, she worked at the International Monetary Fund (IMF), where she served as an adviser in the European Department and led the IMF's Article IV surveillance missions during the global financial crisis to Lithuania and subsequently to Bulgaria. At the IMF, she has also focused on countries in South Asia, Africa, and the Middle East. She received her doctorate in economics from Trinity College, Dublin.

Umar Serajuddin is a senior economist-statistician in the World Bank's Development Data Group, where he leads the socioeconomic and demographic data team and is closely involved with the Bank's Sustainable Development Goal monitoring initiatives. He has also worked as a poverty expert for the World Bank's South Asia and Middle East and North Africa regions. With a doctorate in economics from the University of Texas at Austin, he has published several papers on poverty, inequality, and social protection–related topics.

Eyasu Tsehaye is an economist in the World Bank's Poverty and Equity Global Practice based in Ethiopia. Before joining the World Bank, he worked for various government and research institutions in Ethiopia. He has a master's degree in economics of development from the Institute of Social Studies, the Netherlands.

Matthew Wai-Poi is a senior economist in the World Bank's Poverty and Equity Global Practice, where he leads the analytical work program on poverty, vulnerability, and inequality in Indonesia. He has a doctorate in economics from Columbia University, a master's degree in development economics from Australian National University, and degrees in law and business from the University of Auckland.

Tassew Woldehanna is professor of economics and vice president for research and technology transfer at Addis Ababa University, Ethiopia. His interests include child welfare and poverty, employment, micro- and small-scale enterprise development, entrepreneurship, and food security. He has published several book chapters and articles on areas of poverty, education, and health. He is principal investigator of Young Lives, an international study of childhood poverty following 12,000 children in four countries (Ethiopia, India, Peru, and Vietnam) based at the University of Oxford's Department of International Development. He obtained his doctorate in household economics from Wageningen University, the Netherlands.

Ingrid Woolard is the dean of the Faculty of Commerce and a professor of economics at the University of Cape Town, a research associate of the Southern Africa Labor and Development Research Unit, a senior nonresident research fellow at UNU-WIDER, and a research fellow of the Institute of Labor Economics in Bonn. She is a lead author of the chapter on inequality for the prestigious International Panel on Social Progress Report. Since 2007, she has been one of the principal investigators of South Africa's national household panel survey, the National Income Dynamics Study. In addition, she served from 2011 to 2014 as the chair of the Employment Conditions Commission, which advises the South African Minister of Labor concerning sectoral determinations on working conditions and minimum wages in 11 sectors covering approximately 4 million workers. Since 2013, she has been a member of the Davis Tax Committee, which assesses South Africa's tax policy framework and its role in supporting inclusive growth, employment, development, and fiscal sustainability. Her research interests include labor markets, social protection, poverty and inequality, tax policy, and survey methodology. She holds a doctorate in economics from the University of Cape Town.

Stephen D. Younger is associate director of the CEQ Institute and worked previously at Williams College, Cornell University, the Vrije Universiteit Amsterdam, the Facultad Latinoamericana de Ciencias Sociales, Quito, Ecuador, and Ithaca College, New York. His research focuses on the distributional consequences of public policy in developing countries, especially the nonincome dimensions of well-being as well as multidimensional poverty and inequality. He earned his doctorate in economics in 1986 from Stanford University

Abbreviations

BSM	Poor Education Support (Indonesia)
CEQ	Commitment to Equity (project)
EDRI	Ethiopian Development Research Institute
EEPCo	Ethiopian Electric Power Corporation
ERSS	Ethopian Rural Socio-Economic Survey
FGT	Foster-Greer-Thorbecke (indexes)
GDP	gross domestic product
Geostat	National Statistics Office of Georgia
GST	general sales tax
GTP	Growth and Transformation Plan (Ethiopia)
HBS	Household Budget Survey (Russian Federation)
HCES	Household Consumption Expenditure Survey (Ethiopia)
HEIS	Household Expenditure and Income Survey (Jordan)
HIES	Household Income and Expenditure Survey (Sri Lanka)
IDPs	internally displaced persons
IES	Income and Expenditure Survey (South Africa)
IHS	Integrated Household Survey (Georgia)
ILCS	Integrated Living Conditions Survey (Armenia)
MIP	Medical Insurance Program (Georgia)
MoF	Ministry of Finance
MoFED	Ministry of Finance and Economic Development (Ethiopia)
NAF	National Aid Fund (Jordan)
NIDS	National Income Dynamics Study (South Africa)
NSSRA	National Statistical Service of the Republic of Armenia
PCS	Program of Communal Subsidies (Tbilisi, Georgia)
PIT	personal income tax(es)
PKH	Hopeful Family Program (Indonesia)
PPP	purchasing power parity
PSNP	Productive Safety Net Program (Ethiopia)

RE	redistributive effect
RLMS-HSE	Russian Longitudinal Monitoring Survey of the Higher School of Economics
Rosstat	Russian Federal State Statistics Service
RR	reranking
SAM	social accounting matrix
SSA	Social Service Agency (Georgia)
SSC	Social Security contribution(s)
SUSENAS	National Socioeconomic Survey (Indonesia)
TSA	Targeted Social Assistance (Georgia)
UHC	universal health care (Georgia)
UIF	Unemployment Insurance Fund (South Africa)
VAT	value added tax(es)
VE	vertical equity
WMS	Welfare Monitoring Survey (Ethiopia)

CHAPTER 1

Overview: Fiscal Policy and Redistribution

Gabriela Inchauste and Nora Lustig

Introduction

Governments in low- and middle-income countries (LMICs) are increasingly interested in assessing how effective their current fiscal policies are in promoting growth, expanding opportunities, and accelerating poverty reduction. Although the literature on tax and benefit incidence is vast, few studies have attempted to look at the incidence of both taxes and spending in the context of LMICs.

The tax incidence literature includes a long list of studies with empirical estimates of incidence going back more than half a century (Musgrave 1959; Musgrave, Case, and Leonard 1974; Musgrave et al. 1951; Pechman and Okner 1974). Similarly, on the expenditure side, there is a long tradition using the traditional approach (Meerman 1979; Selowsky 1979) and a behavioral approach (Gertler and Glewwe 1990; Gertler and van der Gaag 1990; Younger et al. 1999).

As Martinez-Vazquez (2008) and Lustig (2017a) argue from a policy viewpoint, net fiscal incidence is the relevant equity measure that government authorities need to use in judging particular policies. For example, an increase in value added taxes (VAT) may be rejected on equity grounds as being regressive, but it may be desirable from an equity standpoint if the resulting revenues are used to finance primary-school services in poor neighborhoods. Taxes may be progressive but, if transfers to the poor are not large enough, worsen poverty.

More generally, governments need to gauge how well they can achieve their distributional objectives. This is especially true given current trends toward slower growth in developed countries, as LMICs will likely need to rely more and

The authors are grateful to Sandra Martinez, Israel Martínez, Luis Felipe Munguía, Ruoxi Li, and Itzel Osorio for their excellent assistance with this chapter. This Overview draws heavily from the Introduction and chapter 1 of the volume edited by Nora Lustig, *Commitment to Equity Handbook: Estimating the Impact of Fiscal Policy on Inequality and Poverty* (Washington, DC: Brookings Institution Press and the Commitment to Equity Institute, Tulane University).

more on their own fiscal resources to finance development objectives that could equalize opportunities. In this context, any effort to mobilize domestic resources requires an evidence base that can guide decision making. In particular, policy makers often want to know the following:

• What are the impacts of taxes and expenditures on inequality and poverty?
• What are the impacts across different demographic groups?
• What are the impacts of individual fiscal interventions on poverty and inequality?
• How does our country compare with others in the redistributive impact of policies, and how can we enhance their redistributive effectiveness?
• Is public spending on education and health both progressive and pro-poor?

However, until the launch of the Commitment to Equity (CEQ) project in 2008, work that analyzed the incidence of both government revenue and spending simultaneously—including net indirect taxes and spending on in-kind services—was less common.[1] Since the CEQ project has developed, this has changed quite strikingly, as evidenced by the publications of Aristy-Escuder et al. (2017); Beneke, Lustig, and Oliva (2017); Bucheli et al. (2014); Cabrera, Lustig, and Morán (2015); Enami (2017a); Higgins and Lustig (2016); Higgins and Pereira (2014); Higgins et al. (2016); Jaramillo (2014); Jellema et al. (2017); Jouini et al. (2017); Lustig (2015, 2016a, 2016b, 2017a, 2017b); Lustig and Pessino (2014); Lustig, Pessino, and Scott (2014); Martínez et al. (2017); Paz Arauco et al. (2014); Pereira (2017); Rossignolo (2017); Scott (2014); Younger, Myamba, and Mdadila (2016); and Younger, Osei-Assibey, and Oppong (2017), as well as the CEQ Working Paper series available at www.commitmentoequity.org.

As in the just-mentioned publications, this volume also showcases the power of undertaking systematic analysis of the distributional impact of taxes and public spending using a common methodological framework developed by the CEQ Institute and presented in the *CEQ Handbook* by Lustig and Higgins (2013) and Lustig (2017a). This volume includes such studies of the following countries[2]: Armenia, Ethiopia, Georgia, Indonesia, Jordan, the Russian Federation, South Africa, and Sri Lanka. It also draws from a larger body of evidence using the same approach. The approach makes three important contributions, showcased throughout the case studies:

• The proposed framework, which aims to be as comprehensive as possible, enables one to estimate the combined impact of taxes and transfers.
• The analysis also includes the estimated marginal contribution of each individual intervention to the reduction in poverty and inequality. In the past, standard incidence analysis often calculated whether a particular intervention was progressive or regressive, but few included the impact on poverty and inequality or the combined redistributive effect.
• The use of a common methodology makes the results comparable across countries.

This approach has already been effective in providing a sound evidence base and spurring national policy dialogues. Earlier versions of some of the case studies in this volume have already contributed in some form to the fiscal policy dialogue within each country. For example, studies in this volume have led to additional diagnostic work and changes in Armenia regarding tax policy (chapter 2) and in Indonesia regarding subsidy policy (chapter 5). This overview chapter describes the common methodology and provides examples of the types of analysis that have been useful to inform policy across a wide set of countries around the world.

At the outset, it is important to describe some important caveats. First, the analysis excludes some important categories of taxes and spending—such as corporate income taxes and spending on infrastructure, defense, and other public goods—because it is difficult to assign these benefits or burdens to any single individual, as the economic burdens (in the case of corporate taxes) or benefits (in the case of spending on public goods) are diffuse. Existing methodologies are not fully developed to credibly incorporate the economic incidence of those categories of taxes and spending.

Second, by considering only the *redistributive* effects of taxes and transfers, the case studies within this volume do not offer a full analysis of whether specific taxes or expenditures are *desirable*. When one type of tax or expenditure is found to be more progressive than another, the temptation is to conclude that the former is preferable. However, redistribution is only one of many criteria that matter when making public policy. Good tax policy will aim to be sufficient, efficient, and simple in addition to being equitable, and public spending will aim to meet a state's core functions by investing in necessary public goods in addition to improving equity. By assessing the equity of taxes and spending, the results of the approach are one input to public policy making—one that should be weighed with other evidence before deciding whether a tax or expenditure is desirable.

Finally, it is important to keep in mind that the approach offers "a picture in time." As such, it cannot inform the trade-offs between spending on (a) current transfers to alleviate poverty in the present and (b) investments in physical and human capital that could lead to large impacts on well-being in the future.

The rest of the chapter is structured as follows: first, the size and composition of taxes and spending are presented across a set of countries for which the proposed analysis has been undertaken, followed by evidence of their redistributive effects. Next, the analysis describes the impact on poverty, highlighting that the effects of tax and spending interventions could be redistributive but poverty increasing. This is followed by a discussion of the marginal contributions to poverty and inequality by individual tax and spending interventions. In addition, the progressivity of government spending on education and health is examined to better understand whether spending on these components reaches not only the middle classes but also the poor. The final section summarizes the volume's main messages and policy implications. Annex 1A presents the methodology used for the analysis, drawing heavily from the *CEQ Handbook* (Lustig and Higgins 2013; Lustig 2017a). Annex 1B presents details of the data and the assumptions used across case studies. Annex 1C presents the redistributive effort of each fiscal intervention, that is, the marginal contribution of taxes and transfers toward reducing inequality.

Budget Size, Social Spending, and Taxation

A country's redistributive potential—that is, its ability to increase household income equality—is determined first and foremost by the size and composition of its budget and how it finances government spending. The size and composition of revenue and expenditures differ in important ways across our sample of countries. Figure 1.1 shows total revenue and primary spending as a share of gross domestic product (GDP) based on data sources that range from 2009 to 2013, depending on the country. Social spending includes direct transfers, noncontributory pensions, and public spending on education and health. It does not include housing subsidies or other forms of social spending.

Figure 1.1 Size and Composition of Government Revenues and Primary Spending as a Share of GDP, in Selected Countries Ranked by GNI per Capita

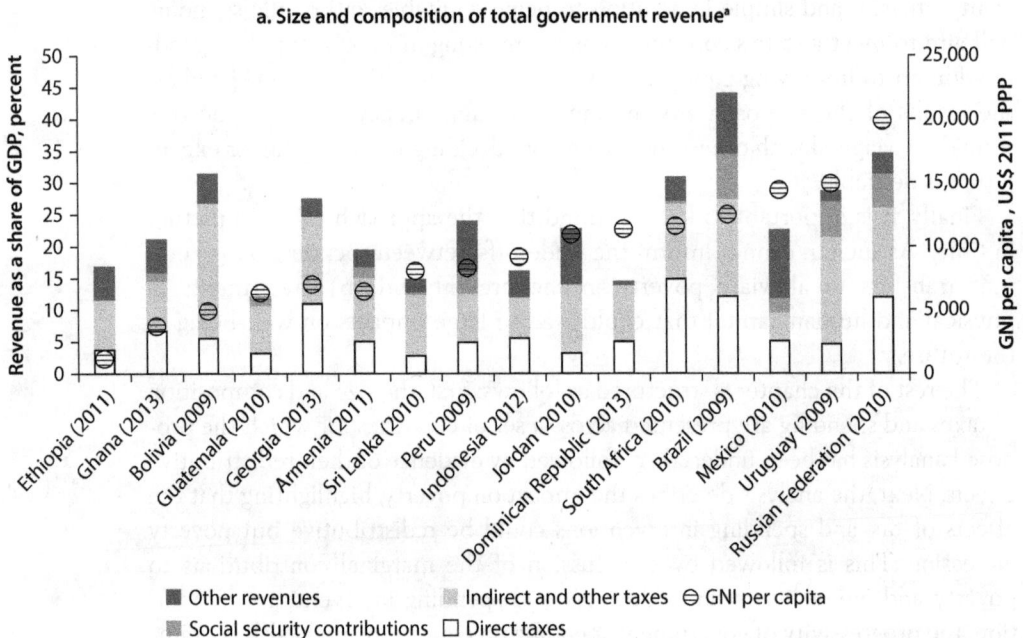

a. Size and composition of total government revenue[a]

figure continues next page

Figure 1.1 Size and Composition of Government Revenues and Primary Spending as a Share of GDP, in Selected Countries Ranked by GNI Per Capita *(continued)*

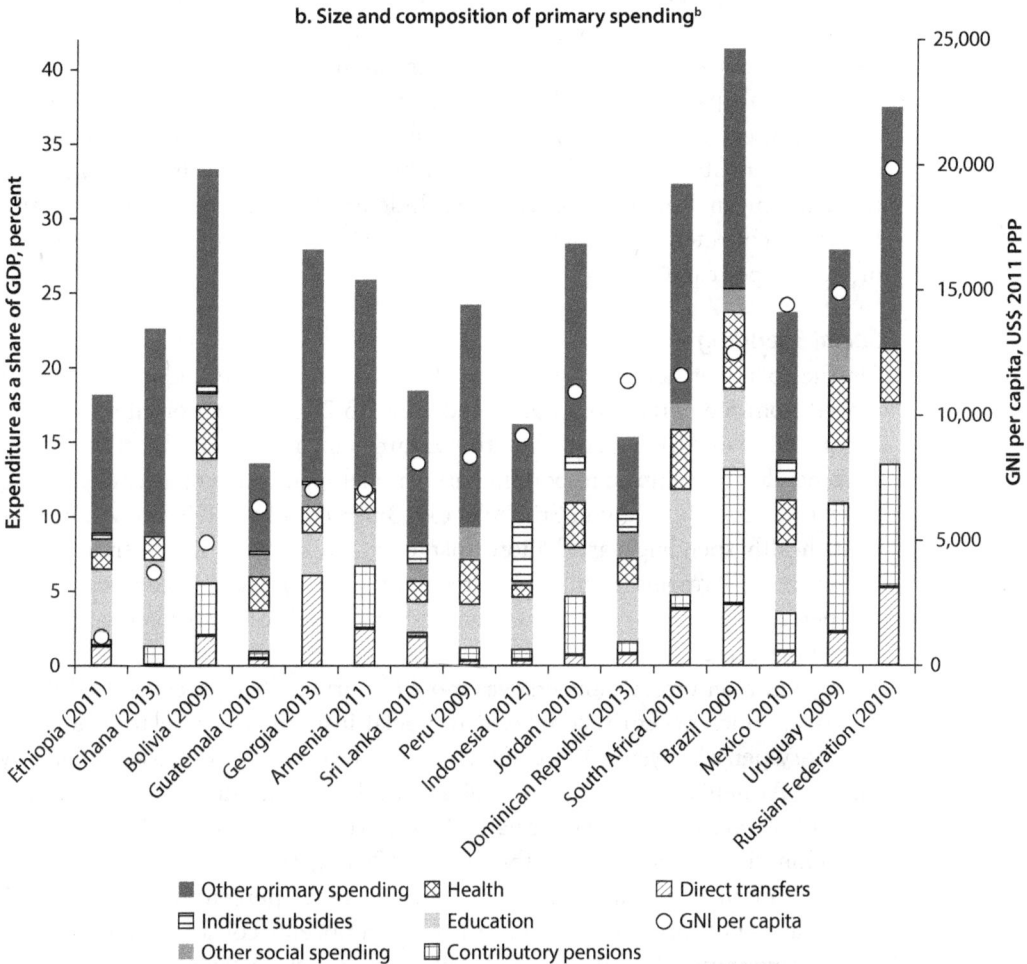

b. Size and composition of primary spending[b]

Legend:
- ■ Other primary spending
- ⊟ Indirect subsidies
- ▦ Other social spending
- ⊠ Health
- ▦ Education
- ▢ Contributory pensions
- ▨ Direct transfers
- ○ GNI per capita

Sources: For Armenia, Ethiopia, Georgia, Indonesia, Jordan, the Russian Federation, South Africa, and Sri Lanka, calculations are based on data in the country-specific chapters in this volume. Additional sources are Bucheli et al. 2014 (Uruguay); Cabrera, Lustig, and Morán 2015 (Guatemala); Aristy-Escuder et al. 2017 (Dominican Republic); Higgins and Pereira 2014, 2016 (Brazil); Jaramillo 2014, 2015 (Peru); Paz Arauco et al. 2014 (Bolivia); Scott 2014 (Mexico); Younger, Osei-Assibey, and Oppong 2017 (Ghana).

Note: The year of each country's household survey is shown within parentheses. The data shown here are administrative data as reported by the source studies. GDP = gross domestic product; GNI = gross national income; PPP = purchasing power parity.

a. "Other revenues" include profits from state-owned enterprises.

b. "Primary spending" is total government spending minus interest payments on domestic and external public debt. "Social spending" includes direct transfers, contributory pensions, education, health, and other social spending (such as housing). Indirect subsidies (in the form of reduced prices for energy or food) are not considered part of social spending.

Revenues

Total revenues range from 12.2 percent of GDP in Guatemala to nearly 35.0 percent of GDP in the Russian Federation (figure 1.1, panel a). Indirect taxes (such as VAT) made up a larger share of total revenue in all countries except Mexico and South Africa, where the largest shares of revenue came from "other revenues" (revenues from state-owned oil company) and from direct taxes, respectively. In fact, in Armenia, Ethiopia, and Guatemala, indirect taxes were more than twice as large as direct taxes (as a share of GDP), whereas in Bolivia, Jordan, Sri Lanka, and Uruguay they were more than three times as large. Oil revenue was an important source of revenue for Indonesia and Russia, whereas grants were relatively important in Ethiopia and Jordan.

The fiscal space afforded by tax collections determines the resources available for fiscal redistribution. In this respect, note that Georgia had higher collections relative to other countries with similar levels of income, whereas the Dominican Republic,[3] Guatemala, Indonesia, Jordan, Mexico, Peru, and Sri Lanka collected less than what would have been expected given their levels of income per capita.

Social Spending

On the spending side, total social spending (which excludes indirect subsidies) ranged from 5.6 percent of GDP in Indonesia to 25.3 percent of GDP in Brazil (figure 1.1, panel b). Regardless of the country's income level, education spending tended to make up an important part of social spending in most cases, ranging from 1.9 percent of GDP in Sri Lanka to 8.3 percent of GDP in Bolivia. In contrast, health spending varied more markedly across countries of similar size: for instance, Armenia spent 1.7 percent of GDP on health compared with 0.9 percent by Indonesia, despite having similar levels of gross national income (GNI) per capita.

Spending on direct transfers was most important (6.1 percent of GDP) in Georgia, which recently converted its social insurance system to a noncontributory pension system). Meanwhile, contributory pensions were relatively large in Armenia, Brazil, Jordan, Russia, and Uruguay. Direct transfers in the form of social assistance were relatively important in Russia and South Africa. In Indonesia, at the time of the survey (2012), the government allocated much more of its resources to energy subsidies (3.7 percent of GDP) than to cash transfers (0.4 percent of GDP), with important consequences in terms of the government's ability to redistribute resources efficiently, as discussed in chapter 5.

Given their size of social spending, Russia and South Africa have the largest amount of resources at their disposal to engage in fiscal redistribution. At the other end of the spectrum are Indonesia and Sri Lanka, with relatively low levels of tax collection and social spending. However, whether Russia and South Africa achieve their higher redistributive potential depends on how the burdens of taxation and the benefits of social spending are distributed, as the next section discusses.

Fiscal Policy and Inequality

What is the impact of taxes and expenditures on inequality? A typical indicator of fiscal policy's redistributive effect is the difference between the Gini coefficient before and after taxes and transfers.[4]

Table 1.1 presents the Gini coefficient for income before taxes and transfers, called "market income." (All of the income concepts are defined in detail in annex 1A.) "Disposable income," which is income after direct taxes and transfers, broadly measures how much income households may potentially spend on goods and services. However, if households completely use their disposable incomes for consumption, actual consumption will depend on the size of indirect taxes and subsidies. Therefore, "consumable income" measures how much individuals can actually consume—that is, consumable income is the net cash position of households after the intervention of taxes and cash transfers. If one adds the value of in-kind transfers such as education and health care, it is possible to measure "final income," which includes the value of these public services if individuals had to pay for those services at the average government cost.

However, there is no clear consensus in how to treat contributory pensions (as opposed to noncontributory pensions, which are always direct transfers). As detailed in annex 1A, one option is to treat these pensions as deferred income—with the corresponding contributions treated as savings (as in table 1.1, panel a). Another option is to treat these pensions as government transfers, with the corresponding contributions treated as direct taxes (as in table 1.1, panel b). Because this issue is unresolved, the studies analyzed here present results for both methods.

Table 1.1 Fiscal Policy and Income Inequality in Selected Countries, by Income Concept
Gini coefficient

a. Contributory pensions treated as deferred income

Country (year of data)	Market income[a] plus pensions	Disposable income[b]	Consumable income[c]	Final income[d]
Armenia (2011)	0.403	0.373	0.374	0.357
Bolivia (2009)	0.503	0.493	0.503	0.446
Brazil (2009)	0.579	0.544	0.546	0.439
Dominican Republic (2013)	0.514	0.502	0.492	0.458
Ethiopia (2011)	0.322	0.305	0.302	0.302
Georgia (2013)	0.507	0.395	0.411	0.383
Ghana (2013)	0.437	0.424	0.423	0.402
Guatemala (2010)	0.551	0.546	0.551	0.523
Indonesia (2012)[e]	0.394	0.390	0.391	0.370
Jordan (2010)	0.342	0.328	0.325	0.319
Mexico (2010)	0.511	0.488	0.481	0.429
Peru (2009)	0.504	0.494	0.492	0.466
Russian Federation (2010)	0.393	0.362	0.366	0.331
South Africa (2010)[f]	0.771	0.694	0.695	0.595
Sri Lanka (2010)	0.371	0.365	0.360	0.344
Uruguay (2009)	0.492	0.457	0.459	0.393

table continues next page

Table 1.1 Fiscal Policy and Income Inequality in Selected Countries, by Income Concept *(continued)*

b. Contributory pensions treated as direct transfers

Country (year of data)	Market income[a]	Disposable income[b]	Consumable income[c]	Final income[d]
Armenia (2011)	0.469	0.373	0.374	0.357
Bolivia (2009)	0.503	0.493	0.503	0.446
Brazil (2009)	0.600	0.541	0.543	0.434
Dominican Republic (2013)	0.514	0.502	0.492	0.458
Ethiopia (2011)	0.322	0.305	0.303	0.302
Georgia (2013)	0.507	0.395	0.411	0.383
Ghana (2013)[g]	n.a.	n.a.	n.a.	n.a.
Guatemala (2010)	0.551	0.546	0.551	0.523
Indonesia (2012)[e]	0.394	0.389	0.390	0.370
Jordan (2010)	0.351	0.328	0.325	0.319
Mexico (2010)	0.509	0.488	0.481	0.429
Peru (2009)	0.503	0.493	0.491	0.464
Russian Federation (2010)	0.491	0.359	0.363	0.323
South Africa (2010)[g]	n.a.	n.a.	n.a.	n.a.
Sri Lanka (2010)[g]	n.a.	n.a.	n.a.	n.a.
Uruguay (2009)	0.527	0.454	0.456	0.386

Sources: For Armenia, Ethiopia, Georgia, Indonesia, Jordan, the Russian Federation, South Africa, and Sri Lanka, calculations are based on the country-specific chapters in this volume. Additional sources are Bucheli et al. 2014 (Uruguay); Cabrera, Lustig, and Morán 2015 (Guatemala); Aristy-Escuder et al. 2017 (Dominican Republic); Higgins and Pereira 2014, 2016 (Brazil); Jaramillo 2014, 2015 (Peru); Paz Arauco et al. 2014 (Bolivia); Scott 2014 (Mexico); Younger, Osei-Assibey, and Oppong 2017 (Ghana).

Note: The Gini coefficient measures a country's level of inequality of income distribution, ranging from 0 (full equality) to 1 (maximum inequality). n.a. = not applicable.

a. "Market income" comprises pretax wages, salaries, income earned from capital assets (rent, interest, or dividends), and private transfers.

b. "Disposable income" = market income − payments for direct taxes + direct cash transfers.

c. "Consumable income" = disposable income − indirect taxes (value added and excise taxes) + indirect subsidies.

d. "Final income" = consumable income + value of in-kind transfers (education and health care).

e. For Indonesia, the fiscal incidence analysis was carried out adjusting for spatial price differences. Personal income tax is imputed to be zero for all National Socioeconomic Survey (SUSENAS) respondents, as further discussed in chapter 5.

f. The fiscal analysis for South Africa assumed that free basic services provided by municipalities (such as power, sanitation, water, and refuse removal) are direct transfers.

g. Panel b excludes the Ginis for Ghana, South Africa, and Sri Lanka for the following reasons: In Ghana, the social security system features a surplus, so there is no scenario in which contributory pensions are treated as a pure transfer. The only contributory pensions in South Africa and Sri Lanka are for public servants and are considered to be part of market income.

Taxes and transfers reduce inequality in all countries. When contributory pensions are treated as deferred income, in-kind transfers typically make most of the difference (figure 1.2, panel a). In contrast, when such pensions are treated as transfers, the redistributive impact of taxes and transfers increases markedly for countries with large contributory systems, such as Armenia, Russia, and Uruguay (figure 1.2, panel b).

However, there is important heterogeneity across countries, with some countries achieving almost all of the fiscal redistribution through in-kind benefits (such as Bolivia and Guatemala) and others achieving most of it through taxes and transfers (such as Georgia and South Africa). It is likely that perceptions about the redistributive impact of the different types of spending will also vary substantially because in-kind transfers are valued at the average government cost of providing health and education services, which may not reflect the value of these services to the individuals who use them.[5]

In Ethiopia, Guatemala, Indonesia, Jordan, and Sri Lanka, fiscal income redistribution is quite limited, reducing the Gini by less than 0.03 Gini points, whereas in Brazil, Georgia, and South Africa, fiscal policy reduces the Gini by more than 0.12 Gini points. The ability to redistribute partly depends on the available resources, but it also depends on how resources are spent. For instance, Bolivia spends more than Georgia as a share of GDP and substantially more than other countries with comparable levels of income, but its redistributive impact is relatively small. Similarly, Armenia and Ghana start out with similar market-income inequality (as shown earlier in table 1.1), but Armenia's fiscal interventions reduce inequality more. Finally, Brazil spends a higher share of GDP on social spending than South Africa, yet is less redistributive. In fact, South Africa is the most redistributive of all the countries examined here. Nevertheless, it remains the most unequal country after taxes and social transfers—even more so than other countries before any fiscal intervention (as indicated earlier in table 1.1, panel a).

Figure 1.2 Redistributive Effects of Taxes and Social Spending in Selected Countries

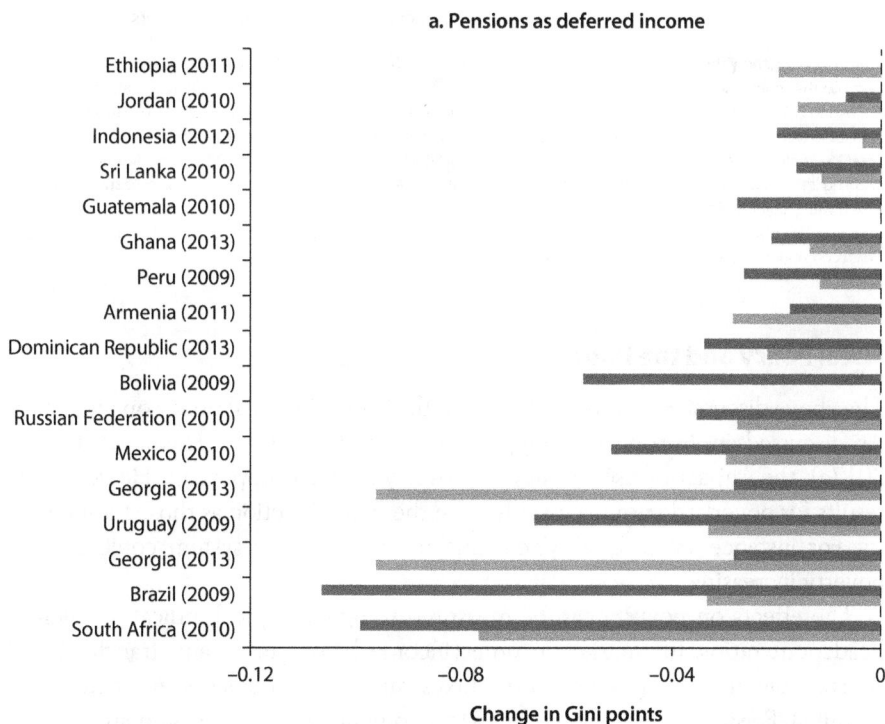

a. Pensions as deferred income

figure continues next page

Figure 1.2 Redistributive Effects of Taxes and Social Spending in Selected Countries *(continued)*

b. Pensions as transfers[a]

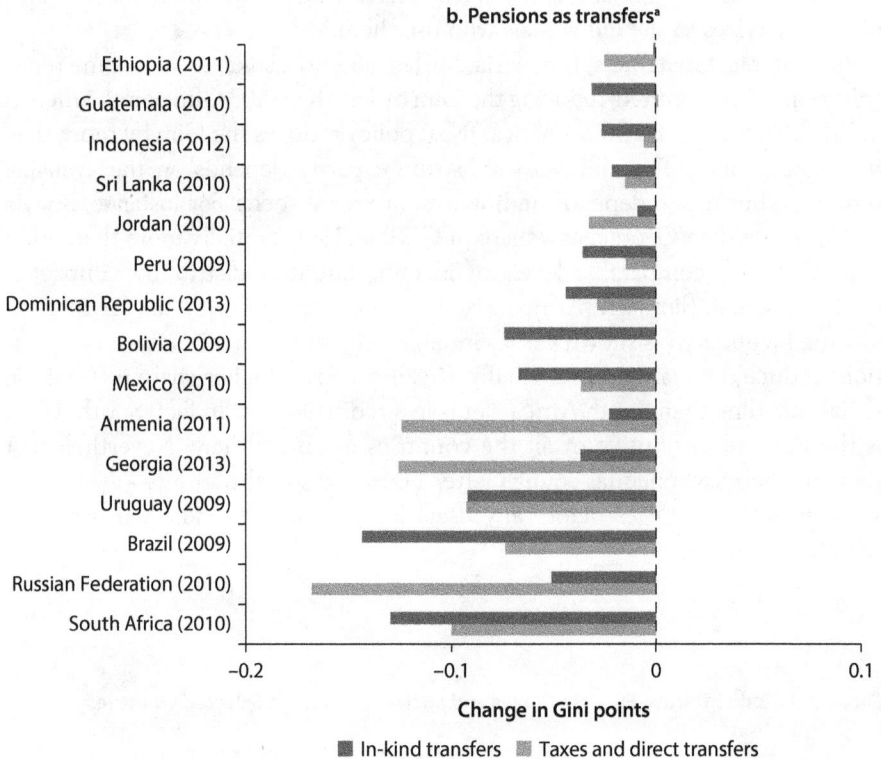

Change in Gini points

■ In-kind transfers   ▨ Taxes and direct transfers

Sources: For Armenia, Ethiopia, Georgia, Indonesia, Jordan, the Russian Federation, South Africa, and Sri Lanka, calculations are based on the country-specific chapters in this volume. Additional sources are Bucheli et al. 2014 (Uruguay); Cabrera, Lustig, and Morán 2015 (Guatemala); Aristy-Escuder et al. 2017 (Dominican Republic); Higgins and Pereira 2014, 2016 (Brazil); Jaramillo 2014, 2015 (Peru); Paz Arauco et al. 2014 (Bolivia); Scott 2014 (Mexico); Younger, Osei-Assibey, and Oppong 2017 (Ghana).
Note: The "redistributive effect" refers to the reduction in inequality, represented by change in the Gini coefficient (a decrease meaning less inequality). For a more detailed discussion, see annex 1A. The year of each country's household survey data is shown within parentheses.
a. Panel b does not include data for Ghana because the social security system features a surplus, so there is no scenario in which contributory pensions are treated as a pure transfer.

Fiscal Policy and the Poor

The above discussion has concentrated on the impact of fiscal policy on inequality. As discussed in Lustig and Higgins (2013) and the *CEQ Handbook* (Lustig 2017a), the impact of fiscal policy on poverty is just as important. However, the results for poverty do not necessarily go in the same direction as those for inequality. For instance, an inequality-reducing tax and transfer system could also be poverty increasing.

The effects on poverty can be measured using the typical indicators, such as headcount ratios, for market income (income before taxes and transfers) and consumable income (income after taxes and direct transfers are taken into account). For instance, to assess the extent to which individuals who are "market income" poor end up being net cash payers to the fiscal system, one can compare the poverty headcount between market income and consumable income.[6] Figure 1.3 shows such a comparison using the US$2.50 per day poverty line (in purchasing power parity [PPP] terms) for all countries except Ethiopia, which is evaluated at the US$1.25 PPP per day poverty line.[7]

The results show that taxes and transfers reduce the poverty headcount ratio in half of the countries: Georgia, Indonesia, Jordan, Mexico, Peru, Russia,

Figure 1.3 Impact of Fiscal Policy on Poverty Reduction in Selected Countries

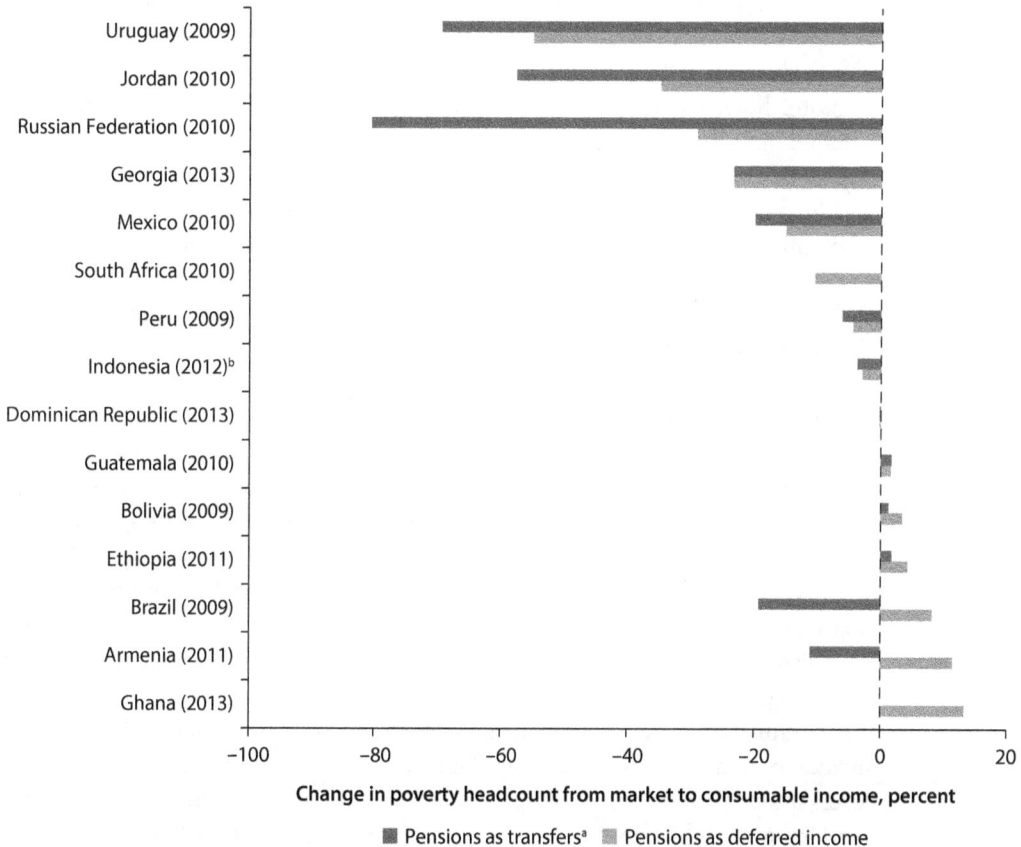

Change in poverty headcount from market to consumable income, percent

■ Pensions as transfers[a] ■ Pensions as deferred income

Sources: For Armenia, Ethiopia, Georgia, Indonesia, Jordan, the Russian Federation, South Africa, and Sri Lanka, calculations are based on the country-specific chapters in this volume. Additional sources are Bucheli et al. 2014 (Uruguay); Cabrera, Lustig, and Morán 2015 (Guatemala); Aristy-Escuder et al. 2017 (Dominican Republic); Higgins and Pereira 2014, 2016 (Brazil); Jaramillo 2014, 2015 (Peru); Paz Arauco et al. 2014 (Bolivia); Scott 2014 (Mexico); Younger, Osei-Assibey, and Oppong 2017 (Ghana).
Note: Figure shows the percentage change in each country's poverty headcount (percentage of population below the poverty line) between "market income" (before taxes or transfers) and "consumable income" (after taxes, direct transfers, and subsidies) under two scenarios: one that treats pensions as deferred income (orange bars) and one that treats pensions as transfers (blue bars). The year of each country's household survey data is shown within parentheses. The poverty line is set at US$2.50 per person per day in terms of 2005 PPP (purchasing power parity), except for Ethiopia where US$1.25 2005 PPP was used. Countries are ranked by poverty reduction (left to right) when contributory pensions as treated as deferred income.
a. Figure excludes "pensions as transfers" results for Ghana, South Africa, and Sri Lanka for the following reasons: In Ghana, the social security system features a surplus, so there is no scenario in which contributory pensions are treated as a pure transfer. The only contributory pensions in South Africa and Sri Lanka are for public servants and are considered to be part of market income.
b. For Indonesia, the fiscal incidence analysis was carried out adjusting for spatial price differences. Personal income tax was imputed to be zero for all National Socioeconomic Survey (SUSENAS) respondents, as further discussed in chapter 5.

The Distributional Impact of Taxes and Transfers • http://dx.doi.org/10.1596/978-1-4648-1091-6

South Africa, and Uruguay. The reductions are especially large in Georgia, Jordan, Mexico, Russia, South Africa, and Uruguay, particularly when pensions are treated as transfers (as in Russia).

However, the results are not so positive elsewhere. Poverty actually increases after direct and indirect taxes in the case of Bolivia, Ethiopia, Ghana, Guatemala, and Sri Lanka, even after taking into account the benefits of direct transfers. In those countries, the burden of indirect taxes is larger than the benefits from direct transfers at the bottom of the distribution. As a result, the net cash position of households worsens. This also happens in Armenia and Brazil when pensions are considered as deferred income. These results highlight that the tax and transfer system can increase poverty even if it is also redistributive.

Note, however, that in some countries, there is a real trade-off between (a) spending on cash transfers that could bring immediate poverty relief, and (b) spending on long-term human capital formation through in-kind education and health services. Although the approach presented here cannot inform the trade-offs between immediate and future spending, it can point to critical hard-ships being felt across the population at a particular point in time. To the extent that fiscal policy today is impoverishing, it can potentially destabilize social cohesion—and, as such, even the best-laid plans to sacrifice today in favor of future well-being could become socially unsustainable.[8]

As a result, governments may wish to better understand who bears the burden of taxes and who receives the benefits. Having estimated the income before and after taxes and transfers for all households, it is possible to further disaggregate the impacts across household types and demographic or age groups. For instance, in the case of Russia (chapter 7), the authors disaggregate their results by house-hold type and demographic group. They find that if contributory pensions are considered as deferred income, households with working-age adults are net pay-ers regardless of whether there are children in the household, whereas pensioner households are the only group that benefits from the fiscal redistribution. When contributory pensions are treated as transfers, the group of beneficiaries grows to include mixed households with working-age people and pensioners. The biggest losers under both scenarios are one- and two-child families and households with working-age adults only. In terms of age groups, adults younger than 30 years old are penalized the most.

The Contribution of Taxes and Transfers

In addition to learning about the impacts of the net fiscal system on inequality and poverty, policy makers are keen to know the impacts of *individual* fiscal interventions on poverty and inequality. As shown in Lambert (2001) and Enami, Lustig, and Aranda (2017), in a world with more than one type of fiscal intervention, determining whether a particular tax or transfer is progressive or regressive in relation to prefiscal income is not enough to figure out its effect on poverty and inequality (as further explained in annex 1A).

For example, a fiscal system that includes a regressive tax can be more equalizing than one that lacks that regressive tax, depending on the characteristics of the tax and transfer system as a whole (Lambert 2001). Under such circumstances, it is best to calculate the marginal contribution of each fiscal intervention to poverty or inequality. The marginal contribution of each intervention can be calculated by taking the difference between the poverty or inequality indicator without and with that intervention.

Figure 1.4 presents marginal contributions for interventions regarding two net fiscal systems: (a) from market to disposable income, and (b) from market to consumable income. Both are presented because existing fiscal redistribution studies often stop at direct taxes and direct transfers.[9] (For detailed results by type of intervention, see annex 1C).

Three results are worth pointing to in particular:

- Direct taxes and direct transfers are generally progressive and equalizing, as expected, whether one calculates their marginal contribution regarding consumable income (after all taxes, direct transfers, and indirect subsidies) or final income (after all taxes, direct transfers, indirect subsidies, and in-kind transfers). Direct transfers exert a particularly high equalizing force in Armenia, Georgia, and South Africa.
- The marginal contribution of direct transfers is usually larger than that of direct taxes, although the difference is not large in Sri Lanka, whereas in Jordan the marginal contribution of direct taxes is slightly larger.

Figure 1.4 Redistributive Effects and Marginal Contributions of Taxes and Transfers, by Type, in Selected CEQ Countries

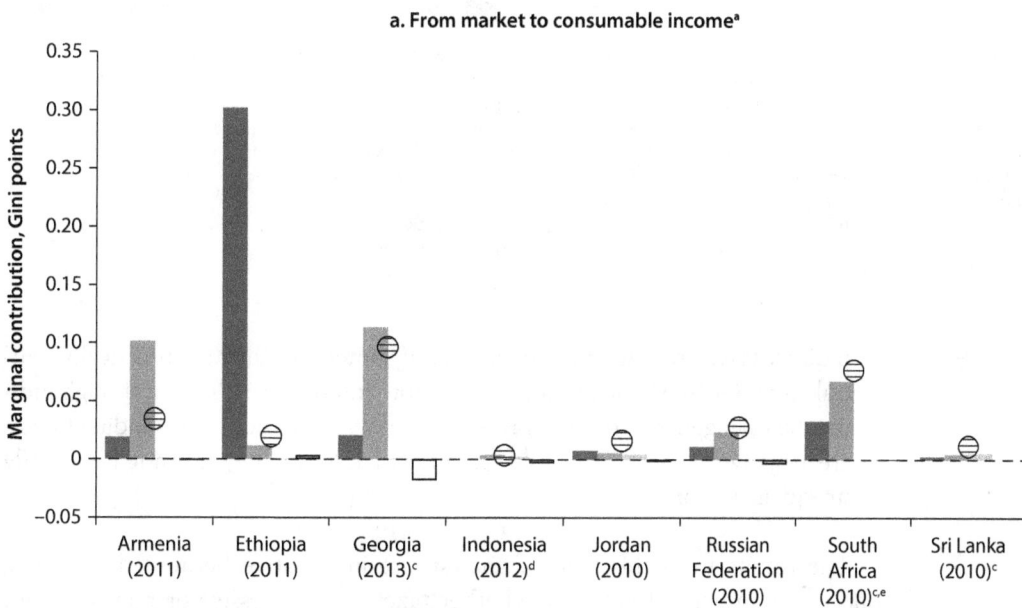

a. From market to consumable income[a]

figure continues next page

Figure 1.4 Redistributive Effects and Marginal Contributions of Taxes and Transfers, by Type, in Selected CEQ Countries *(continued)*

b. From market to final Income[b]

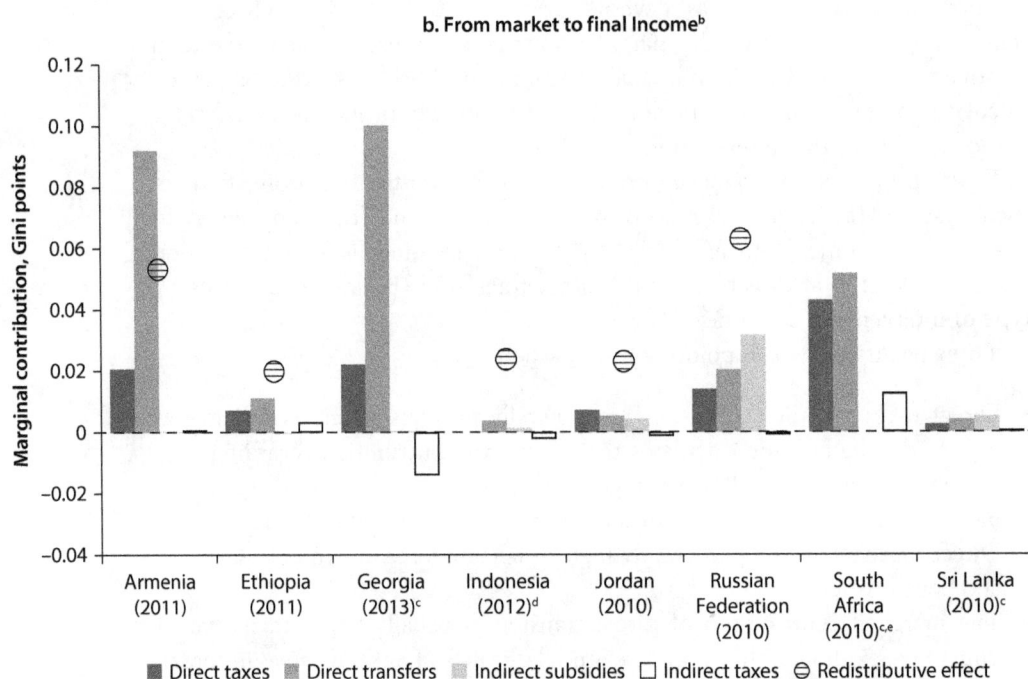

Direct taxes ■   Direct transfers ■   Indirect subsidies ▨   Indirect taxes □   Redistributive effect ⊖

Sources: Based on data in the country-specific chapters in this volume.

Note: Countries shown correspond to the eight country-specific chapters in this volume, with the year of each country's household survey data shown within parentheses. The "marginal contribution" is the difference between the inequality indicator (in this case, the Gini coefficient) with a particular intervention and without that intervention. The "redistributive effect" is the net change in inequality of all the interventions shown. CEQ = Commitment to Equity project.

a. "Market income" is income before taxes and transfers. "Consumable income" adds the effects of direct transfers, all taxes, and indirect subsidies (such as for energy or food).

b. "Final income" includes the effects of all taxes and transfers, including in-kind transfers for education and health services.

c. The results for Georgia, South Africa, and Sri Lanka exclude contributory pensions from direct transfers (instead considering them to be deferred income) for the following reasons: Georgia does not have a contributory pension system. The only contributory pensions in South Africa and Sri Lanka are for public servants; the effects of such pensions were not included in the analysis and are not shown here.

d. For Indonesia, the fiscal incidence analysis was carried out adjusting for spatial price differences. This adjustment, however, does not affect the data shown in this table. Personal income tax was imputed to be zero for all National Socioeconomic Survey (SUSENAS) respondents, as further discussed in chapter 5.

e. The fiscal analysis for South Africa assumes that free basic services provided by municipalities (such as power, sanitation, water, and refuse removal) are like direct transfers rather than indirect subsidies. For a fuller discussion, see chapter 8.

- Indirect taxes are often unequalizing, but sometimes they are practically neutral, as in South Africa and Sri Lanka. More interesting still, even though indirect taxes in general are regressive—the Kakwani coefficients for indirect taxes are negative in both South Africa and Sri Lanka—they are not necessarily unequalizing forces.[10]

The results from this kind of analysis are informative because they enable one to say in general not only whether taxes are progressive or regressive but also whether each specific tax is progressive, equalizing, and poverty reducing.

It is possible, for example, to have a generally progressive direct tax system with small taxes that are unequalizing and poverty increasing, as in the case of land taxes in Ethiopia (chapter 3). The results allow for an evidence-based discussion of the design of each type of fiscal intervention.

Education and Health Spending

Finally, policy makers may wish to know the extent to which the poor benefit from government spending on education and health. Table 1.2 (using the definitions presented in annex 1A, figure 1A.2) summarizes the

Table 1.2 Progressivity and Pro-Poorness of Education and Health Spending, Selected Countries

Country	Education total			Preschool			Primary			Secondary			Tertiary				Health		
	A	B	C	A	B	C	A	B	C	A	B	C	A	B	C	D	A	B	C
Armenia (2011)	+			+			+				+			+				+	
Bolivia (2009)		+		+			+			+				+				+	
Brazil (2009)	+			+			+			+				+					+
Dominican Republic (2013)	+			+			+			+[b]	+[c]			+				+	
Ethiopia (2011)			+	—				+				+			+				+
Georgia (2013)	+			+			+			+				+				+	
Ghana (2013)		—		+			+					+			+	+	+		
Guatemala (2010)		+		+			+				+[b]	+[c]		+					+
Indonesia (2012)		+		—			+				+			+					+
Jordan (2010)[a]	+			+			+			+				+			—		
Mexico (2010)	+			+			+			+				+				+	
Peru (2009)	+			+			+			+				+					+
Russian Federation (2010)	+			—			—			—			—						+
South Africa (2010)	+			+			+			+				+			+		
Sri Lanka (2010)	+			+			+			+				+			+		
Uruguay (2009)	+			+			+			+				+			+		

Sources: For Armenia, Ethiopia, Georgia, Indonesia, Jordan, Russia, South Africa, and Sri Lanka, calculations are based on chapters in this volume. Additional sources are Bucheli et al. 2014 (Uruguay); Cabrera, Lustig, and Morán 2015 (Guatemala); Aristy-Escuder et al. 2017 (Dominican Republic); Higgins and Pereira 2014, 2016 (Brazil); Jaramillo 2014, 2015 (Peru); Paz Arauco et al. 2014 (Bolivia); Scott 2014 (Mexico); Younger, Osei-Assibey, and Oppong 2017 (Ghana).

Note: A = pro-poor (concentration coefficient [CC] is negative), meaning that the share of spending going to the poor is higher than their population share; B = same per capita for all (CC = 0); C = progressive (CC is positive but lower than the market-income Gini coefficient); D = regressive (CC is positive *and* higher than market-income Gini); — = data not available. (All spending that is "pro-poor" is by definition "progressive," but the opposite is not true. "Progressive" spending requires that spending as a share of market income decreases with income, whereas "pro-poorness" refers to the absolute level of spending declining with income.) The year of each country's household survey data is shown in parentheses in the left column.
a. Results concerning health services in Jordan must be taken with caution because the lack of data on the insurance value of health meant the data had to be imputed according to how much people paid. The results are that health spending is slightly unequalizing.
b. Designates lower-secondary school.
c. Designates upper-secondary school.

pro-poorness of government spending on education and health across countries for which comparable analysis is available. As indicated in the chapter by Lustig and Higgins in the *CEQ Handbook* (Lustig, 2017a), pro-poorness here means that per capita spending increases with income; or, alternatively that the share of spending going to the poor is higher than their population share (Lustig, 2017a). Note that all spending that is "pro-poor" is by definition also "progressive" but that the opposite is not true. "Progressive" spending requires that spending, as a share of market income, decreases with income, whereas "pro-poorness" refers to the absolute level of spending declining with income.

The results of a cross-country comparison can be summarized as follows:

- *Total education spending* is pro-poor in all countries where data are available except Bolivia, Guatemala, and Indonesia (where education spending is [approximately] neutral in absolute terms) and in Ethiopia (where education spending is progressive only in relative terms).
- *Preschool spending* tends to be pro-poor in all countries for which data are available, particularly in South Africa.
- *Primary school spending* is pro-poor in all countries for which data are available, except in Ethiopia, where primary education spending is neutral.
- *Secondary school spending* shows a quite heterogeneous pattern: it is progressive in relative terms in Ethiopia, Ghana, and Guatemala; roughly neutral in Armenia and Indonesia; and pro-poor in the rest of the countries for which data are available.
- *Tertiary education spending* is regressive in Ethiopia, Ghana, Guatemala, and Indonesia; it is progressive only in relative terms in the rest of the countries for which data are available.
- *Health spending* is pro-poor in Brazil, the Dominican Republic, Georgia, South Africa, Sri Lanka, and Uruguay; roughly neutral in Armenia, Bolivia, and Mexico; and progressive only in relative terms in Ethiopia, Guatemala, Indonesia, Peru, and Russia. The lowest progressivity is found in Jordan and Indonesia.

Although the results regarding the pro-poorness of spending on education and health are encouraging, guaranteeing access and facilitating the use of public education and health services for the poor are not enough. As long as the government provides low-quality schooling and health care, distortive patterns will be a major obstacle to the equalization of opportunities. However, with the existing information, one cannot disentangle the extent to which the progressivity of education and health spending is a result of differences in family composition—since poorer families tend to have more children and thus benefit more from public education—as opposed to the tendency of many higher-income households to opt out of the public education system because of its poor quality.

Conclusions

What is the role of taxes and social spending in reducing poverty and inequality? Although the literature on tax and benefit incidence is vast, few studies have attempted to look at the incidence of both taxes and spending in the context of developing LMICs. This approach is increasingly important because these countries are likely to rely more and more on their own fiscal resources to finance development objectives that could equalize opportunities. This volume showcases the power of undertaking systematic analysis of the distributional impact of taxes and public spending using a common methodological framework.

The volume presents eight detailed case studies but also draws from a larger body of evidence using the same approach. The approach aims to comprehensively address the impact of taxes and social spending on inequality and poverty; analyze the contribution of each tax and spending intervention to the redistributive and poverty-reducing effort, and assess the extent to which health and education spending are pro-poor. Because a common methodology is used, results are comparable across countries.

The volume's main message is the importance of empirical analysis in gauging the distributional impact of taxes and transfers. Although taxes and transfers are typically equalizing regardless of the size of the economy or the composition of taxes and social spending, there are wide differences across countries. In addition, the varying treatment of contributory pensions can affect the results significantly. When contributory pensions are treated as deferred income, in-kind transfers typically make most of the difference; when pensions are treated as transfers, the redistributive impact of taxes and transfers increases markedly for countries with large contributory systems, such as Armenia and Russia.

Although fiscal policies typically reduce income inequality, their effects are less auspicious in terms of poverty reduction and would have been difficult to predict without the empirical analysis. Although taxes and transfers reduce the poverty headcount ratio in most countries, they are poverty-increasing in some cases (particularly in Jordan, Russia, and Uruguay). This is because indirect taxes such as VAT are large enough at the bottom of the distribution that consumable incomes are lower than market incomes. In these contexts, the approach presented in this volume could be useful to determine the impacts across household types and demographic or age groups.

Moreover, in a world with multiple taxes and transfers and inevitable reranking (RR; households changing places in the income distribution when going from market income to final income), determining whether a particular tax or transfer is progressive or regressive is not enough to figure out its effect on poverty and inequality. We therefore calculate the marginal contributions to poverty and inequality for each tax and spending intervention. For most countries, direct taxes and transfers are generally progressive and equalizing. The marginal contribution of direct transfers is usually larger than the marginal contribution of direct taxes, although the difference is not always large. Indirect taxes are often unequalizing, but in some cases they are practically neutral, as in South Africa and Sri Lanka. Even more interesting, although indirect taxes in general are regressive, they are not necessarily unequalizing forces. In fact, in some cases a regressive tax can be equalizing, but this is difficult to predict unless the empirical work is undertaken.

Finally, policy makers often wish to know the extent to which the poor are benefiting from government spending on education and health. Total spending on education is pro-poor in almost all countries. Preschool is always pro-poor, whereas primary school is pro-poor in all countries except in Ethiopia, where it is neutral. For secondary school, the pattern is quite heterogeneous. In contrast, tertiary education is regressive in Ethiopia, Ghana, Guatemala, and Indonesia and progressive only in relative terms in the other countries. Health spending also has mixed results, being pro-poor in some countries and roughly neutral or progressive in relative terms in others. Although the results regarding the pro-poorness of spending on education and health are encouraging, guaranteeing access and facilitating the use of public education and health services for the poor are not enough to equalize opportunities, especially if the quality of government-provided schooling and health care is low.

Whether the question concerns the distributional impact of a particular fiscal intervention or the overall impact of taxes and transfers on poverty and inequality, this volume shows multiple examples of how a sound evidence base can be a useful input to decision making. Theoretically, a progressive tax or transfer policy could be so small that it makes little difference in terms of poverty and equity. Alternatively, a regressive tax policy could be equalizing—more so than if that tax were absent. The only way to know for sure is to undertake empirical analysis such as that showcased in this volume. Our hope is that a greater number of countries would regularly undertake such evidence-based analysis to inform their policy making.

Annex 1A. Fiscal Incidence Analysis: Methodological Highlights from the *CEQ Handbook*

What Is Fiscal Incidence Analysis?

As discussed in the chapter by Lustig and Higgins in the *CEQ Handbook* (Lustig 2017a), fiscal incidence analysis is used to assess the distributional impacts of a country's taxes and transfers (Lustig 2017a). Essentially, it consists of allocating taxes (particularly personal income tax [PIT] and consumption taxes) and public spending (particularly social spending) to households or individuals so that one can compare incomes before taxes and transfers with incomes after taxes and transfers.[11] Transfers include direct cash transfers; in-kind benefits such as free government education and health care services; and consumption subsidies such as food, electricity, and fuel subsidies.

Income Concepts Defined

As discussed in the *CEQ Handbook* (Lustig 2017a), any fiscal incidence study must start by defining the four basic income concepts used in the CEQ framework (figure 1A.1):[12]

- *Market income*, also called primary or original income, is total current income before direct taxes. It equals the sum of gross (pretax) wages and salaries in the formal and informal sectors (also known as earned income); income from capital (dividends, interest, profits, rents, and so on) in the formal and informal sectors (excluding capital gains and gifts); consumption of own production;[13] imputed rent for owner-occupied housing; and private transfers (remittances, pensions from private schemes, and other private transfers such as alimony).
- *Disposable income* is market income minus direct PIT on all income sources (included in market income) that are subject to taxation plus direct government transfers (mainly cash transfers but also including near-cash transfers such as food transfers, free textbooks, and school uniforms).

Figure 1A.1 Definitions of Income Concepts

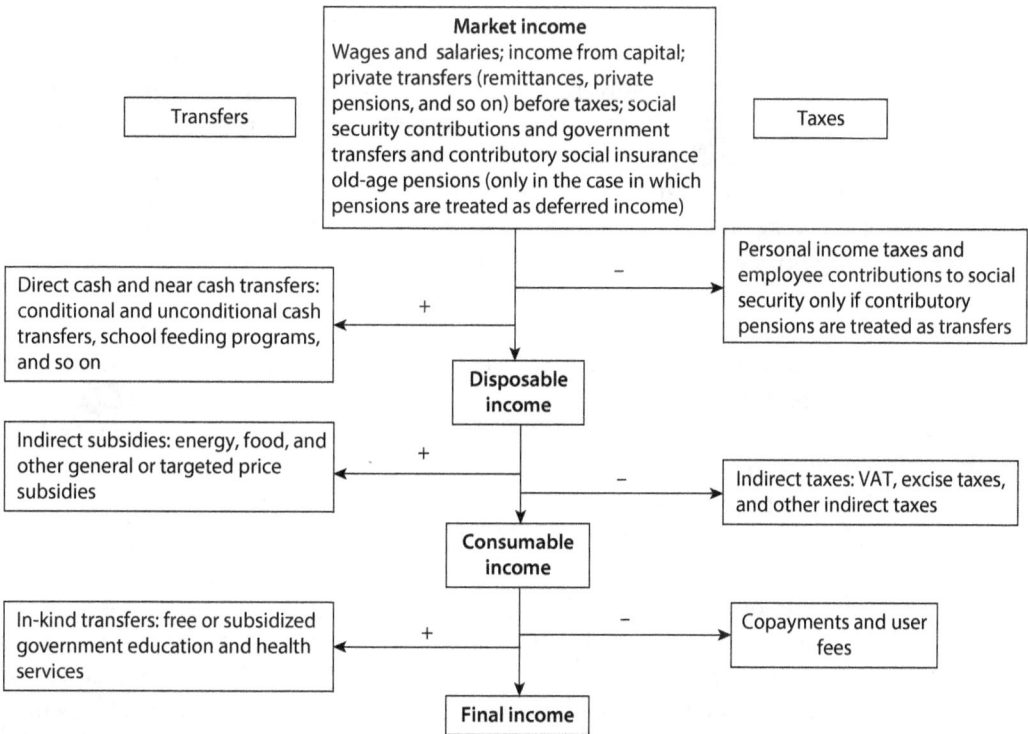

Source: Lustig and Higgins 2013; Lustig 2017a. ©Brookings Institution. Reproduced, with permission, under Creative Commons BY-NC-ND License 4.0.
Note: VAT = value added taxes.

- *Consumable income* is disposable income plus indirect subsidies (such as food and energy price subsidies) minus indirect taxes (such as VAT, excise taxes, and sales taxes).
- *Final income* is consumable income plus government transfers in the form of free or subsidized education and health services, valued at the average cost of provision (Sahn and Younger 2000) (minus copayments or user fees, when they exist).

Treatment of Contributory Pensions

As discussed in Lustig and Higgins (2017a), one area in which the literature presents no clear consensus is on the treatment of pensions from a pay-as-you-go contributory system. Some arguments favor treating contributory pensions as individual savings or deferred income (Breceda, Rigolini, and Saavedra 2008; Immervoll et al. 2009). Others argue that they should be treated as a government transfer, especially in systems with a large subsidized component (Goñi, López, and Servén 2011; Immervoll et al. 2009; Lindert, Skoufias, and Shapiro 2006).

Because this issue is unresolved, the studies analyzed here present results for both methods. One scenario treats social insurance contributory pensions (herewith called "contributory pensions") as deferred income (which in practice means that they are added to market income to generate the original or "pre-fisc" income). The other scenario treats these pensions as any other cash transfer from the government.[14] For consistency, when pensions are treated as deferred income, the contributions by individuals are included under savings (they are mandatory savings); when they are treated instead as government transfers, the contributions are included in direct taxes.

Notably, the treatment of contributory pensions affects not only the amount of spending and how it gets redistributed, but also the ranking of households by original (pre-fiscal) income. For example, under the scenario that considers contributory pensions to be government transfers, households for whom pensions are the main (or sole) source of income will have close to (or just) zero income before taxes and transfers and hence will be ranked at the bottom of the income scale. In contrast, when contributory pensions are treated as deferred income, households receiving contributory pensions will be placed higher in the income scale— sometimes considerably so. Thus, the treatment of contributory pensions in the incidence exercise could have significant implications for the order of magnitude of the "pre-fisc" and "post-fisc" inequality and poverty indicators.

Valuation of In-Kind Transfers

As discussed in Higgins and Lustig (2017), in the construction of final income, the method for estimating the benefit from public education spending consists of imputing a value to the benefit accrued to an individual of going to public school that equals the per-beneficiary input costs obtained from administrative data. For example, the average government expenditure per primary-school student (obtained from administrative data) is allocated to the households based on how many children are reported as attending a public primary school.

In the case of health care, the approach was analogous: the benefit of receiving health care in a public facility equals the average cost to the government of delivering health care services to the beneficiaries.

This approach to valuing education and health care services amounts to asking the following question: how much would a household's income have to increase if it had to pay for the free or subsidized public service (or, in the case of health benefits, the insurance value) at the full cost to the government? To avoid exaggerating the effect of government services on inequality, the totals for education and health spending in the studies reported here were scaled down so that their proportion to disposable income in the national accounts are the same as those observed using data from the household surveys. Such an approach ignores the fact that consumers may value services quite differently from what they cost. Given the limitations of available data, however, the cost-of-provision method is the best available for now.[15] For those who think that attaching a value to education and health services based on government costs is not accurate, the method applied here is equivalent to using a simple binary indicator of whether or not the individual uses the government service.[16]

Measuring the Contribution of Taxes and Transfers

As shown in Lambert (2001) and further developed in the chapter by Enami, Lustig, and Aranda (2017) in the CEQ *Handbook* (Lustig 2017), because the influence of specific interventions may differ from that of the overall fiscal system, a fundamental question in the policy discussion is whether a particular fiscal instrument (or combination of them) is equalizing or unequalizing. In a world with a single fiscal intervention and no RR (meaning that, for all individuals, if one was poorer than another before a fiscal intervention, he or she will remain poorer than the other individual after the intervention), it is sufficient to know whether that particular intervention is progressive or regressive to give an unambiguous response using the typical indicators of progressivity such as the Kakwani index.[17] (The next section further discusses RR in the discussion of horizontal and vertical equity.)

However, in a world with more than one fiscal intervention (even in the absence of RR), this one-to-one relationship between the progressivity of a particular intervention and its effect on inequality breaks down. Depending on certain characteristics of the fiscal system, a regressive tax, for example, can exert an equalizing force over and above that which would prevail in the absence of that regressive tax (Lambert 2001, 277–78).[18]

Lambert's "conundrum"[19] is not equivalent to the well-known (and frequently repeated) result that efficient regressive taxes can be fine as long as, when combined with transfers, the net fiscal system is equalizing (Ebrill et al. 2001; Engel, Galetovic, and Raddatz 1999; Keen and Lockwood 2010). The surprising aspect of Lambert's conundrum is that a net fiscal system with a regressive tax (in relation to market income) is more equalizing than one without it.[20]

The implications of Lambert's conundrum in real fiscal systems are quite profound: namely, that to determine whether a particular intervention (or a particular policy change) is inequality increasing or inequality reducing—and by how much—one must resort to numerical calculations that include the whole system. As Lambert (2001) mentions, the conundrum is "not altogether farfetched": Two renowned studies in the 1980s found this type of result for the United Kingdom and the United States (O'Higgins and Ruggles 1981; Ruggles and O'Higgins 1981). It also made its appearance in a 1990s study for Chile (Engel, Galetovic, and Raddatz 1999).[21]

Lambert's conundrum is a direct result of path dependency. Progressivity indexes such as the Kakwani index measure the characteristic of fiscal interventions, always taking the *pre-fisc income* (called "market income" earlier in figure 1A.1) as the base. However, once other fiscal interventions come into play, whether a particular fiscal instrument is equalizing will no longer just depend on whether it is progressive relative to the *pre-fisc* income but whether it is progressive relative to the income generated with all the other fiscal interventions as well. The income generated with "all other interventions" in the CEQ framework may be disposable income, consumable income, or final income (see definitions above).

Given path dependence, one way to calculate the sign of the effect of a particular fiscal instrument is to calculate the "marginal contribution." The marginal contribution of a tax (or transfer) is the difference between the inequality indicator *without* the tax (or transfer) and *with* it.[22] For example, the marginal contribution of indirect taxes is the difference between (a) the Gini (or any other inequality indicator) for consumable income plus indirect taxes (that is, consumable income *without* the indirect taxes) and (b) consumable income.[23]

One great advantage of calculating the marginal contribution is that it has a straightforward policy interpretation.[24] It is equivalent to asking, "What would the inequality be if the system did not have a particular tax (or transfer) or if a tax (or transfer) were modified? Would inequality be higher, the same, or lower with the tax (or transfer) than without it?"[25]

As shown in Enami (2017b) and Lustig and Higgins (2017), it is important to note that, in addition to the pure case Lambert conundrum, the fact that a progressive (regressive) tax or transfer can be unequalizing (equalizing) can also be the consequence of RR.

Measuring Horizontal and Vertical Equity

As discussed in Enami (2017b) and Lustig and Higgins (2017), a well-recognized form of horizontal inequity is when fiscal interventions arbitrarily alter the relative position of individuals across the distribution—referred to as "reranking." Reranking occurs if individual A was poorer than individual B before a fiscal intervention, but B is poorer than A after the intervention.[26] The definition of horizontal equity postulates that the prefiscal policy income ranking should be preserved (Duclos and Araar 2006). In other words, if individual A was poorer than individual B *before* the fiscal interventions, individual A should continue to be poorer than individual B *after* the interventions.

From theory, we know that the total redistributive effect (RE) can be decomposed into two elements: the change in vertical equity (VE) minus RR

(Duclos and Araar 2006). RE equals the difference between the Gini coefficient for incomes before taxes and transfers, G_m, and the Gini coefficient for incomes after taxes and transfers, $G_{post-fisc}$, or

$$RE = G_m - G_{post-fisc}, \tag{1A.1}$$

Adding and subtracting $\mathbf{C}_{post-fisc}$ (the concentration coefficient [CC] for incomes after taxes and transfers),[27] equation (1A.1) can be decomposed into

$$RE = (G_m - C_{post-fisc}) - (G_{post-fisc} - C_{post-fisc}). \tag{1A.2}$$

Then the redistributive effect can be written as

$$RE = VE - RR, \tag{1A.3}$$

where VE is equal to the difference between the Gini coefficient for incomes *before* taxes and transfers and the CC for incomes *after* taxes and transfers; if there is no RR, RE = VE by definition because the CC for incomes *after* taxes and transfers will be identical to the Gini coefficient for incomes *after* taxes and transfers; and RR is equal to the difference between the Gini coefficient for incomes *after* taxes and transfers and the CC for incomes *after* taxes and transfers.

RR diminishes RE, as clearly shown in equation (1A.3). The VE measure is the Reynolds-Smolensky progressivity index (RS), and the RR measure is known as the Atkinson-Plotnick index of horizontal inequity (Atkinson 1980; Plotnick 1981; Reynolds and Smolensky 1977).

Defining Pro-Poorness of Government Spending

As discussed in Lustig and Higgins (2017), the pro-poorness of public spending here is defined using CCs (also called quasi-Ginis).[28] In keeping with conventions, spending is defined as regressive whenever the CC is higher than the Gini for market income. When this occurs, it means that the benefits from that spending as a share of market income *tend* to rise with market income.[29] Spending is progressive whenever the CC is lower than the Gini for market income. This means that the benefits from that spending as a share of market income tend to fall with market income. Within progressive spending, spending is neutral in absolute terms—spending per capita is the same across the income distribution—whenever the CC is equal to zero.

Spending is defined as *pro-poor* whenever the CC is not only lower than the Gini but also negative. Pro-poor spending implies that the *per capita* government spending on the transfer *tends* to fall with market income.[30] Any time spending is pro-poor or neutral in absolute terms, by definition it is progressive. The converse, of course, is not true.[31] The taxonomy of transfers is synthesized in figure 1A.2.

Figure 1A.2 Progressivity of Transfers: A Diagrammatic Representation

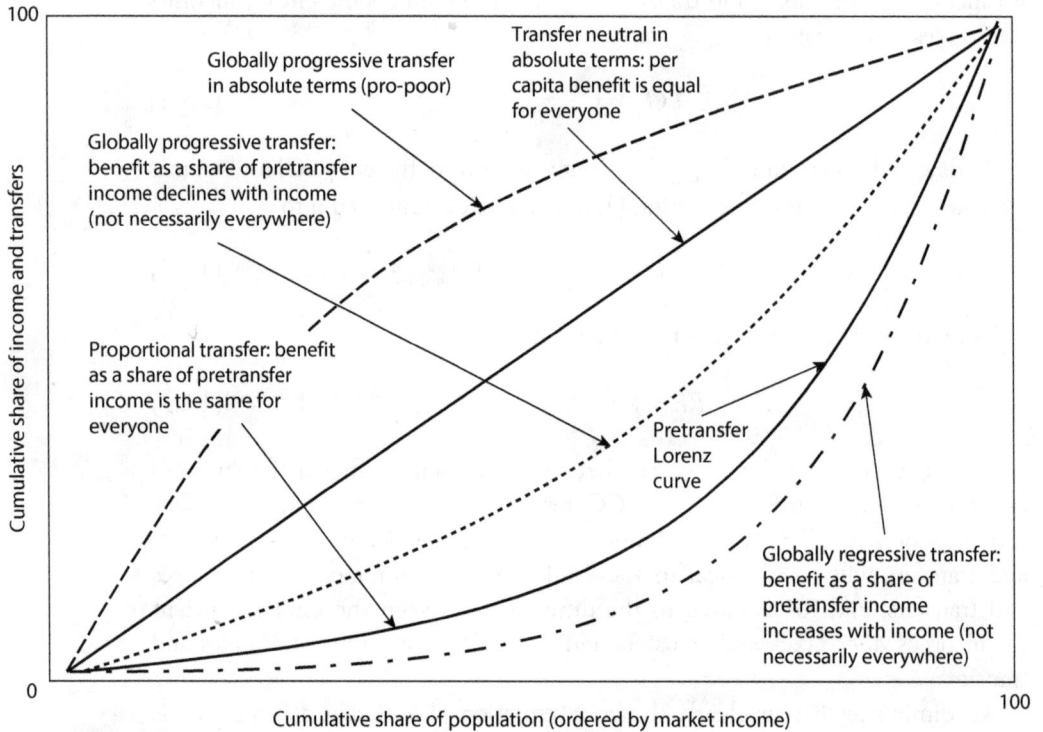

Cumulative share of population (ordered by market income)

Source: Adapted from Enami, Lustig, and Aranda, 2017. ©Brookings Institution. Reproduced, with permission, under Creative Commons BY-NC-ND License 4.0.

Here, households are ranked by per capita market income, and no adjustments are made to their size because of differences in the composition by age and gender. In some analyses, the pro-poorness of education spending, for example, is determined using children—not all members of the household—as the unit of analysis. Because poorer families typically have more children, they would naturally benefit more from spending per child. As a result, pro-poor concentration curves may simply reflect this rather than implying that poorer families receive more resources per child.

Annex 1B. Data and Assumptions

Data Sources

In general, fiscal incidence exercises are carried out using household surveys, as was done here (table 1B.1).[32] Note that empirically one often starts from a concept different from market income. In many income-based surveys, reported income corresponds to (or is assumed to be) market income net of direct taxes (as in Georgia, Russia, and South Africa). Consumption-based surveys, however, often report no income at all. In those cases, the incidence analysis equated

Table 1B.1 Survey Data Sources for Country Fiscal Incidence Studies

Country	Year	Data source
Armenia	2011	Integrated Living Conditions Survey (ILCS)
Bolivia	2009	Encuesta de Hogares (EH) (Household Survey)
Brazil	2009	Pesquisa de Orçamentos Familiares (Household Budget Survey)
Dominican Republic (2013)[a]	2006/07	Encuesta Nacional de Ingresos y Gastos de los Hogares (ENIGH) (National Survey of Household Income and Expenditure)
Ethiopia	2010/11	Household Consumption Expenditure Survey (HCES) and Welfare Monitoring Survey (WMS)
Georgia	2012/13	Integrated Household Survey (IHS)
Ghana	2012/13	Ghana Living Standards Survey (GLSS)
Guatemala	2010	ENIGH (National Survey of Family Income and Expenditure)
Indonesia	2012	Survei Sosial Ekonomi Nasional (SUSENAS) (National Socioeconomic Survey)
Jordan	2010/11	Household Expenditure and Income Survey (HEIS)
Mexico	2010	ENIGH (National Survey of Household Income and Expenditure)
Peru	2009	Encuesta Nacional de Hogares (National Household Survey)
Russian Federation	2010	Russian Longitudinal Monitoring Survey (RLMS-HSE)
South Africa	2010/11	Income and Expenditure Survey (IES) and National Income Dynamics Study (NIDS) 2008, Wave 1, for health expenditures
Sri Lanka	2009/10	Household Income and Expenditure Survey (HIES)
Uruguay	2009	Encuesta Continua de Hogares (Continuous Household Survey)

a. Although the Dominican Republic study analyzes the effects of fiscal policy in 2013, the analysis is based on household income and expenditure survey data gathered in 2006–07.

consumption with disposable income (as in Ethiopia, Indonesia, Jordan, and Sri Lanka). In these cases, market income was generated "backward," applying a "net to gross" conversion (Immervoll and O'Donoghue 2001).

Assumptions

The fiscal incidence analysis used here is point-in-time and does not incorporate behavioral or general equilibrium effects. That is, no claim is made that the original or market income equals the true counterfactual income in the absence of taxes and transfers. It is a first-order approximation that measures the average incidence of fiscal interventions.

However, the analysis is not a mechanically applied accounting exercise. The incidence of taxes is the economic rather than statutory incidence. Consistent with other conventional tax incidence analyses, here we assume that the economic burden of direct PIT is borne by the recipient of income. The burden of payroll and social security taxes is assumed to fall entirely on workers. It is assumed that individual income taxes and contributions by both employees and employers, for instance, are borne by labor in the formal sector. Individuals who are not contributing to social security are assumed to pay neither direct taxes nor contributions. Consumption taxes are assumed to be shifted forward to consumers. In the case of consumption taxes, the analyses take into account the lower incidence associated with own-consumption, rural markets, and informality. These assumptions are strong because, in essence, they imply that labor supply is perfectly inelastic and that consumers have perfectly inelastic demands for goods and services. In practice they provide a reasonable approximation.[33]

Despite these general assumptions, it should also be stressed that each case study reflects the unique characteristics of the tax and benefit system in place. Table 1B.2 presents details on the key assumptions across countries such as assumptions related to the construction of the welfare aggregates as well as regarding how taxes and spending are allocated. For instance, although own-consumption and the imputed value of owner-occupied housing are usually included in market income (Lustig and Higgins 2013; Lustig 2017a), there are some exceptions. In particular, own-consumption data were not considered reliable in the case of South Africa (chapter 8 of this volume), whereas the imputed value of owner-occupied housing is not included in the case of Russia (chapter 7 of this volume).

Similarly, countries differ in their allocation of taxes and transfers. One important difference is in the scope of the analysis. Although in all cases taxes and transfers are included in the analysis, the number of taxes and benefits included in each case is slightly different. For instance, some case studies have been able to include payroll (South Africa) and property (Ethiopia) taxes among direct taxes, whereas others have been able to include customs duties and multiple types of excise taxes into the analysis of indirect taxes (Armenia). Similarly, in terms of benefits, some case studies include careful analysis of indirect subsidies (Indonesia and Jordan), whereas others don't include such subsidies, either because the data are unavailable (Sri Lanka) or because they are not an important source of spending (Armenia). In the case of South Africa, we treat free basic services (municipal provision of power, sanitation, water, and refuse removal) as direct transfers under the benchmark and experiment with treating them as price subsidies under an alternative scenario.[34]

Another source of difference is in the treatment of informality. For example, the Jordan, South Africa, and Sri Lanka case studies do not differentiate between formal and informal workers and assume that all employees pay the statutory PIT rates. However, the Armenia and Russia case studies assume that only formal sector employees pay taxes, and the Georgia and Guatemala case studies assume that employees in small firms and the self-employed do not pay taxes. Similarly, most case studies incorporate the possibility of informality in the analysis of VAT by using effective as opposed to statutory rates, but the Russia and South Africa case studies make no assumptions about informality and use the statutory VAT rates.

Finally, although in all cases we strive to present both a benchmark scenario (that treats contributory pensions as deferred income) and a sensitivity scenario (that treats them as direct transfers), this is not done under specific country circumstances. For instance, in South Africa, the only contributory pensions are for public servants who must belong to the Government Employees Pension Fund (GEPF). Because the government made no transfers to the GEPF in 2010/11, contributory pensions are always treated as deferred income.

Table 1B.2 Key Country Assumptions for Fiscal Incidence Analysis

Assumption type	Armenia (2011)	Ethiopia (2011)	Georgia (2013)	Indonesia (2012)	Jordan (2010)	Russian Federation (2010)	South Africa (2010)	Sri Lanka (2010)
Use of input-output matrix for indirect taxes and subsidies								
Indirect taxes calculated with an input-output matrix?	No	Yes	No	Yes	No	No	Yes	No
Indirect subsidies calculated with an input-output matrix?	n.a.	n.a.	No	Yes, for all except LPG	No	No	No	No
Take-up assumptions								
Take-up of direct transfers—as reported in the survey?	Yes	Yes	Yes	Yes	Yes	Yes, with some exceptions (A random non-take-up is assumed for some simulated benefits.)	Yes	Yes
Take-up of in-kind transfers—as reported by use?	Yes	Yes	Yes	Yes	Yes	Yes	Yes	Yes
SSC, taxes, and subsidies (shifting assumptions)								
SSC: only those paid by employee or both those paid by employee and employer are assumed to be borne by employee?	Both are borne by employee.	n.a.	n.a.	n.a.	n.a.	Both are borne by employee	n.a.	Only employee contribution is included.
Direct taxes: burden of direct PIT assumed to be borne entirely by the recipient of income?	Yes, paid by formal workers.	Yes	Yes	PIT is imputed to be zero for all SUSENAS respondents.	Yes	Yes	Yes	Yes

table continues next page

Table 1B.2 Key Country Assumptions for Fiscal Incidence Analysis *(continued)*

Assumption type	Armenia (2011)	Ethiopia (2011)	Georgia (2013)	Indonesia (2012)	Jordan (2010)	Russian Federation (2010)	South Africa (2010)	Sri Lanka (2010)
Indirect taxes: burden assumed to be borne entirely by the consumer?	Yes	Yes	Yes	Yes	Yes	Yes	Yes	Yes
Indirect subsidies: benefit assumed to be received entirely by the consumer?	n.a.	Yes	Yes	Yes	Yes	Yes	n.a.	Yes

Assumption type	Bolivia (2009)	Brazil (2009)	Dominican Republic (2013)	Ghana (2013)	Guatemala (2010)	Mexico (2010)	Peru (2009)	Uruguay (2009)
Use of input-output matrix for indirect taxes and subsidies								
Indirect taxes calculated with an input-output matrix?	No	Yes	No	Yes	No	No	No	No
Indirect subsidies calculated with an input-output matrix?	No	No	No	No	No	No	n.a.	Not included
Take-up assumptions								
Take-up of direct transfers—as reported in the survey?	Yes	No (imputed)	No (imputed)	No (simulated based on PMT and other program criteria)	Yes	–	–	–
Take-up of in-kind transfers—as reported by use?	Yes	Yes	Yes	Yes (use of the relevant product or service)	Yes	–	–	–

table continues next page

Table 1B.2 Key Country Assumptions for Fiscal Incidence Analysis *(continued)*

Assumption type	Bolivia (2009)	Brazil (2009)	Dominican Republic (2013)	Ghana (2013)	Guatemala (2010)	Mexico (2010)	Peru (2009)	Uruguay (2009)
SSC, taxes, and subsidies (shifting assumptions)								
SSC: only those paid by employee or both those paid by employee and employer assumed to be borne by employee?	n.a.	Yes	Not included	Not included (Assume these are deferred income.)	Yes	Yes	Yes	–
Direct taxes: burden of direct PIT assumed to be borne entirely by the recipient of income?	n.a.	Yes	Yes	Yes, they are paid by formal workers.	Yes	Yes	Yes	Yes
Indirect taxes: burden assumed to be borne entirely by the consumer?	Yes	Yes	Yes	Yes	Yes	Yes	Yes	Yes
Indirect subsidies: benefit assumed to be received entirely by the consumer?	Yes	Yes	Yes	Yes	Yes	–	Yes	Not included

Assumption type	Armenia (2011)	Ethiopia (2011)	Georgia (2013)	Indonesia (2012)	Jordan (2010)	Russian Federation (2010)	South Africa (2010)	Sri Lanka (2010)
Tax evasion assumptions								
Direct taxes	Informal employees and self-employed are assumed to pay no PIT.	None	Tax is evaded for labor income from second jobs or self-employment; tax is evaded for income from abroad.	PIT imputed to be zero for all SUSENAS respondents.	No PIT evasion is assumed.	Only formal sector workers are assumed to pay social insurance contributions and PIT.	None: statutory rates are used.	All high earners are assumed to pay taxes.

table continues next page

Table 1B.2 Key Country Assumptions for Fiscal Incidence Analysis *(continued)*

Assumption type	Armenia (2011)	Ethiopia (2011)	Georgia (2013)	Indonesia (2012)	Jordan (2010)	Russian Federation (2010)	South Africa (2010)	Sri Lanka (2010)
Indirect taxes	Effective rates are used, which implicitly includes evasion.	None	Excise taxes for cigarettes are calculated using administrative sources and adjusted for informal market (scaled up by 9%).	Effective, not statutory, rates are used for VAT; statutory rates are used for tobacco excise.	None	None	None: statutory rates are used.	Effective tax rate is used for VAT and excise taxes.

Assumption type	Bolivia (2009)	Brazil (2009)	Dominican Republic (2013)	Ghana (2013)	Guatemala (2010)	Mexico (2010)	Peru (2009)	Uruguay (2009)
Tax evasion assumptions								
Direct taxes	n.a.	Survey reports taxes are paid.	Self-employed are assumed not to pay PIT.	Self-employed are assumed to pay neither PIT nor SSC, but amounts reported in survey under the HH enterprise questionnaire are included.	PIT is paid by employees and self-employed in firms with fewer than 10 workers; by daily agricultural workers (*jornaleros*); and by the underemployed (reporting less than 40 hours' work per week).	Workers without contributive social security coverage are assumed not to pay direct taxes or SSC.	Survey reports taxes are paid; no assumption is made regarding evasion.	Workers who do not pay SSC do not pay direct taxes.

table continues next page

Table 1B.2 Key Country Assumptions for Fiscal Incidence Analysis (continued)

Assumption type	Bolivia (2009)	Brazil (2009)	Dominican Republic (2013)	Ghana (2013)	Guatemala (2010)	Mexico (2010)	Peru (2009)	Uruguay (2009)
Indirect taxes	None	Effective tax rates take evasion into account.	Goods were classified into four groups: • High propensity for evasion • High propensity to pay ITBIS • Products with estimated compliance rates • Products on which VAT paid as a condition of purchase	Effective tax rates take evasion into account.	Goods exempt by law do not pay VAT. Moreover, assumptions are that some goods are more likely to be sold in informal markets (such as unprocessed food in rural areas) and in some small urban stores. Assumption is that some private services do not pay VAT.	No indirect taxes are paid by either rural consumers or urban buyers from informal sellers (street vendors, farmers markets, and so on).	No taxes are paid by residents of villages with populations below 500 or purchasers from street vendors, farmers markets, or in other informal conditions.	None

Assumption type	Armenia (2011)	Ethiopia (2011)	Georgia (2013)	Indonesia (2012)	Jordan (2010)	Russian Federation (2010)	South Africa (2010)	Sri Lanka (2010)
Scaling-up or scaling-down assumptions								
In-kind education and health services scaled up or down?	In-kind transfers are scaled down in all scenarios.	Scaled down	Scaled down	In-kind transfers scaled down	Scaled down	Education is scaled down; health care is scaled up.	In-kind health care is scaled down.	Scaled down
Other taxes, transfers, and subsidies individually (such as taxes on tobacco) or as a category (such as total indirect taxes) scaled up or down?	PIT and SSC are additionally scaled down in a sensitivity scenario.	n.a.	n.a.	n.a.	n.a.	n.a.	Excise taxes are scaled down.	Excise taxes, free textbooks, free uniforms, and fertilizer subsidy are scaled down.

table continues next page

Table 1B.2 Key Country Assumptions for Fiscal Incidence Analysis (continued)

Assumption type	Armenia (2011)	Ethiopia (2011)	Georgia (2013)	Indonesia (2012)	Jordan (2010)	Russian Federation (2010)	South Africa (2010)	Sri Lanka (2010)
Treatment of administrative costs and capital expenditures								
Cash and near-cash transfers include administrative costs?	No	No	No	No	No	No	No	No
Education and health include administrative costs?	No	Yes	Yes	Yes	No	Yes	No	No
Education and health include capital expenditures?	Yes, albeit they are small ones given stagnant school population and few government-owned health centers and hospitals.	Yes, except they do not include tertiary education.	No	Yes	No	Yes	No	Yes

table continues next page

Table 1B.2 Key Country Assumptions for Fiscal Incidence Analysis *(continued)*

Assumption type	Bolivia (2009)	Brazil (2009)	Dominican Republic (2013)	Ghana (2013)	Guatemala (2010)	Mexico (2010)	Peru (2009)	Uruguay (2009)
Scaling-up or scaling-down assumptions								
In-kind education and health services scaled up or down?	Scaled up	Scaled up; sensitivity analysis #3 uses nonscaled income.	Scaled down	Scaled down; albeit they are small as survey HH consumption is close to national accounts.	Scaled up	Scaled up	Scaled up	Scaled up
Other taxes, transfers, and subsidies individually (such as taxes on tobacco) or as a category (such as total indirect taxes) scaled up or down?	–	–	Indirect taxes are scaled down.	VAT, import duties, and gasoline duties are scaled to match national totals.	Scaled up	–	–	–
Treatment of administrative costs and capital expenditures								
Cash and near-cash transfers include administrative costs?	–	No	No	Yes	No	–	–	–
Education and health include administrative costs?	Yes	Yes	Yes	Yes	Yes	–	–	–
Education and health include capital expenditures?	Yes	Yes	Yes	Yes	Yes	–	–	–

Sources: For Armenia, Ethiopia, Georgia, Indonesia, Jordan, the Russian Federation, South Africa, and Sri Lanka, calculations are based on data in the country-specific chapters in this volume. Additional sources are Buchell et al. 2014 (Uruguay); Cabrera, Lustig, and Morán 2015 (Guatemala); Aristy-Escuder et al. 2017 (Dominican Republic); Higgins and Pereira 2014, 2016 (Brazil); Jaramillo 2014, 2015 (Peru); Paz Arauco et al. 2014 (Bolivia); Scott 2014 (Mexico); Younger, Osei-Assibey, and Oppong 2017 (Ghana).

Note: LPG = liquefied petroleum gas; PMT = proxy means text; PIT = personal income tax; VAT = value added tax; SUSENAS = National Socioeconomic Survey (Indonesia); SSC = social security contributions; HH = household; ITBIS = Tax on Transfer of Industrialized Goods and Services, a value added tax applied to industrialized goods and services; n.a. = not applicable; – = not available.

33

Similarly, in Sri Lanka, the only available pensions are those received by civil servants with more than 10 years of service. As such, these pensions are assumed to be part of their lifelong salaries and therefore always considered as deferred income. In contrast, in Georgia, the government moved away from a contributory pension system, so pensions are always treated as transfers and included as such in both scenarios.

Annex 1C. Redistributive Effort: Marginal Contribution of Taxes and Transfers toward Reducing Inequality

Table 1C.1 Marginal Contribution of Taxes, Transfers, and Subsidies toward Inequality Reduction, Selected Countries

Marginal contribution (contributory pensions as deferred income)	Armenia (2011)[a]	Georgia (2013)[b]	Ghana (2013)	Indonesia (2012)[c]	Jordan (2010)	Russian Federation (2010)	South Africa (2010)[b]	Sri Lanka (2010)
From market income to consumable income[d]								
Redistributive effect[e]	0.035	0.096	0.014	0.004	0.016	0.028	0.0766	0.0115
Direct taxes	0.019	0.021	−0.005	0.000	0.008	0.011	0.0327	0.0025
Direct transfers	0.101	0.113	0.001	0.004	0.006	0.024	0.0672	0.0044
Indirect taxes	−0.001	−0.018	0.001	−0.003	−0.002	−0.004	−0.0002	−0.0003
Indirect subsidies	0.000	0.000	−0.001	0.003	0.005	0.000	—	0.0057
From market income to final income[d]								
Redistributive effect[e]	0.053	0.124	0.035	0.024	0.023	0.063	0.1758	0.0278
Direct taxes	0.021	0.022	−0.006	0.000	0.007	0.014	0.0430	0.0025
Direct transfers	0.092	0.100	0.001	0.004	0.005	0.020	0.0517	0.0041
Indirect taxes	0.001	−0.014	0.002	−0.002	−0.001	−0.001	0.0127	0.0006
Indirect subsidies	0.000	0.000	−0.001	0.001	0.004	0.032	n.a.	0.0051
All in-kind transfers	—	—	0.016	—	0.025	—	0.0992	0.0163
Education	0.014	0.020	0.008	0.019	0.015	0.021	0.0490	0.0105
Preschool	0.001	0.002	0.0014	—	0.000	—	0.0004	0.0108
Primary school	0.005	0.016	0.0132	0.009	0.013	—	0.0298	
Secondary school	—	0.0022	—	0.002	—	0.0166		
Lower secondary	0.006		—	0.008	—	—	—	
Upper secondary	0.002		—	0.002	—	—	—	
Vocational	0.0001** 0.0002++	0.000	0.000	—	0.000	—	—	
Tertiary	0.000	0.001	−0.008	−0.001	0.000	—	−0.0007	−0.0003
Health	0.004	0.008	0.007	0.003	−0.009	0.013	0.043	0.0056
Kakwani coefficient[f]								
Direct taxes	0.096	0.182	—	—	0.594	0.104	0.125	0.5458
Direct transfers	0.660	0.706	0.807	0.640	0.550	0.593	1.042	0.7572
Indirect taxes	−0.129	−0.230	0.002	−0.042	−0.066	−0.072	−0.083	−0.0063
Indirect subsidies	0.382	0.372	−0.011	0.056	0.151	0.213	n.a.	0.3056

table continues next page

Table 1C.1 Marginal Contribution of Taxes, Transfers, and Subsidies toward Inequality Reduction, Selected Countries (continued)

Marginal contribution (contributory pensions as deferred income)	Armenia (2011)[a]	Georgia (2013)[b]	Ghana (2013)	Indonesia (2012)[c]	Jordan (2010)	Russian Federation (2010)	South Africa (2010)[b]	Sri Lanka (2010)
All in-kind transfers	0.473	0.570	0.287	0.344	0.344	0.438	0.8217	0.3916
Education	—	0.541	—	0.363	0.478	0.498	0.8169	0.3892
Preschool	0.442	0.518	0.773	—	0.666	—	0.8852	0.4514
Primary school	0.574	0.585	0.7042	0.471	0.581	—	0.9611	
Secondary school	—		0.3116	—	0.403	—	0.8938	
Lower secondary	0.600		—	0.425	—	—	—	
Upper secondary	0.465		—	0.288	—	—	—	
Vocational	0.870** 0.533++	0.6006	0.0507	—	0.749	—	—	
Tertiary	0.172	0.292	−0.254	−0.085	0.006	—	0.1562	0.0776
Health	0.500	0.636	—	0.273	0.056	0.374	0.8275	0.3963

Sources: For Armenia, Ethiopia, Georgia, Indonesia, Jordan, the Russian Federation, South Africa, and Sri Lanka, calculations are based on data in the country-specific chapters in this volume. For Ghana, see Younger, Osei-Assibey, and Oppong 2017.

Note: The "marginal contribution" equals the difference between the Gini coefficient of the relevant ending income concept without the intervention in question and the Gini coefficient of the relevant ending income concept (which, of course, includes that intervention). By definition, the sum of the marginal contributions does not fulfill the adding-up principle, so it will not be equal to the redistributive effect unless by coincidence. The marginal contributions shown in the table are measured in Gini points. — = not available; n.a. = not applicable (that is, fiscal interventions that do not apply to a particular country).

a. Results for Armenia consider contributory pensions as direct transfers instead of as deferred income.

b. The results for Georgia and South Africa exclude contributory pensions from the analysis for the following reasons: Georgia has only a noncontributory public pension scheme. In South Africa, the only contributory pensions are for public servants, who must belong to the Government Employees Pension Fund.

c. For Indonesia, the fiscal incidence analysis was carried out adjusting for spatial price differences. The PIT is imputed to be zero for all National Socioeconomic Survey (SUSENAS) respondents.

d. "Market income" comprises pretax wages, salaries, income earned from capital assets (rent, interest, or dividends), and private transfers. "Consumable income" = market income − all taxes + direct cash transfers + indirect subsidies. "Final income" = consumable income + value of in-kind transfers (education and health care).

e. The "redistributive effect" refers to the reduction in inequality, represented by change in the Gini coefficient (a decrease meaning less inequality). It equals the difference between the market income plus pensions Gini and the consumable income Gini or final income Gini.

f. The Kakwani coefficient measures whether a fiscal intervention exercises an equalizing or unequalizing force, calculated by subtracting the intervention's concentration coefficient from the market income Gini; progressive interventions have positive Kakwani coefficients, and regressive ones have negative coefficients (Kakwani 1977).

**corresponds to initial vocational education; ++corresponds to secondary vocational education. The year of each country's household survey data from which the analysis was conducted is shown within parentheses.

Notes

1. Led by Nora Lustig since 2008, the Commitment to Equity (CEQ) project works to reduce inequality and poverty through rigorous tax and benefit incidence analysis in low- and middle-income countries and active engagement with the policy community. The project is housed in Tulane University's Commitment to Equity Institute. The Institute has received the generous support of the Bill & Melinda Gates Foundation. In particular, the *Commitment to Equity Handbook* (Lustig 2017a) and the study for Ghana cited in this Overview were possible thanks to this support. For more information, visit http://www.commitmentoequity.org/.

2. Studies included in this volume mostly use the methodology in Higgins and Lustig (2013). Since the Lustig (2017) handbook introduced a series of important revisions to the CEQ methodology, in order to avoid confusion the Lustig and Higgins handbook (2013) is no longer available online; it can be obtained by request by contacting nlustig@tulane.edu.

3. For the Dominican Republic, the study analyzes the effects of fiscal policy in 2013, but the household income and expenditure survey dates back to 2007.

4. The Gini coefficient is the most common measure of the inequality of income (or consumption) distribution within a country. A Gini value of 0 indicates full equality, and 1 (or 100 percent) indicates maximum inequality.

5. For more on this method and its application, see, for example, Demery (2000).

6. This particular comparison does *not* take into account public spending on in-kind services such as health, education, housing, water, sanitation, and so on. It also excludes any benefits from public investment in infrastructure.

7. Ethiopia is evaluated at the US$1.25 PPP per day poverty line, which is closer to the national poverty line given its level of development.

8. For a more thorough discussion of fiscal impoverishment and how it is calculated, see the section on "Measuring Horizontal and Vertical Equity" in annex 1A and particularly the extensive treatment in Higgins and Lustig (2016).

9. See, for example, the EUROMOD statistics on Distribution and Decomposition of Disposable Income, (accessed August 27, 2016), https://www.euromod.ac.uk/.

10. Kakwani coefficients measure whether a fiscal intervention is progressive or regressive, calculated by subtracting the intervention's concentration coefficient from the prefiscal (in our framework, market income or market income plus pensions depending on whether contributory pensions are considered a transfer or deferred income, respectively) Gini for transfers and the converse for taxes. Progressive interventions have positive Kakwani coefficients, and regressive ones have negative coefficients (Kakwani 1977).

11. In addition to the studies cited here and other studies available at www.commitmentoequity.org, see, for example, Förster and Whiteford (2009), Immervoll and Richardson (2011), and OECD (2011).

12. In the case of Indonesia, the surveys do not have income data, so the incidence analysis assumes that consumption in that country equals disposable income.

13. Consumption of own production was not included in the fiscal incidence analysis for South Africa, whose data on auto consumption (also called own-production or self-consumption) were not considered reliable.

14. Immervoll et al. (2009) do the analysis under these two scenarios as well.

15. By using averages, this method also ignores differences across income groups and regions: for example, governments may spend less (or more) per pupil or patient in poorer areas of a country. Some studies in the CEQ project adjusted the estimate of education and health spending for regional differences.

16. Of course, this interpretation is only true within a level of education. A concentration coefficient for total nontertiary education, for example—where the latter is calculated as the sum of the different spending amounts by level—is not equivalent to the binary indicator method.

17. The Kakwani index for taxes is defined as the difference between the concentration coefficient of the tax and the Gini for market income (Kakwani 1977). For transfers, it is defined as the difference between the Gini for market income and the concentration coefficient of the transfer.

18. For a derivation of all the mathematical conditions that can be used to determine when the addition of a regressive tax is equalizing or when the addition of a progressive transfer is unequalizing, see Enami, Lustig, and Aranda (2017).

19. This is Lambert's term (Lambert 2001, 278).

20. It can also be shown that if there is reranking—a pervasive feature of net tax systems in the real world—making a tax (or a transfer) more progressive can *increase* post-tax, post-transfers inequality. In Lambert's example, regressive taxes not only enhance the equalizing effect of transfers, but making taxes more progressive (that is, more dispro-portional in the Kakwani sense) would also result in higher(!) inequality; any additional change (toward more progressivity) in taxes or transfers would just cause reranking and an increase in inequality.

21. As noted in Lustig (2017a), although Engel, Galetovic, and Raddatz (1999) did not acknowledge this characteristic of the Chilean system in their article, an interaction in 2015 between Nora Lustig and the lead author concluded that the Chilean system featured regressive albeit equalizing indirect taxes (Eduardo Engel, pers. comm.).

22. As indicated in Lustig (2017a), the "marginal contribution" should not be confused with the "marginal incidence," the latter being the incidence of a small change in spending. The "marginal contribution" is *not* a derivative.

23. All the theoretical derivations that link changes in inequality to the progressivity of fiscal interventions have been derived based on the so-called family of S-Gini indicators, of which the Gini coefficient is one case. See for example, Duclos and Araar (2006).

24. As shown by Shorrocks (2013) and discussed in Enami, Lustig, and Aranda (2017), because of path dependency, adding up the marginal contributions of each intervention will not be equal to the total change in inequality. Clearly, adding up the sequential contributions will not equal the total change in inequality either. As indicated in Enami, Lustig, and Aranda (2017), one suggested approach to calculate each intervention's contribution such that they add up to the total change in inequality is to use the Shapley value. The studies analyzed here do not have estimates for the Shapley value as its policy interpretation remains elusive.

25. Note that if certain fiscal interventions come in bundles (for example, a tax that only kicks in if a certain transfer is in place), the marginal contribution can be calculated for the net tax (or the net benefit) in question.

26. It is important to note that reranking may occur because individual A could have greater needs—for example, because of his or her health characteristics—than individual B, in which case reranking would *not* be considered a form of horizontal inequity.

27. Recall that a concentration coefficient (also known as quasi-Gini) differs from the Gini coefficient in that the households are still ranked by the income *before* taxes and transfers.

28. A concentration coefficient is calculated in a way analogous to the Gini coefficient. Let p be the cumulative proportion of the total population when individuals are ordered in increasing income values using market income, and let $C(p)$ be the concentration curve, that is, the cumulative proportion of total program benefits (of a particular program or aggregate category) received by the poorest p percent of the population. Then, the concentration coefficient of that program or category is defined as $2\int_0^1 (p - C(p))dp$.

29. For global regressivity or progressivity to occur, it is not a necessary condition for the share of the benefit to rise or fall at each and every income level. When the latter occurs, the benefit is regressive or progressive *everywhere*. Whenever a benefit is *everywhere* regressive or progressive, it will be *globally* regressive or progressive, but the converse is not true.

30. This case is also sometimes called progressive in absolute terms.

31. As mentioned above, care must be taken not to infer that any spending that is progressive (regressive) will automatically be equalizing (unequalizing).

32. The conceptual inputs included in annex 1B come from Lustig and Higgins (2013) and Lustig (2017a).

33. For example, Martinez-Vazquez (2008, 123) finds that "the results obtained with more realistic and laborious assumptions on elasticities tend to yield quite similar results."

34. These free basic services are delivered by municipal governments sometimes at zero cost and sometimes at a subsidized price. Given the difficulty in determining which case applies for households included in the survey, the analysis was carried out in both ways. Results in which the free basic services are considered a subsidy are available upon request.

References

Aristy-Escuder, Jaime, Maynor Cabrera, Blanca Moreno-Dodson, and Miguel E. Sánchez-Martín. 2017. "Fiscal Policy and Redistribution in the Dominican Republic." In *Commitment to Equity Handbook: Estimating the Impact of Fiscal Policy on Inequality and Poverty*, edited by Nora Lustig. Washington, DC: Brookings Institution Press and CEQ Institute, Tulane University. Advance online version available at http://www .commitmentoequity.org/publications/handbook.php.

Atkinson, A. 1980. "Horizontal Equity and the Distribution of the Tax Burden." In *The Economics of Taxation*, edited by H. Aaron and M. Boskin, 3–18. Washington, DC: Brookings Institution Press.

Beneke, Margarita, Nora Lustig, and José Andrés Oliva. 2017. "The Impact of Taxes and Social Spending on Inequality and Poverty in El Salvador." In *Commitment to Equity Handbook: Estimating the Impact of Fiscal Policy on Inequality and Poverty*, edited by Nora Lustig. Washington, DC: Brookings Institution Press and CEQ Institute, Tulane University. Advance online version available at http://www.commitmentoequity.org /publications/handbook.php.

Breceda, Karla, Jamele Rigolini, and Jaime Saavedra. 2008. "Latin America and the Social Contract: Patterns of Social Spending and Taxation." Policy Research Working Paper 4604, World Bank, Washington, DC.

Bucheli, Marisa, Nora Lustig, Máximo Rossi, and Florencia Amábile. 2014. "Social Spending, Taxes and Income Redistribution in Uruguay." *Public Finance Review* 42 (3): 413–33.

Cabrera, Maynor, Nora Lustig, and Hilcías Morán. 2015. "Fiscal Policy, Inequality, and the Ethnic Divide in Guatemala." *World Development* 76 (C): 263–79.

Demery, Lionel. 2000. "Benefit Incidence: A Practitioner's Guide." Working Paper 35117, World Bank, Washington, DC.

Duclos, Jean-Yves, and Abdelkrim Araar. 2006. *Poverty and Equity: Measurement, Policy and Estimation with DAD*. New York: Springer and International Development Research Centre.

Ebrill, Liam, Michael Keen, Jean-Paul Bodin, and Victoria Summers. 2001. *The Modern VAT*. Washington, DC: International Monetary Fund.

Enami, Ali. 2017a. "Measuring the Effectiveness of Taxes and Transfers in Fighting Poverty and Reducing Inequality in Iran." In *Commitment to Equity Handbook: Estimating the Impact of Fiscal Policy on Inequality and Poverty*, edited by Nora Lustig. Washington,

DC: Brookings Institution Press and CEQ Institute, Tulane University. Advance online version available at http://www.commitmentoequity.org/publications/handbook.php.

———. 2017b. "Measuring the Redistributive Impact of Taxes and Transfers in the Presence of Reranking." In *Commitment to Equity Handbook: Estimating the Impact of Fiscal Policy on Inequality and Poverty*, edited by Nora Lustig. Washington, DC: Brookings Institution Press and CEQ Institute, Tulane University. Advance online version available at http://www.commitmentoequity.org/publications/handbook.php.

Enami, Ali, Nora Lustig, and Rodrigo Aranda. 2017. "Analytical Foundations: Measuring the Redistributive Impact of Taxes and Transfers." In *Commitment to Equity Handbook: Estimating the Impact of Fiscal Policy on Inequality and Poverty*, edited by Nora Lustig. Washington, DC: Brookings Institution Press and CEQ Institute, Tulane University. Advance online version available at http://www.commitmentoequity.org/publications /handbook.php.

Engel, Eduardo, Alexander Galetovic, and Claudio E. Raddatz. 1999. "Taxes and Income Distribution in Chile: Some Unpleasant Redistributive Arithmetic." *Journal of Development Economics* 59 (1): 155–92.

Förster, Michael, and Peter Whiteford. 2009. "How Much Redistribution Do Welfare States Achieve? The Role of Cash Transfers and Household Taxes." *CESifo DICE Report* 7 (3): 34–41.

Gertler, Paul, and Paul Glewwe. 1990. "The Willingness to Pay for Education in Developing Countries: Evidence from Rural Peru." *Journal of Public Economics* 42 (3): 251–75.

Gertler, Paul, and Jacques van der Gaag. 1990. *The Willingness to Pay for Medical Care: Evidence from Two Developing Countries*. Baltimore: Johns Hopkins University Press for the World Bank.

Goñi, Edwin, J. Humberto López, and Luis Servén. 2011. "Fiscal Redistribution and Income Inequality in Latin America." *World Development* 39 (9): 1558–69.

Higgins, Sean, and Nora Lustig. 2016. "Can a Poverty-Reducing and Progressive Tax and Transfer System Hurt the Poor?" *Journal of Development Economics* 122 (September): 63–75.

———. 2017. "Allocating Taxes and Transfers, Constructing Income Concepts, and Completing Sections A, B, and C of CEQ Master Workbook." In *Commitment to Equity Handbook: Estimating the Impact of Fiscal Policy on Inequality and Poverty*, edited by Nora Lustig. Washington, DC: Brookings Institution Press and CEQ Institute, Tulane University. Advance online version available at http://www.commit mentoequity.org/publications/handbook.php.

Higgins, Sean, and Claudiney Pereira. 2014. "The Effects of Brazil's Taxation and Social Spending on the Distribution of Household Income." *Public Finance Review* 42 (3): 346–67.

———. 2016. "CEQ Master Workbook: Brazil. Version: January 4, 2016." Commitment to Equity (CEQ) Data Center, CEQ Institute, Tulane University, New Orleans, LA.

Higgins, Sean, Nora Lustig, Whitney Ruble, and Timothy Smeeding. 2016. "Comparing the Incidence of Taxes and Social Spending in Brazil and the United States." *Review of Income and Wealth* 62 (S1): S22–S46. doi:10.1111/roiw.12201.

Immervoll, Herwig, Horacio Levy, José Ricardo Nogueira, Cathal O'Donoghue, and Rozane Bezerra de Siqueira. 2009. "The Impact of Brazil's Tax-Benefit System on Inequality and Poverty." In *Poverty, Inequality, and Policy in Latin America*, edited by Stephan Klasen and Felicitas Nowak-Lehmann, 271–302. Cambridge, MA: MIT Press.

Immervoll, Herwig, and Cathal O'Donoghue. 2001. "Imputation of Gross Amounts from Net Incomes." EUROMOD Working Paper EM1/01, Institute for Social and Economic Research, University of Essex, United Kingdom.

Immervoll, Herwig, and Linda Richardson. 2011. "Redistribution Policy and Inequality Reduction in OECD Countries: What Has Changed in Two Decades?" Discussion Paper 6030, Institute for the Study of Labor (IZA), Bonn.

Jaramillo, Miguel. 2014. "The Incidence of Social Spending and Taxes in Peru." *Public Finance Review* 42 (3): 391–412.

———. 2015. "CEQ Master Workbook: Peru. Version: August 7, 2015." Commitment to Equity (CEQ) Data Center, CEQ Institute, Tulane University, New Orleans, LA.

Jellema, Jon, Astrid Haas, Nora Lustig, and Sebastian Wolf. 2017. "The Impact of Taxes, Transfers, and Subsidies on Inequality and Poverty in Uganda." In *Commitment to Equity Handbook: Estimating the Impact of Fiscal Policy on Inequality and Poverty*, edited by Nora Lustig. Washington, DC: Brookings Institution Press and CEQ Institute, Tulane University. Advance online version available at http://www.commitmento equity.org/publications/handbook.php.

Jouini, Nizar, Nora Lustig, Ahmed Moummi, and Abebe Shimeles. 2017. "Fiscal Incidence and Poverty Reduction: Evidence from Tunisia." In *Commitment to Equity Handbook: Estimating the Impact of Fiscal Policy on Inequality and Poverty*, edited by Nora Lustig. Washington, DC: Brookings Institution Press and CEQ Institute, Tulane University. Advance online version available at http://www.commitmentoequity.org/publications /handbook.php.

Kakwani, Nanak C. 1977. "Measurement of Tax Progressivity: An International Comparison." *The Economic Journal* 87 (345): 71–80.

Keen, Michael, and Ben Lockwood. 2010. "The Value Added Tax: Its Causes and Consequences." *Journal of Development Economics* 92 (2): 138–51.

Lambert, Peter J. 2001. *The Distribution and Redistribution of Income*. 3rd ed. Manchester, U.K.: Manchester University Press.

Lindert, Kathy, Emmanuel Skoufias, and Joseph Shapiro. 2006. "Redistributing Income to the Poor and Rich: Public Transfers in Latin America and the Caribbean." Social Protection Discussion Paper 0605, World Bank, Washington, DC.

Lustig, Nora. 2015. "The Redistributive Impact of Government Spending on Education and Health: Evidence from Thirteen Developing Countries in the Commitment to Equity Project." In *Inequality and the Role of Fiscal Policy: Trends and Policy Options*, edited by Benedict Clements, Ruud de Mooij, Sanjeev Gupta, and Michael Keen. Washington, DC: International Monetary Fund.

———. 2016a. "Fiscal Policy, Inequality and the Poor in the Developing World." Commitment to Equity (CEQ) Working Paper 23, CEQ Institute, Tulane University, New Orleans, LA.

———. 2016b. "Inequality and Fiscal Redistribution in Middle Income Countries: Brazil, Chile, Colombia, Indonesia, Mexico, Peru and South Africa." *Journal of Globalization and Development* 7 (1): 17–60. doi:10.1515/jgd-2016-0015.

———, ed. 2017a. *Commitment to Equity Handbook: Estimating the Impact of Fiscal Policy on Inequality and Poverty*. Washington, DC: Brookings Institution Press and CEQ Institute, Tulane University. Advance online version available at http://www.commit mentoequity.org/publications/handbook.php.

————, ed. 2017b. "Fiscal Policy, Income Redistribution, and Poverty Reduction in Low and Middle Income Countries." In *Commitment to Equity Handbook: Estimating the Impact of Fiscal Policy on Inequality and Poverty*. Washington, DC: Brookings Institution Press and CEQ Institute, Tulane University. Advance online version; available at: http://www.commitmentoequity.org/publications/handbook.php.

Lustig, Nora, and Sean Higgins. 2013. "Commitment to Equity Assessment (CEQ): Estimating the Incidence of Social Spending, Subsidies and Taxes. Handbook." CEQ Working Paper 1, Center for Inter-American Policy and Research; the Inter-American Dialogue; and Department of Economics, Tulane University, New Orleans, LA.

————. 2017. "The CEQ Assessment: Measuring the Impact of Fiscal Policy on Inequality and Poverty." In *Commitment to Equity Handbook: Estimating the Impact of Fiscal Policy on Inequality and Poverty*, edited by Nora Lustig. Washington, DC: Brookings Institution Press and CEQ Institute, Tulane University. Advance online edition available at http://www.commitmentoequity.org/publications/handbook.php.

Lustig, Nora, and Carola Pessino. 2014. "Social Spending and Income Redistribution in Argentina during the 2000s: The Increasing Role of Noncontributory Pensions." *Public Finance Review* 42 (3): 304–25.

Lustig, Nora, Carola Pessino, and John Scott. 2014. "The Redistributive Impact of Taxes and Social Spending in Latin America: Argentina, Bolivia, Brazil, Mexico, Peru, and Uruguay." *Public Finance Review* 42 (3): 287–303.

Martínez, Sandra, Alan Fuchs, Eduardo Ortiz-Juarez, and Giselle del Carmen. 2017. "The Impact of Fiscal Policy on Inequality and Poverty in Chile." In *Commitment to Equity Handbook: Estimating the Impact of Fiscal Policy on Inequality and Poverty*, edited by Nora Lustig. Washington, DC: Brookings Institution Press and CEQ Institute, Tulane University. Advance online edition available at http://www.commitmentoequity.org/publications/handbook.php.

Martinez-Vazquez, Jorge. 2008. "The Impact of Budgets on the Poor: Tax and Expenditure Benefit Incidence Analysis." In *Public Finance for Poverty Reduction: Concepts and Case Studies from Africa and Latin America*, edited by Blanca Moreno-Dodson and Quentin Wodon, 113–62. Directions in Development Series. Washington, DC: World Bank.

Meerman, Jacob. 1979. *Public Expenditure in Malaysia: Who Benefits and Why*. New York: Oxford University Press for the World Bank.

Musgrave, Richard. 1959. *The Theory of Public Finance*. New York: McGraw-Hill.

Musgrave, Richard A., J. J. Carroll, L. D. Cook, and L. Frane. 1951. "Distribution of Tax Payments by Income Groups: A Case Study for 1948." *National Tax Journal* 4 (March): 1–53.

Musgrave, Richard, Karl Case, and Herman Leonard. 1974. "The Distribution of Fiscal Burdens and Benefits." *Public Finance Quarterly* 2 (3): 259–311.

OECD (Organisation for Economic Co-operation and Development). 2011. *Divided We Stand: Why Inequality Keeps Rising*. Paris: OECD Publishing. doi:10.1787/9789264119536-en.

O'Higgins, Michael, and Patricia Ruggles. 1981. "The Distribution of Public Expenditures and Taxes among Households in the United Kingdom." *Review of Income and Wealth* 27 (3): 298–326.

Paz Arauco, Verónica, George Gray Molina, Wilson Jiménez Pozo, and Ernesto Yáñez Aguilar. 2014. "Explaining Low Redistributive Impact in Bolivia." *Public Finance Review* 42 (3): 326–45.

Pechman, Joseph A., and Benjamin A. Okner. 1974. *Who Bears the Tax Burden?* Washington, DC: Brookings Institution.

Pereira, Claudiney. 2017. "Ethno-Racial Poverty and Income Inequality in Brazil." In *Commitment to Equity Handbook: Estimating the Impact of Fiscal Policy on Inequality and Poverty*, edited by Nora Lustig. Washington, DC: Brookings Institution Press and CEQ Institute, Tulane University. Advance online edition available at http://www.commitmentoequity.org/publications/handbook.php.

Plotnick, R. 1981. "A Measure of Horizontal Inequity." *The Review of Economics and Statistics* 63 (2): 283–88.

Reynolds, M., and E. Smolensky. 1977. *Public Expenditures, Taxes, and the Distribution of Income: The United States, 1950, 1961, 1970.* New York: Academic Press.

Rossignolo, Dario. 2017. "Taxes, Expenditures, Poverty, and Income Distribution in Argentina." In *Commitment to Equity Handbook: Estimating the Impact of Fiscal Policy on Inequality and Poverty*, edited by Nora Lustig. Washington, DC: Brookings Institution Press and CEQ Institute, Tulane University. Advance online edition available at http://www.commitmentoequity.org/publications/handbook.php.

Ruggles, Patricia, and Michael O'Higgins. 1981. "The Distribution of Public Expenditure among Households in the United States." *Review of Income and Wealth* 27 (2): 137–64.

Sahn, David, and Stephen Younger. 2000. "Expenditure Incidence in Africa: Microeconomic Evidence." *Fiscal Studies* 21 (3): 329–47.

Scott, John. 2014. "Redistributive Impact and Efficiency of Mexico's Fiscal System." *Public Finance Review* 42 (3): 368–90.

Selowsky, Marcelo. 1979. *Who Benefits from Government Expenditures? A Case Study of Colombia.* New York: Oxford University Press.

Shorrocks, Anthony F. 2013. "Decomposition Procedures for Distributional Analysis: A Unified Framework Based on the Shapley Value." *Journal of Economic Inequality* 11 (1): 99–126.

Younger, Stephen, Flora Myamba, and Kenneth Mdadila. 2016. "Fiscal Incidence in Tanzania." *African Development Review* 28 (3): 264–76.

Younger, Stephen, Eric Osei-Assibey, and Felix Oppong. 2017. "Fiscal Incidence in Ghana." *Review of Development Economics.* Published electronically January. doi:10.1111/rode.12299.

Younger, Stephen, David Sahn, Stephen Haggblade, and Paul Dorosh. 1999. "Tax Incidence in Madagascar: An Analysis Using Household Data." *The World Bank Economic Review* 13 (2): 303–31.

CHAPTER 2

Fiscal Incidence in Armenia

Stephen D. Younger and Artsvi Khachatryan

Introduction

Armenia is an interesting case for an incidence analysis in many ways. Although there are no reliable measures of living standards before independence in 1991, living standards were almost certainly in the middle income range or higher. Social security and social protection systems were well developed, and education and health services were both universal and publicly provided. In short, Armenia almost surely did not look like a low- and middle-income country (LMIC).

The end of the Soviet Union brought independence but also an extraordinary economic crisis. Real gross domestic product (GDP) fell by half from 1991 to 1993 as the economy, once tied to and integrated with the Soviet economy, collapsed. By 1993, GDP per capita was a mere US$565 (constant 2005 U.S. dollars), poor by any standard. This left the government with very limited funds, so social expenditures also suffered greatly.

The economic collapse and political transition did, however, leave the government room to institute radical reforms, which it carried out in many areas, mostly to positive effect. The economy began to grow again in the mid-1990s and accelerated dramatically in the 2000s before the 2008 financial crisis, with concomitant reductions in poverty. Armenia is again a middle-income country,

We have received an enormous amount of help and advice from several quarters. The project's core staff, Nora Lustig and Sean Higgins at the Commitment to Equity (CEQ) Institute, Tulane University, and Gabriela Inchauste and Catherine Lee at the World Bank helped to clarify and resolve many methodological problems and also provided useful comparator information from other country studies. They also made careful comments on previous drafts. Ulrich Bartsch, Nistha Sinha, and Gohar Gyulumyan all provided helpful background information and comments on previous drafts. Many people in Armenia were kind enough to explain the details of tax and expenditure policy to us, including Cristian Aedo, Jhora Asatryan, Susanna Hayrapetyan, Susanna Karapetyan, Lyusya Khachatryan, Arthur Kochnakyan, Diana Martirosova, Astghik Minasyan, Vakhtang Mirumyan, Lilit Petrosyan, Arman Poghosyan, Smbat Sayan, Anush Shahverdyan, Saro Tsaturyan, Zaruhi Tokhmakhian, Vahe Topalyan, and Gevorg Yeghinyan. Finally, we benefited from comments in seminars held at the World Bank's Yerevan office and the American University of Armenia.

but an unusual one. Spending on social protection and social services has recovered but remains small when compared with other middle-income and European and Central Asian countries and probably when compared with Armenia's own past. Tax revenue is also low. As a result, redistribution is not as extensive as one might expect.

This chapter uses household survey data, the 2011 Integrated Living Conditions Survey (ILCS), and budgetary data for the same year to assess the distributional consequences of government taxation and spending. Targeting for most social expenditures and taxes is quite good in Armenia. Expenditures such as education and health care, which should be universal, are spread evenly across the population (although coverage is less than universal in most cases), and programs meant to be targeted toward the poor and disadvantaged by-and-large are. Yet overall, Armenia achieves a redistribution of income through the fisc[1] that is somewhat less than that in most middle-income countries in Latin America and much less than that found in the richer countries of Europe. The main reason that Armenia's better-than-average targeting does not generate more redistribution is that, except for pensions from the social security system, social expenditures are small relative to GDP. Tax incidence is also in line with what one would expect: direct taxes are progressive, whereas indirect taxes are slightly regressive.

Every incidence analysis should include a preemptory caution. When one finds that one tax or expenditure is more redistributive to the poor than another, the temptation is to conclude that the former is preferable. But it is important to remember that redistribution is only one of many criteria that matter when making public policy. Not all redistributive taxes or expenditures are good ones, and not all good taxes or expenditures are redistributive. The results of this study and of all incidence studies are one input to public policy making—one that should be weighed with other goals before deciding that a tax or expenditure is desirable.

Methods and Approach

This chapter uses the standard methods described in Lustig and Higgins (2013b), with one exception: we always treat pensions as transfer payments rather than deferred income. Although Armenia does have a tax on labor income and does pay larger pensions to those who have paid that tax during their working years, the social security system is not independent of the central government budget, which draws on general tax revenues as well as social security taxes to fund pensions. As such, treating pensions as transfers is consistent with the way Armenian officials think about and pay for them. The chapter also includes a sensitivity analysis that treats pensions as deferred compensation and reports key differences between that analysis and our main one.

The survey data for this study come from the 2011 ILCS, the most recent survey to which we have access.[2] In addition, we use 2011 budget information to estimate some of the information needed, most specifically the amount of spending per beneficiary on public education and health services.

Construction of the Income and Expenditure Variables
Disposable Income

Our construction of the five Commitment to Equity (CEQ) income concepts starts with disposable income and works backward to market incomes and forward to final incomes.[3] We assume that incomes reported in the ILCS are closest to disposable income.[4] ILCS income and expenditure data are collected using diaries. Responding households are asked to record all inflows and outflows every day for a month. We count as disposable income all reported inflows except asset sales, loans, and withdrawals from bank accounts. We then add to this 2.75 percent of household expenditures as implicit income from owner-occupied housing. This share is that found for the rental value of owner-occupied housing in the national income accounts in 2011. Most households in Armenia own their home. For the few that do not, we do not make the 2.75 percent adjustment.

Most poverty and inequality analysis done in Armenia is based on household expenditures rather than incomes, so we also include a second "disposable income" variable that is total household expenditures, plus a 2.75 percent adjustment for owner-occupied housing. The correlation between this expenditure measure and the disposable income measure is only 0.40, so even though most CEQ analysis is done in terms of incomes, we carry out a parallel sensitivity analysis based on the expenditure data in Armenia. The expenditure variable that we use is calculated by the National Statistical Service of the Republic of Armenia (NSSRA) and includes expenditures, own-consumption, gifts, and an imputed use value for durable goods.

Net Market Income

To create net market income, we subtract direct monetary transfers from disposable income. The ILCS diary for inflows includes the following categories, which we assume are monetary transfer payments: pensions, compensation for privileges, family benefits, child benefits, unemployment benefits, other benefits, and student stipends.[5]

The diary itself does not allow us to distinguish contributory from noncontributory pensions. However, the main household questionnaire gathers detailed information about "social groups" to which individual household members belong that would entitle them to certain benefits. Among these is a set of "pensioner" characteristics: labor, social, and military. We assume that those who are in the "labor pensioner" group receive contributory pensions, whereas those in the other groups receive noncontributory pensions.

We then construct two direct transfer variables, consistent with the CEQ methodology. The first is all transfers except contributory pensions. This variable treats contributory pensions as deferred compensation (wages) for work done in the past rather than as a transfer payment and therefore part of market income. However, because significant shares of "contributory" pensions are funded through general revenues in many countries, including Armenia, we include a second variable that treats all pensions, including contributory, as transfer payments.

Net market income is then disposable income less these direct transfers. For the second disposable income estimate, based on expenditures, our estimate of net market income can be negative if households' expenditures in the 30 days of the diary are less than their transfer payments. This happens in 0.5 percent of households for the more narrow definition of monetary transfers without contributory pensions and in 7.7 percent of households when we include contributory pensions as transfers. In these cases, we truncate net market income at zero. For the first definition of transfers, exclusive of contributory pensions, this makes very little difference. For the second definition, the truncation raises the average household net market income a little more than 1 percent, but it may have a larger effect on poverty and especially inequality estimates.

In all, we have four net market income variables based on the two-by-two classification of (income vs. expenditure) by (exclude vs. include contributory pensions).

Market Income

Market income is net market income plus all direct taxes and social security contributions (SSC) paid.[6] The ILCS does not ask about taxes paid, so we must simulate these values. We assume that employee income and self-employed income for formal sector workers pay statutory rates for both personal income tax (PIT) and SSC. At the same time, there is widespread agreement that tax evasion through informality is an important problem in Armenia, so we assume that informal self-employed income pays neither PIT nor SSC. It is not possible to identify the owners of corporations in the ILCS, so we do not simulate the corporate income tax.

Our formal–informal distinction uses the NSSRA definition.[7] We should note that wage income in the diary is aggregated across jobs, so workers with two jobs could mix formal and informal income. We assume that if either job is formal, then all wage income is formal and thus taxed. This risks some misclassification, but it will be rare. There are only 461 second jobs in the survey (compared with 12,388 primary jobs), and there are only eight workers whose second job is formal and first job is not.

PIT rates are very simple in Armenia. The tax rate is 10 percent for income up to dram 80,000 (US$289 at purchasing power parity [PPP]) per month and 20 percent for any income in excess of dram 80,000. All tax payers are entitled to a standard personal deduction of dram 32,500 (US$118 at PPP) per month, so this is the threshold at which people begin to pay PIT. The employee share of SSC is also deductible. Withholding is final, so assuming full compliance, our simulations should reflect actual taxes paid accurately.

SSC are also straightforward. Employees pay a flat 3 percent of earnings. Their employers pay dram 7,000 (US$25 PPP) per month plus 15 percent of wages greater than dram 20,000 (US$72 PPP) per month up to dram 100,000 (US$362 PPP) per month. Wages greater than dram 100,000 per month pay dram 19,000 plus 5 percent of wages greater than dram 100,000. We assume that the incidence of both contributions falls entirely on employees.

A few households in the ILCS report lottery winnings. These are taxed at 10 percent if the winnings are greater than dram 10,000 (US$36 PPP) per month. We include these direct taxes in our simulation of PIT.

We add the PIT, SSC, and lottery taxes to the four net market income variables to get four comparable market income variables.

Consumable Income

To calculate consumable income, we return to our disposable income measures and subtract indirect taxes paid. There were no indirect subsidies in Armenia in 2011. Indirect taxes in Armenia include import duties; value added tax (VAT); and excises on petroleum products, alcoholic beverages, and tobacco products.[8]

The VAT system in Armenia is straightforward. The standard rate is 20 percent, with exemptions only for education, books, paper, jewelry, and financial services including insurance. In addition, small firms with revenues of less than dram 58.35 million (approximately US$160,550) per year are not required to pay VAT. Nevertheless, VAT revenue productivity is only about 50 percent in Armenia (IMF 2010). The main problem seems to be the exemption for small firms. Some of these firms, mostly in personal services, pay a presumptive tax in lieu of VAT, PIT, and corporate income taxes. That tax is based on the type of firm. It is impossible to know from the ILCS whether a household has made a purchase from a firm that pays VAT or not. Further, in a standard competitive model, prices at firms that do not pay VAT would be the same as those at VAT-paying firms, with the benefits of nonpayment going to the firm owner rather than customers. Households suffer the incidence of the tax regardless of the tax status of the seller, although not all the benefits go to the fisc; some are captured by small-business owners.[9]

Based on these considerations, we have calculated an effective VAT rate as total VAT collections in 2011 divided by the consumption in the national income accounts that is subject to VAT (that is, all consumption less education, books, paper, jewelry, and financial services). This rate is 10.67 percent, slightly higher than earlier estimates of VAT revenue productivity.[10] We apply this "effective" VAT rate to all household purchases except exempted items. In essence, we assume that all households buy the same share of VAT-paying goods so that the effects of VAT avoidance or evasion on market prices are spread across the population in proportion to each household's expenditures.

One concern with this assumption is the presumption that poorer households have higher food shares and may therefore pay a lower share of their total expenditures in VAT because almost all farms are not subject to that tax. We have not made an adjustment for this concern for two reasons. First, as figure 2.1 shows, the food share varies remarkably little across the income distribution in Armenia.[11] This is actually consistent with our assumption that expenditure shares with respect to VAT-taxable items are constant across the income distribution. The second reason to not make an adjustment for food shares is that 80 percent of food purchases by value are made in shops. Even if farmers do not pay VAT, the shops may well pay it if they are not small businesses.

Figure 2.1 Kernel Regression of Household Food Share on Market Income in Armenia, 2011

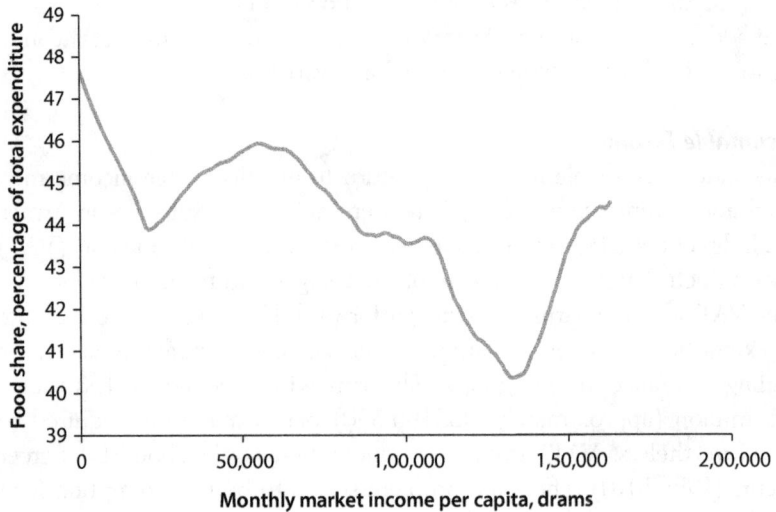

Source: Based on 2011 Integrated Living Conditions Survey (ILCS) database, National Statistical Service of the Republic of Armenia, http://www.armstat.am/en/?nid=246.
Note: "Market income" comprises pretax wages, salaries, income earned from capital assets (rent, interest, or dividends), and private transfers.

Thus, we keep our approach as simple as possible by applying an "effective" VAT rate of 10.67 percent to all VAT-taxable purchases.

Import duties are similarly straightforward in Armenia. All imports are subject to a 10 percent tariff, although the list of exemptions is longer than for the VAT. We calculate an "effective" tariff as the total tariff revenue recorded in 2011 divided by total nonexempted imports. This rate is 3.6 percent, which, again, is slightly higher than previous estimates of import tariff productivity in Armenia. We apply this rate to all purchases of nonexcluded items, whether imported or not. (Indeed, we cannot tell whether a purchase was an import or not in the ILCS.) The logic here is similar to that for the VAT: in competitive markets, import tariffs increase the price of all goods, whether imported or domestic, so households suffer the incidence of the tax regardless of the source of their purchase.

Excise duties are the most complicated of the indirect taxes in Armenia, with different rates depending on the type of product and its source (domestic or imported). Table 2.1 has a complete description. Fortunately, the ILCS expenditure data are quite detailed as to the type of alcohol and tobacco purchased, including distinctions for domestic production versus imports. The ILCS also includes information on physical quantities purchased, so we can apply the excise rates quite precisely.

If we calculate each household's indirect taxes paid based on its consumption expenditures, households with negative savings in the previous month

Table 2.1 Excise Duty Rates in Armenia, 2011

Item	Unit	Domestically produced	Imported
Beer	Liter	dram 70	dram 105
Wine	Liter	10 percent of factory price but not less than dram 100	10 percent of import price but not less than dram 150
Vermouth	Liter	dram 500	dram 600
Vodka, cognac, and other strong drinks	Liter	30 percent of factory price but not less than dram 380	30 percent of import price but not less than dram 600
Ciders and other alcoholic drinks	Liter	dram 180	dram 200
Filtered cigarettes	Cigarette	dram 5.5	dram 7
Unfiltered cigarettes	Cigarette	dram 1.95	dram 3.25
Raw oil and oil materials	Metric ton	dram 27,000	dram 27,000

Source: PwC 2011.

Note: There are other excise duties on other products, but those products cannot be identified from the Integrated Living Conditions Survey (ILCS).

(expenditures greater than income) can have negative consumable incomes. To avoid this, we apply the ratio of indirect taxes paid to expenditure, as described above, to disposable income to estimate indirect taxes paid. This guarantees a positive consumable income. When we use household expenditures rather than income to estimate disposable income, however, we do not make this adjustment.

Final Income

To calculate final income, we add in-kind transfers associated with public provision of education and health care to consumable income. We have not subtracted copayments or fees from these values. Both schools and health care facilities manage their own budgets. The state supports these institutions with transfers that are based on number of students and types of school, number of patients, types of facilities and procedures, and so on.

For education, schools are prohibited from charging extra fees (that is, parent-teacher association dues) for schooling that is publicly supported, so there is nothing to subtract. At universities, the state transfers the tuition of supported students to the institution. Because state-supported students in the ILCS universally report attending for free, we again have nothing to subtract.

For health care, almost all payments from government to providers are inframarginal, that is, they do not cover the full cost of the services provided. For that reason, it seems better to assume that any payments from the patient to the provider bring the full payment up to cost and do not diminish the benefit that the patient receives from the public support to the provider. Thus, we also do not subtract any additional payments from the estimated subsidy per patient.

For schooling, we have two approaches available to calculate the in-kind subsidy for each student. The standard approach takes the budget for 2011 for each type of school and divides by the number of students in those schools, at a national level.[12] The second approach uses the actual per-student funding formula used by the Ministry of Finance (MoF) to make transfers to schools. That formula is quite simple. In 2011, it was (# students) × (dram 105,775) + dram 16,708.

The Distributional Impact of Taxes and Transfers • http://dx.doi.org/10.1596/978-1-4648-1091-6

Several adjustment coefficients are then applied, depending on the school type and location: 2 percent is added for schools in mountainous areas; 20 percent is added for schools in "high mountainous" areas; 20 percent is added for schools that are the only remaining school in a settlement and have fewer than 400 students; and 15 percent is added for high schools. Unfortunately, we cannot identify altitude or school size in the survey, so the best that we can do is to apply the standard formula without the fixed dram 16,708 and with only the adjustment for high schools. This will underestimate the total in-kind subsidies to students. Vocational schools are funded with a different formula that is based on the number and type of classrooms, so we cannot make the same calculation for vocational students. Preprimary schools are funded mostly through local budgets, with no standard per-student transfer.

Table 2.2 presents the estimated in-kind transfer per student using the standard method and the MoF transfer formula. Another useful comparison is a previous benefit incidence study for education in Armenia (AST 2010). That study calculates, for 2008, per-student benefits of dram 205,000 for general education (primary, general secondary, and secondary); dram 265,000 for vocational education; and dram 310,000 for higher education.

Even though use of the MoF transfer formula is conceptually attractive, the fact that its estimates are much lower than the other two methods and cannot be applied to some types of schooling means that we would underweight the importance of transfers for general education if we used the MoF formula for those and the standard method for the others. So we use the standard method in this chapter. This also improves comparability with other CEQ studies. We take both student populations and budgets from standard administrative sources.[13]

Table 2.2 Annual In-Kind Education Benefits per Student in Armenia
drams

Level	Standard method (2011 data)[a]	MoF transfer formula (2011 data)[b]	Advanced Social Technologies (2008 data)
Preprimary	168,406	—[c]	n.a.
Primary (grades 1–4)	223,680	105,775	205,000
General secondary (grades 5–9)	232,081	105,775	
Secondary (grades 10–12)	185,539	121,641	
Secondary vocational	403,300	—[d]	265,000
Secondary professional (college)	386,213	—[d]	
Higher education and postgraduate	504,333	—[d]	310,000

Sources: 2011 Ministry of Finance state budget reports (http://mfe.am/index.php?cat=76&lang=1) and community budget reports (http://mfe.am/index.php?cat=78&lang=1); AST 2010.
Note: MoF = Ministry of Finance; — = not available.
a. The standard formula divides the 2011 budget for each type of school by the number of students in those schools, at a national level. Because the academic year differs from the calendar year, the total number of students includes one-third of the 2010 student population and two-thirds of the 2011 population.
b. The MoF transfer formula in 2011 was (# students) × (dram 105,775) + dram 16,708. Several adjustment coefficients are applied, depending on the school type and location. For more specifics of the MoF funding formula, see http://www.arlis.am/documentview.aspx?docID=65300.
c. No data are available because preprimary schools are mostly funded through local budgets, with no standard transfer per student.
d. The MoF formula applies only to primary and secondary school.

Our treatment of in-kind health benefits also uses the standard method. The schedule of transfers from the State Health Agency to providers is quite detailed, with different amounts for different types of services. We cannot match that detail with information from the type of treatment in the ILCS, so we must use the standard method. We divide treatment into inpatient care at hospitals, which we divide into deliveries and other services, and outpatient care at polyclinics, family doctors, and so on (primary care providers).[14] Budget data come from the MoF, but we encountered dramatically different patient numbers from administrative records (NSSRA 2011) and the ILCS. The administrative data report 13 million visits to primary care providers in 2011, whereas the ILCS has only 3.6 million. Administrative data report 347,000 inpatient visits to hospitals, whereas the ILCS has only 167,000. One possible reason for this discrepancy is that the administrative data count each service that a patient receives as a separate visit, whereas the patient may view them (and report them in the ILCS) as only one visit. If that is true, then it is better to use the ILCS estimates of total patient visits rather than the administrative data. That is the option we have taken. This yields an average in-kind transfer of dram 6,149 for outpatient visits and dram 160,827 for inpatient visits.

The last in-kind benefit that we calculate is free or subsidized rent, usually to soldiers. We calculate this value as 2.47 percent of reported expenditures, which is the share of rental value of owner-occupied housing in consumption in the national income accounts. We apply this only to households that report that their dwelling is "state or municipality rented" and paid no rent.

Consistency between Administrative and Survey Data Sources

It is possible to calculate the total amount that the government spends on certain items and taxes on others using both administrative data (the national accounts, the budget, and so on) and data from the survey (ILCS). These amounts should coincide, but they often do not. This can lead to errors in our estimate of distributional effects if the degree of inconsistency varies among the tax, expenditure, and income variables used in the analysis. For example, suppose that the total value of unemployment benefits in the survey is only half of the amount found in the budget, perhaps because survey respondents are reluctant to report that they receive these benefits. If those benefits go disproportionately to poorer households, which seems likely, then their underreporting in the survey will cause us to underestimate the impact that these benefits have on both inequality and poverty reduction. It is important, then, to try to adjust for discrepancies between the administrative sources and the survey.

In Armenia, by far the largest problem is that the ILCS reports less household expenditures and incomes than do the national accounts. Household expenditures in the survey are only 37 percent of those in the national income accounts.[15] Other items such as pensions, family benefits, and PIT are much closer to the associated administrative accounts. As a result, simply adding or subtracting these items from the very low survey income values to generate the income concepts outlined in the previous section may exaggerate the extent to which these taxes and expenditures affect the distribution of income.

To account for these differences, and to provide some analysis of the sensitivity of our results to possible biases, we sometimes scale up or down certain items in our analysis. In all cases, we scale down the in-kind benefits from health and education spending. This is because our estimate of their monetary value comes entirely from administrative data—the government expenditure per beneficiary. These values are accurate, whereas the income values from the survey are too low. To get the in-kind benefits to a scale similar to the other information in the survey, we scale them down by 0.369, which is the ratio of household expenditures in the survey to those in the national accounts.[16] In addition, we run a sensitivity analysis that scales down PIT (0.753) and SSC (0.497) so that their ratio in the survey is the same as their ratio in the administrative information.[17]

Description of Taxes and Expenditures in Armenia

Tax Revenue Sources

Table 2.3 gives the breakdown of the major government revenue sources in 2011, the year of our ILCS data. Overall revenues are small as a share of GDP (23 percent) compared with other European countries (averaging 40 percent for the EU-28 countries in 2014),[18] a fact that limits government's ability to affect the distribution of income. Most of the taxes are familiar. VAT is by far the most important tax, and SSC, corporate profit, and PIT are also relatively large. Excise duties are levied on cigarettes, alcohol, and petroleum products.

The third column of table 2.3 indicates that not all of these revenue sources can be included in our analysis. To consider the distributional impact of these items,

Table 2.3 Government Revenues in Armenia, 2011

Revenue source	Drams, billions	Included in analysis?	Share of revenue (%)	Share of GDP (%)
Tax revenues	647,809	varies	71	17
Indirect taxes	437,119	varies	47	12
Value added tax	328,483	yes	36	9
Customs duty	36,289	yes	4	1
Excise tax[a]	39,405	yes	4	1
Environmental tax	12,200	no	1	0
Presumptive tax	20,742	no	2	1
Direct taxes	195,226	varies	22	5
Enterprise profit tax	97,842	no	11	3
Personal income tax	81,211	yes	9	2
Property tax	11,794	no	1	0
Land tax	4,429	no	1	0
Simplified tax[b]	−50	no	0	0
Other taxes	15,464	no	2	0

table continues next page

Table 2.3 Government Revenues in Armenia, 2011 *(continued)*

Revenue source	Drams, billions	Included in analysis?	Share of revenue (%)	Share of GDP (%)
State duties	25,703	no	3	1
Social security payments	123,450	yes	14	3
Nontax revenues	69,371	no	8	1
Grants	39,740	no	4	1

Sources: Ministry of Finance state and community budget reports (http://mfe.am/index.php?cat=76&lang=1, http://mfe.am/index .php?cat=78&lang=1); NSSRA 2012a.
Note: GDP = gross domestic product.
a. Includes presumptive tax on cigarettes.
b. "Simplified tax" provides an exemption from value added tax (VAT) and profit tax for small enterprises having turnover on the sale of goods and services (not including VAT) for the previous year of less than dram 30 million (US$51,500). Its contribution to government revenues is negative here because of overpayment refunds.

we must be able to identify them in the ILCS data. That is not always possible. For example, we cannot tell who owns most enterprises or who pays "other taxes" or "state duties." Presumptive taxes are levied on specific types of small businesses. We can identify the self-employed, including those in the informal sector, in the ILCS, but not the specific types of businesses they run. Overall, the analysis accounts for 69 percent of tax revenues, with corporate income tax being the most important omitted tax.

Social Expenditures

It is much more difficult to attribute the expenditure side of the budget to specific beneficiaries. Governments spend significant amounts of their budgets on genuine public goods—national defense, law enforcement, and public administration— that, by their nature, are not attributable to individuals. The areas in which we can identify specific beneficiaries are social expenditures: transfer payments, health, and education.

Table 2.4 gives a breakdown of social expenditures in Armenia in 2011. Overall, these social expenditures account for only 42.5 percent of total expenditures, and the items that we can identify in the ILCS account for 36.6 percent. Health and education spending are noticeably low in Armenia. The large share of old-age pensions also stands out, reflecting Armenia's relatively mature population. Old-age pensions are mostly contributory pensions, that is, pensions paid to retirees who paid social security taxes when they were working. These account for dram 159 billion of the dram 188 billion spent on pensions.

The other large social expenditures are for families and children. In 2011 they included Armenia's only means-tested, unconditional transfer, the Family Benefit (dram 29 billion); one-time payments to mothers upon childbirth (dram 4 billion); and childcare services for participants in the social security system (dram 2.9 billion). It is noteworthy that both unemployment and disability pensions are quite small compared with the other social expenditures (dram 4.1 billion and dram 1.3 billion, respectively).

Table 2.4 Government Social Expenditures in Armenia, 2011

Expenditure type	Drams, millions	Included in analysis?	Share of expenditures (%)[a]	Share of GDP (%)
Total expenditures	1,013,500	varies	100.0	26.8
Health	63,491	varies	6.3	1.7
Outpatient services	22,551	yes	2.2	0.6
Inpatient services	26,891	yes	2.7	0.7
Other health	14,050	no	1.4	0.4
Education	135,071	varies	13.3	3.6
Preprimary	10,694	yes	1.1	0.3
Elementary	30,357	yes	3.0	0.8
General basic	36,022	yes	3.6	1.0
Complete secondary	15,724	yes	1.6	0.4
Initial professional (vocational)	2,180	yes	0.2	0.1
Secondary professional	3,177	yes	0.3	0.1
Higher	7,885	yes	0.8	0.2
Other	29,032	no	2.9	0.8
Social protection	258,336	yes	25.5	6.8
Ailment and disability	1,251	yes	0.1	0.0
Old age	188,396	yes	18.6	5.0
Relative lost persons	190	yes	0.0	0.0
Family members and children	43,596	yes	4.3	1.2
Unemployment	4,115	yes	0.4	0.1
Dwelling provision	815	yes	0.1	0.0
Special social privileges	10,934	no	1.1	0.3
Special protection	9,039	no	0.9	0.2

Source: Ministry of Finance state and community budget reports (http://mfe.am/index.php?cat=76&lang=1, http://mfe.am/index
.php?cat=78&lang=1).
Note: GDP = gross domestic product.
a. The items for health, education, and social protection are not comprehensive and so do not total 100 percent.

Results

Inequality and Poverty

Table 2.5 gives the Gini coefficients and headcount indexes for three different
PPP-based poverty lines for each CEQ income concept. The absolute values of
the Ginis and Foster-Greer-Thorbecke indexes (FGTs)[19] will look unfamiliar
to Armenians accustomed to the NSSRA poverty analyses for four reasons.
First, these variables are based on household incomes, not expenditures. Second,
we use income per capita, not per adult equivalent.[20] Third, the poverty lines
are international "dollar-a-day" lines rather than the cost-of-basic-needs poverty
line that the NSSRA uses in its analysis. And finally, only "disposable income" is
close to the measure that the NSSRA uses in its poverty analysis. All the other
income variables involve the additions and subtractions described in the methodology section.

All of these choices are made to be consistent with other CEQ country
analyses. The most important thing to remember is that although these choices
can have large effects on estimated Ginis and FGTs, the *relative* changes of one

Table 2.5 Gini Coefficients and Poverty Indexes in Armenia, by CEQ Income Concept, 2011

Inequality or poverty indicator	Market income[a]	Net market income[b]	Disposable income[c]	Consumable income[d]	Final income[e]
Gini coefficient[f]	0.469	0.456	0.373	0.374	0.357
Poverty headcount, US$1.25/day PPP (%)	21.3	22.4	9.6	11.9	9.0
Poverty headcount, US$2.50/day PPP (%)	39.3	44.2	28.9	34.9	30.9
Poverty headcount, US$4.00/day PPP (%)	58.3	65.9	55.5	62.7	60.2

Source: Based on 2011 Integrated Living Conditions Survey (ILCS) database, National Statistical Service of the Republic of Armenia, http://www.armstat.am/en/?nid=246.
Note: Income concepts were developed by the Commitment to Equity (CEQ) project to trace "the process by which taxes, subsidies, and transfers are allocated to each household to assess how incomes—and thus inequality indicators—change with fiscal policy" (Lustig and Higgins 2013a), as further described in chapter 1. PPP = purchasing power parity.
a. Market income comprises pretax wages, salaries, income earned from capital assets (rent, interest, or dividends), and private transfers.
b. Net market income subtracts from market income the payments for personal income taxes and employees' social security contributions.
c. Disposable income is constructed by adding direct cash transfers to net market income.
d. Consumable income adds to disposable income the impact of indirect taxes, including value added taxes; import duties; and excises on petroleum products, alcoholic beverages, and tobacco products.
e. Final income adds to consumable income the effects of in-kind transfers for health care and education.
f. The Gini coefficient measures the inequality of income distribution, ranging from 0 (full equality) to 1 (maximum inequality).

measure to the next are much less sensitive to these choices. Thus, the effects of transfers and taxes on poverty and inequality estimated here—the *difference* between the various income concepts—will be quite close to the same effect estimated with the NSSRA welfare measure.[21]

Effects of Direct Taxes
The difference between market income and net market income is direct taxes, which include PIT and SSC in our analysis. Although progressive (see the following section), PIT and SSC are small relative to market income because the tax take of these direct taxes is small (as shown earlier in table 2.3). As a result, the Gini coefficient for net market income is only slightly lower than that for market income.

For headcount poverty, the difference is stronger, especially for the higher poverty lines. This shows that there are households with formal sector workers whose income falls below these lines.[22] This effect for Armenia is larger than that in any of the Latin American economies reviewed in Lustig, Pessino, and Scott (2014); direct taxes move a considerable number of people below the poverty line in Armenia.

Effects of Direct Transfers
The difference between net market income and disposable income is the addition of direct transfers, which include the Family Benefit, childbirth and childcare benefits, unemployment benefits, contributory and noncontributory (social) pensions, student stipends, and a variety of other transfers carried over from previous social protection policies. These transfers lower the Gini by more than 8 percentage points, a sizable decline. Transfer payments also reduce poverty headcounts by large amounts (10–15 percentage points).

These very positive distributional results are driven mostly by contributory pensions. If we consider those pensions to be deferred compensation rather than transfers, the remaining transfers reduce the Gini by only two points and the headcounts from 1.6 to 3.2 points (figure 2A.1). We will show in the next section that these transfers have good-to-excellent targeting, although none of them is very large relative to income, so their overall impact is limited by program size more than targeting. In addition, the diminishing effect as the poverty line increases is because many transfer recipients are below the higher poverty lines both before *and after* the transfer. This, too, reflects the relatively small amounts for these transfers. At every poverty line, direct transfers are sufficient to offset the poverty-inducing effect of direct taxes, although only just so for the highest poverty line.

Effects of Indirect Taxes

Consumable income is disposable income less indirect taxes—VAT, import duties, and excises in our analysis. These taxes barely move the Gini, reflecting the fact that their distribution is similar to the disposable income distribution: in Armenia, the poor and the rich spend similar shares of their incomes on goods and services that pay indirect taxes.

These taxes do, however, increase all three poverty measures substantially. The poor buy goods and services that include indirect taxes and so pay a larger share of these taxes than they do of direct taxes, except at the highest poverty line where the effects are about equal. At the highest poverty line, poverty is higher for consumable income than it is for market income: direct transfers are not sufficient to overcome the poverty-inducing effects of all taxation at this high poverty line, although they continue to be sufficient for the lower poverty lines.

Effects of In-Kind Transfers

Final income is consumable income plus in-kind transfers, mostly health and education in our analysis. Despite the fact that we have scaled down the value of these transfers to be consistent with administrative data, they reduce the Gini coefficient by 1.8 points and also reduce poverty at all three poverty lines.

Overall Effects

The overall effect of the fisc, or rather, the parts that we can measure here, is a significant reduction in the Gini coefficient from 0.469 (market income) to 0.357 (final income). Mostly, this is driven by pensions, a large budget item.

The effect on poverty depends on the poverty line. For the lowest two, the fisc reduces the headcount by a significant amount. For the highest line, however, the effect of taxes overwhelms the transfers, leaving poverty slightly higher post-fisc than pre-fisc. We should note, however, that in-kind transfers are scaled down in this analysis, whereas direct taxes are not.[23] In a sensitivity analysis that scales down direct taxes as well as the overall effect of the fisc on poverty at the US$4.00 per day line, there is a 1 point decline.

Another way to evaluate the overall effect of taxes and expenditures is to ask: at what point in the income distribution do people become net payers to the fisc? Table 2.6 gives the results by income, grouped by international poverty lines in U.S. dollars at PPP.

For the poorest Armenians, the effect is quite positive. Consumable incomes (including all taxes and direct transfers but not in-kind benefits from health and education expenditures) are 208 percent higher than market incomes, and final incomes (including the in-kind health and education benefits) are 247 percent higher. These changes are much larger than those observed in other middle-income countries because Armenia has a large number of pensioner households whose market income is zero but whose pension is reasonably generous, lifting their post-fisc income considerably.

Nevertheless, households become net payers rather quickly as incomes increase. Those with modest incomes in the US$2.50–4.00 range just about break even, whereas those with higher incomes are net payers.[24] It is also interesting to note that those in the highest income group pay a relatively small share of market income in taxes (28 percent).

Incidence Results

For a tax or expenditure to have large distributional impact, it needs to be large relative to income, but it also needs to be strongly targeted to the rich or the poor.[25] Even though the center of the CEQ analysis is a comparison of the five income concepts presented earlier, it is easier to interpret those results if targeting and incidence are understood. To that end, table 2.7 gives Kakwani coefficients calculated for four income concepts and the marginal contributions to changes in inequality for all of the tax and expenditure items included in the analysis.

Table 2.6 Net Impact of Taxes and Social Expenditures in Armenia, by Poverty Group
Percentage of market income

Income group (y)	Change to market income from all taxes	Change to market income from all transfers	Difference between market income and consumable income[a]	Difference between market income and final income[b]
y < $1.25	−42	250	208	247
$1.25 ≤ y < $2.50	−23	43	20	32
$2.50 ≤ y < $4.00	−26	21	−4	2
$4.00 ≤ y < $10.00	−27	9	−18	−15
$10.00 ≤ y	−28	4	−24	−23

Source: Based on 2011 Integrated Living Conditions Survey (ILCS) database, National Statistical Service of the Republic of Armenia, http://www.armstat.am/en/?nid=246.
Note: Income groups stated in terms of U.S. dollars per capita per day at purchasing power parity (PPP). "Market income" comprises pretax wages, salaries, income earned from capital assets (rent, interest, or dividends), and private transfers.
a. Consumable income subtracts from market income tax payments, social security contributions, and indirect taxes (such as value added tax) and adds direct cash transfers.
b. Final income adds to consumable income the effects of in-kind benefits such as health and education.

The Distributional Impact of Taxes and Transfers • http://dx.doi.org/10.1596/978-1-4648-1091-6

Table 2.7 Kakwani Indexes for, and Marginal Contributions of, Specific Taxes and Social Expenditures in Armenia, 2011

	Kakwani coefficients[a]				Marginal contributions[a]		
	Market income[b]	Disposable income[c]	Consumable income[d]	Final income[e]	Market to disposable	Market to consumable	Market to final
Redistributive effect	n.a.	n.a.	n.a.	n.a.	0.096	0.095	0.114
Income (Gini)	0.469	0.373	0.374	0.356	n.a.	n.a.	n.a.
Broad aggregates							
Direct taxes	0.097	0.106	0.099	0.116	0.017	0.019	0.021
Direct transfers	0.660	0.224	0.223	0.207	0.083	0.101	0.092
Indirect taxes	−0.129	−0.005	−0.013	0.002	n.a.	−0.001	0.001
Indirect subsidies	0.381	0.307	0.281	0.259	n.a.	0.000	0.000
In-kind education	0.519	0.473	0.472	0.402	n.a.	n.a.	0.014
In-kind health	0.499	0.346	0.344	0.204	n.a.	n.a.	0.004
Cash transfers							
Family Benefit	0.949	0.646	0.639	0.587	0.012	0.013	0.012
Noncontributory pensions	0.596	0.273	0.272	0.241	0.006	0.007	0.006
Contributory pensions	0.641	0.172	0.172	0.163	0.059	0.073	0.067
Unemployment	0.688	0.506	0.519	0.513	0.001	0.001	0.001
Stipends	0.249	0.011	0.015	−0.074	0.000	0.000	0.000
Special privileges	0.923	0.328	0.348	0.370	0.000	0.000	0.000
Childcare benefits	0.286	0.221	0.218	0.205	0.000	0.000	0.000
Other transfers	0.642	0.041	0.049	0.016	0.000	0.000	0.000
In-kind education benefits							
Preprimary school	0.441	0.436	0.443	0.402	n.a.	n.a.	0.001
Primary school	0.573	0.552	0.551	0.489	n.a.	n.a.	0.005
Middle school	0.599	0.541	0.537	0.465	n.a.	n.a.	0.006
Secondary school	0.464	0.411	0.406	0.354	n.a.	n.a.	0.002
Initial vocational school	0.869	0.630	0.639	0.497	n.a.	n.a.	0.000
Secondary vocational	0.533	0.432	0.435	0.317	n.a.	n.a.	0.000
Postsecondary school	0.172	0.109	0.109	−0.003	n.a.	n.a.	0.000
In-kind health benefits							
Inpatient care	0.496	0.340	0.338	0.128	n.a.	n.a.	0.001
Inpatient, maternity	0.593	0.546	0.546	0.471	n.a.	n.a.	0.001
Primary health care	0.475	0.292	0.290	0.193	n.a.	n.a.	0.002
Other benefits							
Housing subsidies	0.381	0.307	0.281	0.259	n.a.	0.000	0.000
Direct taxes							
Personal income tax	0.209	0.230	0.223	0.242	0.010	0.011	0.012
Social security contributions	0.048	0.052	0.045	0.061	0.007	0.008	0.009

table continues next page

Table 2.7 Kakwani Indexes for, and Marginal Contributions of, Specific Taxes and Social Expenditures in Armenia, 2011 (continued)

	Kakwani coefficients[a]				Marginal contributions[a]		
	Market income[b]	Disposable income[c]	Consumable income[d]	Final income[e]	Market to disposable	Market to consumable	Market to final
Indirect taxes							
Value added tax (VAT)	−0.119	0.010	0.005	0.022	n.a.	0.001	0.002
Import duties	−0.127	0.002	−0.004	0.011	n.a.	0.000	0.000
Gasoline excises	0.110	0.200	0.194	0.220	n.a.	0.000	0.000
Tobacco excises	−0.198	−0.108	−0.134	−0.123	n.a.	−0.002	−0.002
Alcohol excises	−0.069	0.046	0.034	0.049	n.a.	0.000	0.000

Source: Based on 2011 Integrated Living Conditions Survey (ILCS) database, National Statistical Service of the Republic of Armenia, http://www .armstat.am/en/?nid=246.
Note: Kakwani coefficients and marginal contributions are calculated so that equalizing taxes or expenditures produce a positive coefficient. n.a. = not applicable.
a. The "Kakwani coefficients" columns show the difference between the concentration coefficient and the Gini coefficient. The "Marginal contribution" columns show the difference between the Gini coefficients with and without the designated row's tax or expenditure. The Gini coefficient measures inequality of income distribution, from 0 (full equality) to 1 (maximum inequality).
b. Market income comprises pretax wages, salaries, income earned from capital assets (rent, interest, or dividends), and private transfers.
c. Disposable income is market income (a) minus the payments for personal income taxes and employees' social security contributions, and (b) plus direct cash transfers.
d. Consumable income adds to disposable income the impact of indirect taxes, including value added taxes; import duties; and excises on petroleum products, alcoholic beverages, and tobacco products.
e. Final income adds to consumable income the effects of in-kind transfers for health care and education.

Incidence of Direct Transfers

The Family Benefit is the expenditure best targeted to the poor, a result consistent with other studies of this program's targeting (Esado 2012; Karapetyan et al. 2011; Tumasyan 2006). Because it is Armenia's one explicitly need-based public expenditure, this makes sense. Although targeting of the Family Benefit is not perfect—about a third goes to households whose market income is above the US$2.50 per day poverty line—its Kakwani coefficient is higher than those for conditional cash transfer programs in Latin America and better than any other social expenditure in Armenia.

Other transfer payments also go disproportionately to poorer households. "Compensation for privileges" goes primarily to World War II veterans and their children, an elderly population that usually has no other source of income and is thus extremely poor in the absence of this transfer. The same is true for both contributory and noncontributory pensions. Unemployment benefits have significantly negative concentration coefficients as well. None of these transfers is means tested, but all are based on the reasonable presumption that the unemployed and the elderly are likely to be poor before receiving them. Although not universally true, this is certainly true on average and is reflected in the strongly positive Kakwani coefficients.

Among all the direct transfers we can examine, student stipends and childcare benefits have the lowest Kakwani coefficients. Stipends are merit-based, intended to support students based on ability rather than need. That ability is somewhat more common in richer households, especially when ordering the population by final income, which includes the large in-kind benefit of postsecondary education for stipend recipients. Childcare benefits are provided only for mothers who participate in the social security system, that is, those who have a formal job, which explains their households' somewhat higher incomes.

Incidence of In-Kind Benefits

Most in-kind education benefits also go more to poorer households: primary and middle-school education as well as both levels of vocational training all have large Kakwani coefficients, with that for initial vocational training (in years 10–12) being especially high. Secondary schooling and preschool have Kakwani coefficients near the value of the Gini (and so a concentration coefficient near zero). To some extent, this reflects our use of per capita income measures. Households with students are larger and have more members who do not work, giving them lower per capita incomes. But it also reflects the higher-than-average coverage rates of schooling in Armenia, especially at the secondary level. This is not true, however, for university studies, where the Kakwani is much smaller and turns negative when ordering by final income, for the same reason that stipends do.

In-kind health benefits have Kakwani coefficients near the Gini coefficients and so are spread evenly across the income distribution except when ordering by final income (which includes these sometimes large benefits and thus moves the recipients well up the income distribution). Hospital maternity care (deliveries), however, has a somewhat large Kakwani coefficient, indicating that these benefits, which are the most generous in the health care system, go disproportionately to the poor.

All of these health services are supposed to be universal and free. However, the transfers from the State Health Agency to the providers are insufficient to cover costs, so patients sometimes must pay informal fees. Those fees may discourage poorer households from using these services, tilting the beneficiary pool toward richer households. In many LMICs, this effect is more than offset by a flight of richer households from the poor quality of publicly provided services, so that the remaining clientele is relatively poor. In Armenia, however, all primary care providers, public and private, receive the transfer from the State Health Agency for each client that they enroll, so shifts in the type of provider do not alter the income distribution of subsidy recipients.

Incidence of Taxes

As for taxes, both direct taxes (PIT and SSC) and excises on petroleum products[26] have positive Kakwani coefficients, indicating that these taxes are progressive, although only very mildly so in the case of SSC. For market income, the Kakwani coefficients for VAT, import duties, and alcohol excises are all negative, making them (mildly) regressive, a pattern more typical of a developed economy. This changes when we order by the other income concepts, however, because transfer payments, especially contributory pensions, move their recipients significantly higher in the income distribution. Since those pensioners also buy goods and services subject to indirect taxes, their incidence is much more regressive when using market income (which excludes the transfers) than the other income concepts. Tobacco excises are much more regressive than other taxes: smoking is spread more evenly across the population than is income in general.

Sensitivity Analyses of Concentration Coefficients

We have conducted four additional sensitivity analyses to test the robustness of our findings.[27] The first sensitivity analysis changes the treatment of contributory pensions. Rather than viewing them as transfer payments, this run treats them as deferred compensation and thus part of market income. To be consistent, this analysis must also treat SSC as saving rather than a tax, as in the benchmark run. The effect of these alternate assumptions is to move pensioners further up the market income distribution and everyone else down. As a result, benefits that go disproportionately to households receiving contributory pensions—the pensions themselves but also health care—have less positive concentration coefficients in this run and are thus more progressive.

The view of contributory pensions themselves changes dramatically, giving them a much lower Kakwani coefficient. This reflects the fact that contributory pensions, which are the most generous transfer payments in Armenia, move their recipients well up the income distribution. At the same time, benefits that go disproportionately to households that are unlikely to receive a contributory pension—those receiving unemployment benefits or noncontributory pensions and those with students—move down the income distribution, and each of these items has a larger Kakwani coefficient than in the benchmark, although the change is not so large as to change the rankings very much. Other items remain reasonably stable. Initial vocational education actually shows a large decrease in its Kakwani coefficient, but it has a very large standard error (between 0.11 and 0.15) because there are few such students in the sample. One should not read too much into this change.

The second sensitivity analysis alters the construction of the income concepts from an income base to an expenditure base. Most poverty analysis in Armenia is done with consumption rather than incomes. Because the correlation between reported incomes and expenditures is low, it is important to check that a consumption-based welfare variable does not affect the results. Fortunately, that is the case. For this run, we defined disposable income as household total consumption and worked backward to market income and forward to final income in the same way as the base run. Results are very similar to the base run.

The third sensitivity analysis scales household income by the NSSRA adult equivalence scale[28] rather than the number of household members. This, too, has very little effect on the results. This is perhaps surprising but, unlike many other LMIC economies, households with children in Armenia are not especially large.

The fourth sensitivity analysis starts with the pensions-as-transfers scenario and scales down the direct taxes (PIT and SSC) so that the ratio of the total paid to total household income in the survey is equal to the same ratio for administrative data. As noted, household expenditure in the ILCS is only 37 percent of that reported in the national income accounts, and total household income is only slightly larger, but the total household income from formal sector wages, and thus taxes based on them (PIT and SSC), are much closer to the values in administrative accounts. This makes them far too large relative to income in the survey. The scaling down corrects for that.

Whether this is an appropriate adjustment depends on the nature of the underreporting in the surveys. If all households are underreporting their incomes and expenditures, more or less proportionately, then this adjustment will give a more accurate estimate of the concentration coefficients because it also "underreports" direct taxes proportionately. Without it, households that pay direct taxes will move too high in the income distribution, because those direct taxes get added onto observed income to estimate market income. That will make the direct taxes appear too progressive. Although this modification does lower the Kakwani coefficients for PIT and SSC, the effect is not large and both remain progressive taxes.

Overall, then, the results reported in table 2.7 are reasonably robust to alternate approaches and specifications.

Social Expenditure Coverage

A public expenditure's coverage rate is the number of beneficiaries divided by the target population. When subdivided by income groups, this information is a useful complement to the incidence analysis presented so far. In particular, good targeting alone is not sufficient to guarantee high coverage for the poor. The program size (expenditure) must also be sufficiently large. Coverage information can also show leakage of benefits to nontarget populations and indicate whether certain subpopulations are more or less likely to benefit from public services like health and education that should be universal. Table 2.8 gives coverage rates for social expenditures in Armenia.

Preprimary education is not a universal service in Armenia, with public provision provided mostly by local rather than national government. There is a sharp increase in coverage with income, which mostly reflects the Yerevan local government's ability to raise property tax revenue to provide public services, including preschool. Both primary and general secondary schooling have high coverage rates that are evenly balanced across the income distribution. This suggests that the reasons for less than 100 percent coverage are not income related.[29] Higher education is also not a universal service in Armenia; students must pay tuition. Scholarships are available, but they are based on merit, not need. Not surprisingly, coverage rates are much higher for higher-income households. Note, however, that the opposite is true for vocational education.

Health care coverage is difficult to judge because there is no obvious benchmark for the number of health visits per month. The numbers reported are the share of the population that used either a publicly funded outpatient service (at a hospital, polyclinic, family doctor, and so on) or inpatient services (at a hospital) in the previous month (not year). Since not everyone is sick in a month, these rates are far less than 100 percent, as they should be. Overall, however, about 7 percent of the population has contact with the primary health system in a given month.

Table 2.8 Social Expenditure Coverage Rates in Armenia, by Income Group, 2011
Percentage

	Income group (x)					
	x < $1.25	$1.25 ≤ x < $2.50	$2.50 ≤ x < $4.00	$4.00 ≤ x < $10.00	$10.00 ≤ x	Total
	Income share, by group					
Expenditure type	2	8	17	53	20	100
Education[a]						
Preprimary	1.0	5.5	10.2	10.9	27.0	8.0
Primary (I–IV)	89.1	85.4	92.1	89.3	98.3	89.3
General secondary (V–IX)	85.6	83.6	85.9	83.2	73.0	84.0
Secondary (X–XII)	55.7	57.2	64.6	64.9	63.8	61.3
Secondary vocational	1.8	2.6	0.5	0.4	0.0	1.1
Secondary professional (college)	3.1	5.1	2.9	3.7	0.5	3.4
Higher education or post-grad	4.7	4.2	4.7	11.5	13.5	7.9
Health care[b]						
Outpatient care[c]	7.7	6.8	6.9	6.3	5.0	6.7
Inpatient care[d]	3.8	4.3	4.5	3.5	3.7	3.9
Old-age pensions[e]						
Noncontributory[f]	13.0	14.8	10.2	11.5	12.4	12.5
Contributory[g]	86.8	85.0	89.5	87.9	86.5	87.2
Other transfers						
Family Benefit[h]	24.5	13.0	n.a.	n.a.	n.a.	19.2
Unemployment[i]	4.6	3.0	3.2	3.6	2.5	3.6

Source: Based on 2011 Integrated Living Conditions Survey (ILCS), National Statistical Service of the Republic of Armenia, http://www.armstat.am /en/?nid=246.
Note: Income groups stated in terms of U.S. dollars per capita per day at purchasing power parity (PPP). n.a. = not applicable.
a. Education coverage defined as (# students)/(# children of appropriate age + # actual students of other ages).
b. Health coverage defined as people who had one or more consultations divided by population.
c. Outpatient care excludes hospital outpatient care; consultations counted from previous month.
d. Inpatient care is in hospitals only; consultations counted from previous year divided by 12.
e. Old-age pension coverage defined as (number of recipients)/(population 65 or older + actual pension recipients).
f. Noncontributory pensions are "social" pensions.
g. Contributory pensions are from the social security system.
h. Family Benefit coverage is (# household members of recipients) / (# household members in households earning below US$2.50/day).
i. Unemployment coverage is (# recipients) / (# unemployed), which is the NSSRA definition.

Old-age pension coverage is universal. Those who receive a contributory pension cannot receive a noncontributory (social) pension and vice versa, so the fact that the two rows sum almost to 100 percent means that every elderly person is receiving a pension.

Coverage for the other transfers is less impressive. The Family Benefit reaches only 22 percent of people living in households whose market income is less than US$2.50 per person per day. So even though targeting is very progressive for this transfer, it falls far short of covering all those in need. Indeed, there is often a trade-off between better targeting and better coverage in proxy means-tested transfers like the Family Benefit. Tightening the proxy requirements for qualification will generally exclude richer households (which improves targeting) but also some poorer ones (which reduces coverage). Coverage for unemployment compensation is very low.

The Distributional Impact of Taxes and Transfers • http://dx.doi.org/10.1596/978-1-4648-1091-6

Income Mobility

Most fiscal incidence studies focus on expenditures; some examine taxes; but relatively few look at both. Although either expenditures or taxes can be progressive and thus make the income distribution more equal, only expenditures can reduce poverty. Taxes at best leave the income distribution unchanged. This means that the fiscal system as a whole may increase or decrease any individual's income on net, and may move her or him up or down the income distribution. Most measures used to evaluate fiscal incidence are anonymous: they do not consider who is in the pth quantile of the income distribution, only the income that that p^{th} person has.

Lustig and Higgins (2013b) propose the use of mobility matrices to describe the extent to which the fiscal system increases or decreases people's incomes. Table 2.9 gives these matrices for mobility from market income to disposable income and from market income to consumable income. The income ranges are defined by the US$ PPP poverty lines standard to the CEQ analysis.

Table 2.9 Mobility Matrices in Armenia, by Income Concept

Market income[a] group	Disposable income[b] group						Percentage of population	Average market income (drams per month)
	$y < \$1.25$ (%)	$\$1.25 \leq y$ < $\$2.50$ (%)	$\$2.50 \leq y$ < $\$4.00$ (%)	$\$4.00 \leq y$ < $\$10.00$ (%)	$\$10.00 \leq y$ < $\$50.00$ (%)	$\$50.00$ $\leq y$ (%)		
$y < \$1.25$	44	35	13	9	0	0	21	4,231
$\$1.25 \leq y < \$2.50$	2	55	36	7	0	0	18	15,585
$\$2.50 \leq y < \$4.00$	0	10	68	21	0	0	19	26,775
$\$4.00 \leq y < \$10.00$	0	0	13	86	2	0	35	51,421
$\$10.00 \leq y < \$50.00$	0	0	0	38	61	0	7	124,344
$\$50.00 \leq y$	0	0	0	0	58	42	0	520,501
	Consumable income[c] group							
$y < \$1.25$	51	31	13	5	0	0	21	4,231
$\$1.25 \leq y < \$2.50$	6	66	24	5	0	0	18	15,585
$\$2.50 \leq y < \$4.00$	0	24	64	12	0	0	19	26,775
$\$4.00 \leq y < \$10.00$	0	0	25	75	1	0	35	51,421
$\$10.00 \leq y < \$50.00$	0	0	0	56	44	0	7	124,344
$\$50.00 \leq y$	0	0	0	0	58	42	0	520,501

Source: Based on 2011 Integrated Living Conditions Survey (ILCS), National Statistical Service of the Republic of Armenia, http://www.armstat.am /en/?nid=246.

Note: Income groups expressed in U.S. dollars per capita per day at purchasing power parity (PPP).

a. Market income comprises pretax wages, salaries, income earned from capital assets (rent, interest, or dividends), and private transfers.

b. Disposable income is market income (a) minus the payments for personal income taxes and employees' social security contributions, and (b) plus direct cash transfers.

c. Consumable income adds to disposable income the impact of indirect taxes, including value added taxes; import duties; and excises on petroleum products, alcoholic beverages, and tobacco products.

Overall, 34 percent and 36 percent of individuals change income groups in the two analyses, respectively. One can see that the combination of direct taxes and monetary transfers (which constitute the difference between market and disposable income) moves many people to higher income groups, especially those who start with less than US$2.50 per day at PPP. But these taxes and transfers also move a significant number of people to lower income groups, making them "poor." This effect is even stronger when looking at the transition from market to consumable income, which also includes the impact of indirect taxes. Here, even large numbers of those in the US$2.50–4.00 range fall below the US$2.50 poverty line post-fisc.

These results are more dramatic than any reported in CEQ analyses for Latin America.[30] There seem to be three reasons for this. First, this study analyzes taxes that are a larger share of GDP than in most of the other countries (17 percent in Armenia vs. 11 in Bolivia, 25 in Brazil, 9 in Mexico, 9 in Peru, and 15 percent in Uruguay). And social expenditures in Armenia are a smaller share of GDP (7 percent) than in most of the other countries (14 percent in Bolivia, 15 percent in Brazil, 9 in Mexico, 5 in Peru, and 11 percent in Uruguay). In part, this reflects the fact that social expenditures are a smaller share of GDP in Armenia than in the Latin American countries and also that Armenia's largest taxes, VAT, and social contributions are easily identified and modeled.

Second, taxes in Armenia, especially indirect taxes, are very broad-based. This is commendable on efficiency grounds, but it has an equity cost because these taxes do fall, to some extent, on the poor.

Third, Armenia's income distribution is much more concentrated in the lower income groups. Given that only 7 percent of the population has market income greater than US$10.00 per day, it would be impossible to fund the government by taxing only that group. Nevertheless, table 2.9 highlights the stark reality that public spending, including transfer payments, must be funded and that taxation can induce a significant amount of poverty in its own right.

Comparisons with Other Incidence Studies in Armenia

Prior Incidence Analyses

There are several other incidence analyses for Armenia, all done in the past decade. Hovhannisyan (2006) and AST (2010, 2012) examine the distribution of benefits from public expenditures across expenditure quintiles. Harutyunyan and Khechoyan (2008) and NSSRA (2012a) both examine the poverty reduction impact of transfer payments using methods similar to those of this paper. Bouvry-Boyakhchyan (2008) also provides a review of studies that analyze the distributional impact of the Family Benefit. There are no previous studies of tax incidence or the overall distributional effects of the fisc.

Table 2.10 gives the concentration coefficients for the expenditure items analyzed in previous incidence studies.[31] These estimates are not strictly comparable to those presented in table 2.7. Hovhannisyan (2006) appears to use ILCS data, but he gives neither the data sources nor the welfare measure used to establish the quintiles.

Table 2.10 Concentration Coefficients from Previous Incidence Studies of Public Expenditures in Armenia

Expenditure type	Hovhannisyan (2006) data					AST (2010, 2012) data	
	1999	2000	2001	2002	2003	2008/09	2012
Education							
General education	−0.01	0.04	0.04	0.03	0.04	−0.05	−0.08
Vocational education	−0.01	0.05	0.05	0.03	0.02	−0.03	0.04
Higher education	0.12	0.06	0.06	0.12	0.05	0.14	0.13
Health							
Public health primary care services	0.05	—	0.05	0.08	0.04	−0.04	0.01
OB-GYN medical assistance	—	—	—	—	—	−0.07	−0.10
Hospital medical aid services	0.06	—	0.01	0.01	0.04	−0.03	−0.04
Public health services	—	—	—	—	—	−0.01	−0.17
Direct social transfers							
Family Benefit	0.01	—	0.04	0.04	−0.11	—	—
Water							
Drinking water supply	—		—	—	—	0.01	0.01
Sewerage	—		—	—	—	0.01	0.01
Irrigation	—		—	—	—	0.00	0.00

Sources: Based on Hovhannisyan 2006; AST 2010, 2012.
Note: AST = Advanced Social Technologies; — = not available.

AST (2010, 2012) uses its own survey of 1,600 households in each year and an expenditure (rather than income) per capita welfare measure. Nevertheless, with the exception of the Family Benefit, none of these estimates is too different from those derived in this chapter.

General education (which comprises primary and middle school and, in the Hovhannisyan [2006] paper, secondary school) is somewhat less progressive in Hovhannisyan (2006) than our findings suggest, and higher education is more regressive in our study than the previous ones. But for the most part, comparable items give similar results. That is important. One common criticism of studies of this type is that they are "out of date" because they use older survey data. Yet the behavioral patterns that underlie the incidence results are usually slow to change, so that results from previous years are still informative.

The one significant exception is the Family Benefit, which is much more progressive in our study than what Hovhannisyan (2006) found. After its introduction in 1999, the targeting of the Family Benefit was tightened significantly through modification and more careful application of the proxy means test. This had the effect of reducing its coverage and also improving its targeting significantly.

Analyses of Family Benefit Impact on Poverty

There are several papers on the poverty impact and targeting of the Family Benefit. Bouvry-Boyakhchyan (2008) reviews papers that discuss the low coverage rate (only about 30 percent) of the Family Benefit as well as its targeting with an inclusion error of 44 percent early in the 2000s.

NSSRA (2012b) presents results for child poverty (for those under 18 years old), arguing that in 2011, loss of old-age pensions (both contributory and noncontributory) would increase extreme child poverty from the 4.7 percent observed in the 2011 ILCS to 17.0 percent. The loss would also increase child poverty from 41.9 percent to 52.7 percent. For the Family Benefit, the NSSRA results suggest an increase in extreme child poverty from 4.7 percent to 10.3 percent and child poverty from 41.9 percent to 46.6 percent.[32]

These effects are somewhat larger than those that we have estimated in table 2.5 (see change from net market income to disposable income) for all transfer payments. This difference may be due to differences in the welfare variable (NSSRA uses expenditures per adult equivalent) and also different poverty lines (NSSRA uses lines derived with the "cost of basic needs" approach rather than the international lines that we use). One important similarity is that pensions have a larger poverty impact in both studies because, as NSSRA (2012b) notes, they are a much larger budget item.

Harutyunyan and Khechoyan (2008) use the ILCS for 2006 to study the impact of transfer payments on poverty. As in this chapter and the NSSRA (2012b) study, these authors simulate poverty in the absence of transfers by simply reducing observed consumption by the amount of the transfer payments. In table 2.11 (reproduced from Harutyunyan and Khechoyan [2008, table 1]), the authors do not state which poverty lines they use, nor whether they use consumption per capita or per adult equivalent.

To compare with this chapter's table 2.5, the difference between "post-transfers (observed)" and "pre-transfers" here is the same as the difference between net market income and disposable income in table 2.5. To compare "post-transfers (observed)" with "pre-social assistance," look at the sensitivity analysis in annex 2A (figure 2A.1), which treats pensions as market income, and, again, compare net market income with disposable income. In both cases, the results in our paper are somewhat larger, that is, we find that these transfers have a larger effect on the

Table 2.11 Poverty Impact of Social Transfers in Armenia, 2006
Poverty headcount, percentage

Measurement stage	Extreme poverty	Poverty
Income post-transfers (observed)	26.5	4.1
Income pre-transfers	32.8	12.1
Income pre-pension	31.0	8.2
Income pre-social assistance	28.0	7.2
Income pre-Family Benefit	27.8	7.0

Source: Harutyunyan and Khechoyan 2008, table 1.
Note: The Harutyunyan and Khechoyan (2008) study, based on data from the 2006 Integrated Living Conditions Survey (ILCS) does not define the poverty lines used nor whether those lines are defined by consumption per capita or per adult equivalent. However, the National Statistical Service of the Republic of Armenia (NSSRA), which conducts the ILCS, defines poverty based on a "cost of basic needs" approach instead of using standard international lines such as US$1.25, US$2.50, or US$4.00 per person per day. As such, the NSSRA poverty line is dram 30,920 per adult equivalent per month, and the extreme poverty line (or food poverty line) is 17,483 per month.

headcount than do Harutyunyan and Khechoyan (2008), although for social assistance only, the results are quite close.

Conclusions

A CEQ analysis addresses three broad questions about the redistributive effect of taxes and expenditures:

- How much redistribution and poverty reduction is being accomplished in each country through social spending, subsidies, and taxes?
- How progressive are revenue collection and government spending?
- Within the limits of fiscal prudence, what could be done to increase redistribution and poverty reduction in each country through changes in taxation and spending?

The answer to the first question is that a large amount of redistribution occurs. From market income to final income, the Gini coefficient drops by 0.11. This compares with 0.13 in Brazil and 0.15 in the United States, respectively. This is impressive given the small share of GDP (7 percent) dedicated to transfer payments in Armenia.

However, if contributory (social security) pensions are treated as deferred income, the results are much smaller: the fisc reduces the Gini by only 0.05. By comparison, similar analyses for Brazil, Mexico, and the United States find that the fisc reduces the Gini by 0.11, 0.08, and 0.11, respectively. This is not because contributory pensions are the best-targeted social expenditures, but rather because they have by far the largest budget.

Results for poverty reduction are less encouraging. At a poverty line of US$2.50 per day, which is similar to Armenia's national poverty line, the fisc lowers the headcount by 8.4 percent, but at the US$4.00 poverty line, the fisc actually increases the headcount slightly (by 1.9 percent). Even though transfers are reasonably well-targeted in Armenia, taxes (especially indirect taxes) do fall on poorer households, thus offsetting the poverty-reducing effect of public expenditures. Further, the mobility matrices show that the fisc causes a significant amount of downward as well as upward mobility among the poor or near poor, much more so than in Latin American countries where similar analyses have been completed.

As for the second question, expenditure targeting is very good in Armenia. Expenditures that are supposed to help the poor and vulnerable go disproportionately to the poor, as they should. Although it is true that transfer programs in developed countries often have better targeting (with concentration coefficients of −0.8 or lower), the concentration coefficients for most transfers—and the Family Benefit in particular—are as good as or better than those found in other middle-income countries that rely on proxy means tests to identify transfer payment beneficiaries.

At the same time, expenditures on services that should be universal—education and health care—are spread fairly evenly across the population, with concentration coefficients near zero, as they should be. This is not, however, because they are in fact universal. Coverage rates for schooling are less than one and worsen at higher levels. But income and (in)ability to pay for schooling do not seem to be a factor because coverage does not decline with income. The only exceptions to this general finding are for preschool and university, neither of which is meant to be a universal service in Armenia.

Even though transfers other than contributory pensions have good targeting in Armenia, they have a limited effect on income distribution. This holds an important policy implication: large redistribution requires both good targeting and significant expenditures. Armenia has the former but, with the exception of contributory pensions, not the latter.

Coming to the third question, then, the fact that targeting is already good in Armenia means that there is not much scope for improving the distributional effect of fiscal policy by shifting expenditures among items. Although it is true that, say, Family Benefit and unemployment compensation have lower concentration coefficients than noncontributory pensions and other transfers, the fact that the budgets involved are small and that the differences in concentration are not too large means that relatively little could be achieved by shifting expenditures toward the more progressive items. To achieve greater redistribution, Armenia would have to increase social spending. The fact that the one large (and moderately well-targeted) social expenditure—contributory pensions—has a very large redistributive effect underscores this point.

Whether greater distribution is desirable is a question for policy makers and voters. But if the polity feels that the fisc should have a greater influence on the distribution of income in Armenia, the best candidate on the expenditure side of the budget is the Family Benefit, which is more concentrated among the poor than any other social expenditure. This could be achieved by increasing the amount of the benefit or by increasing its coverage, which remains quite low.

On the revenue side, most recent discussion of tax reform revolves around indirect taxes, especially the VAT. This analysis shows that these taxes are significantly less progressive than direct taxes. This is especially true of poverty effects: the poorest households only rarely pay direct taxes in Armenia, but they do pay VAT, import duties, and excises, especially on tobacco. From an equity perspective, then, it would be preferable to consider tax reforms to increase direct taxes either by raising rates or by drawing more workers into the formal economy.

Annex 2A. Sensitivity Analyses

Figure 2A.1 Concentration Coefficients, Sensitivity Analysis 1: Contributory Pensions as Deferred Compensation

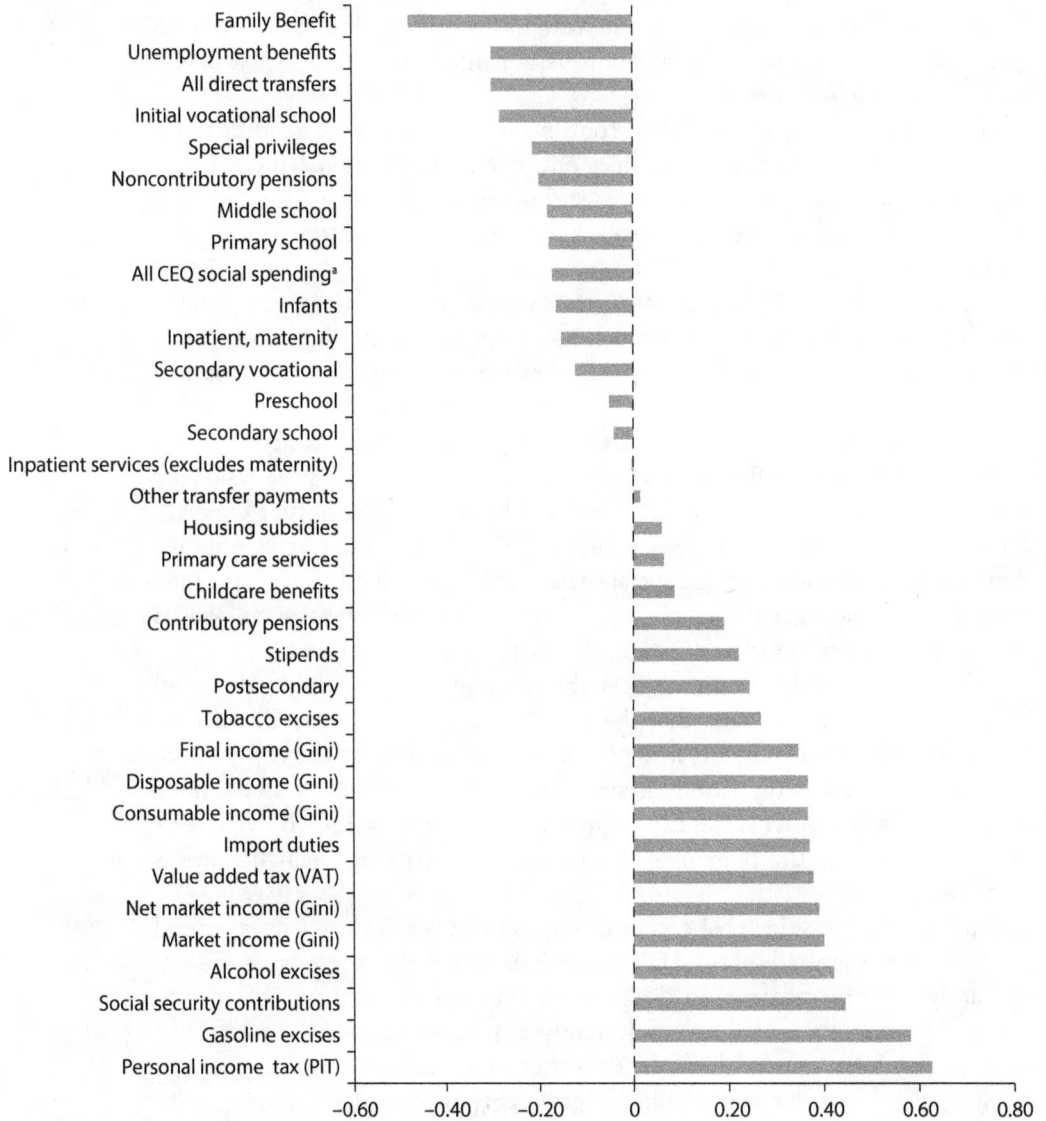

Source: World Bank.
Note: "Gini" refers to a measure of the inequality of income distribution from 0 (full equality) to 1 (maximum inequality). The CEQ (Commitment to Equity project) income concept terms used in the figure are as follows: "Market income" comprises pretax wages, salaries, income earned from capital assets (rent, interest, or dividends), and private transfers. "Net market income" subtracts from market income the payments for personal income taxes and employees' social security contributions. "Disposable income" is constructed by adding direct cash transfers to net market income. "Consumable income" adds to disposable income the impact of indirect taxes, including value added taxes; import duties; and excises on petroleum products, alcoholic beverages, and tobacco products. "Final income" adds to consumable income the effects of in-kind transfers for health care and education.
a. "All CEQ social spending" refers to spending on direct cash transfers and health and education spending as defined by the CEQ project.

Figure 2A.2 Concentration Coefficients, Sensitivity Analysis 2: Disposable Income Estimated with Consumption Rather than Income

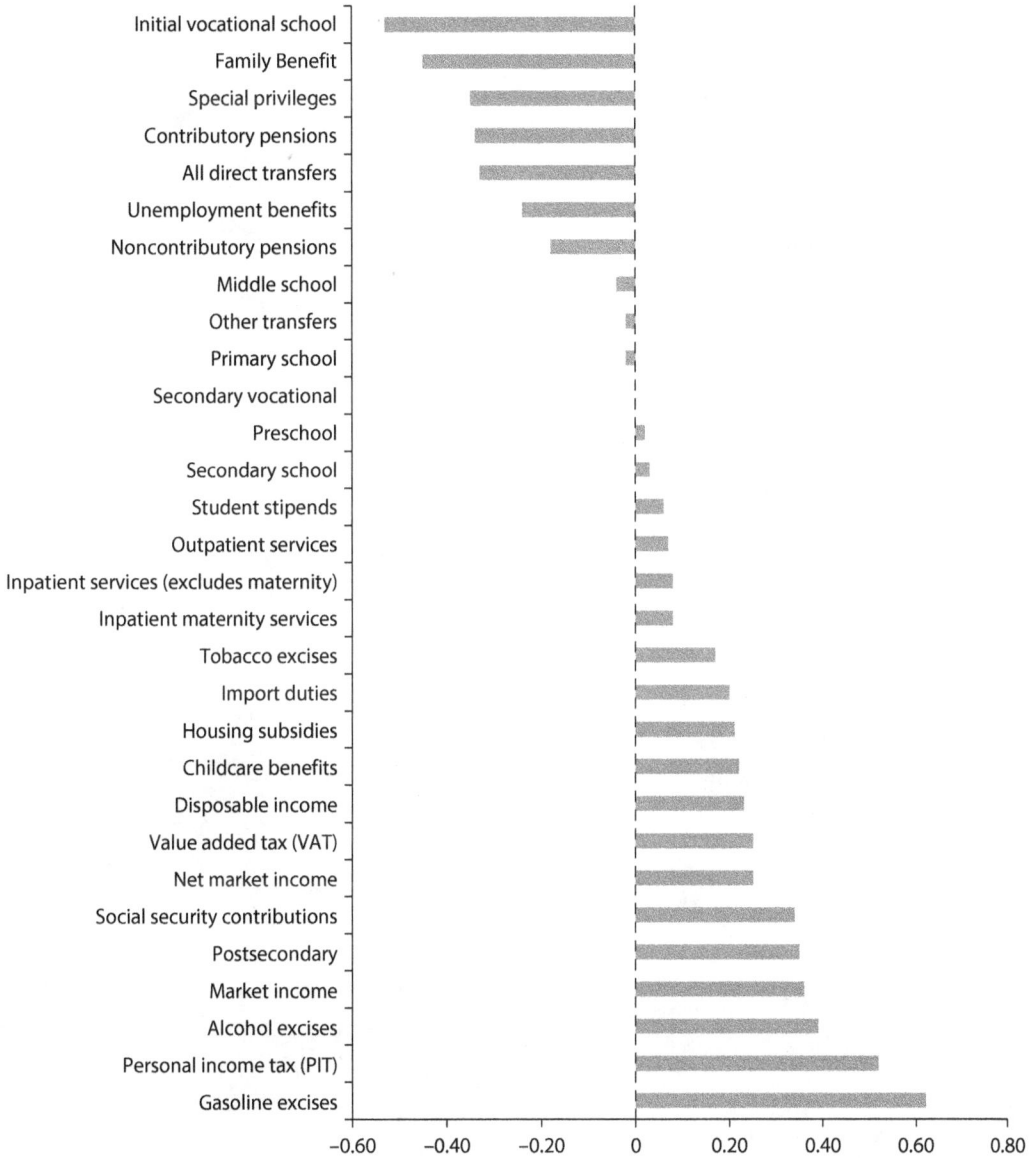

Source: World Bank.
Note: The CEQ (Commitment to Equity project) income concept terms used in the figure are as follows: "Market income" comprises pretax wages, salaries, income earned from capital assets (rent, interest, or dividends), and private transfers. "Net market income" subtracts from market income the payments for personal income taxes and employees' social security contributions. "Disposable income" is constructed by adding direct cash transfers to net market income.

Figure 2A.3 Concentration Coefficients, Sensitivity Analysis 3: Income per Adult Equivalent Rather Than per Capita

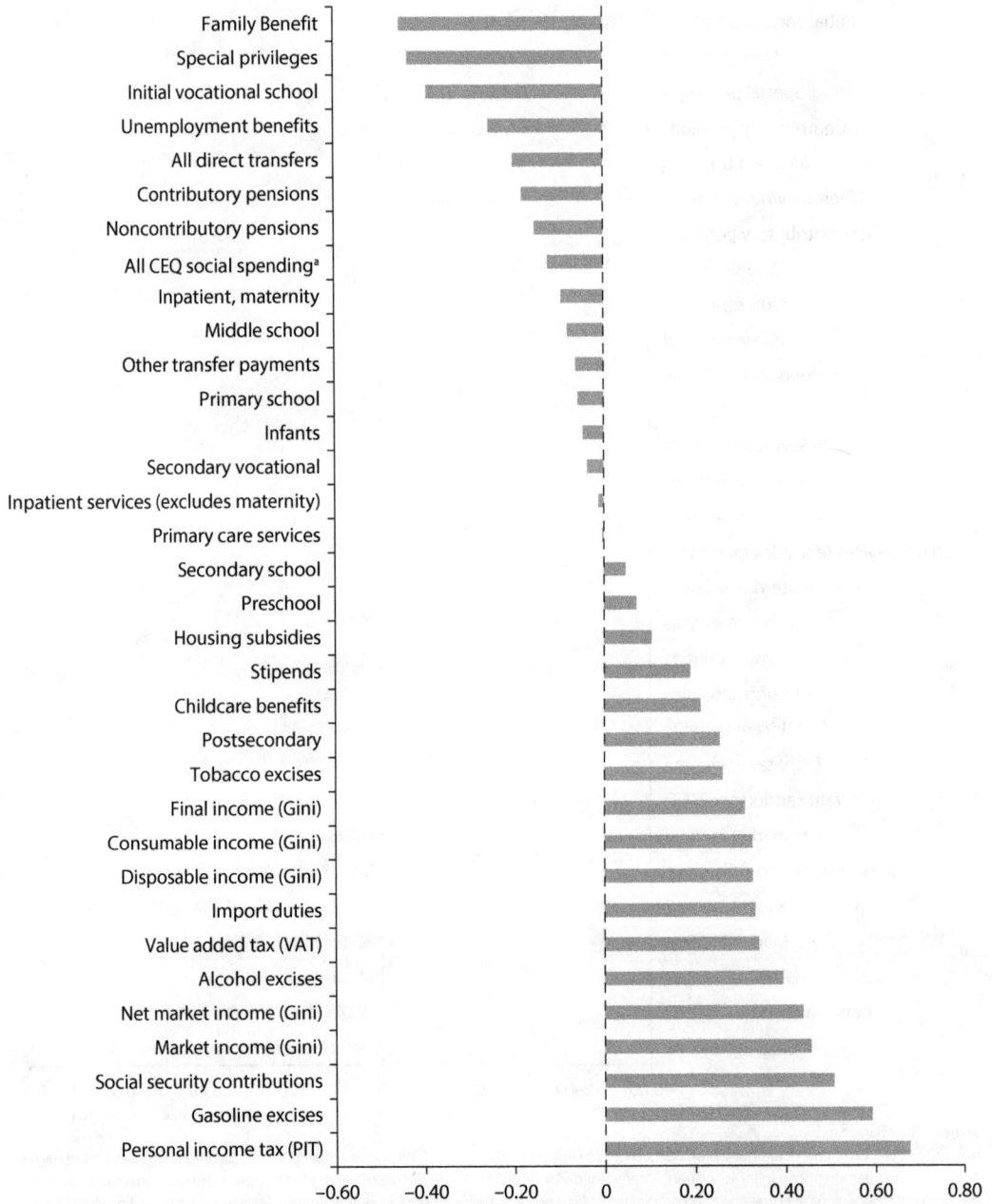

Source: World Bank.
Note: "Gini" refers to a measure of the inequality of income distribution from 0 (full equality) to 1 (maximum inequality). The CEQ (Commitment to Equity project) income concept terms used in the figure are as follows: "Market income" comprises pretax wages, salaries, income earned from capital assets (rent, interest, or dividends), and private transfers. "Net market income" subtracts from market income the payments for personal income taxes and employees' social security contributions. "Disposable income" is constructed by adding direct cash transfers to net market income. "Consumable income" adds to disposable income the impact of indirect taxes, including value added taxes; import duties; and excises on petroleum products, alcoholic beverages, and tobacco products. "Final income" adds to consumable income the effects of in-kind transfers for health care and education.
a. "All CEQ social spending" refers to spending on direct cash transfers and health and education spending as defined by the CEQ project.

Figure 2A.4 Concentration Coefficients, Sensitivity Analysis 4: Direct Taxes Scaled Down to Same Proportion of Household Income Found in National Accounts

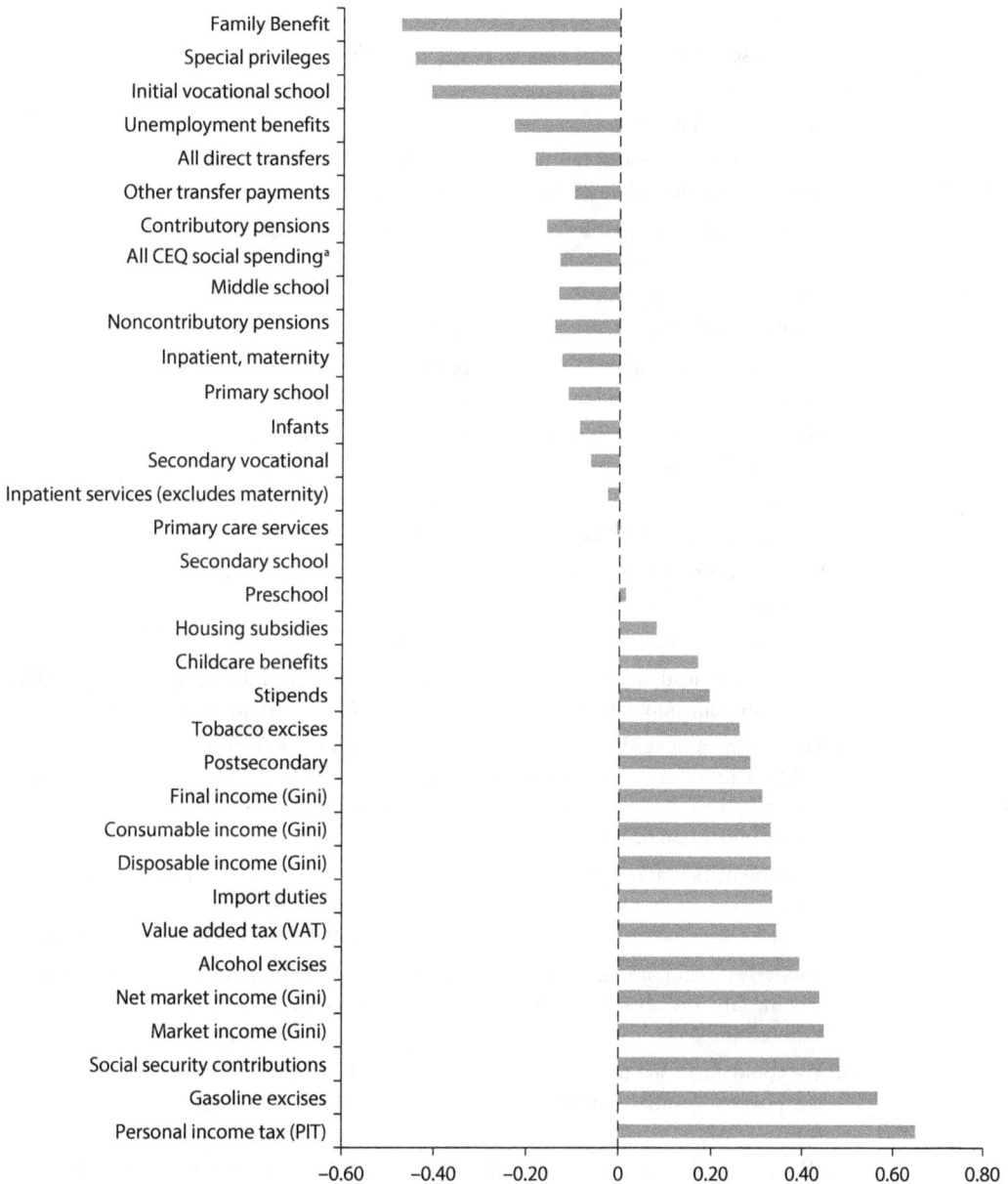

Source: World Bank.

Note: "Gini" refers to a measure of the inequality of income distribution from 0 (full equality) to 1 (maximum inequality). The CEQ (Commitment to Equity project) income concept terms used in the figure are as follows: "Market income" comprises pretax wages, salaries, income earned from capital assets (rent, interest, or dividends), and private transfers. "Net market income" subtracts from market income the payments for personal income taxes and employees' social security contributions. "Disposable income" is constructed by adding direct cash transfers to net market income. "Consumable income" adds to disposable income the impact of indirect taxes, including value added taxes; import duties; and excises on petroleum products, alcoholic beverages, and tobacco products. "Final income" adds to consumable income the effects of in-kind transfers for health care and education.

a. "All CEQ social spending" refers to spending on direct cash transfers and health and education spending as defined by the CEQ project.

The Distributional Impact of Taxes and Transfers • http://dx.doi.org/10.1596/978-1-4648-1091-6

Notes

1. Throughout the chapter, "the fisc" denotes both government revenue collection and expenditure.

2. For a description of the Armenian ILCS, see NSSRA 2012b, 11–13.

3. For a more detailed discussion of the CEQ income concepts used throughout the volume, see chapter 1.

4. This is because we use the income variable constructed by the National Statistical Service of the Republic of Armenia (NSSRA), which includes transfer payments.

5. "Compensation for privileges" refers to carry-over pensions from the Soviet era that are now a small share of all transfer payments.

6. There is one exception: for the sensitivity analysis that treats pensions as deferred income, we do not treat social security contributions as taxes.

7. A formal sector worker is an employee with a written contract, a member of a cooperative, an employer, or an own-account worker whose business is legally registered.

8. The tax on tobacco products is formally a "presumptive" tax, but it applies only to these products, so we treat it as an excise tax.

9. In theory, we could assign these benefits to non-VAT-paying business owners, but there is no way to identify them in the ILCS.

10. Previous estimates were done for earlier tax years, so our calculation may reflect increasing effectiveness of tax administration.

11. The 95th percentile is at dram 90,453, and the 99th is at dram 163,220.

12. Because the academic year is not consistent with the calendar year, we use one-third of the student population in 2010 and two-thirds of the population in 2011.

13. The numbers of students at each level except preprimary come from NSSRA (2010, 2011). The numbers of preprimary students come from NSSRA (2012c). Education budget data come from MoF state and community budget reports, http://mfe.am /index.php?cat=76&lang=1.

14. Outpatient care at hospitals is not subsidized except for nonspecialist care for children under seven years old and beneficiaries of the basic benefit package (BBP). We do include children's and BBP beneficiaries' outpatient hospital visits in the analysis.

15. Similarly direct comparisons for disposable income are more difficult, but disposable income in the ILCS is just 14 percent larger on average than household expenditures.

16. We could also scale up all the survey-based variables, but this would make the resulting poverty results dramatically different from those that are commonly reported from the ILCS.

17. We also explored a technique from Korinek, Mistiaen, and Ravallion (2007) to reweight the ILCS based on the probability that a sampled household will actually agree to be surveyed. That probability, in turn, is a decreasing function of household income. Doing this raises the amount of household consumption in the ILCS to 52 percent of that in the national accounts. As one would expect, it significantly increases estimated inequality and also reduces estimated poverty somewhat. More important for our analysis, though, is that *changes* in inequality and poverty brought about by taxes and public expenditures are very similar in the reweighted sample to the results that we present here. Given that, and in order to keep this analysis as

similar to those in other countries as possible and to also use data familiar to analysts in Armenia, we did not pursue the reweighting approach further.

18. Data for average European revenues as a share of GDP from the Eurostat database, http://ec.europa.eu/eurostat. See total receipts from taxes and social contributions (including imputed social contributions) after deduction of amounts assessed but unlikely to be collected.

19. Foster-Greer-Thorbecke indexes refer to a family of poverty metrics, the most common of which puts higher weight on the poverty of the poorest individuals, making it a combined measure of poverty and income inequality (Foster, Greer, and Thorbecke 1984).

20. Further, we make no adjustment for household members who were absent for part of the preceding month.

21. The one exception to this is the adult equivalence scale. Using per capita income tends to make households with children look poorer, and thus programs directed toward children, like education, look more progressive.

22. Note that taxes cannot *reduce* poverty as they can inequality because they only reduce incomes. The best case from a distributional perspective would be that no poor people pay taxes and the FGT remains unchanged after the tax.

23. Indirect taxes are automatically scaled down because they are estimated as a share of observed expenditures on taxed goods.

24. Recall, however, that analysis includes a considerably larger share of taxes than it does expenditures, so it is biased toward a negative effect of the fisc.

25. Enami, Lustig, and Aranda (2017) show that this statement is not strictly true if the tax or benefit generates a significant reranking of people in the income distribution. They give examples of transfers targeted to the poorest that are large enough to move them well up the income distribution and show that these transfers reduce the Gini less than similarly sized transfers spread more evenly across the population. Nevertheless, the size of taxes and transfers in Armenia are such that the intuition of the text is adequate.

26. We should note that here we are capturing only petroleum products, mostly gasoline, consumed directly by households. This is only a very small part of petroleum consumption in Armenia. Most petroleum products are consumed as intermediate goods, so gasoline excises will affect the price of many goods. We have not been able to trace this effect for lack of a current input-output table, but the concentration coefficient would surely decline if we could do so, since consumption of other goods that use petroleum as an input is more spread across the income distribution than is direct gasoline consumption.

27. All tables and figures for the sensitivity analyses may be found in annex 2A.

28. The adult equivalence scale is (# adults + 0.65 × # children)^0.87, with children being those under 15 years old.

29. Given the way we calculate coverage, it is in fact impossible to have 100 percent coverage if any students are in school outside of the appropriate age. For example, a 12-year-old who is in primary school would count in the denominators of both primary school (actual student) and general secondary school (appropriate age), but only in the numerator of the primary school calculation. In primary, general secondary, and secondary school, respectively, 10 percent, 8 percent, and 16 percent of students are outside the standard ages for those levels.

30. See Lustig, Pessino, and Scott (2014) and the accompanying country papers in *Public Finance Review* (Bucheli et al. 2014; Higgins and Pereira 2014; Jaramillo 2014; Lustig and Pessino 2014; Paz Arauco et al. 2014; Scott 2014).

31. These studies present their results as quintile shares. To condense the table and to make the results comparable to those presented in this study (table 2.7), the concentration coefficients are calculated from these papers' quintile shares. These will be biased toward zero because each person in a quintile is treated as having the same share of benefits.

32. NSSRA uses a poverty line of dram 30,920 per adult equivalent per month and an extreme poverty line (or food poverty line) of dram 17,483 per month.

References

AST (Advanced Social Technologies). 2010. *Benefit Incidence Analysis.* Report for the Global Development Network's "Strengthening Institutions to Improve Public Expenditure Accountability Project," AST, Yerevan. http://www.ast.am/files/BIA,%20 Eng.pdf.

———. 2012. *Benefit Incidence Analysis.* Updated report for the Global Development Network's "Strengthening Institutions to Improve Public Expenditure Accountability Project," AST, Yerevan. http://www.ast.am/files/BIA-AST%202012%20eng.pdf.

Bouvry-Boyakhchyan, Karine. 2008. "Targeting Performance of Main Social Assistance Program." Strategic Objective (SO) 3.4 paper USAID Armenia 111-C-00-06-00067-00 for the Armenia Social Protection Systems Strengthening Project, U.S. Agency for International Development (USAID), Washington, DC.

Bucheli, Marisa, Nora Lustig, Máximo Rossi, and Florencia Amábile. 2014. "Social Spending, Taxes, and Income Redistribution in Uruguay." *Public Finance Review* 42 (3): 413–33.

Enami, Ali, Nora Lustig, and Rodrigo Aranda. 2017. "Analytical Foundations: Measuring the Redistributive Impact of Taxes and Transfers." In *The Commitment to Equity Handbook: Estimating the Impact of Fiscal Policy on Inequality and Poverty*, edited by Nora Lustig, chapter 2. Advance online edition available at Washington, DC: Brookings Institution Press and CEQ Institute, Tulane University.

Esado, Lire. 2012. "Poverty and Distributional Impact of Gas Price Hike in Armenia." Policy Research Working Paper 6150, World Bank, Washington, DC.

Foster, James, Joel Greer, and Erik Thorbecke. 1984. "A Class of Decomposable Poverty Measures." *Econometrica* 3 (52): 761–66.

Harutyunyan, Hovhannes, and Tereza Khechoyan. 2008. "The Impact of Social Transfers on Poverty in Armenia." Paper for the Public Administration Academy of the Republic of Armenia, Yerevan. http://dipse.unicas.it/wb2008/papers/Harutyunyan.pdf.

Higgins, Sean, and Claudiney Pereira. 2014. "The Effects of Brazil's Taxation and Social Spending on the Distribution of Household Income." *Public Finance Review* 42 (3): 346–67.

Hovhannisyan, Shoghik. 2006. "Benefit Incidence Analysis in Armenia." Working Paper 06/04, Armenian International Poverty Research Group, Washington, DC.

IMF (International Monetary Fund). 2010. "How Do Armenia's Tax Revenues Compare to Its Peers?" Unpublished paper, Armenia Country Office, Yerevan.

Jaramillo, Miguel. 2014. "The Incidence of Social Spending and Taxes in Peru." *Public Finance Review* 42 (3): 391–412.

Karapetyan, Susanna, Heghine Manasyan, Nune Harutyunyan, Astghik Mirzakhanyan, and Misak Norekian. 2011. *Armenia: Social Protection and Social Inclusion.* Country Report prepared for the European Commission Directorate-General for Employment, Social Affairs and Inclusion by the Caucasus Research Resource Centers–Armenia, Eurasia Partnership Foundation, Yerevan.

Korinek, Anton, Johan Mistiaen, and Martin Ravallion. 2007. "An Econometric Method of Correcting for Unit Nonresponse Bias in Surveys." *Journal of Econometrics* 136 (1): 213–35.

Lustig, Nora, and Sean Higgins. 2013a. "Commitment to Equity Assessment (CEQ): Estimating the Incidence of Social Spending, Subsidies and Taxes." Handbook and Commitment to Equity Working Paper 1, Center for Inter-American Policy and Research; the Inter-American Dialogue; and Department of Economics, Tulane University, New Orleans, LA.

———. 2013b. "Measuring Impoverishment: An Overlooked Dimension of Fiscal Incidence." Commitment to Equity Working Paper 14, Center for Inter-American Policy and Research; the Inter-American Dialogue; and Department of Economics, Tulane University, New Orleans, LA.

Lustig, Nora, and Carola Pessino. 2014. "Social Spending and Income Redistribution in Argentina in the 2000s: The Increasing Role of Noncontributory Pensions." *Public Finance Review* 42 (3): 304–25.

Lustig, Nora, Carola Pessino, and John Scott. 2014. "The Impact of Taxes and Social Spending on Inequality and Poverty in Latin America: Argentina, Bolivia, Brazil, Mexico, Peru, and Uruguay." *Public Finance Review* 42 (3): 287–303.

NSSRA (National Statistical Service of the Republic of Armenia). 2010. *Social Situation of the Republic of Armenia.* Yerevan: NSSRA.

———. 2011. *Social Situation of the Republic of Armenia 2010.* Yerevan: NSSRA.

———. 2012a. *Social Snapshot and Poverty in Armenia, 2012.* Yerevan: NSSRA.

———. 2012b. *Statistical Yearbook of Armenia.* Yerevan: NSSRA.

———. 2012c. *Social Situation of the Republic of Armenia 2011.* Yerevan: NSSRA.

Paz Arauco, Veronica, George Gray Molina, Wilson Jiménez Pozo, and Ernesto Yáñez Aguilar. 2014. "Explaining Low Redistributive Impact in Bolivia." *Public Finance Review* 42 (3): 326–45.

PwC (PricewaterhouseCoopers). 2011. *Armenia Pocket Tax Book: 2011 Edition.* Guidebook. New York: PricewaterhouseCoopers.

Scott, John. 2014. "Redistributive Impact and Efficiency of Mexico's Fiscal System." *Public Finance Review* 42 (3): 368–90.

Tumasyan, Mushegh. 2006. "Improvement of Social Assistance Targeting in Armenia." Policy Recommendations Paper, Economic Development and Research Center, Yerevan.

CHAPTER 3

Fiscal Incidence Analysis for Ethiopia

Ruth Hill, Gabriela Inchauste, Nora Lustig, Eyasu Tsehaye, and
Tassew Woldehanna

Introduction

Ethiopia has an impressive record of equitable growth. Since the early 1990s,
the country has pursued a "developmental state" model with high public
sector investment to encourage growth and improve access to basic services.
Indeed, strong economic growth[1] and improved public services have been the
primary drivers of poverty reduction over the past decade (World Bank
2015). Ethiopia has not only reduced poverty significantly—from 45.5 percent in 1995/96 to 29.6 percent in 2010/11—but also maintained low
inequality. With a 2011 Gini coefficient of 0.302 (for per capita expenditures), Ethiopia remains one of the less-unequal countries in low- and middle-
income countries.

Despite this progress, the poorest have not fared well in recent years. Although
the incidence of poverty continued to fall in Ethiopia between 2005 and 2011,
the depth of poverty did not fall, and the poverty severity index increased
(World Bank 2015).[2] Even as the government's commitment to poverty reduction remains strong,[3] the challenges have grown. In particular, with a consolidated
primary fiscal deficit at about 4.5 percent of gross domestic product (GDP) in
2013 and a growing debt burden, fiscal space to expand social spending has
become more limited. Despite Ethiopia's progress, it remains one of the world's
poorest countries.[4] In such an environment, the question becomes whether the
government is making the best possible use of fiscal policy to achieve its goal of
reducing poverty, both in the present and in the long term.

In this context, this chapter assesses the impact of fiscal policy on the incidence, depth, and severity of poverty and examines whether there is room for an

increased role for fiscal policy in improving the well-being of the very poorest. Our analysis has three unique features:

- It is the first comprehensive analysis of the impact of fiscal policy on inequality and poverty in Ethiopia.
- It assesses the contribution of each fiscal instrument to the reduction in inequality and poverty.
- Because it applies the Commitment to Equity (CEQ) methodology (Lustig 2017; Lustig and Higgins 2013) to analyze the distributional impact of fiscal policy in a holistic and standardized way, one can compare Ethiopia with other countries to which the CEQ methodology has been applied.[5]

The analysis uses the 2010/11 Household Consumption Expenditure Survey (HCES) and Welfare Monitoring Survey (WMS) collected by the Central Statistical Agency (CSA) of Ethiopia as well as 2011 data from national income and public finance accounts from the Ministry of Finance and Economic Development (now called the Ministry of Finance and Economic Cooperation). In terms of the coverage of fiscal policy components, the analysis includes 83 percent of tax revenue but can only capture 33 percent of government spending even though all government spending on direct transfers and consumption subsidies is included. This is important to keep in mind, as described below.

A tax or expenditure instrument could theoretically be progressive but not have large impacts on equity if it is too small, as further discussed in chapter 1 (also see Duclos and Tabi 1996). More interesting, a tax could be regressive but still equalizing if analyzed in conjunction with other taxes and, especially, transfers.[6] This point is especially important, because a regressive tax could actually end up helping redistribution if it is used to finance highly progressive expenditures. Furthermore, taxes and transfers could be equalizing and yet poverty increasing because inequality depends on *relative* incomes whereas poverty is affected by *absolute* incomes: that is, a tax system could be progressive and equalizing but hurt the poor if they pay more in taxes than they receive through transfers (Higgins and Lustig 2016). With this in mind, the fiscal incidence analysis of Ethiopia yields three main results:

- The tax and social spending system is equalizing overall. Taxes make up a larger percentage of income for wealthier households, and direct transfers are targeted primarily to poorer households. Although subsidies are not always progressive, social spending in general is progressive.
- Taxes and transfers are progressive, and given their size, they help to reduce income inequality and also reduce both the depth and the severity of poverty.
- Despite the progressivity of taxes and spending, because incomes are so low, some households are impoverished as a result of fiscal policy. The analysis finds that poor households pay both direct and indirect taxes, but the transfers and benefits they receive do not compensate all households for the taxes they have paid.

As a result, 1 in 4 of all households are impoverished (either made poor or poorer) after direct taxes are paid and direct transfers received, and nearly 1 in 10 of all households are impoverished when all taxes paid and benefits received (including public spending on education and health) are taken into account.

The analysis highlights two ways in which this negative impact could be reduced: (a) by reducing the incidence of direct tax on the bottom deciles and increasing the progressivity of direct taxes, particularly personal income tax (PIT) and agricultural taxes and (b) by redirecting spending on subsidies to spending on direct transfers to the poorest.

In considering only the redistributive effects of fiscal policy, as chapter 1 further explains, this analysis does not offer conclusions about whether specific taxes or expenditures are desirable. Redistribution is only one relevant criterion in developing good tax or spending policies. The results of this chapter are but one input to public policy making, one to be weighed with other evidence before deciding whether a tax or expenditure is desirable.

Moreover, some of the expenditure items analyzed here have important long-run impacts beyond the short-term distributional impacts. For example, education spending could be seen not only as an investment in individuals' opportunities to earn higher future incomes but also more generally as an investment in the country's productivity as a whole. To the extent that the analysis presented here cannot capture the long-run distributional impact of spending on infrastructure and other public goods, the analysis should be interpreted simply as a picture in time, as the approach is unable to inform the trade-off between current transfers and the long-run impacts of investment in physical and human capital.

The rest of the chapter is organized as follows: The next section describes the structure of taxes and spending in Ethiopia. The "Data Sources and Assumptions" section details the data used and assumptions made in estimating the taxes paid by households and the benefits received. "Overall Impact of Taxes and Spending on Poverty and Inequality" presents the incidence of taxes and spending as well as the impacts of fiscal policy on poverty and inequality. "Progressivity, Marginal Contributions, and Pro-Poorness of Taxes and Transfers" discusses these measurements of each of the fiscal interventions analyzed. The concluding section summarizes the findings and policy implications of the analysis.

Structure of Taxes and Spending

Taxes

On the revenue side, the structure of Ethiopia's tax system shares important features with other CEQ low- and middle-income economies—particularly, their reliance on indirect taxes (figure 3.1) and international trade (Besley and Persson 2009). Of Ethiopia's total tax revenue in 2011, indirect taxes consistently contributed about 67 percent of the general government's tax collection, with the bulk of indirect taxes collected from imports (table 3.1). In 2011, import taxes contributed 40 percent of the total tax collection.

Figure 3.1 Composition of Taxes in Ethiopia and Other Selected CEQ Countries, Ranked by GNI per Capita

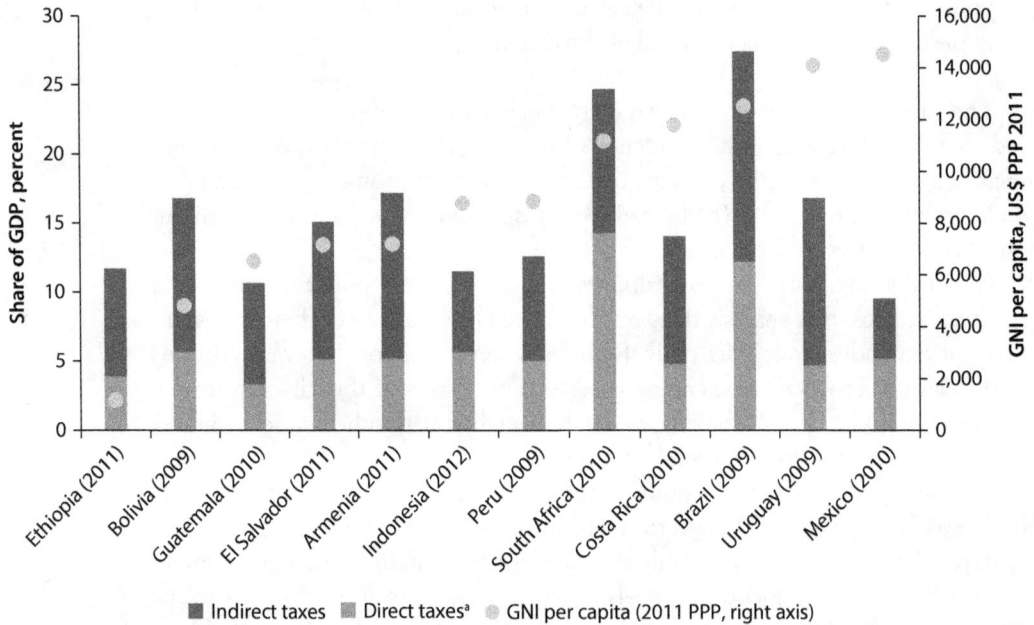

■ Indirect taxes   ▓ Direct taxes[a]   ● GNI per capita (2011 PPP, right axis)

Sources: Beneke, Lustig, and Oliva 2014 (El Salvador); Bucheli et al. 2014 (Uruguay); Cabrera, Lustig, and Morán 2014 (Guatemala); Higgins and Pereira 2014 (Brazil); Jaramillo 2014 (Peru); Paz Arauco et al. 2014 (Bolivia); Sauma and Trejos 2014 (Costa Rica); Scott 2014 (Mexico); World Bank estimates based on 2010/11 Household Consumption Expenditure Survey (HCES) (Ethiopia). Armenia, Indonesia, and South Africa data are from chapters 2, 5, and 8 of this volume, respectively.
Note: The year of each country's household survey is shown within parentheses. CEQ = Commitment to Equity project; GDP = gross domestic product; GNI = gross national income; PPP = purchasing power parity.
a. Direct taxes include both personal and corporate income tax collections.

Table 3.1 Tax Revenue Structure in Ethiopia, 2011

Revenue category	Br, millions	Share of tax revenue (%)	Share of GDP (%)
Total tax revenue	58,986	100.0	11.7
Direct taxes	19,554	33.2	3.9
Personal income tax	5,733	9.7	1.1
Corporate income tax	10,055	17.0	2.0
Agricultural income and rural land use fee	628	1.1	0.1
Rental income	377	0.6	0.1
Other direct taxes	2,761	4.7	0.5
Indirect taxes	39,432	66.8	7.8
Domestic indirect taxes[a]	15,706	26.6	3.1
Import duties, surcharges, and taxes on imports	23,726	40.2	4.7

Source: World Bank estimates based on Ministry of Finance and Economic Development (MoFED) 2011 government finance accounts.
Note: Br = birr.
a. Domestic indirect taxes include local value added, excise, and other sales taxes on domestic goods and services.

Our analysis focuses on the major tax items, namely personal income tax (PIT), land use fees, value added tax (VAT), import duties, and specific excise duties on alcohol and tobacco. The analysis of direct taxes focuses on PIT and land use fees. Corporate taxes are not included given the difficulty of attributing the tax burden to specific households. The analysis of indirect taxes focuses on the VAT, import duties, and excise taxes.

Direct Taxes

PIT is levied on individual taxable income, filing is done individually, and the system does not provide deductions for married persons or children. All formal sector employees must be registered by their employers for PIT, and the employers are responsible for calculating and withholding the PIT payable.

The tax rates were proclaimed in 2002 and have not been adjusted since. As a result, high inflation has caused rises in nominal wages, which have moved income earners upward within the different income brackets.

Beyond the PIT, fees on land use account for about 1 percent of total taxes. These are fees levied for the right to use land in both urban and rural areas. The rates vary by region and depend on the land use type.

Indirect Taxes

The VAT rate of 15 percent is the largest component of indirect taxes, when considering collections from domestic production and imports. The VAT exemptions on various goods and services—most of which are aimed at favoring low-income groups—include unprocessed food items, medicine, kerosene, electricity, water, and transport.[7]

Excise taxes are levied on goods that are deemed to be either luxuries or harmful to health, such as alcoholic beverages, tobacco, electronics, textiles, garments, and motor vehicles (whether imported or produced locally). The rates range from 10 percent (on items such as textile products) to 100 percent (on items such as perfumes, alcohol, tobacco, and high-power personal vehicles, see annex 3A).

Taxes on imports amount to 40 percent of total tax collection, with import duties accounting for 13 percent of tax revenue. The simple average tariff rate is 16.7 percent, and rates reach a maximum of 35 percent depending on the type of commodity. Exemptions from import duties or other taxes are granted for raw materials that are necessary for the production of export goods and selected investment items. In addition to import duty, a 10 percent surcharge on imported consumer goods was introduced in 2007 and has been implemented to date. Together, import duties and surcharges contribute to over 20 percent of total tax revenue. The remaining 20 percent comes from VAT and excise taxes on imports.

Spending

Public spending is guided by Ethiopia's Growth and Transformation Plan (GTP) and is particularly targeted to the pro-poor sectors identified in this plan (MoFED 2010; NPC 2016). The combination of social spending and subsidies in

Ethiopia (7.8 percent of GDP) are about as high as in Armenia (7.7 percent) and higher than in Guatemala or Peru (5.8 percent and 6.3 percent, respectively), all of which have considerably higher incomes per capita and higher tax revenues than Ethiopia (figure 3.2).

The pro-poor sectors identified in the GTP are agriculture and food security, education, health, roads, and water; accordingly, nearly 70 percent of total general government expenditure is allocated to these sectors (table 3.2). Education spending makes up the highest share of total spending (25 percent), followed by roads and agriculture at 20 percent and 15 percent, respectively. About half of the agricultural budget is allocated to ongoing food security and to a large rural safety net program, the Productive Safety Net Program (PSNP). Finally, health spending accounts for about 7 percent of the general government budget.

In addition, the government subsidized electricity, kerosene, and wheat in 2011 through the operations of the Ethiopian Electric Power Corporation (EEPCo), the Oil Stabilization Fund, and the Ethiopian Grain Trade Enterprise (EGTE).

Figure 3.2 Composition of Spending and Subsidies in Ethiopia and Other Selected CEQ Countries, Ranked by GNI per Capita

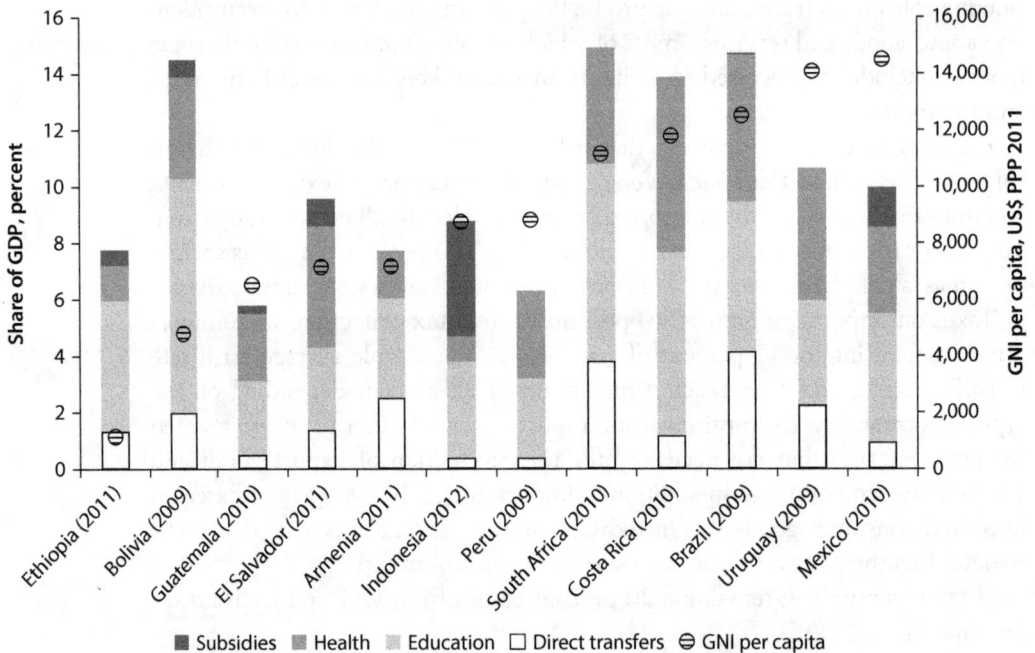

Sources: Beneke, Lustig, and Oliva 2014 (El Salvador); Bucheli et al. 2014 (Uruguay); Cabrera, Lustig, and Morán 2014 (Guatemala); Higgins and Pereira 2014 (Brazil); Jaramillo 2014 (Peru); Paz Arauco et al. 2014 (Bolivia); Sauma and Trejos 2014 (Costa Rica); Scott 2014 (Mexico); World Bank estimates based on 2010/11 Household Consumption Expenditure Survey (HCES) (Ethiopia). Armenia, Indonesia, and South Africa data are from chapters 2, 5, and 8 of this volume, respectively.
Note: The year of each country's household survey is shown within parentheses. CEQ = Commitment to Equity Project; GDP = gross domestic product; GNI = gross national income; PPP = purchasing power parity.

Table 3.2 General Government Expenditure in Ethiopia, 2011

Expenditure category	Br, millions	Share of general government expenditure (%)	Share of GDP (%)
Total general government expenditure	93,831	100.0	18.6
General services	15,655	16.7	3.1
Economic development	38,422	40.9	7.6
Agriculture, of which:	14,183	15.1	2.8
Productive Safety Net Program	5,293	5.6	1.0
Food security	1,510	1.6	0.3
Roads	18,318	19.5	3.6
Other	5,921	6.3	1.2
Social development	32,936	35.1	6.5
Education	23,345	24.9	4.6
Health	6,307	6.7	1.2
Urban development and housing	2,762	2.9	0.5
Labor and social welfare	179	0.2	0.0
Other	343	0.4	0.1
Other	6,818	7.3	1.3
Off-budget indirect subsidies (kerosene, electricity, and wheat)	2,743	n.a.	0.5

Source: World Bank estimates based on Ministry of Finance and Economic Development, 2011 government finance accounts.
Note: Br = birr; GDP = gross domestic product; n.a. = not applicable.

These expenditures (off-budget operations not included in general government finance) were as follows:

- *Electricity* subsidies to households, the primary indirect subsidy, totaled an estimated Br 1.5 billion (equivalent to 0.3 percent of GDP).
- *Kerosene*, subsidized through the Oil Stabilization Fund, amounted to Br 0.7 billion (0.14 percent of GDP).
- *Wheat* was subsidized by government to reduce the effect of food inflation on the urban poor through a program of import and distribution of wheat in Addis Ababa at a subsidized price. The transfer was not targeted, and the sales were rationed to all households of the city through local administrative units (kebeles). The estimated subsidy was Br 150 per quintal of wheat, amounting to total spending of Br 0.5 billion (0.1 percent of GDP).

The incidence analysis covers 33 percent of all government spending (mostly social spending), but it excludes infrastructure spending on education (see annex 3A). It assesses the incidence of spending on education, health, and the PSNP. Spending on general services and roads was not included, given the difficulty of attributing benefits to specific households. Non-PSNP agricultural spending and spending on urban development and housing were not included in the analysis at this stage, given data challenges, but can be considered in future work. However, the fiscal analysis does include the off-budget electricity, kerosene, and wheat subsidies.

Data Sources and Assumptions

Data Sources

Data for fiscal year 2010/11 were used to conduct this incidence analysis study, in line with the availability of survey data. Specifically, we used the 2010/11 HCES[8] and WMS collected by the CSA of Ethiopia. Those surveys are the main data sources used by the Ethiopian government to monitor its poverty reduction strategies. The WMS has detailed information on individual occupations, age, and access to various services including education, health, and agricultural extension. The HCES and WMS data are complemented by the Ethiopian Rural Socio-Economic Survey (ERSS), which is collected by the World Bank in collaboration with the CSA.

Household survey data are combined with data from national income and public finance accounts from the Ministry of Finance and Economic Development (now known as the Ministry of Finance and Economic Cooperation). These accounts provide the public revenue and expenditures corresponding to the 2010/11 Ethiopian fiscal year. Complementing this information are data from the 2010/11 Annual Work Plan for the PSNP and Household Asset Building Program (HABP); the Ministry of Trade; the World Bank's 2013 "Report on Accountability Issues" to EEPCo; and the Ministry of Health. Finally, we use the 2005 social accounting matrix (SAM) produced by the Ethiopian Development Research Institute (EDRI) to estimate the effect of indirect taxes as described below.

Assumptions

Because the HCES does not report income data, the analysis assumes that consumption is equal to "disposable income" and works backward and forward to construct the other CEQ income concepts. The income concept for Ethiopia is based on consumption value from the HCES. Consumption expenditures from all sources are included in the consumption aggregate, including autoconsumption, gifts and proceeds from the sale of durables, and imputed rent for owner-occupied housing. Total household consumption is set to equal disposable income, to which taxes and transfers are subtracted or added to obtain the CEQ income concepts described in chapter 1.

Taxes

We make a simple assumption on the economic incidence of taxes: direct taxes are borne entirely by the income earner and indirect taxes entirely by the consumer. This latter part of this assumption is not entirely appropriate if markets are not competitive—and, in Ethiopia, many are not. However, the extent to which monopolies or oligopolies shift indirect taxes to consumers is not clear; it could be either greater or less than 100 percent depending on the functional form of the demand function (Fullerton and Metcalf 2002). Because we have no information on those functional forms, we assume that 100 percent of taxes are shifted to consumers regardless of market structure.

Direct Taxes

To allocate taxes across households, note that the HCES does not provide information on PIT. Thus, the burden of these taxes had to be simulated. Consistent with other conventional tax incidence analyses, we assume that the economic burden of PIT is borne by the income earner. Tax evasion (the difference between actual PIT collected and estimated tax based on income) is assumed to be borne by all self-employed and employees of the informal sector in proportion to income.

Agricultural income taxes and rural land use fees are calculated on the basis of landholding size reported in the ERSS because the landholding size collected in the 2010/11 HCES often did not record standardized units. The tax schedule for this tax and fee is set by regional and local governments and, as such, varies from locale to locale. However, many of the main tax schedules were examined and found to levy similar per hectare tax rates regardless of land size. A region's total tax revenue was divided by its total agricultural land holdings to generate an average tax rate per hectare. This rate was used with the imputed land size in each region to estimate the amount of agricultural tax paid by each household. This method assumes a constant rate per region, but it takes into account potential evasion as it is based on actual collections.

Indirect Taxes

The burden of indirect taxes is estimated using detailed consumption data in the HCES and the SAM developed in 2006 by EDRI. The SAM's input-output table provides information on indirect taxes collected and the total supply value of each of the 93 commodity accounts. This information is used to calculate an effective tax rate for each of those commodities and to draw a correspondence between the SAM accounts and the item-level consumption in the HCES data. With this, we estimated the price burden on each household based on the proportional increase in the price of each good and service and the household's expenditure on corresponding goods and services, which is assumed to be borne entirely by the consumers. We also estimated the second-round effects of indirect taxes, defined as the price burden on consumers resulting from indirect taxes paid for inputs used in the production process. The input-output table is used to calculate the effect of taxes on intermediate inputs on prices of final goods and services.

For VAT, we consider two scenarios: (a) one in which VAT refunds do not properly work so that VAT works as a sales tax and (b) one in which the indirect effects are only considered in the case of exempt items, since VAT refunds ensure that there is no cascading of nonexempt items. (See annex 3A for more details.)

Transfers

On the spending side, the 2010/11 HCES provides detailed information on which households received PSNP payments and food aid. The beneficiary status of the household and household size were used in conjunction with government expenditure data to impute the value of transfers received by each household, assuming that all food aid and PSNP transfers were distributed equally across beneficiaries.[9]

Indirect subsidies are estimated using item-level HCES data, which provide households' consumption of wheat, kerosene, and electricity. The subsidy per kilogram, liter, and kilowatt-hour for each good, respectively, was then applied to estimate the total value of the subsidy received by the household.

To estimate the incidence of public spending (in-kind transfers) on education and health, we use the "government cost" approach. In essence, we use per beneficiary input costs obtained from administrative fiscal data as the measure of average benefits. This approach is also known as the "classic" or "nonbehavioral approach," and it amounts to asking the following question: how much would the income of a household have to be increased if it had to pay for the free or subsidized public service at the full cost to the government? The WMS provides information on educational enrollment by level and type (public vs. private institutions), which is combined with regional expenditures on education by level. For health spending, curative services are estimated in proportion to households' expenditure on public health fees, whereas preventive service benefits are distributed to all households equally.[10]

General Caveats

To these assumptions, we must add several important caveats about what this fiscal incidence analysis does *not* address:

- It does not take into account behavioral, life-cycle, or general equilibrium effects and focuses on average incidence rather than incidence at the margin. Our tax-shifting and labor-supply response assumptions are strong because they imply that consumers have perfectly inelastic demand and that labor supply is perfectly inelastic, too. In practice, they provide a reasonable approximation, and they are commonly used.
- It does not take into account intrahousehold distribution of consumption.
- It cannot take into account the quality of services delivered by the government.
- It cannot include some important taxes and spending. Corporate income taxes and spending on infrastructure investments, including urban services and rural roads, are excluded even though such taxes and investments affect income distribution and poverty.
- It does not capture the growing debate on how asset accumulation and returns to capital affect income inequality.
- The Ethiopian social security system provides income security in old age, disability, or death only to public servants. As such, contributions are treated as savings and are considered part of market income for public sector workers.

Overall Impact of Taxes and Spending on Poverty and Inequality

Impact on Inequality

Table 3.3 reports Ethiopia's Gini coefficients and the poverty headcount ratios by CEQ income concept. It shows that fiscal policy contributes to reducing Ethiopia's "market income" inequality (market income being income received before any taxes are paid or transfers received).

Table 3.3 Poverty and Inequality Indicators in Ethiopia, by CEQ Income Concept, 2011

Indicator	Market income[a]	Disposable income[b]	Consumable income[c]	Final income[d]
National poverty line[e]				
Poverty incidence[f] (%)	31.2	30.2	32.4	n.a.
Poverty gap[f] (%)	9.0	7.9	8.7	n.a.
Poverty severity[f] (%)	4.3	3.1	3.4	n.a.
US$1.25 a day, 2005 PPP				
Poverty incidence[f] (%)	31.9	30.9	33.2	n.a.
Poverty gap[f] (%)	9.2	8.2	8.9	n.a.
Poverty severity[f] (%)	3.9	3.2	3.5	n.a.
Gini coefficient[g] (%)	0.322	0.305	0.302	0.302

Source: Based on 2011 Household Consumption Expenditure Survey (HCES) and 2011 Welfare Monitoring Survey (WMS) data.
Note: CEQ = Commitment to Equity; n.a. = not applicable (not included in the analysis; see note d); PPP = purchasing power parity.
a. "Market income" comprises pretax wages, salaries, income earned from capital assets (rent, interest, or dividends), and private transfers.
b. "Disposable income" = market income – personal income taxes and social security contributions + direct cash transfers.
c. "Consumable income" = disposable income – indirect (sales and excise) taxes + indirect subsidies.
d. "Final income" = consumable income + in-kind transfers for education and health care. Poverty rates are not calculated by final income because households may not be aware of the amounts spent on their behalf and may not value this spending as much as a direct cash transfer. Hence, the analysis does not assume that this spending improves their welfare by a corresponding amount.
e. The national poverty line is defined by the value that affords consumption of 2,200 kilocalories per day per adult plus essential nonfood expenditure.
f. "Poverty incidence" is the percentage of the population that is poor. The "poverty gap" (or depth) is the average percentage by which individuals fall below the poverty line. "Poverty severity" (or intensity) is calculated as the poverty gap index squared; it implicitly gives greater weight to the poorest individuals, making it a combined measure of poverty and income inequality. These three poverty metrics are known as the Foster-Greer-Thorbecke (FGT) indexes (Foster, Greer, and Thorbecke 1984).
g. The Gini index measures the equality of income distribution, ranging from 0 (perfect equality) to 1 (maximal inequality).

At 0.322, the market-income Gini coefficient is low relative to other countries. The simple worldwide unweighted average was 0.371 in 2013 and 0.438 in Sub-Saharan Africa (World Bank 2016). Using expenditure per capita (instead of income) as the starting welfare indicator, fiscal policy reduces the market-income Gini coefficient from 0.322 to 0.302—a decline of 2 percentage points—when taxes (PIT, land taxes, VAT, import duties, and excise taxes) and transfers (cash transfers, subsidies, and the monetized value of education and health) are taken into account.

Once in-kind transfers are included (as part of "final income"), the net impact of all fiscal policy is progressive, with all but the top 20 percent receiving more benefits relative to their market incomes than the taxes they pay (figure 3.3). As a result, fiscal policy reduces inequality in Ethiopia.

Impact on Poverty

Despite the decline in inequality, the results also show an increase in poverty as a result of taxes and transfers. The combined effect of taxes, cash transfers, and subsidies is to increase the incidence of extreme poverty (at the international per capita poverty line of US$1.25 per day in 2005 purchasing power parity [PPP])

Figure 3.3 Incidence of Taxes and Transfers and Net Fiscal Benefit, by Market Income Decile, in Ethiopia, 2011

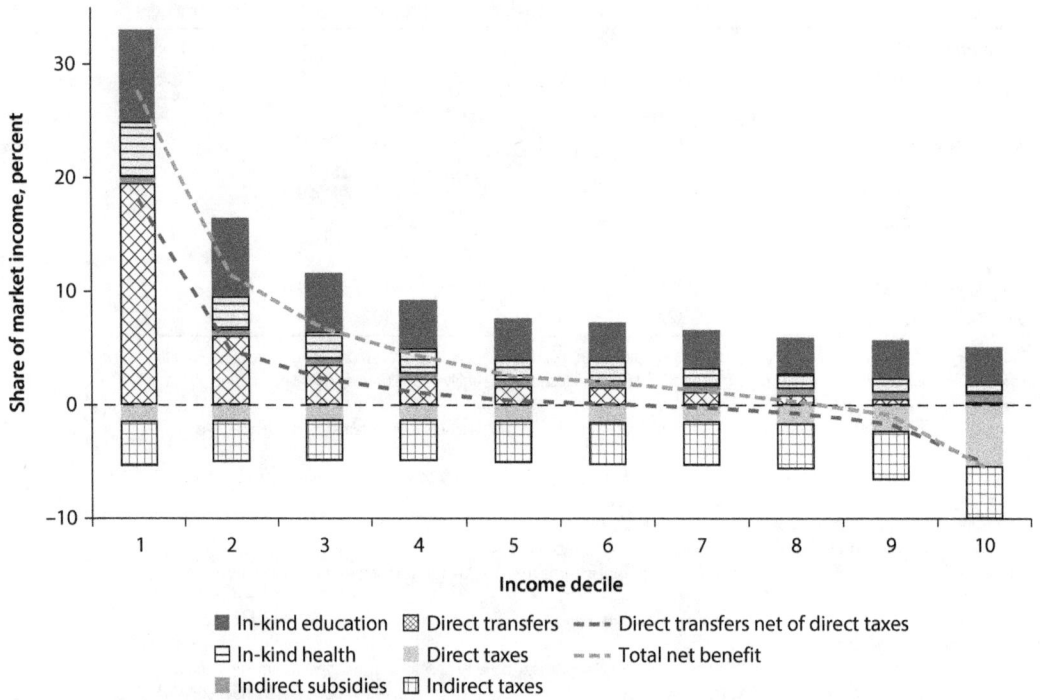

Source: Based on 2011 Household Consumption Expenditure Survey (HCES) and 2011 Welfare Monitoring Survey (WMS) data.
Note: Market income comprises pretax wages, salaries, income earned from capital assets (rent, interest, or dividends), and private transfers. Income deciles range from 1 (poorest) to 10 (richest).

from 31.9 percent (at market income) to 33.2 percent (at consumable income) (table 3.3). The same is true if using the national poverty line: the poverty head-count rate increases from 31.2 percent (at market income) to 32.4 percent (at consumable income)[11]—a signal that total government transfers and subsidies do not make up for the impact of indirect taxes around the poverty line.

Following standard conventions, this analysis refrains from calculating poverty rates after in-kind health and education transfers because households may not be aware of the actual amount spent on their behalf and may not value this spend-ing as much as they would a direct cash transfer. Hence, the analysis does not assume that the monetized value of in-kind transfers improves their monetary welfare by a corresponding amount, nor can it describe the long-run welfare of health and education spending. However, figure 3.3 indicates that spending on education and health does offset the impact of indirect taxes around the poverty line, a point discussed further below.

Note that although the headcount ratio goes up, the poverty gap and poverty severity (the poverty gap squared) are lower for consumable income than for market income. Although this finding is reassuring—indicating that fiscal policy reduces the depth and severity of poverty—it can also be misleading. Standard

Table 3.4 Extent of Impoverishment by Fiscal Policy in Ethiopia, 2011
Percentage of population, by type

Impoverishment headcount index comparison	National poverty line[a]	US$1.25 per day, PPP 2005
Poor population that became poorer		
Market income →(−direct taxes + direct transfers) → disposable income	25.0	25.6
Market income → (− all taxes + direct and in-kind transfers) → final income	9.1	9.3
Nonpoor population that became poor		
Market income → (−direct taxes + direct transfers) → disposable income	0.9	0.9
Market income → (−all taxes + direct and in-kind transfers) → final income	1.1	0.9

Source: Based on 2011 Household Consumption Expenditure Survey (HCES) and 2011 Welfare Monitoring Survey (WMS) data.
Note: The "impoverishment headcount index," developed by Higgins and Lustig (2016), measures the percentage of the population impoverished by the tax and transfer system as a proportion of the post-fisc poor. "Market income" comprises pretax wages, salaries, income earned from capital assets (rent, interest, or dividends), and private transfers. "Disposable income" = market income − direct taxes + direct transfers. "Final income" = disposable income − indirect taxes + indirect subsidies + in-kind transfers. PPP = purchasing power parity.
a. The national poverty line is defined by the value that affords consumption of 2,200 kilocalories per day per adult plus essential nonfood expenditure.

poverty measures can fail to capture the extent to which the poor are further impoverished by tax and benefit systems (Higgins and Lustig 2016). To assess the latter, we use Higgins and Lustig's "fiscal impoverishment headcount index," which measures the percentage of the population *impoverished* by the tax and transfer system as a proportion of the post-fisc poor. "Impoverished" households are those that were either (a) nonpoor before taxes and transfers and made poor by the fiscal system or (b) poor before taxes and transfers and made even poorer by the fiscal system.

Table 3.4 summarizes the impoverishment indexes, at both the national and US$1.25-a-day poverty lines, using two income-concept comparisons: from market to disposable income and from market to final income. This analysis finds that direct taxes made a quarter of the poor population poorer, even when taking direct transfers into account. When all of the measured taxes paid and benefits received are considered (that is, by moving from market income to final income), fiscal policy still further impoverishes 9 percent of the poor. In both income-concept comparisons, about 1 percent of the nonpoor population became poor.

Progressivity, Marginal Contributions, and Pro-Poorness of Taxes and Transfers

To measure the progressivity of particular fiscal interventions, the analysis uses both a standard progressivity measure (the Kakwani coefficient) and a calculation of each intervention's "marginal contribution" to inequality and poverty reduction. The former is calculated by subtracting an intervention's concentration coefficient from the market-income Gini; progressive interventions have positive Kakwani coefficients, and regressive ones have negative coefficients (Kakwani 1977). However, the "marginal contribution" is the difference in the Gini or poverty headcount for an income concept with and without a given intervention.

General Results

Beginning with the Kakwani progressivity index for taxes and transfers and their respective marginal contributions (discussed in further detail below), the results show that both direct taxes and indirect taxes are progressive, with the Kakwani index being positive in both cases (table 3.5).[12] However, among direct taxes, the agricultural income land use fee and the chat tax (a tax on any person transporting or handling chat—the leaves or buds of the plant more commonly spelled "khat," which is chewed or used in tea for its stimulant properties—for commercial purposes) are regressive as well as both inequality and poverty increasing. Interestingly, indirect taxes are redistributive, reducing inequality by 0.339 Gini points. This is not surprising: given that they account for two-thirds of tax revenue collection (as shown earlier in table 3.2), they end up financing a large part of social spending. However, as discussed below, they are also poverty increasing.

Direct cash transfers are progressive in absolute terms. Based on their marginal contribution, they are also strongly redistributive, with the PSNP reducing inequality by 0.993 Gini points. In contrast, the electricity subsidy is regressive and increases inequality by 0.046 Gini points. Kerosene and wheat subsidies are progressive, redistributive, and poverty reducing.

Table 3.5 Marginal Contribution of Taxes and Transfers to Inequality and Poverty Reduction in Ethiopia, 2011

Type of fiscal intervention	Size[a] (%)	Kakwani coefficient[b]	Marginal contribution[c] Redistributive effect[d] (change, Gini points)	Poverty reduction effect[e] (change, pp)
Total from market to consumable income			1.9284	−1.9550
Direct taxes	2.58	0.28	0.7162	−1.1723
Personal income tax	2.39	0.30	0.7216	−1.0127
Agricultural income land use fee	0.08	−0.20	−0.0132	−0.0938
Rental tax	0.07	0.13	0.0030	−0.0545
Chat tax[f]	0.03	−0.05	−0.0005	−0.0318
Direct transfers	1.93	0.69	1.1812	2.0676
Productive Safety Net Program	1.55	0.72	0.9925	1.6274
Food aid	0.38	0.55	0.1616	0.5634
Indirect subsidies	0.56	−0.07	−0.0330	0.3564
Electricity subsidy	0.38	−0.14	−0.0455	0.2257
Kerosene subsidy	0.16	0.07	0.0098	0.1196
Wheat subsidy	0.01	0.04	0.0022	0.0097
Indirect taxes	5.60	0.05	0.3391	−3.6542

table continues next page

Table 3.5 Marginal Contribution of Taxes and Transfers to Inequality and Poverty Reduction in Ethiopia, 2011 *(continued)*

Type of fiscal intervention	Size[a] (%)	Kakwani coefficient[b]	Marginal contribution[c]	
			Redistributive effect[d] (change, Gini points)	Poverty reduction effect[e] (change, pp)
Total from market to final income			2.2072	2.3172
Direct taxes	2.58	0.28	0.7157	−0.9589
Direct transfers	1.93	0.69	1.1032	2.2000
Indirect subsidies	0.56	−0.07	−0.0437	0.3910
Indirect taxes	5.60	0.05	0.3364	−3.6349
In-kind transfers	5.46	0.17	—	n.a.
Education	3.80	0.14	−0.0392	n.a.
Primary school	1.67	0.35	0.5242	n.a.
Secondary school	0.98	0.05	−0.0353	n.a.
Tertiary	1.15	−0.09	−0.5312	n.a.
Health	1.66	0.25	0.3063	n.a.

Source: Based on 2011 Household Consumption Expenditure Survey (HCES) and 2011 Welfare Monitoring Survey (WMS) data.
Note: "Market income" comprises pretax wages, salaries, income earned from capital assets (rent, interest, or dividends), and private transfers. "Consumable income" = market income − direct and indirect taxes + direct cash transfers + indirect subsidies. "Final income" = consumable income + in-kind transfers for education and health care. The Gini index measures the equality of income distribution, ranging from 0 (perfect equality) to 1 (maximal inequality). — = not available (not calculated); n.a. = not applicable (not included in analysis; see note e); pp = percentage points.
a. "Size" equals the ratio of the amount collected or spent divided by total market income.
b. The Kakwani coefficient is calculated by subtracting the concentration coefficient from the market-income Gini; progressive interventions have positive Kakwani coefficients, and regressive ones have negative coefficients (Kakwani 1977).
c. The "marginal contribution" equals the difference between the Gini coefficient or headcount poverty rate of the relevant ending income concept with and without the intervention in question. By definition, the sum of the marginal contributions does not fulfill the adding-up principle, so it will not be equal to the redistributive effect unless by coincidence.
d. The "redistributive effect" equals the difference between market-income Gini coefficient and the relevant ending income concept Gini.
e. The "poverty reduction effect" is based on poverty headcount index using the poverty line of US$1.25 per day in 2005 purchasing power parity (PPP). A negative poverty reduction value indicates an increase in poverty. Poverty rates are not calculated by final income because households may not be aware of the amounts spent on their behalf and may not value this spending as much as a direct cash transfer. Hence, the analysis does not assume that this spending improves their welfare by a corresponding amount
f. The "chat tax" is an excise on any person transporting or handling chat for commercial purposes. Chat is a major psychoactive component of the plant *Catha edulis* (khat). The young leaves of khat are chewed for a stimulant effect.

In-kind health and primary education are equalizing and poverty reducing. However, there is heterogeneity across levels of education, with primary education being strongly progressive and redistributive. In contrast, tertiary education is regressive and unequalizing.

Taxes

Direct Taxes

Typically the collection of direct taxes is low for lower-income countries (Besley and Persson 2009); however, for Ethiopia's level of gross national income (GNI) per capita, direct tax collection is remarkably high (as shown earlier in figure 3.1). For example, direct taxes are a higher share of GDP in Ethiopia (3.9 percent) than in Guatemala (3.3 percent) even though Guatemala's GNI per capita is more than five times higher than Ethiopia's.

Moreover, the share of the tax bill paid by Ethiopian households living on less than US$1.25 per person per day PPP is extremely high (11 percent) relative to other CEQ countries with substantially higher per capita GNI (Armenia, Bolivia, Brazil, El Salvador, Guatemala, and South Africa), as shown in figure 3.4. Thus, even though direct taxes are redistributive and could be used for long-term investments in human and physical capital, they are also poverty increasing in the short term when looking at households' cash position (table 3.4)—highlighting the fundamental challenge of pro-poor revenue generation in a low-income country.

PIT generates most of Ethiopia's direct tax revenue, and although it is progressive and equalizing, it is also poverty increasing (table 3.5), because any personal income above Br 150 per month (or Br 1,800 per year, equivalent to about US$112 in 2011) is taxed.[13] This threshold is much lower than the poverty line of Br 3,781 per adult equivalent, implying that the poor are effectively paying income taxes. Increasing this minimum cutoff would reduce the direct tax burden on the bottom deciles. The consequent loss in tax revenue could be offset by higher PIT rates on higher deciles.

Figure 3.4 Concentration of Total Taxes, by Household Income Group, in Ethiopia and Other Selected CEQ Countries

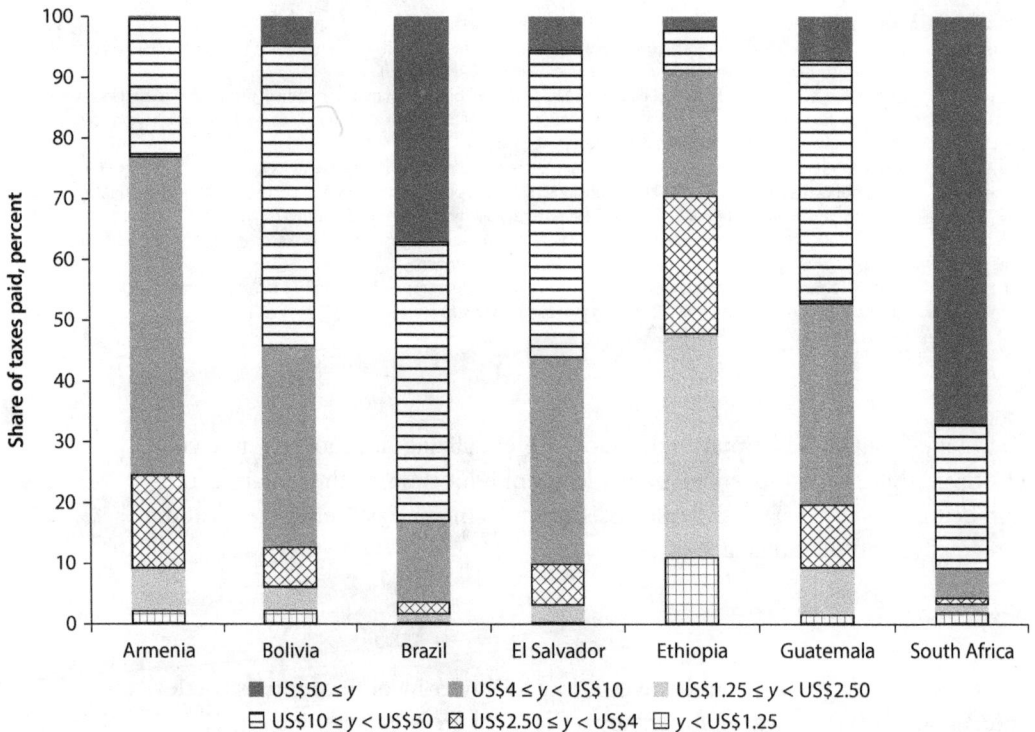

Sources: Beneke, Lustig, and Oliva 2014 (El Salvador); Cabrera, Lustig, and Morán 2014 (Guatemala); Higgins and Pereira 2014 (Brazil); World Bank estimates based on 2010/11 Household Consumption Expenditure Survey (HCES) (Ethiopia). Armenia and South Africa data are from chapters 2 and 8 of this volume, respectively.
Note: Figure shows the share of taxes paid by households in the per capita income groups shown (using internationally comparable per capita income levels at 2005 purchasing power parity, or PPP). y = income group; CEQ = Commitment to Equity project.

In contrast, the agricultural income land use fee is regressive, unequalizing, and poverty increasing (table 3.5), partly because agricultural households are likely to be poorer than nonagricultural households. In addition, agricultural income tax rules are set by regional and local governments and are mainly levied according to landholding size, which does not necessarily determine income earned. In only a few places are assets such as the number of cattle also considered. For the most part, per hectare tax rates do not increase with landholding size, and the estimates here assume that this is the case across the country. (In the Oromia region, they tend to slightly fall with landholding size, as detailed in table 3A.2, so this assumption may underestimate the regressivity of these taxes in Oromia.)

Indirect Taxes

Indirect taxes are progressive and equalizing in Ethiopia as a result of higher tax rates being applied to those goods that are consumed more by richer households. For example, the richest decile spends 10 times more than the poorest decile on alcoholic beverages as a share of total spending, and these products have among the highest excise tax rates. However, indirect taxes are also poverty increasing, with the US$1.25-a-day poverty headcount rate increasing by 3.65 points as a result of these taxes (table 3.5).

Ethiopia's indirect taxes relative to GDP are average compared with other countries (as shown earlier in figure 3.1), but they make up a lower share of market income than in all other countries considered. Although indirect taxes amount to 3 percent of disposable income of the poorest decile in Ethiopia, they amount to 18 percent of the disposable income of the poorest decile in Bolivia, and 11 percent in Brazil.

This highlights the challenge facing Ethiopia: even low and progressive taxes can make many poor households poorer and some nonpoor households poor. To the extent possible, taxes should be made more progressive to limit their impoverishing effect. It is perhaps unlikely that Ethiopia can reduce its reliance on indirect taxes or make them more progressive given how well it compares with middle-income countries on these fronts, but to the extent that direct taxes can be made more progressive, this should be considered. For example, the minimum income above which PIT is levied could be raised along with higher tax rates at the top, and agricultural income taxes can be made more progressive by encouraging a higher per hectare tax rate for households with larger landholdings.

Social Spending

As noted earlier, extreme poverty (measured by the US$1.25-a-day PPP line) was higher for consumable income (after all taxes, direct transfers, and subsidies) than for market income (before taxes or transfers), as shown in table 3.3. In other words, so many poor and near-poor individuals are impoverished by taxes, particularly consumption taxes, that poverty ends up higher after fiscal interventions. Arguably, even if the poor are hurt in cash terms, these poverty-increasing taxes are funding the access of the poor to education and health benefits. Indeed, as seen in figure 3.3, final income shows that the poor benefited—and benefited relatively more than other income groups—from the in-kind transfers in primary education and health, even though the use of services is not universal and many of the poor are still excluded. The subsections below discuss the incidence of spending on direct transfers, indirect subsidies, and in-kind transfers for education and health services.

Direct Transfers

Direct transfers through the PSNP and food aid programs are progressive, equalizing, and pro-poor, with more than 58 percent of the benefits going to households below the national poverty line.[14] PSNP transfers are more progressive and help to reduce inequality and poverty more than emergency food aid (table 3.5), in line with the findings of the broader literature on food aid targeting in Ethiopia and the results of PSNP external evaluations (Gilligan et al. 2010).

Food aid is targeted to communities particularly affected by disasters, and although there is often targeting of poor households within these communities, this is done in an ad hoc fashion to ensure aid is provided in a timely manner. As a result, targeting errors in the selection of individuals at the local level can be quite high. By comparison, the PSNP has clear targeting rules and identification of beneficiaries, resulting in lower targeting errors (Gilligan et al. 2010).

Beyond the fact that direct transfers are progressive and equalizing, PSNP and food aid transfers have a sizable direct effect on poverty, reducing it by 2 percentage points (table 3.5). The direct effect of these transfers was to reduce poverty rates from 33 percent to 31 percent (estimated by comparing consumption with and without the size of the transfer provided). Moreover, the transfers reduced the poverty gap by 1.4 percentage points (to 14.3 percent) and reduced the poverty severity (the poverty gap squared) by 0.9 percentage points (to 21.5 percent). Although small, the marginal contribution of cash transfers to poverty reduction is higher for Ethiopia than for Bolivia, El Salvador, and Guatemala.

In terms of generosity, direct transfers from the PSNP and food aid make up a smaller share of market income of the poorest deciles in Ethiopia than in middle-income countries such as Armenia, Argentina, South Africa, or Uruguay, suggesting there is room to increase the size of direct transfer programs, targeting them to more households. However, they do make up about 20 percent of the poorest decile's market income, which is somewhat comparable to the share of direct transfers in Mexico (31 percent) and more than the shares achieved in Indonesia and Peru (4 percent and 11 percent, respectively).

Indirect Subsidies

Poorer households consume less electricity, kerosene, and wheat than richer households, and as a result, none of these subsidies is pro-poor (figure 3.5). However, wheat and kerosene make up a larger share of spending among poorer households than among richer households, and consequently these two subsidies are progressive in relative terms, meaning that they make up a larger share of the incomes of the poor (figure 3.6). Importantly, they are also equalizing and poverty reducing (as shown earlier in table 3.5). In contrast, electricity makes up a smaller share of spending among poorer households than among richer households; hence, electricity subsidies are regressive and unequalizing (figures 3.5 and 3.6).

The richest 30 percent of the population received 65 percent of the electricity subsidies, whereas the poorest 30 percent—those living below the national poverty line—obtained only 10 percent of the electricity subsidies. Among the three subsidies (electricity, kerosene, and wheat), electricity is the largest. Care should be taken not to assume, however, that the removal of electricity subsidies would not hurt the poor. If not compensated in some other way, some of the poor, especially the urban poor, will become poorer if electricity subsidies are reduced.

In-Kind Transfers

In assessing how much education and health spending benefit the poor, we have to caution that our analysis does not address the quality of such spending. We use government expenditure data on the various forms of education and health services to estimate the unit costs of these programs. The analysis thus assumes that the actual benefit received by individuals is equal to the amount spent per capita. Because the quality of school infrastructure, teachers, and health clinics and hospitals varies across the country, this is a clear limitation of the analysis.

Figure 3.5 Progressivity and Pro-Poorness of Public Spending in Ethiopia, 2011

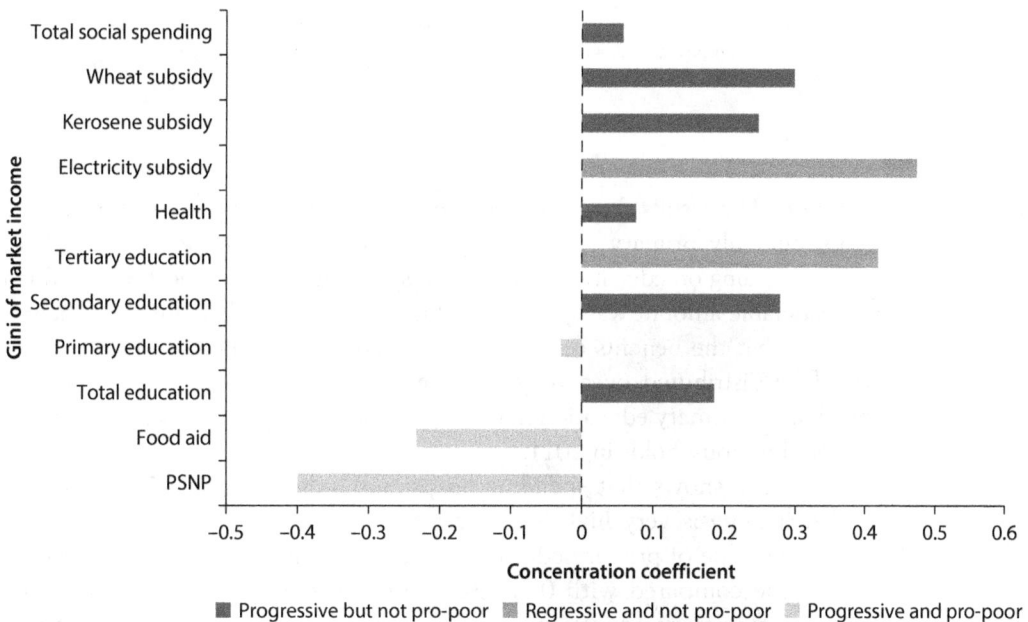

Source: Based on 2011 Household Consumption Expenditure Survey (HCES) and 2011 Welfare Monitoring Survey (WMS) data.
Note: Spending is "progressive" when the concentration coefficient is lower than the Gini coefficient for market income—meaning that the benefits from that spending, as a share of market income, tend to fall with market income. Spending is "pro-poor" when the concentration coefficient is not only lower than the Gini but also negative—implying that the per capita government spending on the transfer tends to fall with market income. (This case is also sometimes called progressive in absolute terms.) "Market income" comprises pretax wages, salaries, income earned from capital assets (rent, interest, or dividends), and private transfers. The Gini coefficient measures the equality of income distribution, ranging from 0 (perfect equality) to 1 (maximal inequality). PSNP = Productive Safety Net Program.

Figure 3.6 Concentration Curves for Indirect Subsidies in Ethiopia, 2011

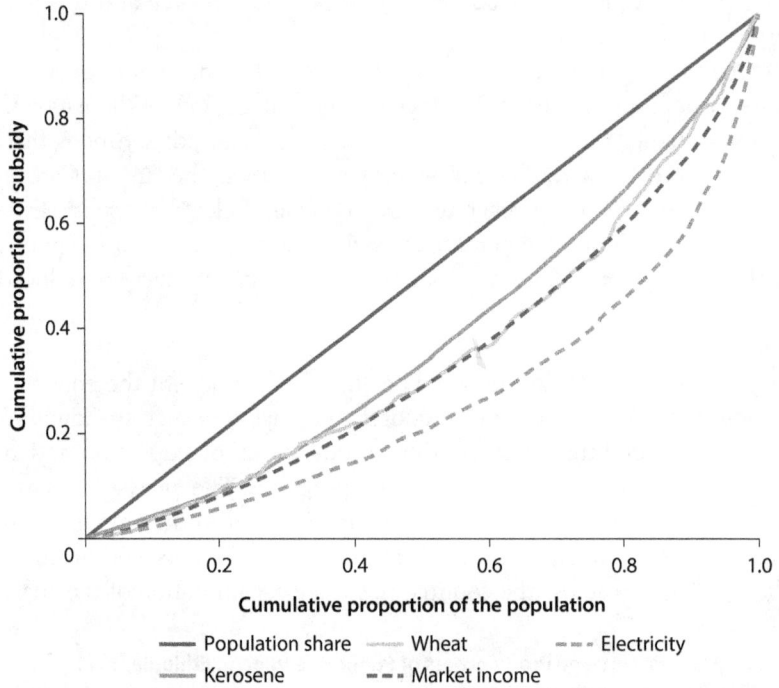

Source: Based on 2011 Household Consumption Expenditure Survey (HCES) data.
Note: "Market income" comprises pretax wages, salaries, income earned from capital assets (rent, interest, or dividends), and private transfers.

Education. The results show that spending on education is progressive in relative terms, but only primary education spending is pro-poor (figure 3.5). Half of public spending on education in 2011 was spent on tertiary education, of which a considerable amount was spent on building universities. Therefore, the analysis assumed that the benefits of investments in university buildings made in 2011 would be distributed over 10 years (see annex 3A). Given this assumption, spending on primary education makes up the largest share of education benefits delivered to households in 2011.

Figure 3.7 shows that spending on primary education as a proportion of market income is very high for poorer households: for those in the poorest decile, the value of primary education benefits received is 5.6 percent of market income compared with 0.5 percent for the richest decile. The absolute amount of primary education benefits received by poor households is also larger than those received by rich households (figure 3.7), and as a result primary education spending is pro-poor in addition to being progressive and equalizing (table 3.5).

Secondary education spending is also progressive in relative terms and equalizing, making up a larger share of market income for poor households than for

Figure 3.7 Concentration Curves for Education Spending in Ethiopia, 2011

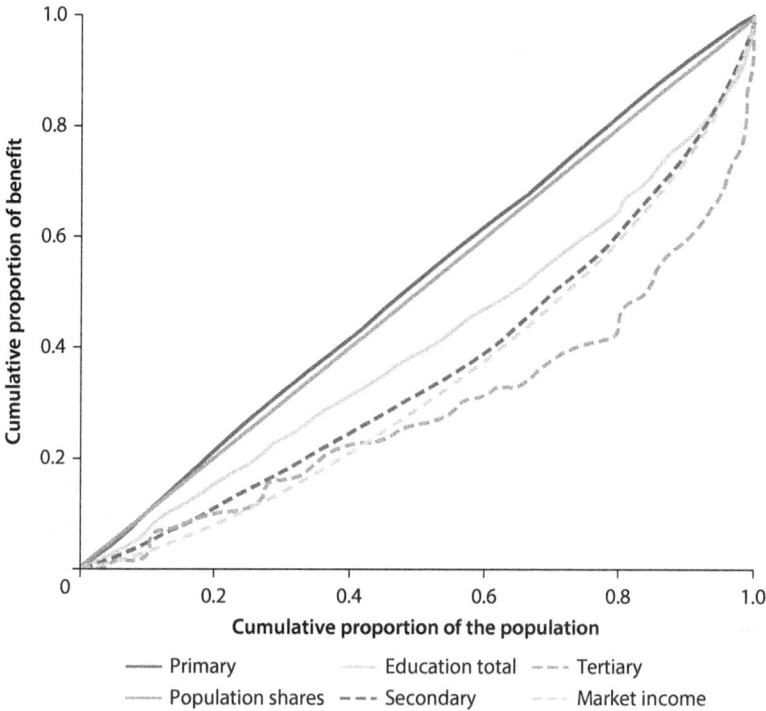

Source: Based on 2011 Household Consumption Expenditure Survey (HCES) data.
Note: "Market income" comprises pretax wages, salaries, income earned from capital assets (rent, interest, or dividends), and private transfers.

rich households, but it is not pro-poor: richer households receive a larger share of the secondary education spending (figure 3.7, table 3.5). In contrast, spending on tertiary education is regressive and unequalizing. Forty percent of spending on tertiary education is received by students in the richest decile, whereas only 2.5 percent of spending is received by the poorest decile. However, spending on tertiary education has beneficial impacts on long-term economic growth rates through technology absorption and innovation, as well as through service delivery (for example, through graduation numbers of new primary school teachers) and should not be reduced; rather, a focus on increased access for poorer families is needed.

Low enrollment rates in secondary and tertiary education limit the progressivity of spending on nonprimary education. Primary education is available in almost all villages in Ethiopia, resulting in high enrollment (reaching 96 percent in 2013), but dropout rates are high and primary completion is very low. This in turn causes secondary school enrollment rates to fall well below those of comparable countries. Children from poorer backgrounds make slower progress through school and are more likely to drop out without completing primary school. They are thus less likely to enroll in secondary school.

It is the opportunity cost of being in school—a need for the child to work to contribute to the family's well-being—that is the main problem (Chaudhury et al. 2006; Weir 2011; Woldehanna et al. 2011). A quarter of total secondary education spending benefits the richest decile, compared with only 5 percent that benefits the poorest decile. Completion of secondary school is a prerequisite for tertiary enrollment, so inequalities in secondary school enrollment are also reflected in tertiary enrollment, despite stipends for attendance available to all households.

The pattern in Ethiopia is not uncommon for low-income countries. As countries become richer, and educational coverage increases at all levels, education spending becomes more progressive. That is, although the average incidence may not be as progressive as in middle-income countries, the marginal incidence is usually increasingly progressive and more equalizing.

Health. Health expenditures are equalizing (table 3.5). Health benefits received by the poorest households are relatively high as a share of their market incomes (figure 3.8). However, these expenditures are not pro-poor: about 9 percent of health spending is concentrated in the poorest decile, whereas 14 percent is concentrated in the richest decile (figure 3.5). Nevertheless, this inequality in the concentration of spending is not as large as in other countries such as Indonesia (7 percent for the poorest, 15 percent for the richest) or Peru (6 percent for the poorest, 15 percent for the richest).

Figure 3.8 Health Spending Concentration and Incidence, by Income Decile, in Ethiopia, 2011

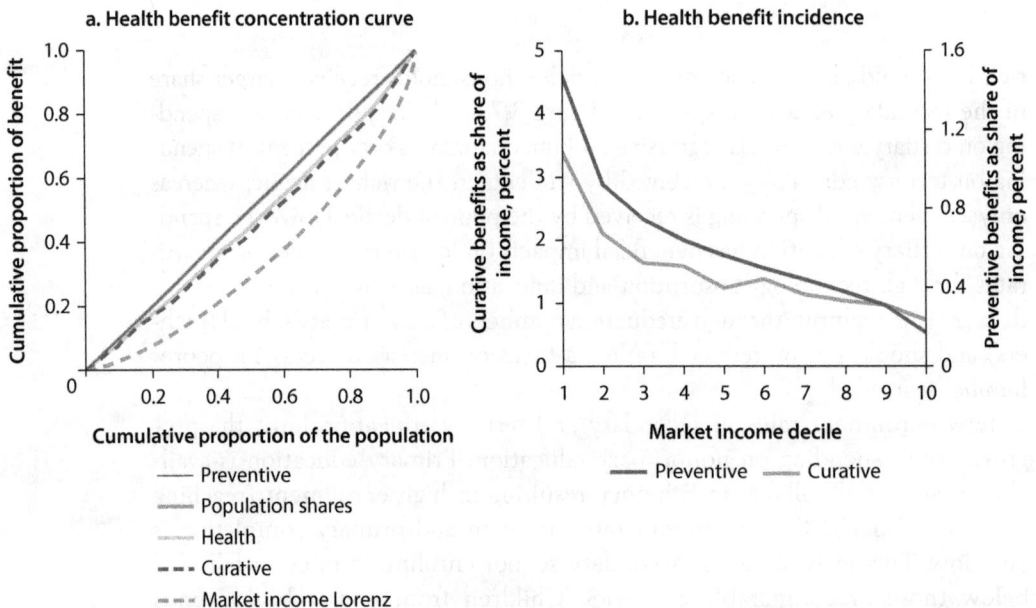

a. Health benefit concentration curve

Preventive
Population shares
Health
Curative
Market income Lorenz

b. Health benefit incidence

Preventive   Curative

Source: Based on 2011 Household Consumption Expenditure Survey (HCES) and 2011 Welfare Monitoring Survey (WMS) data.
Note: "Market income" comprises pretax wages, salaries, income earned from capital assets (rent, interest, or dividends), and private transfers.

Health extension agents are present in all neighborhoods (kebeles) and ensure that a basic range of health services are readily available to all households. This ensures that preventive health care spending—which is about 27 percent of overall health spending—is progressive in relative terms. However, curative health care is less progressive. Although preventive health care services are provided for free, marginal user fees are usually charged for curative public health services, which are much lower than the cost of service. To protect the poor against the financial burden of user fees, there are fee waiver and exemption systems at public health centers and hospitals. However, poorer households do not avail themselves of curative health services to the same extent, resulting in less-progressive public spending relative to preventive services (figure 3.8, panel b).

Overall Incidence of Public Spending

Overall, the progressive nature of taxes in Ethiopia is complemented by progressive social spending, but less than half of the spending analyzed is pro-poor. Of the total social spending included in the study, 81 percent is progressive and equalizing (only 44 percent is progressive and pro-poor), and 19 percent of spending is regressive and unequalizing.

The concentration coefficients (figure 3.5) show that PSNP, food aid, and primary education are the most progressive and pro-poor spending categories. Secondary school, health, wheat and kerosene subsidies, and overall education spending are neutral (that is, their distribution is almost identical to the distribution of market income). Spending on tertiary education and on electricity subsidies is regressive and unequalizing. The regressivity of tertiary education might be associated with low completion rates of primary and secondary education, which implies that a lower share of population may attend tertiary education. The budget allocated to tertiary education is higher than the budget allocated to upper-secondary education, so this result is likely to persist as long as primary and secondary completion rates do not improve. It is important to note that, in general, spending on tertiary education is not regressive in low-income countries. Of 13 low- and middle-income countries analyzed by Lustig (2015), spending on tertiary education around 2010 was unequalizing only in Ethiopia, Guatemala, and Indonesia.

Moving resources from off-budget subsidies (included in this analysis) to direct transfer programs targeted to the poor would improve the progressivity of public spending. If all subsidy financing were used instead to provide transfers to poor households with the same targeting effectiveness as the PSNP, this would further reduce the poverty headcount (at the national poverty line) by 2 percentage points. It would also reduce the poverty gap by 5 percentage points and poverty severity by 12.5 percentage points. Olinto and Sherpa (2014) discuss how a transfer program of 0.2 percent targeted to poorest households in Addis Ababa could cut the city's current poverty rate in half. This is the same as the cost of electricity subsidies to the richest 40 percent.

Conclusion

Fiscal policy in Ethiopia reduces inequality and lowers the depth and severity of poverty but increases the incidence of poverty. Poor households are net beneficiaries of fiscal policy when education and health transfers are taken into account. However, in terms of purchasing power, poor households pay taxes—both direct and indirect—and the transfers and benefits they receive do not compensate all households for the taxes they have paid. As a result, although the depth and severity of poverty fall as a result of fiscal policy, 1 in 4 households are impoverished (either made poor or poorer) after direct taxes are paid and transfers received, and nearly 1 in 10 households are impoverished after all taxes are paid and benefits received (including public spending on education and health).

The analysis in this chapter highlights two areas in which Ethiopia could mitigate the negative impact of taxes and indirect subsidies: (a) by reducing the incidence of direct taxes among the bottom deciles while increasing the progressivity of direct taxes, particularly PIT and agricultural taxes and (b) by redirecting subsidy spending to direct transfers benefiting the poorest.

In Ethiopia, taxes are progressive and equalizing, but their progressivity could be further enhanced. In terms of direct taxes, in addition to PITs, households also pay direct taxes in the form of agricultural and land taxes, particularly households in the bottom deciles. This is particularly costly to the poor in Ethiopia because its bottom deciles are much poorer than in other countries.

Moreover, indirect taxes place a burden on the poor—despite their progressivity—because so many households are poor in Ethiopia, and these taxes are generally levied equally regardless of income level. Although indirect taxes are not regressive, there is a clear trade-off between greater equity and efficiency if the government were to try to collect more direct taxes to improve equity.

On the expenditure side, direct transfers are progressive, pro-poor, and have been effective in reducing poverty and inequality. In contrast, although indirect subsidies are meant to benefit the poor, the top deciles benefit the most from subsidy spending. The electricity subsidy, in particular, is highly regressive and unequalizing, because access to electricity requires an investment that many of the poor cannot afford.

Given the effectiveness of the PSNP, Ethiopia could further reduce poverty if the spending on indirect subsidies were shifted to direct transfers benefiting the poor. As noted, if all subsidy financing were instead used to provide transfers to poor households at the same level of effectiveness as the PSNP's, the population living below the national poverty line would decrease by 2 percentage points. Such a change would also reduce the poverty gap by 5 percentage points and poverty severity by 12.5 percentage points. However, this shift to direct transfers would need to ensure that poor people currently receiving electricity subsidies also get compensated, because the subsidies make up a larger share of their incomes (particularly the urban poor with access to electricity).

Although overall spending on education and health is progressive and equalizing, it is not pro-poor because of limited use by the poor of secondary and tertiary education services. Similarly, there is a limited use of curative health services by the poor. Much progress has been made in increasing coverage of education and health services in recent years, and more progress is needed to further benefit the poor and improve progressivity.

Annex 3A. Methodological Assumptions

Direct Taxes

To estimate household-level PIT, the income tax schedule was applied on the disposable income of urban individuals who were employed by formal private or public organizations (table 3A.1, panel a). Rural individuals were assumed not to be formally employed. For self-employed individuals and those employed in the informal sector, we applied the business tax schedule to determine PIT (table 3A.1, panel b). Tax evasions (calculated as the difference between total actual tax collected and tax estimated based on income) are assumed to be borne by all self-employed and employees of the informal sector in proportion to income.

Agricultural income taxes and rural land used fees are, for the most part, calculated on the basis of landholding size. The tax schedule for this tax and fee is set by regional and local governments and, as such, varies from locale to locale. However, many of the main tax schedules were examined and found to levy similar per hectare tax rates regardless of land size. An example for the Oromia region suggests that, if anything, the per hectare tax rate generally falls with landholding size (table 3A.2).

To estimate agricultural tax and land use fees, we assumed that the rates are always constant per hectare. The landholding size was collected in the 2011 Household Consumption Expenditure Survey (HCES), but standardized units were often not recorded, making the HCES impossible to use. For this reason,

Table 3A.1 Direct Tax Rate Schedules in Ethiopia, 2011

a. Personal or employment income[a]			b. Taxable business income or net profit[b]		
Income bracket (Br per month)	Tax rate (%)	Standard deduction (Br)	Business income or net profit bracket (Br per year)	Tax rate (%)	Deduction (Br)
0–150	Exempted	n.a.	0–1,800	Exempted	n.a.
151–650	10	15.0	1,801–7,800	10	180
651–1,400	15	47.5	7,801–16,800	15	570
1,401–2,350	20	117.5	16,801–28,200	20	1,410
2,351–3,550	25	235.0	28,201–42,600	25	2,520
3,551–5,000	30	412.5	42,601–60,000	30	4,950
Over 5,000	35	662.0	Over 60,000	35	7,950

Source: Ministry of Finance and Economic Development.
Note: Br = birr; n.a. = not applicable.
a. The analysis applied this tax schedule to calculate the personal income tax of urban individuals employed by formal private or public organizations.
b. The analysis applied this tax schedule to calculate the personal income tax on self-employed and informally employed individuals.

Table 3A.2 Land Use Fee and Agricultural Income Tax Schedule in Oromia Regional State, Ethiopia, 2011

Land size (hectare)	Rural land use fee (Br)	Income tax (Br)	Total (Br)	Average tax rate (Br per hectare)
< 0.5	15	Exempted	15	40.0
0.5–1	20	20	40	53.3
1–2	30	35	65	43.3
2–3	45	55	100	40.0
3–4	65	70	135	38.6
4–5	90	100	190	42.2
> 5	120	140	260	34.7

Source: Oromia Regional State, Proclamation to Amend Rural Land Use Payment and Agricultural Income Tax (No. 131/2007), http://extwprlegs1.fao.org/docs/pdf/eth150706.pdf. The tax rate is own calculation.
Note: Br = birr.

the ERSS was used to define the association between land size and consumption in each region, which was then used to impute a land size for each household in the HCES. A region's total tax revenue was divided by total agricultural landholdings in the region to generate an average tax rate per hectare. This rate was used with the imputed land size to estimate the amount of agricultural tax paid by each household. This method implicitly assumes that the average tax rate per hectare is constant across farm size. An example from Oromia (table 3A.2) suggests this is a reasonable assumption. If anything, in Oromia average tax rates decrease with land size, which suggests that the regressivity of agricultural taxes might be underestimated in Oromia.

Indirect Taxes

Indirect taxes are estimated by price multiplier analysis using the SAM developed in 2006 by the EDRI. The SAM has 93 commodity accounts and distinguishes between purchased and own-consumed commodities (77 are purchased, and 16 are own-consumed commodities). The indirect tax account corresponding to each good or service in the SAM represents the actual indirect tax collected. This means that the ratio of the indirect tax to the total supply value of each commodity represents the effective tax rate of each product. For own-consumed commodities, there is no indirect tax in the SAM because the actually collected tax from such commodities is zero.

The second-round effects of indirect taxes are the price burden on consumers resulting from indirect taxes paid for inputs used in the production process. The input-output table is used to calculate the effect of taxes on intermediate inputs on prices of final goods and services. The overall effect is the sum of the direct and indirect effect of indirect taxes. The overall effect of indirect taxes on prices of commodities from the input-output table is simulated, using the World Bank's SimSIP Poverty simulator,[15] to estimate the burden of indirect taxes for each product (as a percentage of the value of supply) in the commodity account. Using item-level consumption in the HCES data, we estimated the price burden on each household on the basis of the proportional increase in the price of each good or service and the household's expenditure on corresponding goods and services, which is assumed to be borne entirely by the consumers (see table 3A.3 for a listing of excise tax rates).

One concern is informality and the potential evasion of consumption taxes. It is impossible to know from the survey whether a household has made a purchase from a shop that pays VAT or not. Further, in a standard competitive model, prices at shops that do not pay VAT would be the same as those at VAT-paying shops, with the benefits of nonpayment going to the firm owner rather than to the government. Households suffer the incidence of the tax regardless of the tax status of the seller, although not all the benefits go to the fiscal authorities. In essence, we assume that all households buy the same share of taxable goods so that the effects of tax avoidance or evasion on market prices are spread across the population in proportion to each household's expenditures.

Table 3A.3 Locally Produced or Imported Goods Subject to Excise Tax in Ethiopia

Ser. no.	Type of product	Excise tax rate (%)
1	Any type of sugar (in solid form) excluding molasses	33
2	Drinks	
2.1	All types of soft drinks (except fruit juices)	40
2.2	Powder soft drinks	40
2.3	Water bottled or canned in a factory	30
2.4	Alcoholic drinks	
2.4.1	All types of beer and stout	50
2.4.2	All types of wine	50
2.4.3	Whisky	50
2.4.4	Other alcoholic drinks	100
3	All types of pure alcohol	75
4	Tobacco and tobacco products	
4.1	Tobacco leaf	20
4.2	Cigarettes, cigar, cigarillos, pipe tobacco, snuff, and other tobacco products	75
5	Salt	30
6	Fuel, including super benzene, regular benzene, petrol, gasoline, and other motor spirits	30
7	Perfumes and toilet waters	100
8	Textile and textile products	
8.1	Textile fabrics, knitted or woven, of natural silk, rayon, nylon, wool or other similar materials	10
8.2	Textile of any type partly or wholly made from cotton, which is grey, white, dyed or printed, in pieces of any length or width (except mosquito net and "Abudgedid") and including blankets, bedsheets, counterpanes, towels, table clothes, and similar articles	10
8.3	Garments	10
9	Personal adornment made of gold, silver or other materials	20
10	Dish washing machines of a kind for domestic use	80
11	Washing machines of a kind for domestic purposes	30
12	Video decks	40
13	Television and video cameras	40

table continues next page

Table 3A.3 **Locally Produced or Imported Goods Subject to Excise Tax in Ethiopia** *(continued)*

Ser. no.	Type of product	Excise tax rate (%)
14	Television broadcast receivers whether or not combined with gramophone, radio, or sound receivers and reproducers	10
15	Motor passenger cars, station wagons, utility cars, and Land Rovers, Jeeps, pickups,	
15.1	similar vehicles (including motorized caravans), whether assembled, together with their appropriate initial equipment	30
15.2	Up to 1,300 c.c.	60
15.3	From 1,301 c.c. up to 1,800 c.c.	
	Above 1,800 c.c.	100
16	Carpets	30
17	Asbestos and asbestos products	20
18	Clocks and watches	20
19	Dolls and toys	20

Source: Proclamation No. 307/2002, Excise Tax Proclamation, Ethiopian Revenues and Customs Authority, http://www.erca.gov.et/index.php /proclamation/38-excise-tax.
Note: c.c. = cubic centimeters (engine size).

A sensitivity analysis uses an alternative way of estimating the impact of indirect taxes. The benchmark estimate included both the first- and second-round effects of all types of indirect taxes (including VAT). This approach considers VAT to be similar to sales tax in which additional taxes are paid in each link of the transaction chain. The alternative approach estimated only the first effect of VAT on prices because, in principle, producers and retailers are entitled to a refund of the VAT payments for input purchases, making intermediate inputs tax-free. The only exception to this concerns items that are VAT-exempt, which would have some indirect impact of VAT on intermediate goods because, if a good is VAT-exempt, producers are not entitled to a VAT refund for the inputs used in producing the item. As a result, in the sensitivity analysis, the first-round effect of VAT is estimated for items on which VAT is levied, and then only the second-round effects are included for goods and services that are VAT-exempt.

Because the sensitivity analysis excludes the second-round effects of VAT on most items, the estimate of indirect tax burden using this method is slightly smaller than the estimate in the benchmark estimate. As a result, the associated income measures of consumable income and final income become slightly higher in the sensitivity analysis. Apart from the slight change in level, the pattern of incidence of indirect taxes on the different income groups based on this method is similar to the pattern in the benchmark estimate. Thus the overall story line of the relative burden of indirect taxes on different income groups does not change, whichever method is used.

Direct Transfers

The 2010/11 HCES identifies households that received payment from the PSNP and households that receive food aid. Both PSNP payments and food aid payments were based on household size, and so the beneficiary status of the households and the household size were used in conjunction with government PSNP and food aid expenditures to impute the value of transfers received by each household. We assume that food aid and PSNP transfers were distributed to all beneficiaries equally.

Indirect Subsidies

Item-level HCES data were used to estimate the amount of households' consumption of wheat, kerosene, and electricity. The subsidy per kilogram, liter, and kilowatt-hour for each good, respectively, was then applied to estimate the total value of the subsidy received by the household.

The wheat subsidy (Br 150 per quintal) was available only to households in the Addis Ababa city administration and so was only applied to households living in Addis Ababa. The electricity subsidy depends on the amount of electricity consumed (table 3A.4). The tariff rate is progressive, but the rates in all ranges are below the unsubsidized tariff. Petroleum prices are regulated by the government, and kerosene was subsidized at Br 2.17 per liter.

In-Kind Transfers
Education
The WMS is used to determine the total number of students enrolled in primary, secondary, and tertiary education in each region. The unit costs of primary, secondary, and tertiary education were obtained by dividing the total regional public spending (Ministry of Finance and Economic Development's [MoFED]) by total regional enrollment.

The monetized value of the in-kind education transfer at the household level is determined by multiplying the number of children enrolled in primary, secondary, and tertiary education in 2010/11 by the unit costs. Public education spending includes salary, wages, and operational costs as well as the administration and capital expenditure for primary and secondary education. For tertiary education, a significant proportion of capital expenditure (amounting to 1.6 percent of GDP) is excluded because there were large expenditures in expansion of higher education infrastructure that will serve another generation in the future. Only 10 percent of the capital expenditure is considered in the analysis to account for the benefits the current students are receiving.

Table 3A.4 Tariff and Subsidy for Household Electricity Consumption in Ethiopia

Monthly consumption		Tariff (Br/kWh/mo.)	Tariff without subsidy (Br/kWh/mo.)	Subsidy (Br/kWh/mo.)
From (kWh)	To (kWh)			
0	50	0.273	0.967	0.694
51	100	0.356	0.967	0.611
101	200	0.499	0.967	0.468
201	300	0.550	0.967	0.417
301	400	0.567	0.967	0.401
401	500	0.588	0.967	0.379
501	1,000,000	0.694	0.967	0.273

Source: World Bank 2013
Note: Br = Birr; kWh = kilowatt-hours; mo. = month.

Health

For health, total public health spending (MoFED 2013) is distributed to all individuals who received public health services as recorded in the WMS. For curative health services, in-kind health benefits are estimated in proportion to households' expenditure on public health fees. For households exempted from user fees, the average benefit is assumed. The WMS is used to identify households that received free health services. For preventive health services, the benefits are distributed to all households equally. Based on the budgets for different health programs, the proportion of preventive and curative health services is estimated to be 27 percent and 73 percent, respectively, of the total government health budget.

Notes

1. Economic growth averaging 10 percent a year between 2007 and 2015 was much higher compared to the average in Sub-Saharan Africa (4.6 percent) and low-income countries (5.4 percent) (World Development Indicators database).

2. Although poverty incidence refers to the basic poverty headcount (percentage of the population that is poor), the depth of poverty (also called the "poverty gap") is the average percentage by which individuals fall below the poverty line. The poverty severity index (also called "poverty intensity") is calculated as the poverty gap index squared; it implicitly gives greater weight to the poorest individuals, making it a combined measure of poverty and income inequality. These three poverty metrics are known as the Foster-Greer-Thorbecke (FGT) indexes (Foster, Greer, and Thorbecke 1984).

3. Ethiopia's first and second Growth and Transformation Plans, for instance, have aimed at sustaining rapid, broad, and equitable economic growth as well as achieving the United Nations Millennium Development Goals (MoFED 2010; NPC 2016). The longer-term objectives are to eradicate poverty, bring about structural transformation of the economy, and reach lower-middle-income status by 2030.

4. Ethiopia's 2015 per capita gross national income of US$590 (using the World Bank's Atlas conversion method) is substantially lower than the 2015 average for Sub-Saharan Africa of US$1,628 (World Bank data, http://data.worldbank.org/?locations =ET-ZG).

5. For more details about the CEQ framework, see chapter 1 and the CEQ Institute website: http://www.commitmentoequity.org.

6. As soon as there is more than one intervention, assessing the progressivity of fiscal interventions individually is not sufficient to determine whether they are equalizing (see, for example, Lambert 2002, 277–78). For a full explanation, see Lustig (2017).

7. VAT-exempted goods and services are the following: sale or transfer of a used dwelling or the lease of a dwelling; financial services; the supply or import of national or foreign currency and of securities; import of gold to be transferred to the National Bank of Ethiopia; services of religious organizations; medicines and medical services; educational services and childcare services for children at preschool institutions; goods and services for humanitarian aid and rehabilitation after natural disasters, industrial accidents, and catastrophes; electricity, kerosene, and water; goods imported by the government, organizations, or institutions or projects exempted from duties and other

import taxes to the extent provided by law or by agreement; postal service; transport; permits and license fees; goods or services by a workshop employing disabled individuals if more than 60 percent of the employees are disabled; books and other printed materials; unprocessed food items; palm oils used for food; bread; and "injera," or milk.

8. Although the survey was conducted in 2010/11, all expenditure data were deflated to December 2010. The PPP conversion is made after adjusting the relative difference between the consumer price index in 2005 and December 2010.

9. It may be that better-off households do not work the same number of days as less-well-off households. If so, the assumption of equal distribution of benefits would make the PSNP appear less progressive than it actually is.

10. Details on the assumptions used for education and health incidence are included in annex 3A.

11. Typically, Ethiopia measures welfare using a household consumption aggregate, which we set as equal to disposable income. Using the national moderate poverty line (2,200 kilocalories per day per adult plus essential nonfood expenditure), the poverty headcount is 30 percent, coinciding with the official headcount rate for 2010/11.

12. We assume that effective tax rates are equal across households, which may underestimate the progressivity of indirect taxes (if richer urban households are more likely to purchase in formal markets).

13. We differentiate between formal and informal or self-employed workers, as further discussed in annex 3A.

14. Spending is considered "progressive" whenever the concentration coefficient is lower than the Gini for market income—meaning that the benefits from that spending as a share of market income tend to fall with market income. Spending is pro poor whenever the concentration coefficient is not only lower than the Gini but also negative— that is, the share of spending going to the poor is higher than their population share. Pro-poor spending implies that the *per capita* government spending on the transfer *tends* to fall with market income.

15. For more information on the simulator, see the "SimSIP Poverty" summary sheet in World Bank (2003, 70).

References

Beneke, Margarita, Nora Lustig, and José Andrés Oliva. 2014. "El impacto de los impuestos y el gasto social en la desigualdad y la pobreza en El Salvador" [The Impact of Taxes and Social Spending on Inequality and Poverty in El Salvador]. Working Paper 26, Commitment to Equity Project of the Center for Inter-American Policy and Research, the Inter-American Dialogue, the Center for Global Development, and Department of Economics, Tulane University, New Orleans, LA.

Besley, Timothy, and Torsten Persson. 2009. "The Origins of State Capacity: Property Rights, Taxation, and Politics." *The American Economic Review* 99 (4): 1218–44.

Bucheli, Marisa, Nora Lustig, Máximo Rossi, and Florencia Amábile. 2014. "Social Spending, Taxes, and Income Redistribution in Uruguay." *Public Finance Review* 42 (3): 413–33.

Cabrera, Maynor, Nora Lustig, and Hilcías Morán. 2014. "Fiscal Policy, Inequality, and the Ethnic Divide in Guatemala." Commitment to Equity Working Paper 20, Center for

Inter-American Policy and Research; the Inter-American Dialogue; and Department of Economics, Tulane University, New Orleans, LA.

Chaudhury, Nazmul, Jeffrey Hammer, Michael Kremer, Karthik Muralidharan, and F. Halsey Rogers. 2006. "Missing in Action: Teacher and Health Worker Absence in Developing Countries." *Journal of Economic Perspectives* 20 (1): 91–116.

Duclos, Jean-Yves, and Martin Tabi. 1996. "The Measurement of Progressivity, with an Application to Canada." *The Canadian Journal of Economics* 1 (special issue: part 1): S165–70.

Foster, J., J. Greer, and E. Thorbecke. 1984. "A Class of Decomposable Poverty Measures." *Econometrica* 3 (52): 761–66.

Fullerton, D., and G. Metcalf. 2002. "Tax Incidence." In *Handbook of Public Economics Volume 4*, edited by A. Auerbach and M. Feldstein, 1787–872. Amsterdam: Elsevier Science.

Gilligan, D., J. Hoddinott, N. Kumar, and A. Taffesse. 2010. "Targeting Food Security Interventions When 'Everyone Is Poor': The Case of Ethiopia's Productive Safety Net Programme." Ethiopia Strategy Support Program Working Paper 24, International Food Policy Research Institute, Washington, DC.

Higgins, Sean, and Nora Lustig. 2016. "Can a Poverty-Reducing and Progressive Tax and Transfer System Hurt the Poor?" *Journal of Development Economics* 122 (September): 63–75.

Higgins, Sean, and Claudiney Pereira. 2014. "The Effects of Brazil's Taxation and Social Spending on the Distribution of Household Income." *Public Finance Review* 42 (3): 346–67.

Jaramillo, Miguel. 2014. "The Incidence of Social Spending and Taxes in Peru." *Public Finance Review* 42 (3): 391–412.

Kakwani, Nanak C. 1977. "Measurement of Tax Progressivity: An International Comparison." *The Economic Journal* 87 (345): 71–80.

Lambert, Peter. 2002. *The Distribution and Redistribution of Income*. 3rd ed. Manchester, U.K.: Manchester University Press.

Lustig, Nora. 2015. "The Redistributive Impact of Government Spending on Education and Health: Evidence from Thirteen Developing Countries in the Commitment to Equity Project." In *Inequality and Fiscal Policy*, edited by Benedict Clements, Ruud de Mooij, Sanjeev Gupta, and Michael Keen. Washington, DC: International Monetary Fund.

Lustig, Nora, ed. 2017. *Commitment to Equity Handbook: Estimating the Impact of Fiscal Policy on Inequality and Poverty*. Washington, DC: Brookings Institution Press and CEQ Institute, Tulane University. Advance online version available at http://www.commitmentoequity.org/publications/handbook.php.

Lustig, Nora, and Sean Higgins. 2013. "Commitment to Equity Assessment (CEQ): Estimating the Incidence of Social Spending, Subsidies and Taxes. Handbook." Commitment to Equity Working Paper 1, Center for Inter-American Policy and Research; the Inter-American Dialogue; and Department of Economics, Tulane University, New Orleans, LA.

MoFED (Ministry of Finance and Economic Development). 2010. "Growth and Trans-formation Plan 2010/11–2014/15." National planning document, MoFED, Federal Democratic Republic of Ethiopia, Addis Ababa. http://www.mofed.gov.et/web/guest/-/gtp-main-document-vol-1?inheritRedirect=true.

MoFED (Ministry of Finance and Economic Development). 2013. "Government Finance Report." MoFED, Federal Democratic Republic of Ethiopia, Addis Ababa.

NPC (National Planning Commission). 2016. "Growth and Transformation Plan II (GTP II) (2015/16–2019/20)." National planning document, NPC, Federal Democratic Republic of Ethiopia, Addis Ababa.

Olinto, P., and M. Sherpa. 2014. "Targeting Assessment and Ex-Ante Impact Simulations of Addis Ababa Safety Net." Background paper for the Ethiopia Poverty Assessment, World Bank, Washington, DC.

Paz Arauco, Verónica, George Gray Molina, Wilson Jiménez Pozo, and Ernesto Yáñez Aguilar. 2014. "Explaining Low Redistributive Impact in Bolivia." *Public Finance Review* 42 (3): 236–45.

Sauma, Pablo, and Juan Diego Trejos. 2014. "Social Public Spending, Taxes, Redistribution of Income, and Poverty in Costa Rica." Commitment to Equity Working Paper 18, Center for Inter-American Policy and Research; the Inter-American Dialogue; and Department of Economics, Tulane University, New Orleans, LA.

Scott, John. 2014. "Redistributive Impact and Efficiency of Mexico's Fiscal System." *Public Finance Review* 42 (3): 368–90.

Weir, Sharada. 2011. "Parental Attitudes and Demand for Schooling in Ethiopia." *Journal of African Economies* 20 (1): 90–110.

Woldehanna, Tassew, Retta Gudisa, Yisak Tafere, and Alula Pankhurst. 2011. *Understanding Changes in the Lives of Poor Children: Initial Findings from Ethiopia.* Round 3 Survey Report for Young Lives: An International Study of Child Poverty, U.K. Department of International Development, University of Oxford.

World Bank. 2003. "A User's Guide to Poverty and Social Impact Analysis." Reference document, World Bank, Washington, DC.

———. 2013. *The Federal Democratic Republic of Ethiopia, Ethiopian Electric Power Corporation, Report on Accountability Issues.* Unpublished report.

———. 2015. "Ethiopia Poverty Assessment 2014." Report AUS6744, World Bank, Washington, DC.

———. 2016. *Poverty and Shared Prosperity 2016: Taking on Inequality.* Washington, DC: World Bank.

CHAPTER 4

The Distributional Impact of Fiscal Policy in Georgia

Cesar Cancho and Elena Bondarenko

Introduction

Georgia is a small lower-middle-income country with a per capita gross domestic product (GDP) of US$3,670 (2014) that ranks among the highest in poverty and inequality indicators in the Europe and Central Asia region (figure 4.1).

The poverty reduction trends have been encouraging since the 2000s. In 2000, 51 percent of the population in Georgia lived on less than US$2.50 per person per day.[1] By 2002, poverty had fallen to 46 percent but remained around the same level until 2011, when it fell slightly to 45 percent of the population. Since then, poverty has fallen more rapidly, reaching 32 percent in 2014.

In contrast, inequality has persisted. Estimates of inequality have persisted at about 40 Gini points since 2000, up from estimates of around 30 points in the late 1980s.[2] Since 2000, Gini estimates have oscillated between 39 and 40 points, registering 40 points in 2013 and 2014. The high-inequality indicators over this period are explained in part by the prolonged period of social system restructuring that followed the collapse of the Soviet Union in 1991 and dismantling of the universal social protection it had offered.

After declaring independence from the Soviet Union in 1991, Georgia inherited the Soviet social protection and health system model comprising primarily free

This chapter is based on "Enhancing Equity with Fiscal Policies," previously published as chapter 2 of the 2015 "Georgia Public Expenditure Review: Selected Fiscal Issues" (World Bank 2015a). Some indicators differ slightly from those used in that work because of the use of per capita aggregates in this chapter (instead of the "per adult equivalent" scale) and because of refinements to the definitions of income aggregates. The authors are grateful to Congyan Tan and Mariam Dolidze of the World Bank's Macroeconomics and Fiscal Management Global Practice (GP), who led the project; to Gabriela Inchauste, Lidia Ceriani, and Nistha Sinha of the Bank's Poverty GP; and to Nora Lustig and Sean Higgins of Tulane University and the Commitment for Equity Project—all of whom provided valuable advice and guidance. The authors are also grateful to Irina Capita for assistance with the administrative fiscal data.

Figure 4.1 Georgia Poverty and Inequality Trends and Regional Country Comparisons

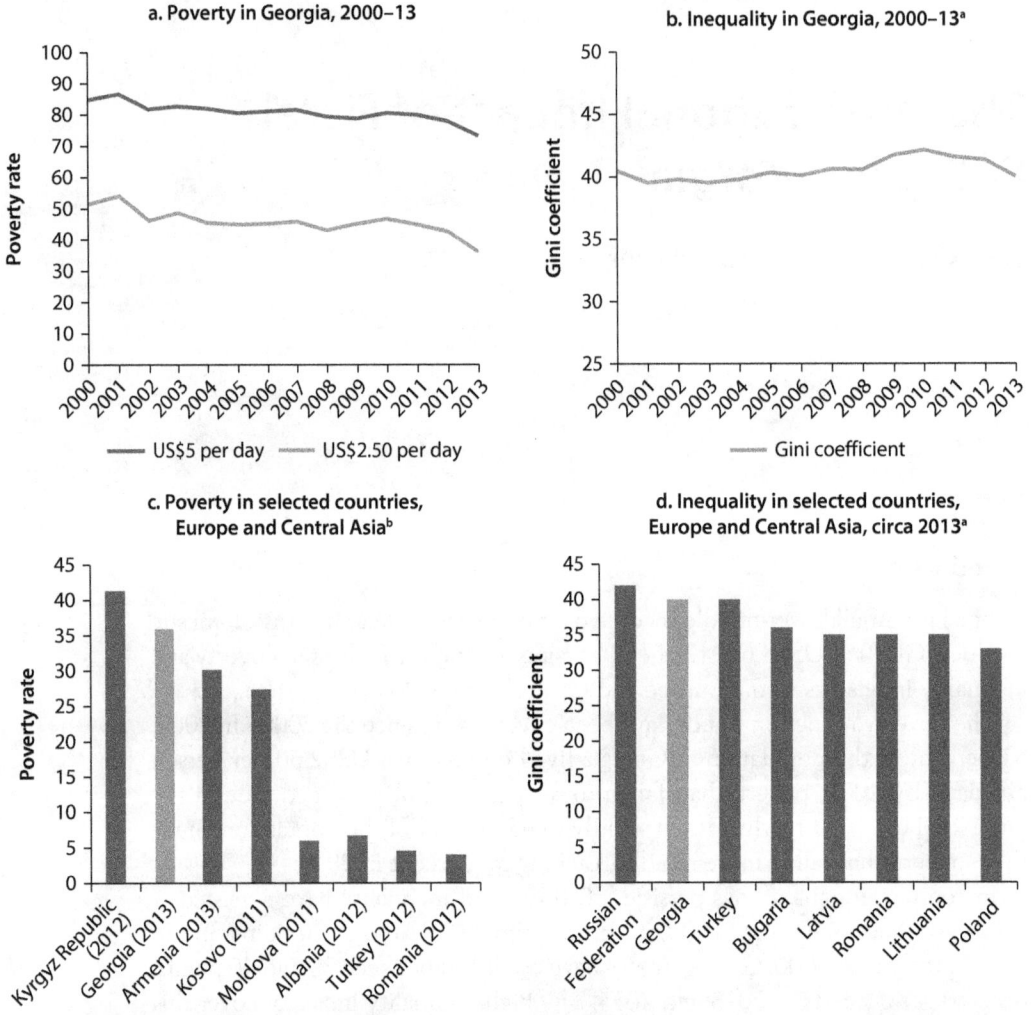

a. Poverty in Georgia, 2000–13

b. Inequality in Georgia, 2000–13[a]

c. Poverty in selected countries, Europe and Central Asia[b]

d. Inequality in selected countries, Europe and Central Asia, circa 2013[a]

Source: World Bank 2015b.

a. The Gini coefficient indicates the inequality of income distribution, ranging from 0 (full equality) to 100 (maximum inequality).

b. Poverty is defined as US$2.50 per person per day at 2005 purchasing power parity (PPP). Country-specific years of data are within parentheses.

health care, a state insurance system, and a pension system. Overall, the system continued to work under its own inertia until 1994, but the expenditures had not met actual needs since 1992, public financing declined, and the order of the system was distorted. The social burden fell almost completely on individuals: social protection programs were limited, pensions were paid irregularly, and individuals were responsible for mandatory health insurance premiums and copayments, which resulted in lower affordability of health services and higher poverty.

The first wave of system changes was characterized by extensive health care reforms during 1995–2003, followed by deep pro-market reforms and expansion of the social protection system in the mid-2000s. The government started introducing various social transfers; improving pension provision; enhancing health care accessibility for the population living below the poverty line; and extending the coverage, quality, and quantity of social programs (Gzirishvili 2012).

Since 2012, Georgia has been shifting fiscal policy toward greater prioritization of social spending on pension, health, and targeted social programs—expanding these programs to include more beneficiaries and scaling up expenditures as follows:

- *All social transfers were increased,* including the universal, noncontributory old-age pensions (the largest social assistance program, covering close to 20 percent of the population). In addition, the Targeted Social Assistance (TSA) allowance, which supports about 10 percent of the population, was doubled.[3] In fact, previous research has shown that most of Georgia's poverty reduction in 2010–12 is attributable to the expansion of social assistance, with the labor market playing a relatively limited role (World Bank 2014c).
- *Health care program eligibility was expanded.* From February 2013, all citizens who were not enrolled in the targeted Medical Insurance Program for the poor (MIP) Program were eligible for the state-funded, noncontributory Universal Health Care (UHC) program.
- *Other expenditure increases* included indirect compensation through transfers for small farmers.

On the tax side, the government introduced personal income tax (PIT) refunds for low-wage earners in 2013. The main efforts in tax policy were directed toward sustaining the stability of the tax system. The Economic Liberty Act, adopted in 2011 and entering into force in 2014, introduced the constitutional referendum requirement for new state taxes or increases in existing taxes (except for the excise tax), thus preserving a regulatory policy that helps maintain low pressure on taxation (Government of Georgia 2011).

In this context of expanding social policies, this chapter examines how effectively these social transfers and the collected taxes redistribute income from the top to the bottom and lift households out of poverty. In concrete, we seek to answer the following: How much income redistribution and poverty reduction does the government accomplish through taxes, social transfers, and subsidies? How progressive are the government's revenue collection and spending practices? And what are the individual impacts of taxes and transfer policies on inequality and poverty, given the fiscal resources used?

Along those lines, the main contribution of this work is to provide systematic empirical evidence on the progressivity of the fiscal interventions. Although similar studies exist for other countries in the region (for example, Armenia and the Russian Federation),[4] this study is the first comprehensive examination of Georgia's fiscal instruments and their ability to redistribute income and reduce poverty that—by using a harmonized methodology developed under the Commitment to

Equity (CEQ) project (Lustig and Higgins 2013)—allows researchers to produce comparative analytics with other countries in the region and the world.[5]

In the case of Georgia, the main results of this analysis are threefold:

- *The tax system is regressive overall on account of indirect taxes.* Although direct taxes are progressive because their burden falls mostly on formal workers at the top of the income distribution, indirect taxes are more widespread along the distribution and represent a heavier relative burden at the bottom.
- *Social spending is reasonably targeted to the bottom of the distribution, effectively acting as a safety net protecting the poor from negative shocks.* The TSA program is, by and large, the most progressive social expenditure, and old-age pensions are the most important for poverty reduction.
- *Current fiscal policy reduces income inequality and poverty.* The joint analysis of taxes and transfers shows that inequality and poverty decrease after all the government interventions are applied, although there is some heterogeneity in the specific impact of different interventions.

The chapter is structured as follows: The next section provides an overview of tax and social spending systems that were implemented by the Georgian government in 2013. The "Methodology, Data, and Assumptions" section describes the data and covers the framework and assumptions used for each fiscal intervention in the analysis. The "Main Results" section outlines the redistributive and poverty effects as well as the marginal contributions of individual taxes and transfers. This section also analyzes the progressivity of taxes and social spending by looking at the incidence of each element independently and the impact of all interventions as a whole. "Concluding Remarks" summarizes the chapter's findings, noting the current role of government expenditures in reducing poverty and sharing prosperity and proposing policy options to increase the effectiveness of redistribution policies. This section includes recommendations for tax and spending reforms that are in line with fiscal sustainability.

Fiscal Instruments to Tackle Poverty and Inequality

Georgia generated total revenues of about 28 percent of GDP in 2013, which is below the average overall revenue reported by middle-income countries in the Europe and Central Asia region. Total general government spending in Georgia is also lower than the regional average, amounting to about 29 percent of GDP in 2013.[6] Tables 4.1 and 4.2 in this section show the 2013 breakdown of the major government tax revenue and public spending, respectively, and identify which taxes and transfers were included in the incidence analysis.

Taxes

Tax revenue represents a significant portion of fiscal revenues in Georgia.[7] Taxes account for about 25 percent of GDP, with value added taxes (VAT) and PIT being the most important. There are six taxes in Georgia, of which five

Table 4.1 Tax Revenues in Georgia, by Category, 2013

Category	Share of total (%)	Share of GDP (%)	IAª (% of GDP)
Total tax revenues	100	24.8	21.4
Indirect taxes	55.0	13.6	13.3
Value added tax	42.8	10.6	10.6
Excise taxes	10.8	2.7	2.7
Import taxes	1.3	0.3	n.a.
Direct taxes	44.6	11.1	8.1
Personal income tax	29.0	7.2	7.2
Corporate income tax	12.1	3.0	n.a.
Property tax	3.5	0.9	0.9
Other taxes	0.4	0.1	n.a.
Social security contributionsᵇ	—	—	—

Source: Based on data from the Ministry of Finance website, http://www.mof.ge/en/.
Note: GDP = gross domestic product; n.a. = not applicable (not included in the analysis); — = not available.
a. IA = included in the incidence analysis.
b. Georgia does not have a contributory social security system; therefore, data for "social security contributions" are not available.

(PIT, corporate income tax [CIT], VAT, excise tax, and import tax) are nation-wide; one (property tax) is a local tax. There are no capital gains,[8] inheritance, gift, wealth (except for property), property transfer, social, branch remittance, or other taxes imposed in Georgia.

Based on available data in the household survey, the analysis looks primarily at four major taxes: PIT; property tax; VAT; and excise duties on alcohol, tobacco, and fuel (table 4.1). Together they make up about 86.2 percent of total general government tax revenues, with the indirect taxes making up almost 54 percent of the total and direct taxes making up a little over 32 percent. The CIT, other nonclassified taxes, and revenues from other sources that are not captured by Georgia's Integrated Household Survey (IHS) are not part of the analysis. Customs duty is omitted because it is not possible to identify whether a purchase was imported; moreover, duties represent only a small share of government revenues.

Georgia relies more on consumption or indirect taxes and less on direct taxes or PIT to finance its public expenditure. Obtaining higher revenue by raising tax rates is restricted; the Economic Liberty Act of 2011 bans the introduction of new state taxes or increases in existing taxes without a nationwide referendum, except for the excise tax. This feature and institutional restriction, along with smaller average revenue than Georgia's peers in Europe and Central Asia, limits the government's ability to affect the distribution of income.

Personal Income Tax

The PIT structure for 2013, the year of the IHS data, is straightforward in Georgia. Employees pay a flat income tax rate of 20 percent. PIT is levied on individual taxable income, which is the difference between the gross income and

Table 4.2 Government Spending in Georgia, by Category, 2013
Percentage of GDP

Category	Total	IAª
Total government spending[b]	28.8	12.0
Primary government spending[c]	27.9	12.0
Social spending (incl. contributory pensions)[d]	12.1	11.0
Social spending (excl. contributory pensions)[e]	12.1	11.0
Total cash transfers	6.1	6.0
Cash transfers (excl. all pensions)	1.8	1.8
Noncontributory pensions[f]	4.3	4.3
Total in-kind transfers[g]	5.2	4.1
Education	2.8	2.5
Tertiary education	0.3	0.3
Health	1.8	1.6
Contributory[h]	n.a.	n.a.
Noncontributory	1.8	1.6
Other social spending[i]	0.8	0.8
Contributory pensions[j]	n.a.	n.a.
Nonsocial spending	15.8	0.7
Agricultural Cards	0.7	0.7
Indirect subsidies	0.3	0.3
Other subsidies	1.7	—
Other nonsocial spending[k]	13.3	—
Debt service	0.9	—

Source: Ministry of Finance budget data, http://www.mof.ge/en/4539.
Note: GDP = gross domestic product; n.a. = not applicable; — = not available.
a. IA = included in the incidence analysis.
b. Total government spending = primary government spending + debt service (interest and amortization).
c. Primary government spending = social spending including contributory pensions + nonsocial spending.
d. Social spending (including social contributions) = total cash transfers + total in-kind transfers + other social spending + contributory pensions.
e. Social spending (excluding social contributions) = total cash transfers + total in-kind transfers + other social spending.
f. Noncontributory pensions are those to which the pensioner (or employee) makes no contributions. In Georgia, pensions are funded from general government revenues.
g. Total in-kind transfers include government expenditure on health and education programs.
h. Contributory health spending is not applicable to Georgia, where employees do not make contributions toward health spending.
i. "Other social spending" includes a considerable number of small social assistance programs that were not possible to identify in administrative sources and therefore not included in the analysis using the data from the 2013 Integrated Household Survey (IHS).
j. Georgia does not have a contributory social security system; therefore, data for "social security contributions" are not available.
k. "Other nonsocial spending" includes spending on general public services, defense, public order and safety, economic affairs, environmental protection, recreation, culture, and religion.

deductions during a calendar year. Gross income includes income from employment (salaries, wages, benefits, and other income); income earned from economic activity not related to employment; and income earned from other sources (for example, properties, dividends, and shares).

The PIT system has a number of deductions and exemptions applied in the analysis. Individuals whose taxable income earned as salary does not exceed GEL

6,000 (US$2,506)[9] in a calendar year are entitled to a deduction of GEL 1,800 (US$752) from employment income and can claim a tax refund by filing a tax return with the Georgian tax authorities. Dividends distributed by Georgian companies are subject to a 5 percent withholding tax at the source. Interest payments are subject to a 5 percent withholding tax. Capital gains realized by a resident from the sale of tangible assets are subject to a 20 percent tax.

Certain types of salaries are exempt from income tax: (a) income from the primary supply of agricultural products produced in Georgia if the gross income does not exceed GEL 200,000 (US$83,530); (b) the first GEL 3,000 (US$1,253) of income earned by single mothers; and (c) the first GEL 6,000 (US$2,506) of income earned by a person with a disability. Other tax exemptions are applied to grants, state and private pensions, state compensation, state scholarships, and alimony.[10] If an income tax payer is eligible to more than one tax privilege (exemption), only the highest privilege is applied.

Property Taxes

Property taxes are levied on taxable property and land, including agricultural, nonagricultural, and forest land. Tax rates are set locally and differentiated according to the income earned by the taxpayer's family. Family income includes taxable income earned from economic activity, any other income (including income not related to economic activity), and gross salary.

A person's taxable property is tax-exempt if the person's gross family income during the year preceding the tax year does not exceed GEL 40,000 (US$16,706). In addition, property possessed or owned by a person and parcels of land attached to it are exempt from the property tax if such a person cannot use such property because it is being used as a dwelling for internally displaced persons (IDPs) and if the property has been registered as a unit of "compact accommodation" of IDPs.

Real estate tax is applied to the imputed values of properties, unfinished construction, buildings, or their parts.[11] For families with annual income of GEL 40,000–100,000 (US$16,706–41,765), the tax rate is 0.05–0.2 percent of the market value of the taxable property. For families with income equal to or greater than GEL 100,000, the tax rate is 0.8–1.0 percent of the market value of the taxable real estate.

Tax rates on agricultural land and forest land used for cultivation (arable, homestead, grassland, and pastureland) are differentiated according to administrative-territorial unit and land category and are applied to the land size reported in the survey. The tax is calculated in lari per hectare for the regions analyzed in the survey, varying between GEL 13 and GEL 100 (US$5.40–42.00) per hectare, depending on the region and type of land. Parcels of agricultural land of up to five hectares are exempt from the property tax.

The basic tax rate on land not used for cultivation is GEL 0.24 per square meter of land per year, which is adjusted by the territorial coefficient (up to 1.5) fixed by the local government. However, at the time of this analysis, local territorial coefficients data were not available. This study assumed the basic tax rate for land not used for cultivation.

Value Added Tax

The standard rate of VAT on domestic sales of goods and services and the importation of goods is 18 percent. In most cases, the amount of VAT is determined on the basis of the transaction price.

Some transactions are exempt from VAT without the right to claim input tax credits. The exemptions relevant for this study include financial services; supply or importation of goods (books, newspapers and magazines, and music); medical services; care services in children's homes; care of the sick, disabled, and elderly; and public procurement of goods and services related to health care programs or educational services.

In addition, there are a number of exemptions for supply and importation of the following agricultural products: agricultural produce of Georgia (other than eggs), live plants and vines, fertilizers of animal or vegetable origin, plant or animal products obtained by mixing chemical treatments, agrarian pesticides and agrochemicals, and seed and plant materials of agricultural plants.

Excise Tax

Georgia applies excise tax to the traditional excisable products (alcohol, tobacco products, means of transport, and various petroleum products) and also on mobile communication service. The tax rates vary by the type of product, as follows:

- *Alcohol:* Ranging from GEL 2.50 per liter (for wine and champagne) to GEL 4.60 per liter (for liqueurs and cordials)
- *Tobacco products:* GEL 0.75 per pack (for filtered cigarettes) and GEL 0.20 per pack (for unfiltered cigarettes)
- *Oil and fuel products:* GEL 0.16 per liter (for fuel and gasoline products), GEL 0.12 per liter (for kerosene and diesel fuel), and GEL 0.33 per cubic meter (for liquefied petroleum gas)
- *Mobile communications services:* A 10 percent excise tax, introduced in September 2010

Social Spending

The new government of Georgia that took power in 2012 has shifted fiscal policy toward greater social spending to address poverty and inequality. During the years that followed, the government expanded social programs to include more beneficiaries; increased universal noncontributory pensions and TSA benefits; and, in 2013, introduced UHC.

Georgia's social protection system is financed entirely out of general revenues and accounts for about 42 percent of total public spending and 12 percent of GDP—one of the highest shares of GDP in the region—with social benefits, especially pensions, being the largest component (table 4.2).[12] Most of the poverty reduction seen over 2013–14 is attributable to social assistance, with the labor market playing a relatively limited role (World Bank 2014c).

Direct Transfers: Social Assistance

Direct transfers in Georgia are the highest in the region, accounting for 6.1 percent of GDP (World Bank 2014c, 17). Compared with the largest "spenders" identified in the CEQ analysis—Bolivia, Brazil, Costa Rica, and South Africa—Georgia spends twice as much on direct transfers as a percentage of GDP (Lustig 2015).

Pensions. Unlike all other countries in the Europe and Central Asia region, Georgia's pension system is financed entirely out of general revenues; the employers' social contribution tax was abolished in 2006.[13] In particular, Georgia has a noncontributory public pension scheme that provides a flat universal pension to all elderly people at the replacement rate of about 19 percent of the 2013 average wage. This pension is the largest social assistance program by its budget and coverage, accounting for 4.3 percent of GDP and covering 686,675 beneficiaries in 2013, according to Ministry of Labor, Health and Social Affairs of Georgia.[14]

With the coverage to all pensioners, pension payments start at 65 years of age for men and 60 years of age for women. The basic pension was GEL 150 (US$63) per month in the first eight months of 2013. The level was raised by 2.6 percent, to GEL 154 (US$64.68), in September 2013.

Targeted Social Assistance. The analysis includes TSA, Georgia's second-largest social assistance program, which aims to reduce poverty and inequality. TSA is a pecuniary social assistance program (subsistence allowance) to provide income support and help with consumption smoothing among the poor households and various vulnerable groups in Georgia.[15] The program supports about 10 percent of the population (454,000 beneficiaries in 150,607 households) and amounted to 1.7 percent of GDP as of 2013.[16]

The base TSA allowance for the oldest household member was GEL 30 (US$12.50) per month, and each additional household member received GEL 24 (US$10) during the first half of 2013. In July 2013, the base benefit rose to GEL 60 (US$25) per month plus GEL 48 (US$20) for each additional member. TSA eligibility is defined by a special formula that includes a number of objective and subjective criteria and calculates a score for registered households based on provided information. All households with a score below 57,000 are eligible for TSA.

Other Social Spending. A variety of other pensions and social packages available to different groups in 2013 were also included in the analysis. Overall, these "other social spending" transfers accounted for 0.8 percent of GDP. Pensions for disabled individuals without other means of support were paid to 122,940 individuals. Loss-of-breadwinner pensions (survivor's pensions) were distributed to 27,080 surviving individuals or family without other means of support.[17]

The government also subsidized temporary disability benefits, designed for employed persons who are temporarily out of work due to sickness (sickness benefits), childbirth (maternity benefits), or other reasons (needy residents benefits).

In addition, the analysis included pensions of disabled veterans, participants in a war, and other special (individual) pensions; social (household) assistance for single pensioners and disabled persons; and assistance for IDPs. Other cash transfers included academic scholarships and monetary benefits for Tbilisi residents to cover utility costs during the winter months.

In-Kind Transfers

Public Education System. The system of education in Georgia consists of preschool; general education (primary, basic, and secondary); and tertiary and vocational education.[18] At all levels of education there are two systems: a free, public education system and a private system. The education sector is dominated by public schools and universities but with a growing share of the private sector in higher and vocational education.

In 2013, Georgia's 2,103 public and 283 private general education schools and universities were teaching more than 700,000 students (World Bank 2014b). For the academic year 2012/13, nearly 88 percent of the students were enrolled in public schools at the preschool, general, and higher education levels while the rest were in private schools. Private education prevails in vocational education institutions, with only 40 percent of the vocational students enrolled in public schools. The total public educational budget accounted for 2.8 percent of GDP in 2013.[19]

Preschool education was cofinanced to the extent of 30 percent by parental contributions until September 2013, when contributions were abolished. The annual total cost per student varied widely across preschools in different municipalities. The country average was GEL 744 (US$310) in 2013. The parental copay was differentiated: most families would pay about GEL 60 (US$25) per month, property tax payers (with annual income above GEL 40,000, or US$16,800) paid around GEL 80 (US$33) per month, and TSA recipients were exempt from the copay.[20] These rates are for Tbilisi preschools, and other municipalities have similar schemes with slightly lower rates. The total budget for preschool education was 0.25 percent of GDP and was allocated for 91,300 preschool students in 2013.

General education in public schools is free, whereas universities' tuition is usually merit-based and paid with state grants. Grants are allocated only for students with high scores on national entrance examinations. The grant amount ranges between 30 percent and 100 percent of total tuition. Schools receive direct fund transfers from the Ministry of Education and Science based on the number of students in a given year. These transfers cover salaries, utilities, and routine maintenance costs. More than 70 percent of all higher education students studied in public universities in 2013, and about a third received state grants to finance education, in part or in full, of which 3 percent received a need-based tuition grant.[21] The total budget for general and higher education was 2.2 percent of GDP.

The cost of university education is high and difficult to afford for a large part of the population. During 2009–13, the annual tuition fee in most public universities was GEL 2,250 (US$1,350) per year and ranged roughly between USD$1,200 and USD$6,424 in private institutions. As a share of GDP per capita, this annual tuition in private institutions represents 37 percent in public institutions, 94 percent in private research universities, and 51 percent in private teaching universities (World Bank 2014a). This level of tuition fees is common to some post-Soviet countries (Azerbaijan, Armenia, and Kazakhstan) but very high relative to countries in Europe and North America as well as other developed countries (Australia, Japan, the Republic of Korea). This puts Georgia among the countries with the highest tuition fees both in public and private tertiary institutions (Salmi and Andguladze 2011; World Bank 2014a).[22]

Public vocational educational institutions include community and vocational colleges that offer preparatory general education programs and vocational education programs and training. Public institutions are financed through a voucher system, and private operators charge tuition fees. Some students are eligible to receive the state voucher and attend private institutions. The eligibility for vouchers is determined by the students' socioeconomic background and educational standing.[23]

Public Health System. The health care system in 2013 comprised two major programs: the State Health Insurance Program (or MIP) and UHC. Combined, this noncontributory health spending accounted for 1.8 percent of GDP in 2013 (as shown earlier in table 4.2).

MIP, launched in June 2011, was designed mostly for the poor, aiming to provide medical services free of charge and without limitation by covering the premiums for health insurance provided by private companies. The beneficiaries of MIP included in the analysis and directly identifiable in the survey are socially vulnerable families,[24] IDPs, teachers and administrative-technical staff of public schools and vocational training centers, all pensioners, children under 6 years of age, students, and military servants. MIP funds outpatient services; laboratorial and instrumental examinations and tests; medical referrals and prescriptions; and inpatient services, including emergency treatment, hospitalization, surgical intervention, and medical facility expenses.

Following the October 2012 elections, the government announced that all Georgians, refugees, or stateless persons would be eligible for state-funded health care—that is, UHC. At the end of February 2013, the uninsured population was extended a package that included basic primary health care services paid via capitation to primary care providers by the Social Service Agency (SSA) and coverage of emergency or trauma care at hospitals paid via fee-for-service reimbursement by SSA. In July 2013, this package was expanded to include a comprehensive range of services very similar to those covered by the MIP program already available to the poor, pensioners, teachers, and children.

The program coverage varied by type of beneficiary and type of service. Veterans and individuals reaching retirement age received 100 percent coverage for all services. Other individuals received full coverage for the minimum package (regular outpatient services), preventive services, and most tests, while receiving about 70–80 percent coverage for other services (surgeries, emergency, delivery, and specific tests). These packages mostly exclude an outpatient drug component, on which very high out-of-pocket spending was registered. These services were also reimbursed on a fee-for-service basis by SSA according to the claims submitted by providers.

Nonsocial Spending: Subsidies and Agricultural Cards
Subsidies
This study includes two subsidies administered by Tbilisi, the capital of Georgia, specifically for Tbilisi residents: the Program of Communal Subsidies (PCS) and the Subsidy for Public Transportation.[25] The PCS subsidizes the cost of utilities for selected households during the winter months, including electric energy, cleaning, and water payments. Households and families registered in the "Socially Unprotected Households Database in Tbilisi" with a rating score up to 1.2 times the threshold for qualifying for TSA are eligible for the PCS in January, February, March, November, and December. All other Tbilisi households receive the PCS in January, February, and March. The PCS covered 382,000 households and accounted for about 0.08 percent of GDP in 2013.

Public transportation in Tbilisi is provided either free or subsidized for eligible individuals (pensioners, teachers, IDPs, people with disabilities, and employees of various ministries including defense) when using the city bus transport, underground electric transport (metro), and cable car. This analysis includes subsidies for retired and socially vulnerable individuals, who pay a reduced fare of GEL 0.20. (The general amount of municipal travel fare equals GEL 0.50, thus 60 percent of total cost of transportation is subsidized.) The total number of beneficiaries in these categories in 2013 was 226,596 (retired) and 164,338 (socially vulnerable). The total Subsidy for Public Transportation budget for all categories of eligible individuals accounted for 0.24 percent of GDP.

Agricultural Cards
Agricultural development is one of Georgia's strategic, high-priority issues, and adequate development of the sector can contribute to rapid economic growth and significant improvement of living standards. Under the initiative of the Ministry of Agriculture and with the financial support from the Rural and Agricultural Development Fund (launched in 2013), the Small Landowner Farmers Supporting Spring Project was designed to stimulate farmers' involvement in production of one-year and perennial crops if farmers use or actually own up to 5 hectares of agricultural land.

In the 2013 Spring Project, 710,479 beneficiaries (farmers) received assistance in the form of Agricultural Cards worth GEL 195,551,811 (US$82.1 million), which is about 0.73 percent of GDP. Agricultural Cards worth GEL 190,120,332 (US$79.9 million), amounting to 0.71 percent of GDP, were cashed by the agricultural goods suppliers and service provider companies by the end of 2013, and 207,326 hectares of beneficiary-owned land were plowed within the project.[26]

Agricultural Cards came in four types with various benefit amounts and eligible purchases. The benefit amount depended on the crop type (perennial or one-year crop) and the land area. Eligible purchases included plowing and disking the soil, farming goods, agricultural materials, and equipment. Some of the qualified farmers did not receive the benefits in 2013 because of identification issues. The list of potential beneficiaries was expanded to 800,000 farmers for the Spring Project of 2014.[27]

Methodology, Data, and Assumptions

Methodology

Following the recommendations of the CEQ project's state-of-the-art incidence analysis, here we describe the methodology followed to construct the five key income concepts: market income, net market income, disposable income, consumable income, and final income.

We assume that the income reported by each household in the IHS comes from labor, capital, and property incomes net of taxes. We also assume that the burden of taxes falls entirely on the household in the form of lower income or increased prices. Thus, the analysis starts by identifying "net market income" as the aggregation of net labor income, net income from capital, and net income properties and private transfers. From net market income, we construct "market income" by grossing up by the amount paid in direct taxes. Therefore, market income comprises gross (pretax) wages, salaries, and income earned from capital assets (rent, interest, profits, or dividends). Pensions are not treated as part of market income.[28]

In addition, we include in market income the value of self-production (also referred as autoconsumption), imputed rent for owner-occupied housing, private transfers (remittances and other private transfers such as alimony), and income from the sale of agricultural production. The value of self-production is calculated based on reported products of own production (or received free of charge) valued at median local market prices. The imputed value of owner-occupied housing is estimated using national accounts information, which estimates this value at 4.4 percent of total household expenditures. Income from the sale of agricultural products is collected in the IHS, and thanks to the survey design (rotating panel) and available data for the previous and following year, we are able to capture sales for the whole year, avoiding seasonality issues. Market income is then divided by the number of members in each household to arrive at per capita market income.

"Disposable income" is constructed by adding direct cash transfers to net market income. These transfers mainly include pensions, assistance for socially vulnerable families (TSA), Agricultural Cards, the monetary benefits for families in need in Tbilisi, and other minor transfers.

Next, we create "consumable income" (also sometimes called postfiscal income) by (a) subtracting from disposable income the impact of indirect taxes (VAT and excise taxes) and (b) adding to disposable income the subsidies distributed by the municipality of Tbilisi for utilities and transportation.

We obtain "final income" by adding to consumable income in-kind benefits—in this case, free or subsidized health and education services. The specific assumptions regarding tax shifting, tax evasion, program take-up, and monetization of in-kind transfers in education and health are presented in the "Assumptions" subsection below.

There are some important caveats about what the fiscal incidence analysis does *not* address. We are unable to include some important taxes and spending that are included in the general government budget. Revenues such as corporate income and international trade as well as spending categories such as infrastructure investments (including urban services and rural roads, for example) are excluded even though they affect income distribution and poverty.[29] In addition, since the analysis focuses on tax and spending programs that are on-budget and are part of the general government, it excludes operations of state-owned enterprises.

Data

The income concepts are built using the 2013 IHS microdata collected by the National Statistics Office of Georgia (Geostat). The survey is representative at the national level, for urban and rural areas, and at most administrative divisions (all nine regions and one city, Tbilisi).[30] It contains data on household income, expenditures, cash transfers, utilization of health and educational services, and characteristics of households and their members for 11,102 households and 39,926 individuals.

Data on government revenues and expenditures for 2013 come from the Ministry of Finance (MoF), the MoF's Treasury Service, and the SSA. Data on education enrollments and spending come from the MoF and the Ministry of Education and Science of Georgia. Aggregate data on other macroeconomic variables (GDP, population, consumption, and so on), poverty, and inequality variables are obtained from Geostat, the World Bank's World Development Indicators database, and the World Bank's Europe and Central Asia Team for Statistical Development.

Georgia's national accounts and administrative fiscal data are used to map the taxes and transfers to individual members in a household. In some instances, as in the case of most transfers, information reported in the IHS matches quite closely with the administrative records. In other instances (for example, income taxes and subsidies), no information is available in the survey, and the household-level information is imputed based on usage data, consumption data, or the reported use of public services by individual households. By assigning or using the taxes and transfers reported in the survey, we are able to construct the four different income categories required for the analysis.

Assumptions

Taxes

Tax assumptions are as follows. The PIT burden is borne by the income recipient. PITs are not reported in the IHS; therefore, we simulated them based on the reported earned income, which is assumed to be net of taxes (net market income). In the case of labor income, we assumed a rate of 20 percent withheld by employers, applying tax deductions and exemptions to qualified households in accordance with the tax code (low-wage earners, single mothers, and persons with disabilities). Our incidence analysis assumed that individuals receiving income from self-employment or from a secondary job evade taxes. Income earned abroad is not subject to income taxation.

Property taxes on real estate were estimated by applying statutory tax rates to the imputed real estate property value. Property values were imputed using a model for real estate property values—a linear regression on the logarithm of the dwelling price, against characteristics of the dwelling, household income per capita, and location dummies (region and urban/rural). All variables are reported in the survey.[31] Property taxes on land were also estimated by applying tax rates to the land area reported in the survey.

The burden of consumption taxes were assumed to fall entirely on the consumers in the form of increased prices. To take into account informality and ineffective tax administration, effective tax rates were applied to all household purchases excluding exempt goods.[32] The effective rate of the VAT was calculated as a ratio of total VAT revenue collections in 2013 to the consumption in the national income accounts that was subject to VAT.[33] The tax was estimated by applying the effective tax rates to household expenditures, excluding the exemptions provided by the tax code. Excise rates were also applied to household purchases using effective rates. The effective tax rates were obtained as a ratio of total excise revenue collections to the consumption data.[34] Excise taxes paid were estimated based on the type and the quantity of the excisable product consumed (as provided in the survey) using effective tax rates.

Transfers

Direct Transfers. The direct transfers collected in the IHS are the old-age pension; disability pension; IDP benefits; assistance for socially vulnerable families (TSA); and other, smaller transfers.[35]

In addition, we considered the Agricultural Cards to be a direct transfer. The money received through this program can only be used for agricultural production–related items such as seeds or plowing equipment, so it is not a traditional cash transfer program whereby the recipient can freely spend the money. However, we categorize it as a direct transfer because its definition is closest to that of the other types of transfers and subsidies defined by the CEQ methodology. The beneficiaries were identified using the eligibility rules of the program, and the transfers adjusted proportional to the size of the plot, as stipulated by the program.

The monetary benefits distributed in Tbilisi through the PCS are not reported in the IHS and were assigned to TSA beneficiaries, following the program eligibility criteria. Therefore, the analysis also includes them among the direct transfers.

In contrast with in-kind transfers, direct transfers reported directly in the IHS were not scaled down but were left as reported in the survey because the aggregate information in terms of beneficiaries and distributed amounts matched reasonably well with the administrative records.[36] Robustness checks indicated that scaling down direct transfers would lead to similar qualitative results, albeit with smaller magnitudes.[37]

In-Kind Transfers. In-kind education benefits are calculated as the average government spending per student by type of educational institution (preschool, primary, secondary, tertiary, and vocational), defined as ratio of the budget for each type of school and the number of students. The data on government spending is obtained from the MoF and enrollment data from the Ministry of Education and Science of Georgia.

Since parental copayments for preschool were abolished in September 2013, for simplicity we assumed that households benefited from free preschool during the whole year. To identify preschool, general, higher, and vocational education students, we used information from the household roster in the IHS. However, since the survey reports only attendance but not *who* attended public institutions, we used data available in the 2011 IHS to identify the percentage of students who attend public schools. Using data on tuition payments in 2013 IHS, we assigned the students with the highest tuition payments to private education until the 2011 percentage was matched.

We used an imputation method and insurance values to estimate in-kind health benefits. For the targeted MIP, which covers the cost of health insurance premiums for families in need, we used information from the household roster, where insurance is reported at the individual level, to identify beneficiaries and assign the national average premium paid by the government to each beneficiary (GEL 150, or US$63 per year). In addition, we included people who satisfied the eligibility criteria (that is, children, IDPs, or people with disabilities).

In contrast, for UHC, which directly covers health care expenses, we identified beneficiaries using information from the household roster ("Other forms of health insurance") and information on the use of health services in accordance with the rules of the UHC program.[38] Each beneficiary is assigned the annual average cost (GEL 350, or US$147) obtained from the Ministry of Labor, Health and Social Affairs, using benefit amounts for inpatient and outpatient services.

Subsidized public transportation in Tbilisi for pensioners and TSA beneficiaries are estimated using the cost of travel on intraurban and local transportation directly identified in the IHS.[39] The subsidized tariff is equal to 40 percent of the total cost of transportation. The benefits from the PCS program in Tbilisi are imputed using administrative tariffs and eligibility criteria. We use the administrative amounts of subsidized utilities allocated per eligible household per month to calculate the implicit subsidy for TSA beneficiaries and helpless families who applied for assistance to the SSA.

Other considerations included scaling down the in-kind transfers (health and education) and Agricultural Cards. These benefits were scaled down to better match administrative data, using the ratio between households' consumption reported in the IHS and the national accounts. Spatial deflators were used as a robustness check, and the results were consistent with those without the use of deflation.

Main Results

Redistributive and Poverty Effects

Table 4.3 illustrates how fiscal interventions affect different quintiles of the per capita income distribution. The income of the bottom 60 percent increased moving from market income to final income, with the largest increase experienced by the poorest 20 percent. The top 40 percent, in contrast, are net payers. Although indirect taxes reduced the incomes of the poor, social spending raised their incomes considerably.

Comparing market income with consumable (postfiscal) income, which accounts for direct and indirect taxes and cash transfers, the bottom 40 percent saw their income almost double their initial market income. After incorporating in-kind transfers, the income of the bottom 40 percent grew even further, with final income more than doubling their initial market income.

The overall fiscal system in Georgia contributes to reducing poverty and improving equity. Georgia's Gini coefficient falls by more than 0.12 points when moving from market income to final income (table 4.4). Relative to other countries in CEQ sample, Georgia's reduction in inequality was above average.[40]

Poverty rates are also considerably affected by taxes and transfers. Poverty at the US$2.50 per day line falls from 39.2 percent to 30 percent when moving

Table 4.3 Distributional Impact of Fiscal Policies in Georgia, by Income Quintile, 2013

Measurement	Quintile					All
	1 (poorest)	2	3	4	5 (richest)	
Population (no.)	734,738	735,268	734,902	734,754	735,416	3,675,078
Market income[a] (US$/day p.c.)	0.6	1.9	3.4	5.5	13.1	4.9
Net market income[b] (US$/day p.c.)	0.6	1.8	3.2	5.1	11.4	4.4
Change wrt market income (%)	−0.4	−2.1	−5.5	−8.8	−12.8	−9.8
Disposable income[c] (US$/day p.c.)	2.1	2.9	4.0	5.8	12.0	5.4
Change wrt market income (%)	267.3	54.1	19.4	4.3	−8.3	9.6
Consumable income[d] (US$/day p.c.)	1.8	2.5	3.5	5.1	10.9	4.8
Change wrt market income (%)	216.4	34.2	4.2	−7.7	−17.1	−2.7
Final income[e] (US$/day p.c.)	2.2	2.8	3.8	5.4	11.1	5.1
Change wrt market income (%)	276.3	51.2	13.5	−2.4	−15.3	3.5

Source: Based on 2013 Integrated Household Survey (IHS) data.
Note: Income was measured as daily per capita income in U.S. dollars, 2005 purchasing power parity (PPP). p.c. = per capita; wrt = with respect to.
a. "Market income" comprises pretax wages, salaries, income earned from capital assets (rent, interest, or dividends), and private transfers.
b. "Net market income" = market income − direct taxes and contributions.
c. "Disposable income" = market income − direct taxes and contributions + cash transfers (including noncontributory pensions).
d. "Consumable income" = disposable income − indirect taxes (value added, import duties, and excises) + indirect subsidies.
e. "Final income" = consumable income + in-kind transfers (such as health care and education expenditure).

Table 4.4 Impact of Fiscal Policy on Inequality and Poverty in Georgia, by Income Concept, 2013

Indicator	Market income[a]	Net market income[b]	Disposable income[c]	Consumable income[d]	Final income[e]
Inequality					
Gini coefficient[f]	0.507	0.489	0.395	0.411	0.383
Ratio p90/p10[g]	18.7	16.5	6.2	7.0	5.8
Poverty headcount (FGT0)[h]					
US$2.50/day PPP (%)	39.2	40.7	23.3	30.0	n.a.
US$5.00/day PPP (%)	67.1	70.4	61.5	67.6	n.a.
Poverty gap (FGT1)[h]					
US$2.50/day PPP	20.6	21.0	8.1	11.6	n.a.
US$5.00/day PPP	37.5	39.1	25.8	31.2	n.a.
Poverty intensity (FGT2)[h]					
US$2.50/day PPP	14.1	14.3	4.2	6.6	n.a.
US$5.00/day PPP	26.3	27.1	14.4	18.6	n.a.

Source: Based on 2013 Integrated Household Survey (IHS) data.
Note: PPP = purchasing power parity; n.a. = not applicable (not included in table estimates; see note "h" below).
a. "Market income" comprises pretax wages, salaries, income earned from capital assets (rent, interest, or dividends), and private transfers.
b. "Net market income" = market income − direct taxes and contributions.
c. "Disposable income" = market income − direct taxes and contributions + direct cash transfers (including noncontributory pensions).
d. "Consumable income" = disposable income − indirect taxes (value added, import duties, and excises) + indirect subsidies.
e. "Final income" = consumable income + in-kind transfers (such as public health and education expenditure).
f. The Gini coefficient measures the inequality of income distribution, from 0 (full equality) to 1 (maximum inequality).
g. Ratio p90/p10 = ratio of 90th percentile to 10th percentile.
h. FGT refers to Foster-Greer-Thorbecke indexes, a family of poverty metrics that presents poverty along three dimensions: The "poverty headcount" (FGT0) is the percentage of the population that is poor. The "poverty gap" (FGT1) is the average percentage by which individuals fall below the poverty line. "Poverty intensity" (FGT2), calculated as the poverty gap index squared at the household level, implicitly gives greater weight to those furthest below the poverty line. The FGT indexes are not estimated here under final income because final income adds only the effects of in-kind transfers, which do not affect household spendable income.

from market to consumable income (table 4.4)—the largest reduction in poverty among countries for which CEQ analysis was performed.[41] Using the regional moderate poverty line in use by the World Bank (US$5 per day), poverty remains at almost the same level when moving from market income (67.1 percent) to consumable income (67.6 percent).

An analysis of households' position income distribution under the different income aggregates shows that only the three top deciles and the households with per capita earnings above US$5 per day are net payers, registering final incomes lower than their market incomes (figure 4.2). Similar dynamics in poverty and inequality reduction are observed when using "per adult equivalent" measures of income distribution. The Gini coefficient falls by about 0.10 points when moving from market income to final income (from 0.483 to 0.374). The poverty rate (at US$2.50 per day) declines from 20.3 percent to 7.7 percent when moving from market income to consumable income (World Bank 2015a).

The considerable redistribution attained by the fiscal interventions is explained mostly by reductions in vertical equity (VE) rather than by reranking (RR) of the households. (For more about how VE, reranking, and horizontal equity are defined and used in the analyses throughout this volume, see chapter 1.)

Figure 4.2 Income Aggregates as a Percentage of Market Income in Georgia, by Household Income Decile, 2013

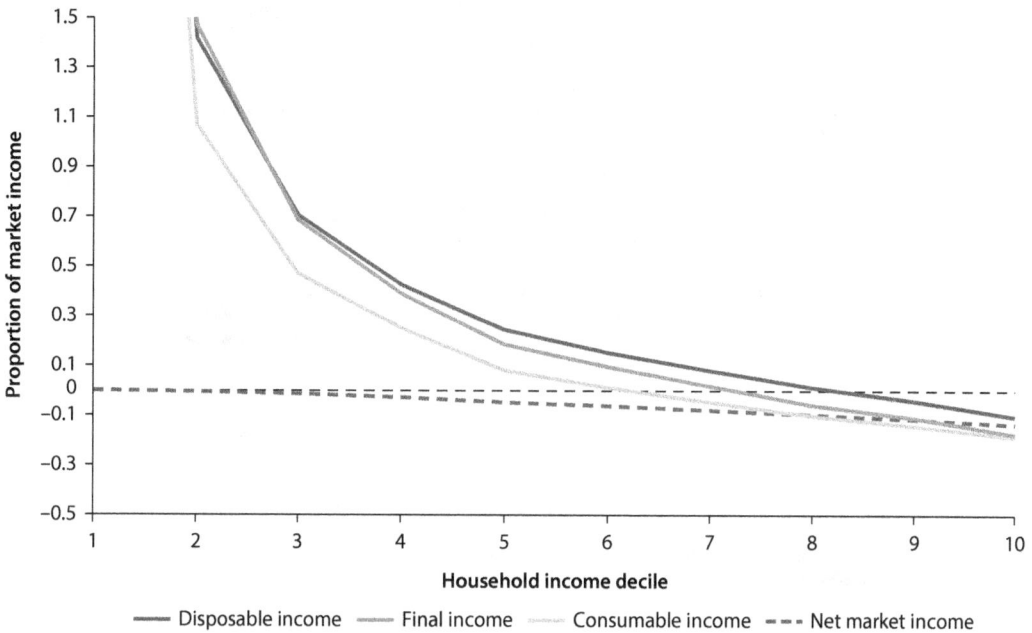

Source: Based on 2013 Integrated Household Survey (IHS) data.

Note: The income aggregates are as follows: "Market income" comprises pretax wages, salaries, income earned from capital assets (rent, interest, or dividends), and private transfers. "Net market income" = market income – direct taxes and contributions. "Disposable income" = market income – direct taxes + cash transfers (including noncontributory pensions). "Consumable income" = disposable income – indirect taxes (value added taxes, import duties and excises) + indirect subsidies. "Final income" = consumable income + in-kind transfers (such as public health and education expenditure).

RR represents approximately 20 percent, 27 percent, and 21 percent of the VE reduction when moving from market income to disposable income, consumable income, or final income, respectively (table 4.5).

A complementary measure of fairness of the fiscal interventions, "fiscal impoverishment" (based on Higgins and Lustig 2015), indicates the extent to which households are actually hurt by the interventions—in the case of Georgia, whether the tax and transfer system pushes some nonpoor households below the poverty line. Depending on the income aggregates used for this comparison, the percentage of households whose incomes decrease such that they fall below the poverty line (US$2.50 per day per capita) is either 2 percent (from market income to disposable income); 13 percent (from market income to consumable income); or close to 7 percent (from market income to final income).

The monetary loss is minimal for those who become fiscally impoverished in the change from market income to disposable income (0.2 percent of market income). However, the monetary loss is higher for those who become fiscally impoverished in the other comparisons: it is close to 4 percent from market income and consumable income and 2 percent from market income to final income.

Table 4.5 Redistributive, Vertical Equity, and Reranking Effects of Fiscal Policy in Georgia, 2013

Indicator	Disposable income[a] change wrt market income[b]	Consumable income[c] change wrt market income	Final income[d] change wrt market income
Redistributive effect (change in Gini)[e]	0.113	0.096	0.124
Vertical equity (VE)[f]	0.140	0.131	0.157
Reranking effect (RR)[g]	0.028	0.035	0.033
Horizontal inequity (RR/VE)[h]	20.3	26.7	21.1

Source: Based on 2013 Integrated Household Survey (IHS) data.

Note: wrt = with respect to.

a. "Disposable income" = market income − direct taxes and contributions + cash transfers and noncontributory pensions.

b. "Market income" comprises pretax wages, salaries, income earned from capital assets (rent, interest, or dividends), and private transfers.

c. "Consumable income" = disposable income − indirect taxes (value added taxes, import duties, and excises) + indirect subsidies.

d. "Final income" = consumable income + in-kind transfers (such as public health and education expenditure).

e. "Redistributive effect" refers to the change in inequality associated with fiscal policy (direct and indirect taxes, direct transfers, and subsidies) as shown in the change in the Gini coefficient (a measure of the inequality of income distribution, ranging from 0 for full equality to 1 for maximum inequality).

f. Vertical equity (VE) refers to the change in Gini due to adding different fiscal interventions, while keeping the original ranking fixed. It is equal to the difference between the Gini coefficient for incomes *before* taxes and transfers and the concentration coefficient for incomes *after* taxes and transfers.

g. The reranking effect (RR) is a measure of inequity that shows whether the fiscal system changes the ordering of households in the income distribution. It is equal to the difference between the Gini coefficient for incomes *after* taxes and transfers and the concentration coefficient for incomes *after* taxes and transfers.

h. Horizontal inequity is calculated as the RR effect as a proportion of the VE effect, or RR/VE.

Progressivity, Marginal Contributions, and Pro-Poorness of Taxes and Transfers

Overall, Georgia's fiscal system is equity enhancing, although the effects of different taxes and transfers vary in sign and magnitude. Consumable and final income as percentages of market income for different income groups show that the bottom benefits relatively more than the top from these interventions (figure 4.3). This redistributive effect is driven by the transfers and subsidies in place, although taxes partially offset this effect at the bottom.

Taxes

There is a stark contrast between direct and indirect taxes in their distributional effect: direct taxes are progressive (concentrating more in the top deciles), whereas indirect taxes are more evenly distributed. Together the result is a regressive tax system, especially for the lowest deciles of the income distribution, whereas it is almost neutral for the top deciles based on market income.[42]

Georgia's direct tax system is progressive, as shown in the concentration curves for taxes (figure 4.4). Among direct taxes, PIT is the largest component and is largely progressive despite being a flat-rate tax (of 20 percent). Other direct taxes are also concentrated in the upper section of the income distribution, hence making direct taxes as a group progressive. In addition, household surveys usually do not capture the top of the income distribution well—where property tax,

Figure 4.3 Taxes, Transfers, Consumable Income, and Final Income Relative to Market Income in Georgia, by Income Group, 2013

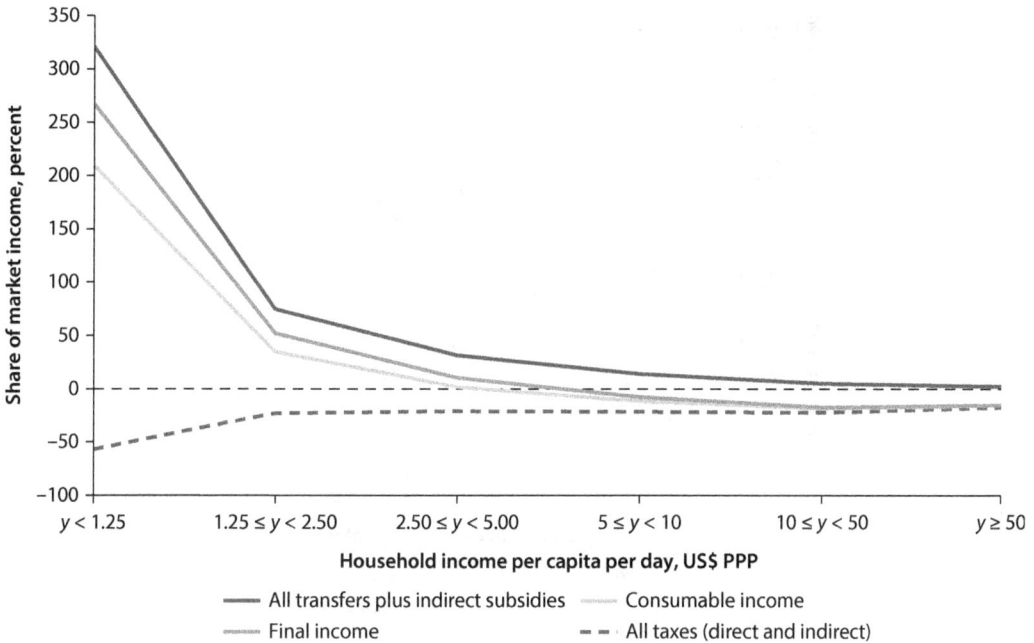

Household income per capita per day, US$ PPP

— All transfers plus indirect subsidies   Consumable income
— Final income   – – All taxes (direct and indirect)

Source: Based on 2013 Integrated Household Survey (IHS) data.
Note: Figure shows curves for transfers, taxes, consumable income, and final income relative to market income, by household income group (*y*). "Market income" comprises pretax wages, salaries, income earned from capital assets (rent, interest, or dividends), and private transfers. "Consumable income" = market income – direct and indirect taxes + direct cash transfers (including noncontributory pensions) and indirect subsidies. "Final income" = consumable income + in-kind transfers (such as public health and education expenditure). "Indirect subsidies" include subsidies for utilities and transportation. "Direct taxes" include income, capital gains, and property taxes. "Indirect taxes" include value added taxes (VAT) and excise taxes.

capital gains tax, and property income tax payments are mostly concentrated—which means that the progressivity of those taxes may be underestimated. Finally, the PIT exemption for low-income earners introduced in 2013 enhanced the progressivity of PIT; without the exemption, PIT would still be progressive but less so.

In addition, the Kakwani index for direct taxes confirms their progressivity (table 4.6). Marginal contributions also allow us to conclude that the fiscal system is more equalizing thanks to the progressivity of direct taxes. The marginal contribution of direct taxes to the reduction in the Gini index is close to 0.2 points. Direct taxes increase poverty somewhat, though, increasing the poverty headcount (at per capita income of US$2.50 per day) from 40.3 percent to 41.9 percent when direct taxes are subtracted from market income. However, this impact is quite small and largely compensated for by other fiscal interventions.

As for indirect taxes, Georgia's system is regressive. Although the VAT, excise taxes, and indirect taxes overall are more concentrated in the highest deciles, their distribution is less proportional than disposable income, meaning that the

Figure 4.4 Progressivity of Taxes in Georgia, 2013

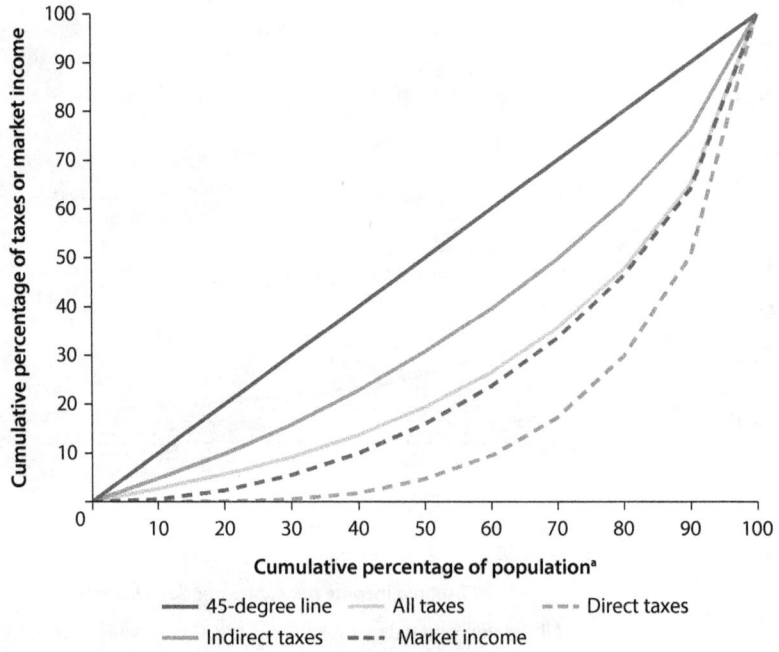

Source: Based on 2013 Integrated Household Survey (IHS) data.
Note: Figure shows concentration curves for taxes and Lorenz curves representing the distribution of "direct taxes," "indirect taxes," "all taxes," and "market income." "Market income" comprises pretax wages, salaries, and income earned from capital assets (rent, interest, or dividends) and private transfers. "Direct taxes" include income, capital gains, and property taxes. "Indirect taxes" include value added and excise taxes.
a. The cumulative proportion of the population is ordered by market income.

Table 4.6 Kakwani Indexes for, and Marginal Contributions of, Taxes and Social Expenditures in Georgia, 2013

| | Kakwani index[a] | Marginal contribution, by income concept[b] (change in Gini index) | | |
		Market to disposable	Market to consumable	Market to final
Redistributive effect (all interventions)	n.a.	0.1125	0.0961	0.1244
Direct taxes	0.1818	0.020	0.021	0.022
PIT	0.1829	0.020	0.020	0.022
Direct transfers	0.7064	0.094	0.113	0.100
Old-age pensions	0.6584	0.052	0.062	0.057
TSA	1.0781	0.016	0.018	0.015
Indirect taxes	−0.2297	n.a.	−0.018	−0.014
VAT	−0.2151	n.a.	−0.014	−0.010
Excises	−0.3108	n.a.	−0.006	−0.005
Indirect subsidies	0.3715	n.a.	−0.000	0.000

table continues next page

Table 4.6 Kakwani Indexes for, and Marginal Contributions of, Taxes and Social Expenditures in Georgia, 2013 *(continued)*

	Kakwani index[a]	*Marginal contribution, by income concept*[b] *(change in Gini index)*		
		Market to disposable	*Market to consumable*	*Market to final*
In-kind education	0.5415	n.a.	n.a.	0.020
Preschool	0.5176	n.a.	n.a.	0.002
General	0.5851	n.a.	n.a.	0.016
Higher	0.2915	n.a.	n.a.	0.001
In-kind health	0.6360	n.a.	n.a.	−0.008
MIP	0.7004	n.a.	n.a.	−0.007
UHC	0.3717	n.a.	n.a.	−0.001

Source: Based on 2013 Integrated Household Survey (IHS) data.

Note: MIP = Medical Insurance Program for the poor; PIT = personal income tax; TSA = Targeted Social Assistance; UHC = Universal Health Care; VAT = value added tax; n.a. = not applicable.

a. Kakwani coefficients measure whether a fiscal intervention exercises an equalizing or unequalizing force, calculated by subtracting the intervention's concentration coefficient from the market income Gini; progressive interventions have positive Kakwani coefficients, and regressive ones have negative coefficients.

b. The "marginal contribution" columns show the degree of change in the Gini coefficient from one income concept to another when the designated tax or transfer is taken into account (the Gini being a measurement of income inequality ranging from 0 for full equality to 1 for maximum inequality). The income concepts are as follows: "Market income" comprises pretax wages, salaries, and income earned from capital assets (rent, interest, or dividends) and private transfers. "Disposable income" = market income − direct taxes and contributions + direct cash transfers (including noncontributory pensions). "Consumable income" = disposable income − indirect taxes (value added taxes, import duties, and excises) + indirect subsidies. "Final income" = consumable income + in-kind transfers (such as public health and education expenditure).

poor tend to spend a higher percentage of their income than the rich on indirect taxes. The Kakwani index is negative for indirect taxes (table 4.6), confirming their regressive nature.

Even though VAT has a number of exemptions, they do not influence the progressivity of the tax. VAT exemptions are distributed across the income distribution in almost the same way as the VAT itself. The exemptions in value terms benefit the upper end of the income distribution the most and, relative to market income, do not quite improve the progressivity of the VAT. Therefore, exemptions, especially the least pro-poor of them, could be eliminated to improve equity and enhance collections.[43]

Georgia's excise taxes are more regressive than the VAT. Excises are the only taxes the government can levy under the Economic Liberty Act without a referendum, but because of their regressive nature, a universal increase of tax rates would make the poor bear a heavier burden.

Overall, the net fiscal system is more unequalizing with the current system of indirect taxes than with direct taxes. The marginal contribution of indirect taxes to the Gini index is estimated at 0.018 if we consider all taxes and transfers except in-kind transfers (consumable income) and 0.0145 when we also include the incidence of in-kind transfers (final income). Indirect taxes also increase poverty, explaining almost entirely the increase in poverty observed between disposable and consumable income (only marginally affected by indirect subsidies).

Direct Transfers and Indirect Subsidies

Direct transfers in Georgia are progressive in absolute terms: per capita transfers decline with income, as shown in the concentration curves for transfers (figure 4.5). The TSA is clearly progressive, concentrating on the bottom deciles of the distribution. Old-age pensions are also progressive in absolute terms, and, being the largest program (representing 62 percent of all direct transfers), they influence the final shape of the consolidated Lorenz curve for "all direct transfers."

The Agricultural Card program—with a concentration coefficient close to zero (figure 4.6) and a concentration curve almost equal to the diagonal (figure 4.5)—is near neutral in absolute terms: that is, the per capita transfer is the same for everybody.[44] Overall, however, the direct transfers are progressive in absolute terms, and they help to increase considerably the market income of those in the bottom decile in Georgia.

The Kakwani indexes and marginal contributions of cash transfers (as shown earlier in table 4.6) imply that the progressive nature of cash transfers reduce poverty and inequality in Georgia. Direct transfers are responsible for the large decrease in poverty observed between net market and disposable income

Figure 4.5 Progressivity of Selected Direct Transfers and Indirect Subsidies in Georgia, 2013

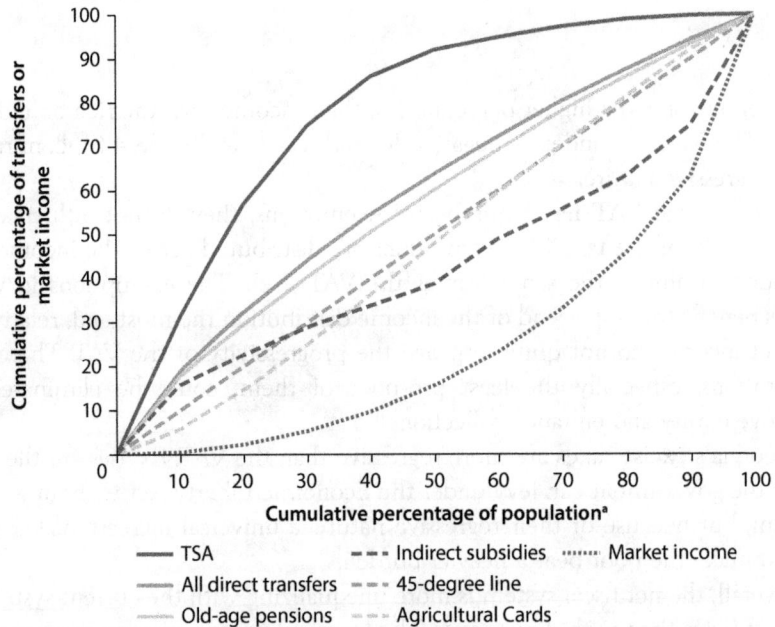

Source: Based on 2013 Integrated Household Survey (IHS) data.
Note: Figure shows concentration curves for spending and Lorenz curves representing the distribution of "all direct transfers" and "market income," which comprises pretax wages, salaries, and income earned from capital assets (rent, interest, or dividends) and private transfers. "Direct transfers" include old-age pensions, TSA, and Agricultural Cards. "Indirect subsidies" include subsidized utilities and public transportation for Tbilisi residents. TSA = Targeted Social Assistance.
a. The cumulative proportion of the population is ordered by market income.

Figure 4.6 Concentration Coefficients of Social Spending Categories in Georgia, 2013

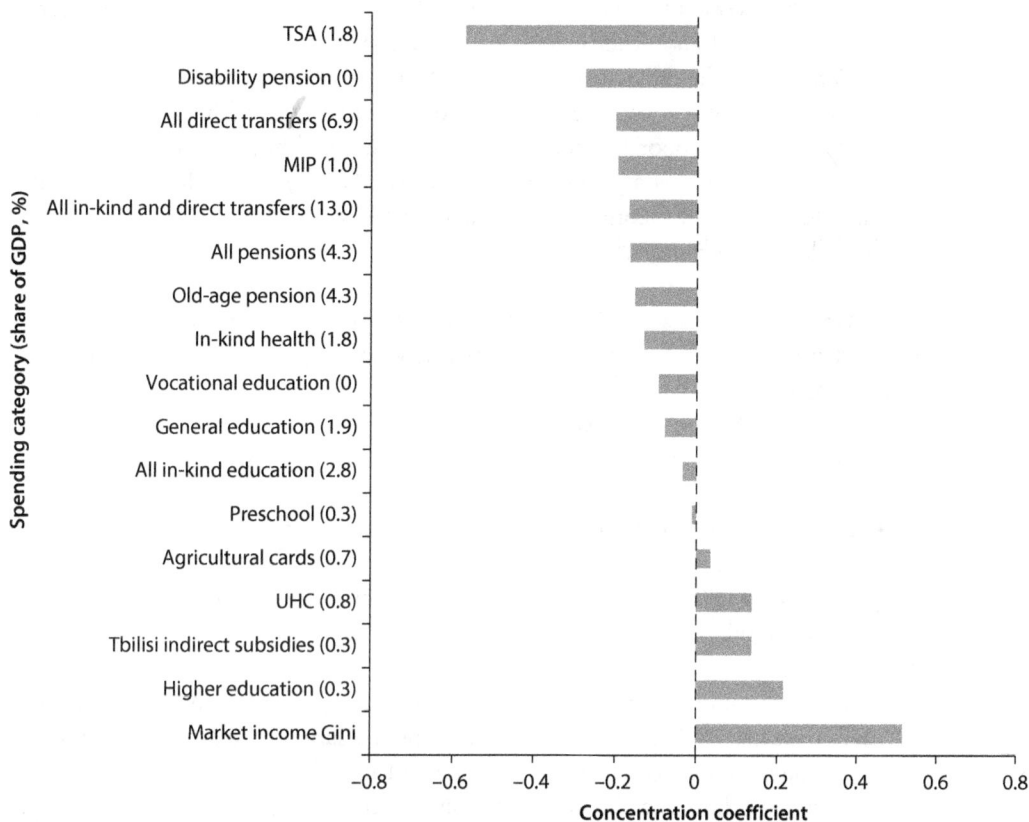

Source: Based on 2013 Integrated Housing Survey (IHS) data.
Note: Figure shows the concentration coefficient for each type of social spending relative to its equivalent percentage of GDP (shown in parentheses after each category) when households are ordered by market income (comprising comprises pretax wages, salaries, income earned from capital assets, and private transfers). As further discussed in chapter 1, spending is "progressive" when the concentration coefficient is lower than Georgia's market-income Gini (0.51); it is also "pro-poor" when the concentration coefficient is not only lower than the market-income Gini but also negative. GDP = gross domestic product; MIP = Medical Insurance Program for the poor; TSA = Targeted Social Assistance; UHC = Universal Health Care.

(18 percentage points), and they also reduce the Gini index by close to 0.10 point. Pensions, in particular, play an important role in diminishing poverty, given their magnitude. Rough estimations indicate that pensions are responsible for two-thirds of the observed reductions assigned to direct transfers.[45]

The Tbilisi indirect subsidies are progressive in relative terms—as indicated by their Kakwani index (table 4.6) and by the shape of their concentration curve, which is predominantly below the 45-degree line (figure 4.5)—but they are not pro-poor.[46] Although there is some concentration of beneficiaries at the bottom, which drives the curve to go above the 45-degree line for the lowest levels of concentration, most benefits do not go to the bottom of the income distribution. Moreover, these subsidies (the only indirect subsidies considered in this analysis) are only given in Tbilisi, which does not represent the bottom of the national income distribution.

In comparing the values of the concentration coefficients, TSA again is noticeable for the scope of its concentration coefficient, which is much more progressive than that of any other Georgian transfers (figure 4.6).

Considering the efficiency of the direct transfers altogether in terms of reducing poverty, they cover a considerable share of the poverty gap (the average percentage by which the poor fall below the poverty line), although many resources go beyond what is necessary to overcome poverty. The poverty reduction efficiency and effectiveness of Georgia's direct transfers, taken together, can be quantified by the following indicators:[47]

- *Vertical expenditure efficiency:* 54.9 percent of direct transfers go to those identified as market-income poor (those who are poor before receiving direct transfers).
- *Poverty reduction efficiency:* 34.1 percent of the direct transfers are needed to bring the market-income poor up to the per capita poverty line of US$2.50 per day.
- *Spillover:* 37.8 percent of the direct transfers benefit the market-income poor after they have reached the poverty line.
- *Poverty gap efficiency:* 61.3 percent of the direct transfers cover the gap between poor households' incomes and the poverty line.

The vertical expenditure efficiency, roughly 55 percent, signals that although more than half of direct transfers go to the poor, a large share does not. This result is consistent with having old-age pensions (a transfer by design not targeted to the poor) as the main direct transfer and a number of other programs such as the TSA or Tbilisi TSA supplement that effectively benefit the bottom of the distribution.

The poverty reduction efficiency, about 34 percent, shows that roughly a third of the direct transfers go toward moving poor households up to the US$2.50-per-day poverty line (or at least increasing the incomes of poor households that, after the transfers, remain below the poverty line). Consistent with this result, the spillover of almost 38 percent indicates that more than a third of the resources delivered to the poor through direct transfers are spent moving formerly poor households *beyond* the poverty line, which can be considered wasteful. Finally, the poverty gap efficiency, roughly 61 percent, shows that direct transfers cover a large portion of the existing gap between poor households' incomes and the poverty line.

In-Kind Transfers
In-kind transfers—free public services valued at cost, including education and health care—are also progressive as a group, but results for their components differ.

Education. Education in-kind transfers as a whole are progressive, although the general, preschool, and higher education components have different levels of progressivity.

General education, which comprises the primary and secondary levels, is progressive in absolute terms, reporting a concentration coefficient of −0.08 when households are ordered by market income (as shown in figure 4.6). Being the largest component of educational expenses (67 percent), it influences strongly the final progressivity of education expenses. Preschool education is also progressive, although it is slightly more concentrated in the upper deciles of the income distribution (figure 4.7), its concentration coefficient being very close to zero (as shown earlier in figure 4.6).

Finally, the concentration curve for higher education is much closer than the other levels to the curve for market income but is still consistently above it, meaning that although the benefits from higher-education spending are concentrated more heavily among the upper income groups than other educational spending, it is still much less heavily concentrated than market income itself. This last result is consistent with international evidence that higher education is accessible mainly for the middle and upper sections of the income distribution. Representing 10 percent of the budget for education, higher education contributes toward making educational expenses less progressive, but the effect of general education is predominant. When looking at the marginal contributions, overall education reduces inequality by close to 0.2 points in the Gini index, largely driven by the contribution of general education (0.16).

Figure 4.7 Progressivity of Education Spending in Georgia, 2013

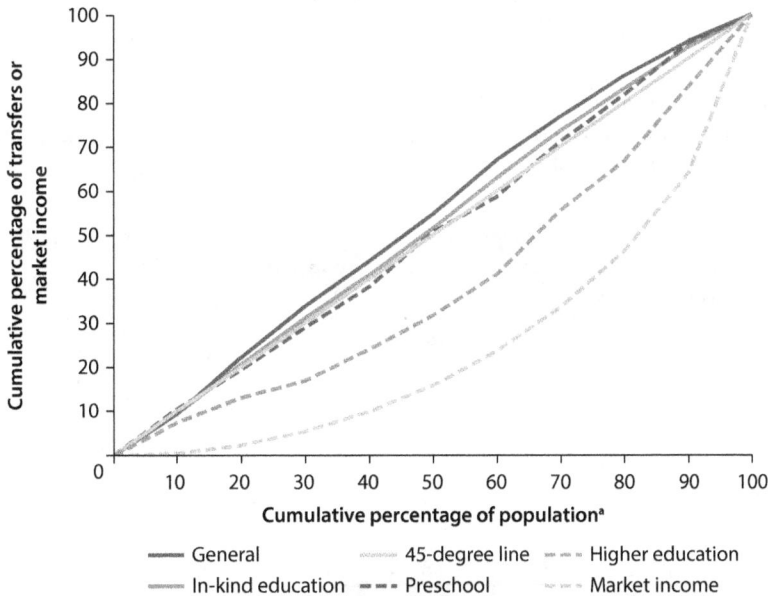

Source: Based on 2013 Integrated Household Survey (IHS) data.
Note: In-kind education benefits are calculated as the average government spending per student by type of educational institution. Data on government spending are obtained from the Ministry of Finance, and enrollment data come from the Ministry of Education and Science of Georgia.
a. The cumulative proportion of the population is ordered by market income.

A public expenditure's coverage rate is the percentage of a qualifying population that benefits from the expenditure. An analysis of the coverage of public education among the households with children of normative age range shows that general education has a very large coverage, reaching close to 90 percent of potential beneficiary households, whereas preschool and higher education show lower but still considerable coverage rates, at 36 percent and 23 percent, respectively (table 4.7).[48]

The distribution of the coverage by income group shows a more nuanced story. In the case of general education, the highest coverage rates are reached at the lowest income level (less than US$1.25 per day in per capita income). In contrast, for preschool and higher education, the highest rates are reported in the middle and higher brackets, respectively, although the levels of coverage for the lowest bracket are always significant: about 34 percent for preschool and 18 percent for higher education. These patterns reflect (a) that the government is reaching the bottom of the distribution, although there is still considerable room for improvement, and (b) that programs designed to be universal (such as educational programs) will inevitably devote resources to nonpoor households, as is evident by the coverage rates of the upper income brackets.

Health Care. Health in-kind transfers are progressive in absolute terms, but different components show different degrees of progressivity. The targeted MIP program is progressive in absolute terms—not surprising in that it covers mainly TSA beneficiaries. UHC, introduced in mid-2013 to provide medical coverage to large population segments that had lacked health insurance, is more concentrated in the upper deciles of the distribution, albeit to a lesser degree than market income.

A consolidation of all of these programs results in a progressive concentration curve, largely driven by the effect of the MIP (figure 4.8). The curve for the consolidated health care program is located between the two individual ones,

Table 4.7 Education Coverage in Georgia, by Level and Income Group, 2013
Percentage of potential beneficiary households

Educational level by normative age range	Income group (US$ per day)						All income groups
	< 1.25	1.25 ≤ y < 2.50	2.50 ≤ y < 5.00	5 ≤ y < 10	10 ≤ y < 50	≥ 50[a]	
Preschool (ages 1–5)	33.8	32.7	39.2	38.9	31.7	n.a.	36.1
General (primary and secondary) (ages 6–17)	91.4	89.4	92.2	88.8	79.6	n.a.	89.8
Tertiary (ages 18–23)	18.0	12.4	22.5	29.1	33.1	0.0	22.6
Total households	2.5	7.1	20.9	31.8	36.7	1.1	100.0

Source: Based on 2013 Integrated Household Survey (IHS) data.
Note: "Education coverage" refers to the percentage of a qualifying group benefiting from public education expenditure. For example, among households living on per capita income of less than US$1.25 per day, 33.8 percent of children ages 1–5 years receive government-funded preschool education. n.a. = not applicable (see note "a").
a. The survey captured very few households in this income group, and among those households, no children of preschool or general-education age are reported.

Figure 4.8 Concentration Curves for MIP, UHC, and Consolidated UHC

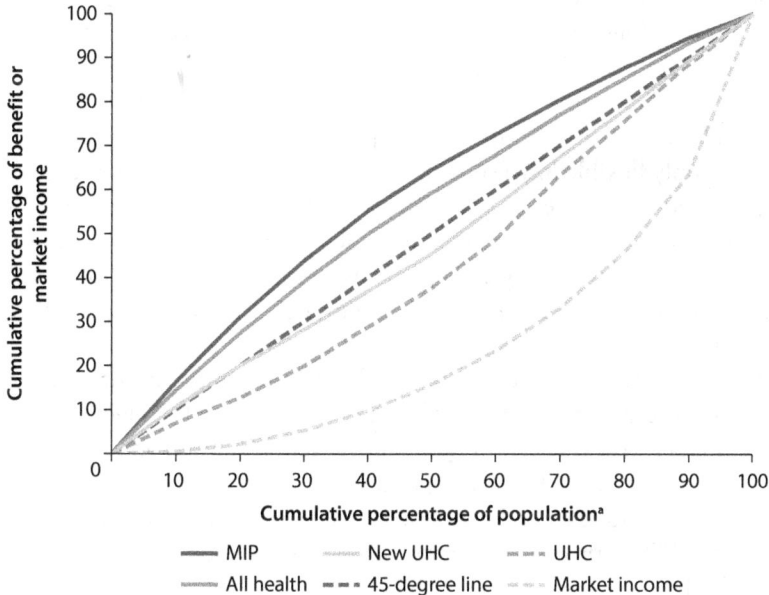

Source: Based on 2013 Integrated Household Survey (IHS) data.
Note: "New UHC" refers to a simulated UHC covering all qualifying beneficiaries in the country, including those currently covered by the MIP. MIP = Medical Insurance Program for the poor; UHC = Universal Health Care.
a. The cumulative proportion of the population is ordered by market income.

gaining progressivity compared with the original UHC because it incorporates both TSA and MIP beneficiaries. The Kakwani indexes also show that Georgia's in-kind transfers in health are progressive, while the marginal contribution results show that in-kind health transfers reduce inequality (by 0.008 Gini points), largely driven by the effect of MIP (0.007 Gini points).

Concluding Remarks

This chapter analyzed the progressivity of tax and transfer systems in Georgia using the 2013 IHS and administrative data, applying the CEQ methodology (Lustig and Higgins 2013). A wide range of fiscal activities were analyzed, among them taxes (personal income, property, value added, and excise taxes); direct transfers (pensions and social assistance programs); in-kind transfers (preschool, general, and tertiary education, UHC, and targeted medical insurance); the Agricultural Card program; and Tbilisi city benefits and subsidies.

Results indicate that Georgia's social spending system is progressive overall, whereas its tax system is regressive overall. In addition, the transfers system is effective at decreasing income inequality and poverty, although the reduction is partially offset by indirect taxes. Government programs vary in their impact on poverty and inequality. TSA is one of the programs that best targets the poorest, and pensions play an important role in reducing poverty in spite of not being the most efficient program in doing so. Pensions are responsible for two-thirds of the observed poverty reduction due to direct transfers.

The analysis suggests that although the fiscal system is progressive, the tax system can be improved further toward more equity. Specific actions concerning indirect taxation could include refocusing VAT exemptions on basic goods heavily consumed by the poor or limiting the imposition of new excise taxes. The excise tax was the only flexible instrument left after the Economic Liberty Act restricted raising rates on other taxes, but the analysis shows that it is quite regressive. The government has been using excises, but in the future it could consider using them only to levy taxes on items not heavily consumed by the poor. For the VAT, it is advised from an equity standpoint that exemptions that are not pro-poor could be eliminated to improve its progressivity.

Actions concerning direct taxation could include enhancing the property tax by lowering the payment threshold and intensifying PIT collection efforts to broaden the tax base, especially among the better-off households. From an equity perspective, giving direct taxes a bigger role will make the tax system even more progressive.[49] Although the Economic Liberty Act rules out the possibility of raising either PIT or property tax rates without referendum, there is still space to enhance both.

Finally, regarding in-kind transfers (and in line with the government's intention of creating fiscal space without a drag on growth), the government could introduce a mechanism that encourages the most affluent sectors of the society to use private services, which can reduce the burden on the public budget that these programs represent (for example, private health insurance).

Notes

1. As this chapter was written, new international poverty lines were reestimated at US$1.90 and US$3.10 per person per day, using 2011 purchasing power parity (PPP) exchange rates. This chapter uses the previous US$1.25 and US$2.50 per day poverty lines based on 2005 PPP exchange rates.

2. Gini index data for Georgia come from the World Income Inequality Database of the United Nations University–World Institute for Development Economics Research (UNU-WIDER), https://www.wider.unu.edu/data.

3. Social program data come from the Government of Georgia's Social Service Agency database, http://ssa.gov.ge.

4. Regarding Armenia, see Younger and Khachatryan, see chapter 2 of this volume. Regarding the Russian Federation, see chapter 7 of this volume.

5. Led by Nora Lustig since 2008, the Commitment to Equity (CEQ) project is a joint initiative of the Center for Inter-American Policy and Research (CIPR); the Department of Economics at Tulane University; and the Inter-American Dialogue. For more details, see http://www.commitmentoequity.org.

6. Average general government revenue in middle-income countries in Europe and Central Asia amounted to 34.9 percent of GDP in 2013 (World Bank 2014b). The average general government expenditure in those countries was 36.6 percent of GDP in 2013.

7. All information in this section about Georgia's tax structures, exemptions, and rates is taken or paraphrased from the Tax Code of Georgia (Document 3591, issued September 17, 2010), https://matsne.gov.ge/en/document/view/1043717.

8. Capital gains used in the analysis are tax-exempt; however, some capital gains are subject to tax. For more information, refer to the Tax Code of Georgia (Document 3591, issued September 17, 2010), https://matsne.gov.ge/en/document/view/1043717.

9. The exchange rate of 1 GEL = US$0.42 as of May 10, 2015, is used.

10. The list includes only the exemptions applied in the analysis. For full list of exemptions, refer to the Tax Code of Georgia (Document 3591, issued September 17, 2010), https://matsne.gov.ge/en/document/view/1043717.

11. The value of property (that is, property subject to real estate tax) is imputed using dwelling and household characteristics reported in the IHS. See the methodology section for more details.

12. In this analysis, social spending includes social benefits as well as wages, goods and services, subsidies in the form of cash, grants, gross acquisition of nonfinancial assets, and other expenses, per the CEQ methodology.

13. See, for instance, Nutsubidze and Nutsubidze (2015).

14. All social assistance data in this subsection come from the Social Service Agency of the Ministry of Labor, Health, and Social Affairs of Georgia, http://ssa.gov.ge/index.php?sec_id=610&lang_id=ENG.

15. Vulnerable groups are identified under the assessment system; no specific group is preselected. The eligibility of applicant households is determined through a proxy means test that uses a complex formula to measure the welfare of a specific household. If the test score is below a certain threshold, the household automatically gets access to benefits.

16. Beneficiary and share-of-GDP data from the Social Service Agency of the Ministry of Labor, Health, and Social Affairs of Georgia (http://ssa.gov.ge/index.php?lang_id=ENG&sec_id=35) and the National Statistics Office of Georgia (Geostat) (http://www.geostat.ge/index.php?action=page&p_id=200&lang=eng).

17. Pension beneficiary data from the Social Service Agency of the Ministry of Labor, Health, and Social Affairs of Georgia: http://ssa.gov.ge/index.php?sec_id=610&lang_id=ENG.

18. The educational system descriptions and public statistics are based on World Bank (2014b).

19. Educational budget data are from the Geostat database, National Statistics Office of Georgia (http://www.geostat.ge/index.php?action=0&lang=eng), and from the Ministry of Education and Science of Georgia (http://www.mes.gov.ge/?lang=eng).

20. The copay for *all* payers was abolished, so copayments are not included in the calculation of "net" in-kind transfers for preschool education.

21. A need-based state grant is available for students from minority-language schools, schools in remote areas, students from conflict zones, students who are either orphans or have several siblings, students eligible for social assistance, and so on. The allocation of the need-based grants also has a merit component in it: students with the highest scores receive the grant.

22. Gross transfers were used in this calculation, but using net transfers does not change the result qualitatively for any educational level.

23. Only 41 of the approximately 11,000 households interviewed in the survey reported having a member attending vocational education. Because representativeness would

be an issue, vocational education was not analyzed independently but only jointly with other educational levels.

24. "Socially vulnerable" families are those that are registered in the "unified database of socially vulnerable families" with a rating score not exceeding 70,000 units.

25. All subsidy beneficiary and cost information comes from Tbilisi City Hall, unpublished data. Share of GDP from World Bank calculations.

26. Spring Project data from "The Land-Poor-Farmers Assistance 2014 Spring Project," Government of Georgia website (accessed May 2, 2016), http://gov.ge/print .php?gg=1&sec_id=288&info_id=41117&lang_id=ENG. Unfortunately, information is unavailable on the average total farming cost for farmers with less than 5 hectares of land, to account for the percentage covered by the Agricultural Card program.

27. The Ministry of Agriculture and Project Management Agency, with the help of local governments, specified the list of potential beneficiaries.

28. The CEQ framework (Lustig and Higgins 2013) recommends doing the fiscal incidence analysis under two main assumptions for contributory pensions: (a) a "benchmark scenario," under which contributory pensions are assumed to be deferred income and are counted as part of market income, and (b) a "sensitivity analysis," under which contributory pensions are treated as any other direct cash transfer. Because Georgia does not have a contributory pension system, our study treats all pensions as transfers.

29. The empirical tools necessary to undertake incidence analysis of corporate taxes and investment spending are not well established in the literature and were beyond the scope of what could be done in this study.

30. Georgia is geographically divided into nine regions, one city, and two autonomous republics. The Abkhazia and South Ossetia regions are not covered in the survey.

31. Close to 20 percent of observations report a selling price. This information was used to project price to the rest of the sample.

32. We didn't estimate the indirect effects of VAT due to cascading because our household survey includes a relatively small number of exempt goods. The effective tax rates account for unreported consumption of alcohol and cigarettes. The calculations are based on the data from Ericksen et al. (2015); Geostat (http://www.geostat.ge /index.php?action=0&lang=eng); Ng et al. (2014); the MoF's Treasury Service (http:// www.mof.ge/en/4513); and WHO (2015).

33. Effective tax rate calculations included not only the de facto tax revenue but also underreported consumption of alcohol and cigarettes (Ericksen et al. 2015; WHO 2015).

34. The data on per capital alcohol consumption in 2010 come from WHO (2015) and were used with revenue data for 2010 to calculate effective excise tax rates for alcoholic beverages. The data on per capita consumption of cigarettes come from Ericksen et al. (2015) and Ng et al. (2014). Consumption data on oil, oil products, and telecommunication services come from Geostat: http://www.geostat.ge/index.php?action =0&lang=eng. Revenue data are from the MoF's Treasury Service: http://www.mof.ge /en/4513.

35. The other, smaller transfers include the loss-of-breadwinner (survivor's) pensions; scholarship; temporary disability benefits (because of illness or childbirth); pensions of disabled veterans, participants in a war, or pensions of persons equal to them, and other special (Ministry of Internal Affairs, personal) pensions; social (household) assistance for single pensioners and disabled persons; and other income. The number of beneficiaries obtained in the survey aligned with those reported in administrative sources.

36. For more about the rationale and methodology for scaling up or scaling down certain transfers in the calculation of the income aggregates, see chapter 1.

37. Scaling down the direct transfers reported in the survey (see endnote 36), as done for in-kind transfers, would have led to a smaller change in the Gini coefficient from market income to disposable income (a fall of 8.4 Gini points instead of 11.2), although a roughly similar final income Gini (39.6 against the current 38.3). Qualitative results on the progressivity and regressivity of taxes and transfers would remain the same.

38. Outpatient and prevention services were covered between March and June 2013, and outpatient, preventive care, surgeries, and other inpatient care were covered from July 2013. The IHS reports the following expenditures on health care: outpatient treatment for chronic or disabled patients; outpatient treatment for any disease (excluding chronic); and inpatient treatment, maternal and child health, dental services, preventive inspection, therapeutic appliances, and equipment.

39. Expenses for local and intraurban transportation are reported at the household level in the IHS. The only provider of this service is the municipality.

40. For instance, Brazil (2009) and South Africa (2010) observed Gini reductions of 0.14 and 0.175, respectively, while Ethiopia (2011), Indonesia (2012) and Armenia (2011) registered reductions of 0.024, 0.026, and 0.046, respectively (World Bank 2015a).

41. For most countries, poverty reduction from market to consumable income is only a few percentage points.

42. For definitions and methodologies regarding the assessments of progressivity, regressivity, and pro-poorness of the fiscal interventions examined in this volume, see chapter 1.

43. This chapter does not assess the progressivity of individual VAT exemptions and the consumption share by the poorest decile of population to determine which of the exemptions are the least pro-poor and therefore the best candidates for elimination. However, because a fairly wide range of goods and services are VAT-exempt (from agriculture produce to imported goods and financial services), the impact of VAT exemption is unlikely to be confined to a specific income category.

44. Small plots are widespread because of state property transfer to households during the reforms of the 1990s. Tax schemes may also create an incentive to keep plots small. In addition, it is not uncommon for urban household to own plots of cultivable land, which makes them also eligible for the agricultural card.

45. Similar to the problem encountered with microdecompositions in trying to disentangle the effect of different income components on poverty reduction (see, for instance, Azevedo et al. 2013), contributions of specific programs under this framework cannot rely on sequential calculations because there is path dependency. We could use marginal contributions, but because they do not add up to the total change, one cannot calculate shares of a contribution to the total change. The most proper way to identify this contribution is probably by using some Shapley-style averages. In this case, the estimation is a rough approximation, where pensions are added to net market income first, and poverty reduction is compared with the total reduction and then added after all other components have been added. Because pensions are much larger than the other transfers, we would expect this result to be robust under different specifications.

46. As further discussed in chapter 1, spending is "progressive" when the concentration coefficient is lower than the Gini for market income: that is, the benefits from that spending as a share of market income tend to fall with market income. Spending is defined as "pro-poor" when the concentration coefficient is not only lower than the

Gini but also negative. Pro-poor spending implies that the *per capita* government spending on the transfer *tends* to fall with market income.

47. The indicators of poverty reduction efficiency and effectiveness are defined by Beckerman (1979) and Immervoll et al. (2009).

48. Coverage is calculated in relation to the relevant age group, namely ages 1–5, 6–17, and 18–23 years.

49. This chapter does not address tax efficiency, and the measures introduced could lead to changes in efficiency.

References

Azevedo, J. P., G. Inchauste, and V. Sanfelice. 2013. "Decomposing the Recent Inequality Decline in Latin America." Policy Research Working Paper 6715, World Bank, Washington, DC.

Beckerman, W. 1979. "The Impact of Income Maintenance Payments on Poverty in Britain, 1975." *Economic Journal* 89 (354): 261–79.

Ericksen, M., J. Mackay, N. Schluger, F. I. Gomeshtapeh, and J. Drope. 2015. *The Tobacco Atlas*. 5th ed. Atlanta, GA: American Cancer Society.

Government of Georgia. 2011. "Georgia Adopts the Economic Liberty Act." Press Release, July 11.

Gzirishvili, David. 2012. *Independent Georgia—Health and Social Protection Systems. Analytical Review*. Tbilisi: Open Society Georgia Foundation.

Higgins, Sean, and Nora Lustig. 2015. "Can a Poverty-Reducing and Progressive Tax and Transfer System Hurt the Poor?" Commitment to Equity Working Paper 33, Center for Inter-American Policy and Research; the Inter-American Dialogue; and Department of Economics, Tulane University, New Orleans, LA.

Immervoll, H., H. Levy, J. R. Nogueira, C. O'Donoghue, and R. Bezerra de Siqueira. 2009. "The Impact of Brazil's Tax-Benefit System on Inequality and Poverty." In *Poverty, Inequality, and Policy in Latin America*, edited by S. Klasen and F. Nowak-Lehmann, 271–302. Cambridge, MA: MIT Press.

Lustig, Nora. 2015. "Inequality and Fiscal Redistribution in Middle Income Countries: Brazil, Chile, Colombia, Indonesia, Mexico, Peru and South Africa. Evidence from the Commitment to Equity Project (CEQ)." CEQ Working Paper 31, CEQ Institute, Tulane University, New Orleans, LA.

Lustig, Nora, and Sean Higgins. 2013. "Commitment to Equity Assessment (CEQ): Estimating the Incidence of Social Spending, Subsidies and Taxes—Handbook." CEQ Working Paper 1, Center for Inter-American Policy and Research; the Inter-American Dialogue; and Department of Economics, Tulane University, New Orleans, LA.

Ng, M., M. Freeman, T. Fleming, M. Robinson, L. Dwyer-Lindgren, B. Thomson, et al. 2014. "Smoking Prevalence and Cigarette Consumption in 187 Countries, 1980–2012." *Journal of the American Medical Association* 311 (2): 183–92.

Nutsubidze, T., and K. Nutsubidze. 2015. "The Challenge of Pension Reform in Georgia: Non-Contributory Pensions and Elderly Poverty." Working Paper 2015-18, Center for Retirement Research, Boston College.

Salmi, Jamil, and Natia Andguladze. 2011. "Tertiary Education Governance and Financing in Georgia." Draft policy report for the World Bank, Tbilisi.

WHO (World Health Organization). 2015. "Regional Alcohol Per Capita (15+) Consumption by WHO Region." Global Health Observatory Data Repository, WHO, Geneva. http://apps.who.int/gho/data/view.main.52325.

World Bank. 2014a. *Georgia Education Sector Policy Review: Strategic Issues and Reform Agenda.* Report ACS11059, Georgia: Technical Assistance to Support Preparation of Education Sector Strategy, World Bank, Washington, DC.

———. 2014b. *Georgia Public Expenditure Review: Strategic Issues and Reform Agenda.* Report No. 78143-GE, Vol. 1, World Bank, Washington, DC.

———. 2014c. "Georgia: Winds of Optimism." Georgia Economic Report 6, Working Paper 91697, World Bank, Washington, DC.

———. 2015a. *Georgia Public Expenditure Review: Selected Fiscal Issues.* Report 96524, World Bank, Washington, DC.

———. 2015b. *World Development Indicators 2015.* Washington, DC: World Bank.

Younger, S. D., and A. Khachatryan. 2017. "Fiscal Incidence in Armenia." In *The Distributional Impact of Taxes and Transfers: Evidence from Eight Low- and MIddle-Income Countries,* edited by Gabriela Inchauste and Nora Lustig. Washington, DC: World Bank.

CHAPTER 5

The Distributional Impact of Fiscal Policy in Indonesia

Jon Jellema, Matthew Wai-Poi, and Rythia Afkar

Introduction

Fifteen years of sustained income growth helped Indonesia cut its poverty rate by more than half since the beginning of the new millennium: it stood at just over 11 percent of the population in 2014, down from 24 percent during the 1997–98 Asian Financial Crisis (World Bank 2016).[1] However, the benefits from expanding, more efficient macroeconomic conditions have been shared disproportionately: between 2003 and 2010, real per capita consumption of the richest 10 percent of Indonesians grew by over 6 percent per year, but consumption of the poorest two-fifths of the population grew by less than 2 percent per year (World Bank 2016).

This disparity explains a recent uptick in inequality in Indonesia: the Gini coefficient increased by approximately 10 percentage points, from approximately 0.30 in 2000 to 0.41 in 2014.[2] Worsening inequality has alarmed the public and politicians alike: nearly 90 percent of Indonesians recently said it was "urgent" that the government address inequality. The executive administration implemented significant fuel subsidy reforms in late 2014 and early 2015 and reallocated expenditures to programs that reduce inequality and foster balanced economic growth (World Bank 2016).

To illuminate the impact of fiscal policies and public programs on poverty and inequality in Indonesia, we catalogue the distributional welfare consequences of Indonesia's public revenues and expenditures, quantify the impact of these fiscal activities on both inequality and poverty, and estimate how effectively they

The authors wish to thank Luky Alfirman (head of Macroeconomic Policy Center), Arti Dyah Woroutami (head of Welfare and Labor Subdivision), and Ahmad Fikri Aulia (executive of Welfare and Labor Subdivision) of the Indonesian Ministry of Finance; Gabriela Inchauste, Vivi Alatas, Violeta Vulovic, and Ahya Ihsan of the World Bank; and Nora Lustig, Sean Higgins, and the rest of the Commitment to Equity Institute team.

redistribute income between the rich and the poor. We generate these estimates using the Commitment to Equity (CEQ) analytical methodology as described in the CEQ Assessment Handbook (Lustig and Higgins 2013) as well as in chapter 1 of this volume.

The CEQ project uses standard fiscal incidence analysis to allocate to the representative individuals in a national household survey both the burdens of household-based revenue collection instruments (direct and indirect taxes) and the benefits from direct, indirect, and in-kind transfers financed by public expenditures.[3] The magnitude of total burdens and benefits are taken directly from budget figures and administrative data, and their distribution among individuals in the household survey is informed by program rules, policy statements, and relevant regulations. Verified, cumulative expenditure and revenue figures and the microlevel distribution of individuals are equally important empirical keystones in the CEQ method. This creates an opportunity for straightforward international comparison and the incorporation of differing income levels, spending priorities, and socioeconomic composition via a common *empirical* methodology.

Indonesia-based researchers have traced the distributional consequences of a generalized fiscal process as well as some individual fiscal policy elements. For example, Damuri and Perdana (2003) apply a computable general equilibrium (CGE) model to estimate the impact of general fiscal expansion on poverty and welfare across the entire income distribution; their results indicate that urban households and nonagricultural rural households benefit the most from expansionary fiscal policy. Hadiwibowo (2010) suggests that "development expenditures" *specifically* increase investment and accelerate economic growth, with positive domino effects on poverty.

Dartanto (2013) examines the impact of Indonesian energy subsidies (also through a CGE model) and finds that reducing the then-current fuel subsidy by 25 percent would have contributed to an increase in the headcount poverty rate by just less than one quarter of a percentage point, whereas foregone subsidy expenditures would have—had they been reallocated as general government expenditures—reduced poverty incidence by just over one quarter of a percentage point.

This report builds on previous findings by empirically generating a greater range of fiscal policy impacts on poverty and inequality, both overall and from individual revenue and expenditure components. Nationally representative macrodatasets and microdatasets are used in one empirical analytical framework to estimate and describe the contribution of the main components of fiscal policy to the reduction of both poverty and inequality. The analysis covers about 44 percent of total tax revenues and 56 percent of primary government expenditures. It also includes the user fees collected directly from individuals using public health and education services as well as the indirect impacts of energy subsidies and consumption-based indirect taxes on household welfare. In other words, the analysis summarized here provides more details on the impact of each fiscal policy element while preserving generality and the ability to aggregate those impacts to describe fiscal policy generally—in so doing, accommodating a greater empirical range of sources of potential welfare impacts.

Our findings indicate that despite a relatively low social spending base and relatively little revenue collection from direct income taxation, Indonesia's fiscal policy does reduce both inequality and poverty. However, those fiscal policy impacts are modest: poverty or inequality statistics measured *after* the application of fiscal policy are only slightly reduced from those measured on the basis of prefiscal-policy incomes. If we look at "consumable" transfers only,[4] nearly two-fifths of individuals who are poor at the level of "consumable income"[5] have paid more in taxes than they have received in transfers: in other words, nearly 40 percent of the consumable-income poor have been impoverished by fiscal policy in Indonesia.[6]

A second striking result is that although local, unregulated user fees for publicly delivered health and education services are a significant cost for most users regardless of income level, in practice the burden of such fees is distributed to slightly reduce inequality.[7] In other words, in a highly decentralized administrative and executive framework (such as Indonesia's), local public bodies can alter the effect of centrally determined policy.

The rest of the chapter proceeds as follows: the next section provides an overview of the key fiscal tools used by government as well as the mechanisms by which those tools redistribute income between the rich and the poor. The "Data, Assumptions, and Income Concepts" section summarizes the data sources, discusses the construction of the CEQ income concepts, and describes the allocative assumptions used in the analysis. The "Results Overview" presents the findings concerning the progressivity of fiscal policy, the fiscal system's impact on horizontal equity, the effectiveness of spending, and whether the reduction in poverty or inequality achieved is commensurate with the amount spent. The concluding section summarizes the findings, compares them with others in the CEQ country set, and briefly points toward policy changes that could further reduce poverty and inequality in Indonesia.

The Government's Fiscal Toolkit

In the aftermath of the 1997–98 Asian Financial Crisis and the political and social upheaval that ended the Suharto dictatorship at the end of the 20th century, Indonesia has steadily strengthened its democratic institutions and decentralized its fiscal and administrative framework. Not unrelatedly, it has also expanded social spending on public goods and services as well as a social safety net specifically for the poor and vulnerable: social assistance expenditures have nearly doubled, from approximately 0.35 percent of gross domestic product (GDP) in 2004 to approximately 0.70 percent of GDP in 2014.

This era coincided with robust macroeconomic growth and sound fiscal management: growth in real GDP per capita averaged 5.4 percent between 2000 and 2014, whereas the annual fiscal deficit never exceeded 2 percent (of GDP) from

2001 to 2012. Hence, the increased social spending was easily absorbed into regular budgets; in fact, the debt-to-GDP ratio has fallen from a peak of 82 percent in 2001 to a roughly stable 30 percent (or less) since 2008.

Taxes

By the standards of most middle-income countries, Indonesia's tax system generates comparatively few resources (table 5.1): within the CEQ country set, only Mexico raises less of its public expenditures from taxes.[8] Approximately three-quarters of all public revenues in Indonesia come from taxes (and the remainder through natural resource rents and royalties), so the public revenue base is low compared with the rest of the CEQ country set.[9]

Within the total set of tax revenues, approximately equal shares are generated from direct taxes on incomes (of individuals and corporate entities) and indirect taxes on individuals' and corporate entities' expenditures (table 5.1). Approximately 80 percent of direct taxes are generated from corporate income taxes, whereas about 70 percent of indirect taxes (primarily value added and excise taxes) are generated from individual or household expenditures.

Table 5.1 also shows the share of total government revenues (about 36 percent) included in the current incidence analysis. As in most of the CEQ country set, indirect taxes are relatively more important than direct taxes for public revenue generation. This means that the average Indonesian household's tax burden is primarily from indirect consumption and expenditure taxes.

Table 5.1 Government Revenues in Indonesia, 2012
Percentage of GDP

Revenue source	2012	Included in incidence analysis
Total general government revenue	16.2	5.3
Tax revenue	11.9	5.2
Direct taxes	5.6	0.0
Personal income tax	1.2	0.0[a]
Corporate income tax	4.4	n.a.
Indirect taxes	5.9	4.0
Value added taxes (VAT)[b]	4.1	2.9
Specific excise duties	1.2	1.2
International trade taxes	0.6	n.a.
Other taxes	0.4	n.a.
Nontax revenue[c]	4.3	0.1

Source: BPK 2013.
Note: GDP = gross domestic product; n.a. = not applicable.
a. The personal income tax burden is imputed to be zero for all households represented in the National Socioeconomic Survey (SUSENAS) survey. For a more detailed discussion, see the "Data, Assumptions, and Income Concepts" section of this chapter.
b. VAT revenues *not included* in the incidence analysis are those collected from nongovernmental organizations, corporate consumption activities, and other nonhousehold sources.
c. Nontax revenue includes natural resource royalties, social security contributions, and user fees paid for publicly provided health and education services. Only social security contributions and user fees are included in the incidence analysis.

Direct personal income taxes (PIT) are commonly engineered to be progressive in that the share paid in direct taxes rises with the taxpayer's income. The amount of revenue collected from Indonesia's direct taxes (combining personal and corporate income taxes) is, at 5.6 percent of GDP, on par with Chile, Colombia, Mexico, or Peru (Lustig 2014). However, the share of total direct taxes from PIT in Indonesia, at about 20 percent, is lower than in those other countries: in Peru, for example, the PIT share is 30 percent, and in Mexico it is 44 percent.

This report also analyzes the value added tax (VAT)[10] and tobacco excise taxes, which impose significant burdens on the households represented in the National Socioeconomic Survey (SUSENAS).[11] We calculate and apply an effective VAT rate, defined as the value of VAT collections (as reported in budget documents) divided by the total sales value of all goods subject to VAT (the taxable base). In 2012, this effective VAT rate was, at about 5.2 percent, approximately half the policy VAT rate of 10 percent.

Collectively, the VAT and tobacco excise taxes represented nearly 45 percent of all tax revenues, and 33 percent of total government revenues, in 2012. PIT burdens—representing approximately 10 percent of all tax revenues and 7 percent of total government revenues, in 2012—were not allocated because the narrow, de facto application of PIT collection means that households represented in SUSENAS have zero expected income tax burdens.[12]

Expenditures

Government expenditures in Indonesia are small relative to the other members of the CEQ country set, which is unsurprising given the country's small revenue base, its nearly balanced budget condition, and its declining debt stock. For example, total primary government spending came to about 16 percent of GDP in 2012 (table 5.2). Social expenditures alone (direct cash transfers plus all in-kind transfers) were smaller (5.6 percent of GDP) and subsidy spending higher (4.1 percent of GDP) in Indonesia in 2012 than in any of the other CEQ countries (Lustig 2014). For example, in Chile, Colombia, Mexico, and Peru, social spending ranged from 9 percent to 13 percent of GDP (including spending on subsidies of 0–1.4 percent of GDP).

In 2012, approximately one quarter of public expenditures went to social spending, and about 70 percent of that amount was for education.[13] Less than 0.5 percent of GDP was dedicated to direct cash transfers to individuals (table 5.2). Indonesia is one of only three CEQ countries that spends less than 1 percentage point of GDP on cash transfers (the others being Guatemala and Peru).

Indonesia's subsidized rice program, known as Raskin, which distributes centrally purchased rice to local marketplaces where it is sold at subsidized prices, is treated as a direct cash transfer for the following reason: recent and historical estimates indicate that rice distributed through Raskin represents less than 10 percent of the market for rice, and because there are no formal or practical restrictions on Raskin rice resale, Raskin rice is for most individuals an asset that can quickly be turned into cash (Jellema and Noura 2012).[14]

Other social spending items include in-kind transfers in health, education, and housing. As mentioned earlier, most social spending goes toward public education.

This study uses analysis to allocate, among a household income and expenditure survey population, direct cash transfers incidence, contributory pensions, and in-kind transfers in the form of health and education; these items (excluding contributory pensions and housing/urban in-kind expenditures) account for 98 percent of social spending. (The rightmost column of table 5.2 indicates how much of spending is included in the current incidence analysis.) We also allocate energy subsidy expenditures even though they are not strictly "social" spending. With energy subsidies included, about 57 percent of total primary government spending is covered in the incidence analysis.

Table 5.2 Government Expenditures in Indonesia, 2012
Percentage of GDP

Expenditure type	Total	Included in incidence analysis
Total expenditures[a]	17.47	9.06
Primary government spending[b]	16.25	9.06
Social spending[c]	4.86	4.61
Total cash transfers	0.39	0.33
Raskin rice subsidies[d]	0.23	0.23
Poor Student Education Support (BSM)	0.08	0.08
Conditional cash transfer (Hopeful Family Program, or PKH)	0.02	0.02
Noncontributory pensions	0.06	n.a.
In-kind transfers	4.47	4.28
Education	3.40	3.40
Health	0.88	0.88
Housing and urban	0.19	n.a.
Other social spending[e]	n.a.	n.a.
Contributory pensions	0.76	0.76
Nonsocial spending (incl. public sector pensions)	10.63	3.69
Indirect subsidies	4.08	3.69
Energy	3.69	3.69
Others	0.39	n.a.
Other nonsocial spending[f]	6.55	n.a.
Debt service	1.23	n.a.

Source: BPK 2013.
Note: GDP = gross domestic product; n.a. = not applicable.
a. Total expenditures = primary government spending + debt service (interest and amortization).
b. Primary government spending = social spending + contributory pensions + nonsocial spending.
c. Social spending = total cash transfers (including noncontributory pensions) + total in-kind transfers + other social spending.
d. The Raskin rice subsidy program is treated as a direct cash transfer because the subsidized rice distributed through the program is often resold for cash.
e. "Other social spending" includes a considerable number of small social assistance programs that could not be identified in administrative sources and thus could not be included in the analysis.
f. "Other nonsocial spending" includes, among other things, public sector pensions, infrastructure, administration, and law, order, and justice.

Data, Assumptions, and Income Concepts

To determine the size of the transfer received or the taxes contributed by households and individuals, taxes and transfers are allocated to individual households. To accomplish this we use the September 2012 SUSENAS, which contains data on household expenditures, cash transfers, and utilization of educational and health services collected from approximately 71,000 representative households across the country over a period of 12 months. Per capita values are obtained by dividing the total tax paid or transfer received by the total number of permanent household members. To calculate the indirect burdens and benefits of indirect consumption taxes or subsidies, we use a year-2011 input-output table for the Indonesian economy.[15]

Construction of Income Concepts and Income Tax Variables

Available SUSENAS data do not contain individual or household income reports or any of the CEQ "market income" components (wages and salaries, investment income, or pension income, for example). Therefore we derive the CEQ "market income" measure—our primary income concept (that is, the income concept that is free of direct fiscal policy impacts)—from consumption expenditures instead.

We derive the other income concepts from this total consumption expenditure by either subtracting or adding various fiscal interventions. These interventions include, but are not limited to, direct cash transfers, pension contributions, direct taxes, and the imputed rental value of owner-occupied housing.[16] "Net market income" (or income after taxes) is simply consumption expenditures minus direct cash transfers; and "disposable income" is equal to consumption expenditures.

Indonesia's direct PIT is assumed to be borne entirely by the income recipient.[17] PIT in Indonesia is levied on gross income from all sources less exemptions and deductions (for example, for child dependents, pension income, occupational expenses, or pension contributions). Because SUSENAS does not report gross or net-of-tax incomes nor PIT paid, we use the derived market income measure to impute the expected household PIT burden.

Relative to the derived market incomes of those households represented in the SUSENAS survey, PIT statutes detail a high "tax threshold" (the income level above which individuals are required to register with the tax authorities and file tax returns). For example, the individual tax threshold is approximately US$5.60 per day in 2005 purchasing power parity (PPP) terms; there are no representative individuals in the 2012 SUSENAS with derived market incomes exceeding this level. For a two-parent, two-child, two-income household, the threshold is approximately US$8,116 PPP annually (about Rp 50 million); there were 25,000 to 35,000 households in SUSENAS with estimated total income at or exceeding that level. However, pension contributions can be deducted, and pension incomes are exempt (up to a limit), so some of these households will have paid no income taxes.

Additionally, tax directorate records indicate that the income group with the largest single contribution (31 percent) to total PIT revenues is a very rich group of approximately 4,000 individuals (less than 0.01 percent of approximately 60 million Indonesian households), whereas a 25 percent share of total PIT revenues (in 2012) is attributed to a rich group of approximately 32,000 individuals (again less than 0.1 percent of Indonesian households) whose reported incomes start at 10 times median income. In other words, over half of PIT revenues appear to be contributed by fewer than 0.5 percent of Indonesian households, whose incomes are at least 10 times the median income. Secondary sources indicate that 80 percent or more of PIT revenues come from less than 2 percent of the population. Both of these observations imply that the average SUSENAS respondent will not be liable for income taxes, whereas even a "90th percentile" SUSENAS respondent may either not be liable for taxes (depending on his or her household composition) or may not arrange withholding (if self-employed).

Tax directorate records also indicate that PIT filers in the lowest reported-income group provide about 12 percent of total PIT collections, and we estimate (based on the 25,000–35,000 households with household income above the PIT threshold) that we could find in SUSENAS proxy households for at most 1.5 percent of the 2.6 million verified filers in that group. So we would be able to sensibly allocate within SUSENAS at most 0.2 percent of total PIT collections. This in turn would mean allocating approximately US$21 million among 24 million individuals (in the richest SUSENAS expenditure decile), or about US$0.90 per individual (per year) in the richest SUSENAS decile. That figure is less than 0.01 percent of per capita income in that decile. Hence, we imputed PIT to be zero for all households represented in SUSENAS.[18]

Allocating Contributory Pensions and Cash Transfers

Indonesia's public expenditures include a contributory pension scheme for civil servants (including formally contracted teachers, the police, and the military). The fiscal incidence literature sometimes incorporates contributory pensions as part of market income (deferred income) and sometimes as separate revenue and expenditure streams (a tax-and-transfer scheme).[19] The results discussed below include a benchmark case in which contributory pensions are treated as part of market income and a sensitivity analysis where pension incomes are classified as government transfers and pension contributions as a direct tax (one's market income is lowered by exactly one's pension contribution amount to arrive at net market income).[20]

Pension status is not recorded in SUSENAS, so individuals *potentially* making contributions to (as well as those *potentially* receiving income from) the pension system were identified using individual characteristics such as relationship to household head, age, education, sector of work, and most important, participation in other benefit schemes for civil servants. Both less- and more-restrictive condition sets were used, and the final number of *potential* pension system participants was adjusted in line with the other taxes and transfers analyzed.

Contribution and benefit amounts were adjusted using parameters from an imputed wage regression carried out in a secondary labor force survey.[21]

In contrast, for nearly all direct cash or near-cash transfers included in the incidence analysis,[22] we can use *direct identification* to determine whether a household received a benefit and the magnitude of the benefit received: there are SUSENAS questions that ask the respondent to indicate which transfers were received, how much was received (when a particular transfer was received), and which subsidized items were consumed.[23] Two important exceptions are contributory pensions (covered directly above) and Indonesia's conditional cash transfer (CCT), known locally as the Hopeful Family Program (*Program Keluarga Harapan*, or PKH).

To allocate PKH transfers, we first generated household per capita consumption deciles in the 2013 SUSENAS, which directly identifies CCT receipt. Because no planned (or actual) CCT coverage increases occurred between 2012 and 2013, we applied the 2013 CCT shares (by region and by household per capita consumption expenditure decile) to the 2012 CCT administrative records to generate a 2012 CCT "quota" for each region and, within each region, for each decile. We then allocated that region-decile quota randomly among all CCT-eligible households[24] in each region-decile. In essence, we are "backcasting" directly identified CCT concentration shares (in 2013) onto the 2012 distribution of households.[25] The eligible 2012 households that were allocated the CCT received the observed (from administrative records) *average* transfer amount.

Allocating Energy Subsidies and Indirect Taxes

Consumption taxes and subsidies—Indonesia's VAT, tobacco excise tax, and 2012-era subsidies for fuels and electricity—are shifted forward to consumers, meaning that we assume consumers have perfectly inelastic demands for goods and services. For the direct effect of the VAT and energy subsidies, we calculate household burdens or benefits by multiplying total household expenditures by the *effective* tax or subsidy rate[26] but make no further adjustments to, for example, expenditures made in rural areas or areas where some sellers are informal and therefore not registered for VAT.

For the indirect effects of the VAT regime (which exempts foods considered basic necessities and basic financial, health, and education services) and the fuel subsidy regime, we use a "cost push" assumption for all economic sectors: if input prices change for producers *as a result of policy or regulatory decisions*, those producer price changes will be pushed on to the final sale price of the good or service in question. For the direct effect of the tobacco excise, we use an average of statutory rates for the most commonly sold types of cigarettes; neither the household data nor the budget data would allow calculation of an effective tobacco excise.[27]

Allocating In-Kind Health and Education Transfers

The monetized value of in-kind public education and health benefits is generated by the "government cost" approach. In essence, we use per-beneficiary input costs obtained from administrative fiscal data as the measure of average benefits. This approach is equivalent to asking the following question: how much would the income of a household have to be increased if it wanted to consume the subsidized public service at the full cost to the government?

SUSENAS provides information on educational enrollment by level and type (public vs. private institutions), so in-kind education benefits are equal to the average public spending per student by level (preschool, primary, lower-secondary, upper-secondary, and tertiary) and by type (public or private). Indonesia provides public revenues to some private education providers through the placement of civil servant teachers as well as through "operational grants" that are available to all schools providing Indonesia's "basic" nine-year education (the primary through lower-secondary level). We therefore generated an algorithm (based on estimated total public education expenditures arriving at private school facilities) to generate average public spending in private schools per private student by level.[28]

SUSENAS also provides partial information on the use of inpatient or outpatient health facilities at public or private providers.[29] Because the administrative and operational borders between public and private services are porous—some private services can be acquired at public service-provider locations, and publicly subsidized services can be acquired at private service-provider locations—the rough typology of utilization contained in SUSENAS is likely in error part of the time.

For publicly provided services, service provider-specific fees are common and unavoidable in both the education and health sectors in Indonesia. For health in particular, the border between "publicly" and "privately" provided services is porous, and a determination of whether the fees paid end up as "private" income or as "public" revenues cannot be made without some assumptions. We developed an algorithm that allocates the fees paid (for health or education services acquired) to the public or private provision systems.[30] For health care service fees, the algorithm allocates incompletely classified health fees[31] paid on the basis of observed health service consumption in which the service type and service provider type are clearly indicated (and the individual's consumption expenditure is known). Basically, we take all instances where a household recorded consumption of a private or public inpatient or outpatient service to calculate "unit fees" (for each market income decile) paid by a household for a service. We also calculate health care visit frequencies by provider and service type (again for each market income decile). We then allocate total health care service fees paid to each health care service–utilizing household according to these frequencies and unit costs by decile, by provider type, and by service type.

We treat these user fees in two different ways: as a baseline case and in an alternative scenario. Our baseline case assumes the fees are an excise tax on the service acquired; when they are so treated, we update the benefit provided to be equal to the government's "unit cost" for services provided (as discussed earlier) *minus* this "excise tax" paid to the public provision system. Although fees are charged and collected by a lower level of government than the level providing the in-kind transfer (which we value at the average unit expenditure), our baseline scenario implicitly treats these two different levels as one overarching public sector; to access the public sector benefit, individuals must pay a fee to the public sector, which reduces the net benefit received.

An alternative scenario, which we discuss further near the end of the "Results Overview" section, treats payments of public service provider fees as disposable income (which would have been spent in the same amounts and on the same services in the absence of public expenditures on the same services). When we make this alternative assumption, consumable and final incomes are neither decreased nor increased by the imposition of these fees. As a consequence, final incomes are *larger* (for households who consumed public services) than in the baseline scenario because the value of the in-kind transfer is not reduced. The consequences of these alternative assumptions as well as the progressivity and marginal impacts of public service fees are explored in the next section.

Results Overview

Fiscal policy reduces both inequality and poverty in Indonesia (table 5.3).[32] For example, the Gini coefficient is reduced from 0.394 at "market income" (the "before taxes and transfers" welfare indicator) to 0.370—that is, a decline of approximately 2.5 percentage points—after all taxes (PIT, VAT, and excises) and transfers (including cash transfers, consumption subsidies, and the monetized value of education and health care)[33] are applied to compute the "final income" concept. From market to consumable income, the headcount extreme poverty rate (the percentage of the population with incomes below US$1.25 per day in PPP exchange rate terms) falls from approximately 12.0 percent to 10.5 percent, whereas the incidence of poverty measured at the national poverty expenditure line[34] falls from 12.9 percent to 11.4 percent.[35]

In 2012, the net positive redistribution implemented through Indonesia's fiscal systems, from market income to disposable income, adds about US$11 to those in the bottom decile (those with per capita market incomes of Rp 2.4 million per year, or US$274). At the median, the net positive redistribution is valued at approximately US$6.50, whereas the market income in that decile is Rp 5.1 million (US$567) per year.

The bottom two sets of rows of table 5.3 present the overview for two different sensitivity analyses: (a) one that considers pensions to be government transfers (and pension contributions a tax on market income) and (b) one that does not treat public service fees (for public health or public education service access) as taxes. Because the reductions in equality are nearly equivalent[36] in both our benchmark scenario and the first sensitivity analysis (which treats pensions as transfers and pension contributions as a direct tax), we will not discuss these minor differences in great detail. However, the latter sensitivity analysis (which treats public service fees as in-kind transfers instead of as an indirect tax) is discussed in greater detail near the end of this chapter.

Table 5.3 Poverty and Inequality in Indonesia, by Income Concept

Indicator	Market income[a]	Disposable income[b]	Consumable income[c]	Final income[d]
Inequality indicators				
Gini coefficient	0.394	0.390	0.391	0.370
Theil index[e]	0.308	0.302	0.301	0.272
90/10 ratio[f]	5.05	4.92	4.97	4.52
Poverty headcount				
National poverty line (%)	12.9	11.6	11.4	—
National extreme poverty line (%)	4.7	3.9	3.9	—
US$1.25 PPP per day (%)	12.1	10.8	10.5	—
US$2.50 PPP per day (%)	56.4	55.9	54.8	—
Sensitivity analysis: pensions treated as transfer				
Gini coefficient	0.394	0.389	0.390	0.370
National poverty line (%)	13.4	11.7	11.4	—
US$1.25 PPP per day (%)	12.6	10.8	10.6	—
Sensitivity analysis: public service fees not treated as a tax				
Gini coefficient	0.394	0.389	0.390	0.369
National poverty line (%)	13.4	11.7	11.4	—
US$1.25 PPP per day (%)	12.6	10.8	10.6	—

Source: Based on BPK 2013 and 2012 National Socioeconomic Survey (SUSENAS) data.
Note: PPP is in 2005 U.S. dollars. The Gini coefficient is an indicator of inequality, ranging from 0 (full equality) to 1 (maximum inequality). The national poverty line in 2014 was defined as expenditure of Rp 302,735 (US$25) per person per month. The national extreme poverty line is 80 percent of the poverty line, so Rp 242,188 (U$20) "US$1.25 PPP per day" and "US$2.50 PPP per day" refer to international extreme poverty and poverty lines, respectively, in terms of per capita income. PPP = purchasing power parity; — = not available.
a. "Market income" comprises pretax wages, salaries, income earned from capital assets (rent, interest, or dividends), and private transfers.
b. "Disposable income" = market income − payments for personal income taxes + direct cash transfers to net market income.
c. "Consumable income" = disposable income − indirect taxes (VAT and excises) + indirect subsidies.
d. "Final income" = consumable income + value of in-kind transfers (such as for education and health care). Poverty headcounts at "final income" are not available because the net addition to household income from the consumption of publicly provided in-kind services is not available.
e. The Theil index, a measurement of economic inequality and other economic phenomena, is a member of the family of generalized entropy inequality measures (Theil 1967).
f. The 90/10 ratio measures how the relatively rich fare compare with the relatively poor. It is calculated as the average income of those in the 90th percentile divided by the average income of those in the 10th percentile (Lustig and Higgins 2013).

Indonesia's fiscal policy provides net positive transfers (on average) for any household regardless of its position in the income distribution and at every income concept (figure 5.1).[37] In other words, on average, disposable incomes are higher than market incomes, consumable incomes are higher than disposable incomes, and final incomes are higher than consumable incomes for households anywhere in the market income distribution. Because nontax revenues (primarily resource rents) are approximately as large as total VAT or total corporate income tax collections[38] and are much larger than excise or PIT collections, a significant portion of public expenditures are financed from instruments that do not create a direct burden on households. In addition, PIT is largely paid by wealthier Indonesians who are largely not captured in SUSENAS; these tax revenues are not part of the current incidence analysis. These facts both explain (in part) why most Indonesian households—and all the representative households captured in SUSENAS—receive net positive transfers from Indonesia's fiscal system.

Figure 5.1 Extent to Which Disposable, Consumable, and Final Income Exceed Market Income in Indonesia, by Income Decile, 2012

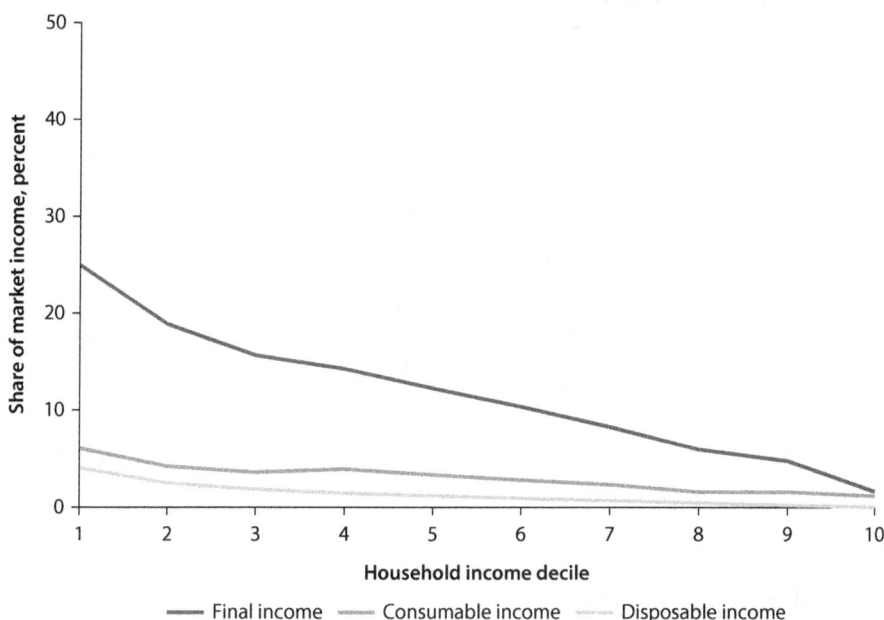

Source: Based on 2012 National Socioeconomic Survey (SUSENAS) data.
Note: "Market income" comprises pretax wages, salaries, income earned from capital assets (rent, interest, or dividends), and private transfers. "Disposable income" = market income − payments for personal income taxes + direct cash transfers to net market income. "Consumable income" = disposable income − indirect taxes (value added tax and excises).

Relative to other countries in the CEQ set, a larger share of the Indonesian population is net recipients: for example, in Armenia in 2011, fourth-decile households are already net contributors to public revenues (and all wealthier deciles remain net contributors), whereas in Brazil (2009), South Africa (2010), and Uruguay (2009), eighth-decile households turn net contributors (Woolard, Zikhali, and Maboshe 2014 and references therein).

It is somewhat surprising—given that an average SUSENAS household in any decile is a fiscal policy net "winner"—that the rate at which fiscal policy makes individuals poor is significant. The figures for fiscal impoverishment and fiscal gains to the poor[39] summarize how many of the poor lost or gained via the application of fiscal policy elements as well as the magnitudes of those losses or gains (table 5.4). When we define poverty as per capita income of less than US$1.25 per day PPP, after the fiscal instruments mentioned above are applied, nearly 40 percent of individuals who are measured as poor at consumable income have been impoverished by fiscal policy (not including in-kind transfers in health and education). In other words, they have paid more in taxes than they have received in direct or indirect cash or near-cash transfers.[40] That approximately two-fifths of poor individuals are impoverished by fiscal policy indicates that a progressive, poverty-reducing fiscal system like Indonesia's does not necessarily produce net positive transfers for all poor households.

Table 5.4 Fiscal Loss or Gain at Consumable Income, by Income Level, in Indonesia, 2012

Per capita income (US$ per day PPP)	Fiscal impoverishment[a]		Fiscal gains[b]	
	Postfiscal losers (%)	Average loss (% of market income)	Postfiscal gainers (%)	Average gain (% of market income)
1.25 (extreme poor)	39	3.7	72	7.1
2.50 (poor)	35	4.0	67	7.3
4.00 (upper-bound poor)	36	4.0	65	7.2
10.00	36	3.9	64	7.1
50.00	36	3.9	64	7.1

Source: Based on 2012 National Socioeconomic Survey (SUSENAS) data.

Note: The table shows loss and gains based on households' "consumable income" (or "postfiscal" income), which is defined as market income – direct and indirect tax payments + direct transfers. It excludes in-kind transfers (for education or health care). "Market income" (or "prefiscal" income) comprises pretax wages, salaries, income earned from capital assets (rent, interest, or dividends), and private transfers. PPP = purchasing power parity, in 2005 U.S. dollars.

a. "Fiscal impoverishment" is the extent to which fiscal system (of taxes and transfers) either (a) make a substantial portion of the poor even poorer, of (b) make the nonpoor poor. In other words, if the poor pay more in taxes than they receive in transfers, they are fiscally impoverished (Higgins and Lustig 2016).

b. "Fiscal gains to the poor" is the opposite of fiscal impoverishment, representing more in gains from transfers than they pay in taxes (Higgins and Lustig 2016).

Fiscal impoverishment is not uncommon. In a recent 17-country study for example, all countries demonstrated *some* fiscal impoverishment, whereas all of the lower-middle-income countries demonstrated fiscal impoverishment of 16 percent or greater (Higgins and Lustig 2016). Indonesia's rate of fiscal impoverishment (39 percent) falls between that of Sri Lanka (36 percent) and Armenia (52 percent). In Indonesia, the fiscal gains to the poor are greater (in sum) than the fiscal losses among the impoverished.

Equity of Fiscal Policy between Similar Households

As shown in table 5.4, some, but not all, poor households are impoverished by fiscal policy (excluding in-kind transfers). This finding indicates that horizontal equity (the degree to which individuals with similar income levels have similar transfer receipts and tax burdens) is incomplete. This incomplete horizontal equity limits the total redistributive effect of fiscal policy,[41] and the overall redistributive effect of fiscal policy in Indonesia is small (as shown earlier in table 5.3). Table 5.5 quantifies the impact of incomplete horizontal equity on this redistributive effect.

Table 5.5 indicates that although reranking (RR, a measure of horizontal inequity) in Indonesia is relatively small, so too is the vertical equity (VE) component: RR is about two-fifths the size of VE in Indonesia, which is a larger relative share than in Brazil and South Africa, where fiscal policy has a much larger total redistributive effect (from market to postfiscal income). One of the consequences of Indonesia's fiscal system—in which major transfers (energy subsidies) and taxes (VAT and excise taxes) are universal but do not cover everyone with equal net transfer amounts—is that some fiscal redistribution occurs between similar households.

Table 5.5 Redistributive, Vertical Equity, and Reranking Effects of Fiscal Policy in Indonesia Relative to Other CEQ Countries

Indicator	South Africa (2010)	Bolivia (2009)	Brazil (2009)	Indonesia (2012)
Gini (market income)[a]	0.771	0.503	0.579	0.394
Gini (consumable income)[b]	0.695	0.503	0.546	0.391
Redistributive effect[c]	0.077	0.000	0.033	0.004
Vertical equity (VE)[d]	0.083	0.003	0.048	0.006
Reranking effect (RR)[e]	0.006	0.003	0.014	0.003
Horizontal inequity (RR/VE)[f]	0.075	1.000	0.300	0.418

Sources: World Bank estimates based on 2012 National Socioeconomic Survey (SUSENAS) data (Indonesia); Higgins and Pereira 2014 (Brazil); Paz Arauco et al. 2014 (Bolivia). South Africa data from chapter 8 of this volume.
Note: Indicators are calculated from income-based data for Bolivia, Brazil, and South Africa and from consumption-based data in the case of Indonesia. The Gini coefficient measures the inequality of income distribution. A value of 0 indicates full equality, and 1 indicates maximum inequality. CEQ = Commitment to Equity project.
a. "Market income" comprises pretax wages, salaries, income earned from capital assets (rent, interest, or dividends), and private transfers.
b. "Consumable income" = market income − direct taxes and indirect taxes (value added and excise) + direct cash transfers + indirect subsidies.
c. The "redistributive effect" refers to the change in inequality associated with direct and indirect taxes as well as direct transfers and subsidies. It is calculated as the difference between the market income and consumable income Gini coefficients.
d. "Vertical equity" refers to the proportionality and progressivity of taxation, whereby the taxes paid increase with the amount of earned income.
e. The "reranking effect" is when fiscal interventions alter the relative position of individuals across the distribution (for example, if individual A was poorer than individual B *before* a fiscal intervention, but B is poorer than A *after* the intervention for no good reason).
f. "Horizontal inequity" refers to a situation where prefiscal and postfiscal income rankings are not preserved, calculated as the RR effect as a proportion of the VE effect, or RR/VE.

Fiscal policy has only a modest impact on the poverty headcount in Indonesia, but table 5.6 below shows that Indonesia is one of the rare CEQ countries where net indirect consumption taxes do not increase the poverty headcount (fiscal impoverishment notwithstanding). Net indirect subsidies are positive for every decile (as shown earlier in figure 5.1), meaning households in every decile *collectively* received more subsidy benefits (through consumption) than they paid in taxes (on consumption) on average.

Marginal Contributions of Fiscal Policy Elements to Income Redistribution
The Kakwani progressivity index for taxes and transfers indicates that only two spending items (pension income and tertiary education spending) are regressive in Indonesia, and only the tobacco excise tax is absolutely regressive (table 5.7).[42] Civil servant pensions were not designed as a social policy instrument but are a nonsalary benefit for government employees; and regressivity in tertiary education expenditures is driven by enrollment—the small number of students reaching the tertiary level are disproportionately nonpoor—rather than by program design.

Table 5.7 also summarizes marginal impacts on inequality (as summarized by the Gini coefficient) along with the magnitude of tax revenues collected

Table 5.6 Poverty Headcount in Selected Countries, by Income Concept
Percentage living on US$2.50 per person per day PPP

Country	Market income[a]	Disposable income[b]	Consumable income[c]
Armenia (2011)	31.3	28.9	34.9
Bolivia (2009)	19.6	17.6	20.2
Brazil (2009)	15.1	11.2	16.3
Costa Rica (2010)	5.4	3.9	4.2
El Salvador (2011)	14.7	12.9	14.4
Ethiopia (2011)	81.7	82.4	84.2
Guatemala (2010)	35.9	34.6	36.5
Indonesia (2012)	56.4	55.9	54.9
Mexico (2010)	12.6	10.7	10.7
Peru (2009)	15.2	14.0	14.5
South Africa (2010)	46.2	33.4	39.0
Uruguay (2009)	5.1	1.5	2.3

Sources: Beneke, Lustig, and Oliva 2016 (El Salvador); Bucheli et al. 2014 (Uruguay); Cabrera, Lustig, and Morán 2015 (Guatemala); Higgins and Pereira 2014 (Brazil); Jaramillo 2014, 2015 (Peru); Paz Arauco et al. 2014 (Bolivia); Sauma and Trejos 2014 (Costa Rica); Scott 2014 (Mexico). World Bank estimates based on 2012 National Socioeconomic Survey (SUSENAS) data (Indonesia). Armenia, Ethiopia, and South Africa data from chapters 2, 3, and 8 of this volume, respectively.
Note: PPP = purchasing power parity, in 2005 U.S. dollars.
a. "Market income" comprises pretax wages, salaries, income earned from capital assets (rent, interest, or dividends), and private transfers.
b. "Disposable income" = market income – direct taxes + direct cash transfers.
c. "Consumable income" = disposable income – indirect taxes (value added and excise) + indirect subsidies.

or transfer expenditures made. Direct transfers—PKH, Raskin, and Poor Student Education Support (BSM)—collectively have a larger marginal impact on inequality than do energy subsidies, but subsidies receive a budget allocation that is 10 times the allocation for direct transfers. Likewise, education (cumulatively) has an impact on inequality more than 10 times the impact of energy subsidies, but subsides receive a budget allocation that is one-third again as large as that for education. Inequality is neither much increased nor decreased *even though* most policy instruments available do reduce inequality.

Cash and near-cash transfers, energy subsidies, and in-kind transfers (in health and education) are all progressive with respect to market income. But notice that transfers provided via subsidy spending or in-kind provision of services are received indirectly through consumption, which means that households consuming either more (as in the case of energy subsidies) or higher-valued types (as in the case of tertiary education or health) will receive proportionately larger shares of the transfers available.

Indonesia's direct transfers do reduce poverty by approximately 1 percentage point although little is spent on them (table 5.8). Within the set of direct transfers, the subsidized rice program's (Raskin) impact on poverty is two to three times that of PKH although the expenditures are over 10 times as high.

Table 5.7 Marginal Contributions of Expenditures and Taxes to Inequality Reduction in Indonesia, 2012

Fiscal intervention	Kakwani[a]	Magnitude (% of GDP)	Marginal inequality reduction, from market income[b]		
			Disposable income[c]	Consumable income[d]	Final income[e]
Redistributive effect	n.a.	n.a.	0.0043	0.0036	0.0237
Contributory pension[f]	−0.209	0.76	0.0002	0.0001	−0.0001
Direct transfers	0.640	0.33	0.0042	0.0041	0.0037
PKH	0.854	0.02	0.0008	0.0008	0.0007
Scholarships	0.669	0.08	0.0003	0.0003	0.0003
Raskin[g]	0.596	0.23	0.0030	0.0030	0.0028
Indirect taxes	−0.042	5.30	n.a.	−0.0031	−0.0022
VAT	0.015	4.10	n.a.	0.0010	0.0015
Tobacco excise	−0.134	1.20	n.a.	−0.0043	−0.0038
Indirect subsidies	0.056	3.70	n.a.	0.0026	0.0014
In-kind education	0.363	2.70	n.a.	n.a.	0.0193
Primary	0.471	0.85	n.a.	n.a.	0.0089
Lower-secondary	0.425	1.05	n.a.	n.a.	0.0083
Upper-secondary	0.288	0.34	n.a.	n.a.	0.0023
Tertiary	−0.085	0.37	n.a.	n.a.	−0.0007
In-kind health	0.273	0.89	n.a.	n.a.	0.0031

Source: Based on 2012 National Socioeconomic Survey (SUSENAS) data.
Note: PKH = Hopeful Family Program (*Program Keluarga Harapan*); VAT = value added taxes; n.a. = not applicable.
a. The Kakwani coefficient is a typical measure of progressivity, using market income as the base. For taxes, it is the difference between the concentration coefficient of the tax and the Gini for market income. For transfers, it is the difference between the Gini for market income and the concentration coefficient of the transfer. (See chapter 1 for a further explanation.)
b. "Market income" comprises pretax wages, salaries, income earned from capital assets (rent, interest, or dividends), and private transfers.
c. "Disposable income" = market income − payments for personal income taxes + direct cash transfers.
d. "Consumable income" = disposable income − indirect taxes (VAT and excises) + indirect subsidies.
e. "Final income" = consumable income + value of in-kind transfers (such as for education and health care).
f. The marginal contribution of the contributory pension system is the cumulative impact of pension contributions made by households and pension benefits received by households. The marginal impact of pension benefits by themselves is *negative,* meaning income inequality is higher when pension income is added.
g. The Raskin rice subsidy program is treated as a direct cash transfer because the subsidized rice distributed through the program is often resold for cash.

The same pattern happens across transfer types as well: although energy subsidies' impact on poverty reduction (4 percentage points) is approximately four times the impact of direct transfers (1 percentage point), the budget allocation for subsidies exceeds the budget allocation for direct transfers by a factor greater than 10. So, not all poor households are covered by direct transfer initiatives, and direct transfer beneficiaries receive amounts that are small (relative to their own incomes); consequently the impact on poverty from direct transfer expenditures is modest. The impact on poverty is greater from energy subsidy programs, but the magnitudes of those subsidy expenditures are several times greater (proportionally) than are direct transfer magnitudes.

Table 5.8 Marginal Contributions of Transfers, Taxes, and Subsidies to Poverty Reduction in Indonesia, 2012

Fiscal intervention	Magnitude (% of GDP)	Marginal poverty reduction, from market income[a] Disposable income[b]	Consumable income[c]
Poverty reduction impact (at income of US$1.25 per day PPP)	n.a.	0.0124	0.0153
Direct transfers	0.33	0.0118	0.0113
PKH	0.02	0.0025	0.0027
Scholarships	0.08	0.0012	0.0011
Raskin[d]	0.23	0.0079	0.0081
Indirect taxes	5.30	n.a.	−0.0273
VAT	4.10	n.a.	−0.0145
Tobacco excise	1.20	n.a.	−0.0157
Indirect subsidies	3.70	n.a.	0.0410

Source: Based on 2012 National Socioeconomic Survey (SUSENAS) data.

Note: PKH = Hopeful Family Program (*Program Keluarga Harapan*); PPP = purchasing power parity (in 2005 U.S. dollars); VAT = value added taxes; n.a. = not applicable.

a. "Market income" comprises pretax wages, salaries, income earned from capital assets (rent, interest, or dividends), and private transfers.

b. "Disposable income" = market income − payments for personal income taxes + direct cash transfers.

c. "Consumable income" = disposable income − indirect taxes (VAT and excises) + indirect subsidies.

d. The Raskin rice subsidy program is treated as a direct cash transfer because the subsidized rice distributed through the program is often resold for cash.

Effect of Social Spending on Incomes

We generate Beckerman-Immervoll efficiency indexes for marginal poverty reduction contributions (from market to disposable income) in table 5.9. The vertical expenditure efficiency (VEE) indicator shows that less than one quarter of total direct cash benefits available (PKH, BSM, Raskin) are transferred to the poor (at the national poverty line). The larger transfers (BSM and Raskin) both have target beneficiaries defined as eligible households or individuals who are "poor or near poor," so we also look at VEE at the national vulnerability line: nearly two-fifths (37 percent) of direct transfers reach the moderate-poverty-line poor.[43]

The spillover (S) index, at 0.12, indicates that direct-transfer magnitudes rarely exceed the strictly necessary amount required for poor beneficiaries to reach poverty-line income; in other words, transfer levels are appropriately specified *given coverage*.[44] The poverty reduction effectiveness (PRE) indicator, which is the product of VEE times (1-S), shows that in Indonesia only 20 percent of direct transfer spending actually helped reduce the head-count poverty rate, and only 35 percent helped to reduce the vulnerability rate. The poverty gap efficiency (PGE) indicator shows that in Indonesia the distribution of direct transfers eliminates 16 percent of the (pretransfer) poverty gap. Indonesia's PGE confirms two weaknesses constraining the impact of direct transfers on poverty reduction: coverage is low, meaning the

Table 5.9 Direct Transfers and Poverty Reduction

Beckerman-Immervoll indicator	National poverty line[a]	National vulnerability line[b]
VEE	0.22	0.37
S	0.12	0.06
PRE	0.20	0.35
Change in poverty rate (%)	−1.3	−1.3
PGE	0.16	0.10
Change in poverty gap (%)[c]	−0.4	−0.5

Source: Based on 2012 National Socioeconomic Survey (SUSENAS) data.

Note: PGE = poverty gap efficiency, the extent to which transfers cover the gap between poor households' incomes and the poverty line (Beckerman 1979; Immervoll et al. 2009); PRE = poverty reduction effectiveness, the percentage of reduction in the poverty headcount rate; S = spillover, the share of transfer expenditures that move households that are over the poverty line, thus benefiting those who are no longer poor; VEE = vertical expenditure efficiency, the percentage of direct transfers that go to the poor.

a. The 2014 national poverty line was expenditure of about Rp 302,735 (US$25) per person per month.

b. The 2014 national vulnerability line is 1.5 times the poverty line, or Rp 454,103 per person per month (US$37.50).

c. The poverty gap is the average percentage by which poor individuals fall below a given poverty line.

majority of poor households' incomes or expenditures are unchanged after direct transfers are distributed, and transfer values are small for those who actually receive them.

Ultimately, households in the poorest decile receive direct transfers, indirect subsidies, and in-kind transfers that are worth 30 percent of their market income; indirect taxes represent about 7 percent of their market income. So, in net terms—and again for the poorest decile—direct transfers boost market income by approximately 4 percent, net subsidies provide a boost of approximately 2 percent, and net in-kind transfers provide a boost of approximately 19 percent.[45] For the richest decile, the analogous numbers are 0.05 percent, 1.00 percent, and 3.00 percent—meaning that the survey households in the richest decile are cumulative recipients of public expenditures rather than net contributors to public revenues (as shown earlier in figure 5.1).

In-Kind Transfers and the Distribution of Utilization

In-kind transfers of health and education services are the largest social expenditures we consider; the only other public expenditure category of commensurate magnitude is subsidies. Because receipt of in-kind transfers requires use of the services provided, and we value those services at the (uniform, average) cost to the government of providing them, the redistributive effect of this set of transfers is driven entirely by the distribution of use: if certain income groups use the service with greater frequency (or if they consume higher-valued types of the public service with greater frequency), they will receive greater shares of total in-kind expenditures.

Enrollment rates are high for all income groups in Indonesian primary schools and then decline rapidly for lower-income students from primary to lower-secondary; from lower- to upper-secondary; and from upper-secondary to tertiary (figure 5.2). The rate of tertiary enrollment in the poorest three deciles is

Figure 5.2 Gross School Enrollment Rates in Indonesia, by Income Decile, 2012

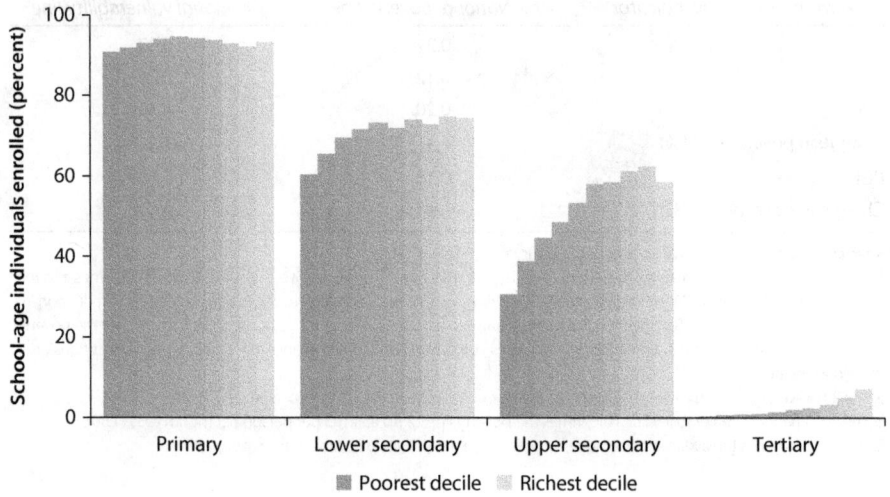

Source: Based on 2012 National Socioeconomic Survey (SUSENAS) data.

Figure 5.3 Health Care Service Utilization Rates in Indonesia, by Income Decile, 2012

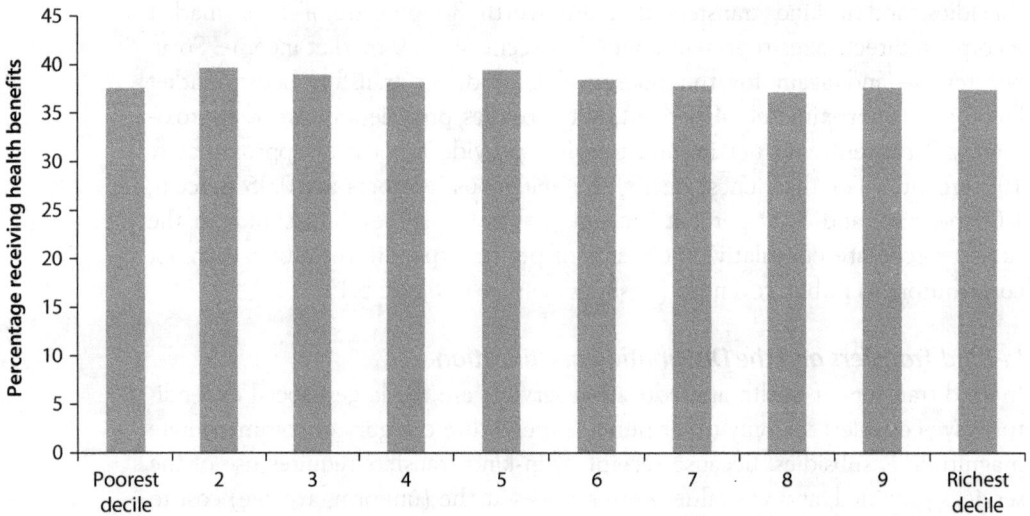

Source: Based on 2012 National Socioeconomic Survey (SUSENAS) data.

essentially zero; whereas few SUSENAS individuals overall are enrolled in tertiary education. Nearly 100 percent of those enrolled in tertiary education come from households with *at least* median per capita incomes.

Use of health care services, conversely, is distributed approximately uniformly across income deciles (figure 5.3).

As table 5.7 indicated earlier, cumulative public education services do reduce inequality, but the results vary noticeably by education level.[46] For example, the marginal impact of primary and lower-secondary education transfers are estimated to be nearly 1.0 percentage point, whereas for upper-secondary the estimated marginal impact is closer to 0.2 percentage points. Tertiary education expenditures have a negative estimated marginal impact that is nevertheless small (less than 0.1 percentage point). This across-education-levels pattern can be predicted from figure 5.2, which shows that education utilization gaps between poorer and richer households are smallest for primary education and grow steadily larger from lower-secondary to tertiary levels. Public health services provided have a positive marginal impact on inequality, but the impact is smaller than that for education.

Most individuals using public health and education services in Indonesia pay non-negotiable fees to access those systems; such fees are most often charged by the unit providing the service (such as the school, hospital, or clinic). This practice indicates that centrally provided public expenditures do not completely cover the locally prevailing *inclusive* cost of public provision. Our baseline scenario treats them as excise taxes (levied at the public service provider), whereas the centrally budgeted expenditures accruing to a particular service are treated as a subsidy, so that to each public health care or education service accrues a "net" subsidy (equal to the central-level unit subsidy minus the local-level tax).[47] It is this "net" subsidy that was summarized earlier in table 5.8 and in the text preceding table 5.7.

We can also treat the payment of non-negotiable, unregulated fees as disposable income (which would have been spent in the same amounts and on the same services in the absence of public expenditures on the same services). Theoretically, these "membership" or access fees are unrelated to the central government's cost of providing the health care or education services utilized.[48] When we treat these fees as the price of access to the public provision system (rather than as an indirect tax on the consumption of public services), we can then also provide to households the full cost of provision of public services (rather than the "net" subsidy as described above); our third sensitivity analysis does exactly that.

To summarize this alternative conceptualization (which forms one of the sensitivity analyses in our analytical framework), table 5.10 presents the Gini and concentration coefficients for the distribution of disposable income before and after these fees are paid as well as the distribution of the in-kind health and education transfers with respect to disposable income.

Public education access fees have a negative Kakwani coefficient, indicating that those with higher income shares pay decreasing shares of these fees. This result is due in part to a higher rate of private education among richer households: fees paid for privately provided education do not contribute to public revenues and therefore cannot be turned into public expenditures. Fees paid for public health system access are progressively distributed *and* pro-poor in that the fee shares are smaller (for all but the richest decile) than market income or disposable income shares.[49]

Table 5.10 Marginal Contributions of In-Kind Transfers to Inequality Reduction in Indonesia, by Income Concept, 2012

In-kind transfer type	Kakwani[e]	Magnitude (% of GDP)	Marginal inequality reduction, from market income[a]		
			Disposable income[b]	Consumable income[c]	Final income[d]
Redistributive effect					
In-kind fees as tax	n.a.	n.a.	0.0043	0.0036	0.0237
In-kind fees as income	n.a.	n.a.	0.0051	0.0044	0.0258
In-kind fees as income					
Public health fees	0.271	0.15	0.0019	0.0019	0.0020
Public education fees	−0.170	0.52	−0.0027	−0.0026	−0.0009
In-kind public spending					
In-kind health spending	0.284	0.9	n.a.	n.a.	0.0028
In-kind education spending	0.361	2.7	n.a.	n.a.	0.0174
All in-kind spending + fees	0.495	4.2	n.a.	n.a.	0.0197

Source: Based on 2012 National Socioeconomic Survey (SUSENAS) data.
Note: GDP = gross domestic product; n.a. = not applicable.
a. "Market income" comprises pretax wages, salaries, income earned from capital assets (rent, interest, or dividends), and private transfers.
b. "Disposable income" = market income − payments for personal income taxes + direct cash transfers.
c. "Consumable income" = disposable income − indirect taxes (value added taxes and excises) + indirect subsidies.
d. "Final income" = consumable income + value of in-kind transfers (such as for education and health care).
e. The Kakwani coefficient is a typical measure of progressivity, using market income as the base. For taxes, it is the difference between the concentration coefficient of the tax and the Gini for market income. For transfers, it is the difference between the Gini for market income and the concentration coefficient of the transfer. (For further explanation, see chapter 1.)

The Gini coefficient on disposable income measured *without* these public service fees included is approximately three-tenths of a percentage point higher (at 0.3934) than the Gini coefficient on disposable income measured *with* public service fees included (0.3899). This indicates that the reduction in the Gini coefficient is larger when these fees are levied; without public health and education service access fees, measured inequality (at disposable income) would be greater.[50]

Conclusions

This report assesses the distributional impact of a subset of the public revenue collection and spending instruments and finds that fiscal policy does reduce both poverty and inequality in Indonesia. However, the magnitudes are modest. Indonesian fiscal policy does not harm many individuals: fiscal impoverishment is low when in-kind transfers are included. However fiscal impoverishment is much higher when we examine only those tax and expenditure instruments that have a direct impact on consumable income: nearly 40 percent of poor individuals (at postfiscal, consumable income) have been impoverished by fiscal policy.

We have allocated just over 70 percent of total tax revenue collected from households (and about 44 percent of total tax revenues) including VAT and excise taxes; PIT burdens are expected to be zero *for SUSENAS households*. We have allocated 56 percent of primary government expenditures with a focus on social spending including direct cash transfers, health and education spending, and nonsocial fuel subsidy spending.

Summary of Fiscal Impacts

Indonesia's (2012-era) fiscal policy reduced poverty and inequality through a slightly regressive indirect tax system and slightly progressive social spending. Everyone in Indonesia contributes consumption-based tax revenues, and those resources are redistributed as government expenditure on direct and indirect transfers and in-kind spending that raises incomes for everyone—raising incomes for the poorest individuals proportionately more than for the richest individuals. Approximately 3.6 million individuals were lifted out of poverty (at the US$2.50 or US$1.25 per day PPP lines or at the prevailing national poverty line) as a result of the tax-and-transfer system.

Fiscal resources are replenished with household contributions, mainly from taxes on consumption. Total consumption taxes actually increase inequality (marginally). The larger of the taxes (VAT) has a positive marginal impact on inequality, whereas the smaller tobacco excise has a negative marginal impact on inequality. Kakwani coefficients (as shown in table 5.7) indicate that VAT is progressively distributed (with respect to market income): the share of total VAT paid rises with market income.

Direct transfers are equalizing and more effectively target the poor than in-kind transfers or subsidies. They are also quite small in magnitude—total spending on all direct transfers representing less than half a percentage point of GDP—and either provide relatively small benefit packages or do not have very broad coverage (or both). The marginal inequality and poverty reduction impacts of these direct transfers are therefore muted.

In-kind benefits, which are much larger in both expenditure and coverage magnitudes, are received only by individuals using a publicly provided service. Poorer households in Indonesia have far lower rates of access to secondary- and tertiary-level education (and approximately equal rates of access to health care services) than do rich households. Even so—and because the lower-cost types of such public services (elementary education or outpatient health care, for example) have positive marginal inequality reduction impacts—overall the public provision of services, and especially the provision of basic education, are equalizing. The combination of social spending (direct and in-kind transfers) and energy subsidies is modestly inequality and poverty reducing.

Energy subsidies and education spending alone account for approximately 80 percent of all public expenditures analyzed here. Energy subsidies in 2012 had a positive marginal impact on inequality reduction. As a consequence, the resulting net subsidy on consumption (subsidies received through consumption minus taxes paid through consumption) is slightly progressive (with respect to disposable income) and poverty-reducing. Because very few individuals pay more in taxes than they receive in transfers, Indonesia's fiscal system boosts market income (on average) not just among poor households, but also among middle-income and rich households.

CEQ Comparison and Policy Implications

Compared with the rest of the CEQ country set, Indonesia has relatively low prefiscal inequality (in terms of market income). However, Armenia and Ethiopia (for example), which have similarly low prefiscal inequality, surpass Indonesia in terms of poverty or inequality reduction through fiscal policy although spending similarly low amounts.

The particularly modest impacts on inequality and poverty of Indonesia's fiscal practices have to do in part with a low revenue base: Indonesia's PIT collections and the effective indirect tax rate (on consumption) are both low by CEQ-country standards. These modest impacts also stem from Indonesia's prioritization of energy subsidies: its untargeted energy subsidies have broad coverage among poor, middle-income, and rich households and account for total expenditures more than 10 times as large as the country's direct transfers. Regardless of the optimal magnitude of fiscal expenditures in Indonesia, then, policy makers can still reduce income equality and reduce the number of impoverished citizens by shifting fiscal priorities away from untargeted subsidies and toward targeted transfers.

Notes

1. The poverty rate is defined as the percentage of population living below the national poverty line of Rp 302,735 (US$25) per person per month (in 2014). Real gross domestic product (GDP) per capita grew by 5.4 percent annually (on average) between 2000 and 2014. This growth has also helped create a larger consumer class than ever before: 45 million people—approximately 18 percent of all Indonesians—are now "economically secure," defined as middle-class households that are economically secure from poverty and vulnerability; the economic security line in 2014 was about Rp 1 million (US$83) in consumption per person per month (World Bank 2016).

2. The Gini index is measured in Indonesia in terms of the distribution of per capita consumption rather than distribution of per capita income. See World Bank (2016) for an extended discussion.

3. For the Indonesia CEQ assessment, we use household survey data from the 2012 National Socioeconomic Survey (SUSENAS) conducted by the Central Statistics Agency (http://microdata.bps.go.id/mikrodata/index.php/catalog/SUSENAS). Public expenditure and revenue magnitude data come from fiscal year 2012 audited budget and administrative data (BPK 2013).

4. "Consumable" transfers include direct and indirect cash (or near-cash) transfers because they can be directly transformed into goods and services the household wishes to consume. "In-kind transfers" (such as for education and health care) are not "consumable" in the same way.

5. In general, "consumable income" = market income (pretax wages, salaries, income earned from capital assets, and private transfers) – direct and indirect taxes paid + cash

transfers + indirect subsidies. (For a more detailed discussion of how the CEQ income concepts are constructed, see chapter 1 and Lustig and Higgins [2013].) "Poor" is defined here as those whose consumable income is less than or equal to US$1.25 per day in 2005 purchasing power parity (PPP) terms.

6. The "consumable income" poor headcount (at the US$1.25 PPP per day poverty line) is approximately 10.5 percent, and approximately 40 percent of those individuals are impoverished by Indonesia's fiscal policy interventions. However, if we include the monetized value of in-kind public health and education services—large expenditures (in magnitude) that cover significant portions of the poor, near-poor, and nonpoor populations—there are very few net fiscal payers.

7. The magnitude and pervasiveness of local, unregulated user fees—often charged by the unit actually providing the service—is unique to Indonesia within the CEQ country set, but worldwide this empirical fact is likely seen in other fiscal systems.

8. The CEQ set includes 26 countries, with per capita incomes ranging from less than US$2,000 to over US$14,000 in 2005 PPP terms (Lustig 2014). The World Bank classifies middle-income countries as having a per capita gross national income in 2014 of US$1,046–US$12,735 (see http://data.worldbank.org/about/country-and-lending -groups). Under World Bank's definitions, Indonesia is classified as a lower-middle-income country, whereas Mexico is classified as an upper-middle-income country.

9. Coupled with Indonesia's consistently low fiscal deficits and now-stable debt burdens, this low revenue base in turn means there are few public revenues available to turn into public expenditures, as further discussed in the next section.

10. In Indonesia, food goods that are considered necessities (rice, corn, sago [palm starch], soybeans and soy products, and salt) and basic essential services (health care, education, banking and other financial services, and other public services) are VAT-exempt. The standard VAT rate (in 2012) was 10 percent, although some firms and activities are subject to output VAT based on a deemed percentage of transaction value; such firms and activities do not claim refunds for input VAT.

11. The analysis summarized in this report excludes public revenues generated from corporate or industry income tax payments (4.5 percent of GDP in 2012) as well as nontax revenues (4.3 percent of GDP in 2012).

12. Most of Indonesia's PIT is paid by high-income, formal wage earners (or formal business owners), of whom very few are represented in the SUSENAS national household survey (as discussed further in the "Data, Assumptions, and Income Concepts" section).

13. Beginning in 2009, Indonesia implemented (within a national budget) a constitutional amendment requiring that a minimum of 20 percent of total budgeted government expenditures go to education.

14. The agency responsible for stockpiling rice for distribution, as Raskin rice, to local marketplaces also sets a farm-gate price floor and has sole control and responsibility for rice imports, meaning that in some years it may be providing a subsidy to rice suppliers as well as to rice consumers (Jellema and Noura 2012).

15. For more details about the use of input-output tables in the CEQ analyses, see Lustig and Higgins (2013).

16. There is concern that SUSENAS does not adequately contact or receive information from households at the top of the income distribution. The absence of such households means the upper end of the SUSENAS-based market income distribution is

truncated; this is true whether market income is directly reported or derived from consumption expenditures. Together with the Bank Indonesia (the country's central bank) and the Finance Ministry's Fiscal Policy Office, the Poverty Global Practice in the World Bank's Jakarta office is assembling a framework for incorporating these wealthy households into SUSENAS-based analysis (Wai-Poi, Wihardja, and Mervisiano, forthcoming).

17. There were no payroll or social security taxes in Indonesia in 2012.

18. We do not propose that no SUSENAS household pays PIT. Rather, SUSENAS does not record actual PIT payments made, so we estimate the magnitude of the total PIT payments generated from SUSENAS households. However, the estimate of total PIT payments generated from SUSENAS households is small enough that all SUSENAS households would rationally have an empirical expectation of zero for their own PIT burden.

19. For references on both sides, see Lustig and Higgins (2013).

20. We do not include an incidence analysis of the pension contributions paid by the *employer* (the government of Indonesia) but potentially borne by the *employees* (civil servants) in the form of lower wages. Although these contributions are not shown in the tables and graphs, additional results for the case in which pensions are a transfer are available upon request.

21. The National Labour Force Survey (*Survei Angkatan Kerja Nasional*, or SAKERNAS) also does not contain pension status information.

22. Allocative assumptions for indirect transfers—consumption subsidies—are covered at the beginning of this section.

23. Even when the "event" of paying a tax or receiving a benefit can be identified directly, it is not always possible to directly identify the amounts paid or received. When inference or imputation is needed to estimate a value of a tax or benefit for a directly identified payer or recipient, the "CEQ Master Workbook: Indonesia" provides the details on the algorithms used to estimate these values (Afkar, Jellema, and Wai-Poi 2015).

24. Eligibility conditions were also not revised between 2012 and 2013.

25. In other words, we are simulating an observed conditional distribution of benefits and beneficiaries in a new sample of households with a similar distribution of characteristics that underlie the observed conditional distribution.

26. For energy subsidies, we calculate the rate as the difference between the government's "reference" price (available in official decrees or administrative documentation) and the sale price (which is widely publicized and easily verified) as a percentage of the reference price.

27. Processed tobacco is not used as an input in any other economic sector represented in Indonesia's input-output table, so the indirect effects of the tobacco excise are assumed to be zero.

28. For details on the algorithms used to estimate these values, see the "CEQ Master Workbook: Indonesia" (Afkar, Jellema, and Wai-Poi 2015).

29. SUSENAS does not always contain complete utilization information for all four combinations of service and service-provider types.

30. For details on the algorithms used, see the "CEQ Master Workbook: Indonesia" (Afkar, Jellema, and Wai-Poi, 2015).

31. In contrast, concerning observed education fees, there is complete information on the service provider type, so an allocative algorithm is unnecessary.

32. As Bibi and Duclos (2010) and Lustig (2014) explain, the potential impact of any individual intervention should not be calculated by taking the difference between consecutive pairs of income concepts. For example, taking the difference between the Gini coefficient for postfiscal income (or consumable income) and disposable income is *not* equal to the contribution of indirect subsidies and indirect taxes to the decline of inequality from market income to postfiscal income. Because (a) the contribution of each intervention is path dependent; (b) we are showing one possible path; and (c) the actual path is unobserved, there is an error component to our estimates when they are arranged sequentially. We *can* compare, however, the impact of interventions on any indicator with respect to market income (which is what we do in this section). Therefore, perhaps a more precise way of stating our result is the following: without the redistributive process set in motion (via taxes and transfers) by Indonesia's fiscal policy, measured inequality would be higher (in a static setting).

33. The quality or effectiveness of publicly provided health and education services varies widely in Indonesia, whereas the available outcome measures indicate that health and education service quality is uncorrelated with official public expenditure levels (Jellema and Noura 2012). We do not have primary or secondary source information that would allow us to make quality adjustments to services provided or to calculate the government's cost for an "effective" or "standard" unit of health care or education. Because any public service will contain more or less of an effective unit of the service, we are misestimating the distribution of these effective units by making the "government cost" assumption. However, by including the unofficial fees paid into public provision systems, we are lowering our misestimate by lowering the value of the government's contribution (or lowering the effective units provided) in proportion to the unofficial fees paid by the individual.

34. The national poverty line in Indonesia is calculated by expenditure level rather than income level. As of 2014, the poor were those living below expenditure of about Rp 302,735 (US$25) per person per month (Aji 2015; World Bank 2016).

35. The poverty calculations include the combined effect of all taxes, cash transfers, and indirect subsidies. In line with international practice, we exclude the monetary value of education and health services in calculating the impact of fiscal policy on poverty rates because households are unaware of how much the government spends on these services and as a result do not view these services as part of their income.

36. And the headcount poverty rates are predictably larger when income is reduced by, for example, excluding pensions from market income or excluding pension contributions from disposable income.

37. Caveats are necessary here: this is true for the set of representative households that appear in the SUSENAS survey and for which the direct PIT is assumed to be zero. PIT is assumed to be zero because the vast majority of households have implied market incomes below the tax threshold (as discussed earlier in the "Data, Assumptions, and Income Concepts" section).

38. These three instruments (nontax revenue, VAT, and corporate income tax) each contribute approximately one-quarter of all public revenues (table 5.1).

39. See Higgins and Lustig (2016) for the elaboration of the fiscal impoverishment and fiscal gains to the poor indexes.

40. The headcount poverty rate is estimated at approximately at 12.1 percent at market income (prefiscal income) and 10.5 percent at consumable income.

41. For a more detailed discussion of vertical equity (VE), reranking (RR), and redistributive effects, see chapter 1 in this volume and Duclos and Araar (2006), chapter 8.

42. Table 5.7 shows the marginal impact of pension income. For the pension *system* (that is, the cumulative impact of pension contributions made by households and pension benefits received by households) the marginal impact on inequality reduction is positive (at disposable, consumable, and final income). The VAT regime does include exemptions for basic foodstuffs, public transport, and other necessities and is likely better described as "neutral," rather than regressive, in both design and operation. Furthermore, the Kakwani index for total indirect taxes is approximately zero, indicating a neutral indirect tax regime. (For a further explanation of the Kakwani index, see chapter 1.)

43. The "national poverty line" in Indonesia is calculated by expenditure level rather than income level. As of 2014, the poor were those living below expenditure of about Rp 302,735 (US$25) per person per month (Aji 2015; World Bank 2016). The "national vulnerability line" is set at 1.5 times the poverty line, or Rp 454,103 per person per month (US$37.50).

44. However, the objective of Indonesian social assistance programs is not solely to put the poor over the poverty line; that is, they are not designed to have no "spillover."

45. Because indirect taxes and public service access fees are a burden (and subsidies and in-kind benefit transfers become a benefit) conditional on consumption, it is easier to express indirect subsidies or taxes and in-kind transfers or access fees in "net" terms.

46. The private education sector in Indonesia also benefits from public education spending primarily through the placement of civil servant teachers (provided to all education levels) and an "operational funds" budget that is provided on a per-student basis to both private and public education providers at the primary and lower-secondary levels.

47. An implication of this scenario is that households or individuals acquiring public services value the service acquired at some level higher than the central government's cost of provision; the "tax" paid by service-utilizing individuals is treated as revenue by the government.

48. This alternative scenario may capture a form of "insurance" provided by the fee-collecting institution. Theories of administrative and political decentralization propose that local-level actors have more and higher-quality information regarding local preferences and budgets on both the supply and demand sides of any transaction. Indonesia's fee system—which is a burden on users only and which allows for price discrimination under limited competition—can be regarded as a locally determined and affordable "premium" charged to likely users that ensures the continued effective operation of the facilities users visit. The costs of "continued effective operation" include (but are not limited to) capital depreciation as well as maintaining a sufficient labor productivity level. (Under limited competition, skilled health care service labor will have outside options.) In other words, the fees charged to users insure those same users against decreasing productivity or the facility going offline altogether. If the fees charged do accomplish this insurance function, then in the event that such fees were abolished, the poverty headcount (as measured by expenditure levels) would not necessarily change although health status might decline (on average), leading to lower broadly measured welfare, particularly among those households unable to afford the nonsubsidized cost of provision.

49. Some individuals may not be accessing health care service providers because of anticipated fees. If individuals constrained in this way are more often from poorer deciles, poorer households bear a greater burden (from these fees) than the statistics in table 5.10 indicate. The SUSENAS household survey does not allow us to identify individuals who *did not visit* health care providers because of anticipated fees. The same caveats apply to fees charged by public education providers.

50. Inequality (as measured by the Gini coefficient) is slightly lower at final income under this alternative scenario than under our benchmark case (where public service fees are treated as an indirect tax on public service consumption), shown earlier in table 5.3. This result is logical because, in the alternative scenario, we do not remove the equalizing effect of the public service fees through their characterization as an indirect tax.

References

Afkar, Rythia, Jon Jellema, and Matthew Wai-Poi. 2015. "CEQ Master Workbook: Indonesia. Version: March 15, 2015." Commitment to Equity (CEQ) Data Center, CEQ Institute, Tulane University, New Orleans, LA.

Aji, Priasto. 2015. "Summary of Indonesia's Poverty Analysis." ADB Papers on Indonesia No. 4, Asian Development Bank, Manila.

Beckerman, W. 1979. "The Impact of Income Maintenance Payments on Poverty in Britain, 1975." *Economic Journal* 89 (354): 261–79.

Beneke, Margarita, Nora Lustig, and José Andrés Oliva. 2016. "The Impact of Taxes and Social Spending on Inequality and Poverty in El Salvador." Commitment to Equity (CEQ) Working Paper No. 57, Center for Inter-American Policy and Research; the Inter-American Dialogue; and Department of Economics, Tulane University, New Orleans.

Bibi, Sami, and Jean-Yves Duclos. 2010. "A Comparison of the Poverty Impact of Transfers, Taxes and Market Income across Five OECD Countries." *Bulletin of Economic Research* 62 (4): 387–406.

BPK (Audit Board of the Republic of Indonesia). 2013. "Laporan Keuangan Pemerintah Pusat Tahun 2012." Annual audit report, BPK, Jakarta. http://www.bpk.go.id/lkpp.

Bucheli, Marisa, Nora Lustig, Máximo Rossi, and Florencia Amábile. 2014. "Social Spending, Taxes, and Income Redistribution in Uruguay." *Public Finance Review* 42 (3): 413–33.

Cabrera, Maynor, Nora Lustig, and Hilcías E. Morán. 2015. "Fiscal Policy, Inequality, and the Ethnic Divide in Guatemala." *World Development* 76 (C): 263–79.

Damuri, Yose Rizal, and Ari A. Perdana. 2003. "The Impact of Fiscal Policy on Income Distribution and Poverty: A Computable General Equilibrium Approach for Indonesia." Economics Working Paper No. WPE068, Center for Strategic and International Studies, Jakarta, Indonesia.

Dartanto, Teguh. 2013. "Reducing Fuel Subsidies and the Implication on Fiscal Balance and Poverty in Indonesia: A Simulation Analysis." *Energy Policy* 58 (July 2013): 117–34.

Duclos, Jean-Yves, and Abdelkrim Araar. 2006. *Poverty and Equity: Measurement, Policy, and Estimation with DAD.* New York: Springer and International Development Research Centre.

Hadiwibowo, Yuniarto. 2010. "Fiscal Policy, Investment and Long-Run Economic Growth: Evidence from Indonesia." *Asian Social Science* 6 (9): 3–11.

Higgins, Sean, and Nora Lustig. 2016. "Can a Poverty-Reducing and Progressive Tax and Transfer System Hurt the Poor?" *Journal of Development Economics* 122 (September 2016): 63–75.

Higgins, Sean, and Claudiney Pereira. 2014. "The Effects of Brazil's Taxation and Social Spending on the Distribution of Household Income." *Public Finance Review* 42 (3): 346–67.

Immervoll, Herwig, Horacio Levy, José Ricardo Nogueira, Cathal O'Donoghue, and Rozane Bezerra de Siqueira. 2009. "The Impact of Brazil's Tax-Benefit System on Inequality and Poverty." In *Poverty, Inequality, and Policy in Latin America*, edited by Stephan Klasen and Felicitas Nowak-Lehmann, 271–301. Cambridge, MA: MIT Press.

Jaramillo, Miguel. 2014. "The Incidence of Social Spending and Taxes in Peru." *Public Finance Review* 42 (3): 391–412.

———. 2015. "CEQ Master Workbook: Peru. Version: August 7, 2015." Commitment to Equity (CEQ) Data Center, CEQ Institute, Tulane University, New Orleans, LA.

Jellema, Jon, and Hassan Noura. 2012. "Protecting Poor and Vulnerable Households in Indonesia." Public Expenditure Review, World Bank, Washington, DC.

Lustig, Nora. 2014. "Taxes, Transfers, Inequality and the Poor in the Developing World. Round 1." Commitment to Equity Working Paper No. 23, Center for Inter-American Policy and Research; the Inter-American Dialogue; and Department of Economics, Tulane University, New Orleans, LA.

Lustig, Nora, and Sean Higgins. 2013. "Commitment to Equity Assessment (CEQ): Estimating the Incidence of Social Spending, Subsidies and Taxes." Handbook and Commitment to Equity Working Paper No. 1, Center for Inter-American Policy and Research; the Inter-American Dialogue; and Department of Economics, Tulane University, New Orleans, LA.

Paz Arauco, Verónica, George Gray Molina, Wilson Jiménez Pozo, and Ernesto Yáñez Aguilar. 2014. "Explaining Low Redistributive Impact in Bolivia." *Public Finance Review* 42 (3): 326–45.

Sauma, Pablo, and Juan Diego Trejos. 2014. "Social Public Spending, Taxes, Redistribution of Income, and Poverty in Costa Rica." Commitment to Equity Working Paper No. 18, Center for Inter-American Policy and Research; the Inter-American Dialogue; and Department of Economics, Tulane University, New Orleans, LA.

Scott, John. 2014. "Redistributive Impact and Efficiency of Mexico's Fiscal System." *Public Finance Review* 42 (3): 368–90.

Theil, H. 1967. *Economics and Information Theory*. Chicago: Rand McNally and Company.

Wai-Poi, Matthew, Monica Wihardja, and Michaelino Mervisiano. Forthcoming. "The Problem with Taxes: Estimating Top Incomes in Indonesia." Working Paper, World Bank, Jakarta.

Woolard, Ingrid, Precious Zikhali, and Mashekwa Maboshe. 2014. "CEQ Master Workbook: South Africa. Version: September 30, 2014." Commitment to Equity Data Center, CEQ Institute, Tulane University, New Orleans, LA.

World Bank. 2016. "Indonesia's Rising Divide: Why Inequality Is Rising, Why It Matters and What Can Be Done." Research project report, World Bank, Jakarta.

CHAPTER 6

The Distributional Impact of Fiscal Policy in Jordan

Shamma A. Alam, Gabriela Inchauste, and Umar Serajuddin

Introduction

Jordan's economy grew at an average of 6.7 percent a year between 2000 and 2008. This performance was better than the average of the Middle East and North Africa region as a whole, which grew at a rate of about 4.5 percent a year (World Bank 2012b). Jordan's economic growth declined sharply between 2008 and 2009, coinciding with the global financial crisis: real gross domestic product (GDP) growth fell from almost 7.2 percent in 2008 to 2.3 percent in 2010 (IMF 2012).

With strong economic growth in the earlier part of the decade, the country made important social gains. For example, Jordan's growth was accompanied by a large reduction in poverty (DOS and World Bank 2009; Mansour 2012). Even with the decline in per capita output growth in 2009 and 2010, the poverty rate had fallen by an estimated 5 percentage points between 2008 and 2010 (World Bank 2012a), and unemployment remained stable during this period (Inchauste, Mansur, and Serajuddin 2017).

Despite the progress in poverty reduction, the downturn in Jordan's economy starting at the end of 2008 placed its fiscal accounts under pressure as both tax revenues and external grants fell (Inchauste, Mansur, and Serajuddin 2017). This downturn necessitated efforts to streamline government spending and institute reforms. At the same time, popular perceptions regarding Jordan's progress in poverty reduction over this period remained typically pessimistic (DOS and World Bank 2009; Mansour 2012), making reform efforts challenging. Moreover, the regional wave of civil uprisings in 2011 that became

The authors acknowledge detailed comments and suggestions from Nora Lustig and Sean Higgins. We thank Chadi Bou Habib, Eric Le Borgne, Jon Jellema, Lea Hakim, Paolo Verme, Tamer Samah Rabie, and Yusuf Mansur for helpful discussions. We thank Morad Abdel-Halim for his help on administrative data collection and data analysis. We are grateful to Mukhallad Omari, Zein Soufan, and Orouba Al Sabbagh of the Ministry of Planning and International Cooperation of the Government of Jordan for helpful discussions and for sharing data. Any errors in this chapter are solely ours.

known as the Arab Spring placed even stronger demands on the government for populist policies.

In the presence of such economic and social uncertainty, there is significant interest in examining not only the costs and benefits of different policy options but also their equity-enhancing attributes. This chapter focuses on the latter, examining the distributional impact of Jordan's key fiscal policies on both the tax and the social spending sides. We use data from Jordan's 2010 Household Expenditure and Income Survey (HEIS) in conjunction with data from administrative accounts, applying the Commitment to Equity (CEQ) methodology in our analysis (Lustig [forthcoming]).[1] We cover the impacts of the primary fiscal policies employed by the government, such as direct taxes (personal income taxes); indirect taxes (sales taxes); direct transfers; indirect subsidies (subsidies for food, oil, electricity, and water); and in-kind benefits (benefits for education and health).

Although the data for the study may appear a bit dated, they correspond to the country's most recent official poverty estimates. Major changes have taken place since 2010—the influx of Syrian refugees perhaps being the most notable—and Jordan currently grapples with how to provide services to its citizens as well as to the refugees. The country has also initiated several ambitious reform efforts, such as drastically reducing subsidies on petroleum products in November 2012 (Atamanov, Jellema, and Serajuddin 2015; Inchauste, Mansur, and Serajuddin 2017).

At the same time, the government's commitment to equity has remained strong. In May 2015 the government launched an economic blueprint—"Jordan 2025: A National Vision and Strategy"—that proposes a 10-year strategy for economic and social development (Government of Jordan 2015). Important targets of this blueprint include halving poverty rates and enhancing equality of opportunity for citizens. In the context of such targets, the study presented in this chapter can serve as a benchmark for assessing the equity or distributional aspects of existing policies and for subsequently assessing the equity aspects of alternative policies.

Our analysis results in several main findings. Among them, we find that the Jordan's fiscal system is mostly progressive, as it decreases the poverty headcount and inequality in the country. More specifically, direct taxes (personal income taxes), direct cash transfer programs, and in-kind education benefits are very progressive. In contrast, indirect taxes appear to be regressive in Jordan, as they seemingly increase income inequality. This suggests that the poor and the middle class could potentially benefit from changes in the general sales tax (GST) system, because they currently spend a greater fraction of their incomes on indirect taxes than do the wealthier households.

We organize this chapter as follows: The next section discusses the fiscal instruments the Jordanian government uses to tackle poverty and inequality, including the income tax, the GST, the direct transfer program, the subsidy program, the pension system, and in-kind benefits such as education and health care. The "Data, Methodology, and Assumptions" section explains the data set and methodology used for our analysis and clarifies the underlying assumptions behind the analysis. The "Results" section presents our findings, focusing on topics such as (a) how inequality changes across different concepts of household income, (b) the details of poverty and inequality measures, (c) the progressivity of Jordan's fiscal system, and (d) the income mobility of poor households. Finally, the "Conclusion" summarizes the chapter's findings.

Fiscal Instruments to Tackle Poverty and Inequality

Taxes

Tax revenues account for a significant fraction of Jordan's GDP—for about 15.9 percent of GDP in 2010—their two largest components being direct taxes (including the payroll tax) and the GST (table 6.1). Our analysis focuses on these two tax items, which directly affected people and accounted for around 34 percent of the government's tax revenue. In addition to these two items, the government also collects corporate taxes from private firms and indirect taxes on the commercial sector.

It is important to note that in addition to the GST, the government collects customs duty on imported goods. We cannot include this in our analysis because the household survey data do not identify whether certain expenditures were made for imported goods or services.

Table 6.1 Government Revenue in Jordan, by Source, 2010

Revenue source	Total (JD, millions)	Share of GDP (%)	Share of total included in analysis (%)
Total government revenue[a]	4,642.1	24.7	22.3
Tax revenues[b]	2,986.0	15.9	34.7
Taxes on income and profits	624.6	3.3	24.4
Personal income tax	152.3	0.8	100.0
Corporate taxes from private firms	472.3	2.5	0.0
GST and other indirect taxes	1,997.8	10.6	43.2
Sales tax on imported goods	819.4	4.4	0.0
Sales tax on domestic goods	463.3	2.5	100.0
Sales tax on services	400.4	2.1	100.0
Sales tax on commercial sector	304.2	1.6	0.0
Tax on air fares	10.5	0.1	0.0
Other taxes[c]	363.6	1.9	5.7
Of which: Pension contributions	20.7	0.1	100.0
Foreign grants	401.7	2.1	0.0
Other revenues[d]	1,254.4	6.7	0.0

Source: MoF 2013.
Note: The table does not include customs duties on imports because household survey data do not identify whether expenditures were for imported goods or services. GDP = gross domestic product; GST = general sales tax; JD = Jordanian dinars.
a. Total government revenue = tax revenues + other revenues + foreign grants.
b. Tax revenues = taxes on income and profits + GST and other indirect taxes + other taxes.
c. "Other taxes" includes custom duties and fees.
d. "Other revenues" includes revenue from selling goods and services, income from property ownership, mining revenues, and other miscellaneous revenues.

Direct Taxes

The Jordanian government collects two forms of direct taxes: personal income taxes for individuals and corporate taxes from the private sector. Since only the income tax directly affects individuals, we examine the effect of income taxes on poverty and inequality in Jordan.

Jordan's income tax system is designed to be progressive: the first JD 12,000 of an individual's income is not taxed; individual income between JD 12,000 and JD 24,000 is taxed at 7 percent, and individual income above JD 24,000 is taxed at 14 percent. The burden of the tax is fully borne by the worker, not the employer. The tax system does not provide deductions for married persons or children.

Indirect Taxes

Jordan's GST system plays a role similar to that of a value added tax. Although certain items are zero-rated, certain other items are exempted from taxes altogether. Overall, three different rates of GST are applied across goods and services: 0 percent, 4 percent, and 16 percent.[2]

Social Spending

The government of Jordan spends a significant amount on different social programs—equivalent to about 30 percent of the country's GDP in 2010 (table 6.2). The following subsections provide more detail on each of these programs.

Direct Transfers

Jordan has an unconditional cash transfer program, the National Aid Fund (NAF), which accounted for about 0.4 percent of GDP in 2010. NAF's target population includes families taking care of orphaned children, elderly individuals, persons with disability, families headed by divorced or abandoned women, women with young children, families whose breadwinner is in prison, humanitarian cases, abandoned women, persons receiving assistance and rehabilitation loans, families of seasonal workers, families of missing and absentee fathers, and persons with no income (Silva, Levin, and Morgandi 2013).

To receive NAF benefits, a household's income must be below a preset per capita threshold. All NAF beneficiaries also are automatically eligible for health insurance. The fund provides the beneficiaries with monthly cash transfers ranging from JD 40 to JD 180 depending on income, assets, and family circumstances. Approximately 88,000 families benefit from this program each year (Silva, Levin, and Morgandi 2013).[3]

Another small cash transfer program is the Zakat Fund, which provides direct monetary assistance to the poor, with a specific focus on orphans and children in targeted families.[4] Its scope is far smaller than the NAF's, providing cash assistance only to extremely poor individuals.

Besides these cash transfer programs, the government provides other transfers to certain poor and vulnerable populations through four programs: Handicapped

Table 6.2 Government Spending in Jordan, by Category, 2010

Category	Total (JD, millions)	Share of GDP (%)	Share of total included in analysis (%)
Total government spending[a]	5,708.0	30.4	43.0
Primary government spending[b]	5,310.5	28.3	46.3
Social spending[c]	1,708.6	9.1	89.2
Total cash transfers	136.0	0.7	100.0
Direct cash transfers (NAF)	77.4	0.4	100.0
Other transfers	58.6	0.3	100.0
Total in-kind transfers[d]	1,388.2	7.4	100.0
Education	597.3	3.2	100.0
Health	581.2	3.1	100.0
Contributory	215.0	1.1	100.0
Noncontributory	366.2	2.0	100.0
Housing and urban	209.8	1.1	100.0
Other social spending	184.4	1.0	0.0
Nonsocial spending[e]	2,856.9	15.2	100.0
Indirect subsidies	191.2	1.0	100.0
On final goods	123.8	0.7	100.0
On inputs/oil	67.4	0.4	100.0
Other nonsocial spending	2,666.0	14.2	0.0
Contributory pensions	745.0	4.0	100.0
Interest payments	397.5	2.2	0.0

Source: MoF 2013.

Note: GDP = gross domestic product; JD = Jordanian dinars; NAF = National Aid Fund.

a. Total government spending = primary government spending + interest payments on debt.

b. Primary government spending = social spending + nonsocial spending + contributory pensions.

c. Social spending = total cash transfers + total in-kind transfers + other social spending.

d. Total in-kind transfers = education + health + housing and urban.

e. Nonsocial spending = indirect subsidies + other nonsocial spending.

Affairs, Social Defence, Community Development and Combating Poverty, and Family and Childhood Protection.[5] These programs help households with wide-ranging issues and include assistance to combat poverty; assistance to ensure the well-being of people with disabilities through rehabilitation services, education, and institutional care; assistance to families in the upbringing of children; assistance to protection of families from disintegration; awareness programs for needy families; and assistance to improve the housing conditions of the poor. In addition to these transfers, the King's funds provide further assistance to the needy.

In-Kind Transfers

Public education. Jordan's government spent an amount equivalent to 3.2 percent of the country's GDP on education in 2010. The country's education system consists of kindergarten, basic schooling, and secondary schooling. Basic schooling (primary and middle school) and secondary schooling are free; at the same time, education is compulsory for all children until the age of 15 (Al Jabery and

Zumberg 2008; DOS 2012). An estimated 71 percent of all students go to public schools for basic schooling, and 86 percent go to public schools for secondary schooling (DOS 2012).

After completing basic schooling, the students continue on one of two secondary-school tracks: either an academic track or a vocational track (Al Jabery and Zumberg 2008). In the academic track, students complete secondary school with a general secondary school examination. The vocational track consists of specialized courses and aims to prepare students for employment as skilled labor.

Health benefits. Jordan has one of the most modern health care infrastructures in the Middle East (WHO 2006). In 2010 the government spent an amount equivalent to 3.1 percent of the country's GDP on health benefits. These expenditures include the costs of highly subsidized health care at public primary health care centers and hospitals as well as investments in research and development (MoH 2012; WHO 2006).

Jordan's public health insurance program covers about 40 percent of the population, mostly civil servants and the very poor (MoH 2012; WHO 2006). The insurance coverage is expected to expand substantially in the coming years.

Indirect Subsidies
As it does for health and education benefits, Jordan also provides significant indirect subsidies on food, petroleum products, electricity, and water.[6]

Food Subsidies. The government sells imported wheat and barley to consumers at a subsidized price. A World Bank study shows that completely removing wheat subsidies would increase its price by 68 percent and adversely affect the poorer population if unaccompanied by any offsetting measures (World Bank 2012b). The government also subsidizes flour and bread so that people can buy such items at a low price. Although barley is not directly consumed by households, it is consumed by animals such as livestock, and subsidized barley puts a downward pressure on the price of meat in Jordan (World Bank 2012b).

Fuel Subsidies. In 2011, government subsidies on petroleum products—liquefied petroleum gas, kerosene, gasoline, and diesel—amounted collectively to about 2.8 percent of GDP. The government provided these subsidies to energy companies to cover the difference between the cost of production and the selling price (World Bank 2012b).

Electricity Subsidies. Electricity subsidies in 2010 amounted to around 1 percent of GDP, but in 2011 they rose to about 5.5 percent of GDP because political unrest disrupted the supply of natural gas from the Arab Republic of Egypt, causing Jordan to abruptly switch to imported oil products (heavy fuel oil and diesel) to produce electricity (Atamanov, Jellema, and Serajuddin 2015).

Water Subsidies. Jordan subsidizes water consumption and provides water subsidies through discounts on water bills depending on the amount of consumption. A World Bank study estimated that removal of this subsidy would cause the water price to increase by 257 percent (World Bank 2012b).

Pensions

Jordan has a public contributory pension (pay as you go) system, with three types of pensions in place. The Social Security Corporation manages the national pension system for private sector workers, for public employees who joined the civil services after 1995, and for army personnel recruited after 2002.[7] The current mandatory contribution rate is set at 14.5 percent of the worker's salary, of which 5.5 percent is paid by employees and the rest by the employer. It is now a mandatory scheme for all employers. Self-employed workers have to pay the entire 14.5 percent of their income on their own. However, government employees recruited before 1995 are covered by the Civil Pension System, and members of the military recruited through 2002 are covered under the Military Pension System.[8]

Data, Methodology, and Assumptions

Data

As mentioned earlier, our study uses data from the HEIS, conducted by Jordan's Department of Statistics. This survey interviewed around 11,000 households over the course of 12 months from April 2010 to March 2011. It contains detailed data on household expenditure and income as well as data on potential sources of income, direct transfers, and household use of education and health services. Additionally, we use 2010 administrative and national accounts data that broadly coincide with the time frame of the household survey.

Methodology and Assumptions

Income Concepts

Our incidence analysis is conducted in the context of the five CEQ income concepts, as described in Lustig (forthcoming): market income, net market income, disposable income, consumable income, and final income. Because income is typically presumed to be underreported in household survey data (Atkinson and Brandolini 2001; Deaton 1997; Ravallion 2003; Thomas, Strauss, and Henriques 1991), we start our computation by equating household total expenditure with "disposable income." From that, we subtract direct transfers to generate "net market income." To this we add the amounts paid in direct taxes to generate "market income." We also compute household "consumable income" by adding indirect subsidies and subtracting indirect taxes from disposable income. Last, we produce household "final income" by adding in-kind health and education benefits and subtracting user fees for using such services from consumable income.[9]

Next we explain how we assigned monetary values to the government's different fiscal interventions, broadly categorized as taxes (income and sales taxes) and transfers (direct transfers, pensions, indirect subsidies, and in-kind transfers).

Taxes

Because HEIS does not report household taxes, we simulate the income tax paid by households by assuming that households follow the income tax code. Although tax evasion could be potentially large, we cannot model these evasions for lack of data. Following the tax code, for individual incomes below JD 12,000 (which are tax exempt), we assume that individuals paid no income tax. For individual income between JD 12,000 and JD 24,000, we apply a marginal tax rate of 7 percent; for additional income above JD 24,000, we apply a marginal tax rate of 14 percent.

In the absence of GST data, we simulate the sales taxes paid by the households using the government's statutory rates. Because the HEIS data do show itemized household expenditures, we can impose the sales tax rates for the different items, which allows us to simulate the total sales tax paid by the households on all items. Sales taxes are probably not paid on expenditures in informal markets, but because we cannot identify such expenditures, it is not possible to calculate the evasion of such sales tax payments.

Transfers

The HEIS data include household income generated from direct transfer programs. The survey asked households about their previous year's earnings from the NAF program as well as the amount of transfers they had received from other government institutions.

We can also identify directly from the HEIS data whether an individual is receiving a pension and, if so, the amount. Throughout this chapter we treat pensions only as deferred income.

Moreover, the HEIS data include the amounts of household expenditures on the various items receiving indirect subsidies (including food, fuel, electricity, and water). From these item-specific expenditures we impute the direct and indirect benefits households receive from indirect subsidies.

Because the HEIS data do not include the in-kind transfers received in the form of education or health benefits, we simulate these benefits as described below.

Education. The household survey data include whether an individual goes to a public school or university and, if so, the level of education that the individual is receiving (kindergarten, primary, secondary, vocational, or university). Additionally, from national accounts, we have data on government expenditure on education allocated by different levels of education.

The national accounts also provide data on the total number of students at the different education levels, enabling us to estimate the education benefits received by each student. Then we impute these education benefits per student to the corresponding students in the household survey. In addition to the benefits arising from these government expenditures, there are infrastructure costs that are not allocated by education level in the national accounts. We apportion those costs equally among all the students receiving education in public schools.

Finally, because our total income in the household data is significantly less than the total income in administrative data, we have scaled down the education benefits imputed to the households.[10] We do so by multiplying the imputed education benefits by the ratio of survey-data income to administrative-data income.

Health. The HEIS data include information on households' health expenditures, including expenditures related to visits to public hospitals. Most households visiting public hospitals had to pay at least a small user fee. Such fees vary greatly, possibly indicating the variation in the severity of illness and the benefit the individual is receiving. We assume that an individual who is paying a higher fee is likely to receive greater health benefits (because higher fees may indicate a greater severity of illness and greater use of health facilities) than an individual paying lower fees. Therefore, we impute larger health benefits for households that paid higher user fees, with the imputed health benefits increasing proportionally with the amount of user fees paid. Then we subtract the user fees from the health benefits received by the individual.

Although our assumptions regarding the imputation of health benefits are strong, it is important to note that we lack both government expenditure data and survey data on the *types* of health services received (medical checkups, hospitalization, and so on). That is why we allocate the benefits according to the health expenditure made by individual households. As with the education benefits, we have scaled down the health benefits imputed to the households by the ratio of income reported in survey data to income in administrative data.

Results

Changes in Inequality across Income Concepts

We start our analysis by exploring how fiscal interventions affected the share of cumulative income in Jordan earned by the poorest, the middle, and the richest income groups. To conduct this analysis, we first rank households by income decile. Then we examine the percentage of cumulative income in Jordan earned by each decile under the following three income concepts: market income, consumable income, and final income. If households in the lower deciles earn a greater percentage of the cumulative income in their final income relative to their market income, it would suggest that the fiscal interventions are helping to reduce inequality in the country.

Figure 6.1 Share of Total Household Income in Jordan, by Decile and Income Concept, 2010

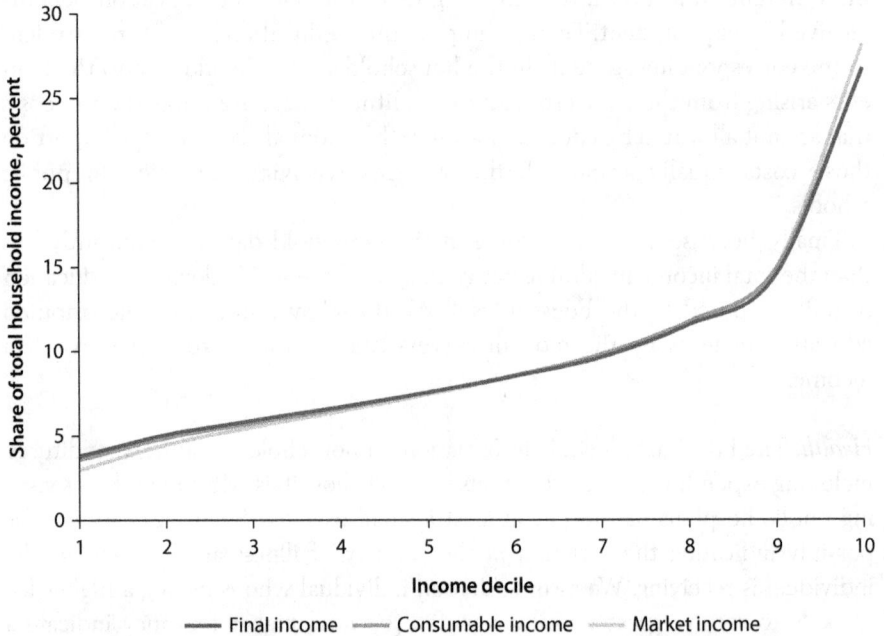

Legend: Final income — Consumable income — Market income

Source: 2010 Household Expenditure and Income Survey (HEIS) data and Jordan Department of Statistics national accounts database, http://web.dos.gov.jo/sectors/national-account/?lang=en.
Note: "Market income" comprises pretax wages, salaries, income earned from capital assets (rent, interest, or dividends), and private transfers. "Consumable income" is constructed by (a) subtracting from market income the payments for personal income taxes, social security contributions, and sales taxes; and (b) adding direct cash transfers. "Final income" adds to consumable income the benefits of in-kind transfers for education and health care.

We present the results in figure 6.1. The results suggest that the poorest three deciles are slightly wealthier according to their final income than according to their market income. In contrast, the richest decile is slightly less wealthy in final income relative to market income. Interestingly, we find no significant difference between market income, consumable income, and final income for the middle deciles. Overall, the graph suggests that Jordan has a slightly progressive fiscal policy in place.

A deficiency in such an analysis by income decile is that it does not tell us the within-decile impacts. Nor does it tell us the specific impact of the fiscal policy on the poor, as defined by a poverty line. To better understand this impact on the poor, we divide Jordan's population into six income groups for analysis under two income concepts: market income and consumable income.

Based on per capita income per day (in 2005 purchasing power parity [PPP] prices) the six income groups are as follows: less than US$1.25; US$1.25–US$2.50; US$2.50–US$4; US$4–US$10; US$10–US$50; and more than US$50. Figure 6.2 presents the fraction of Jordan's population within each income group by income concept.

The result clearly demonstrates that fewer people are below the poverty lines of US$2.50 and US$4 a day according to their consumable income than they are

Figure 6.2 Share of Population in Different Income Groups in Jordan, by Income Concept, 2010

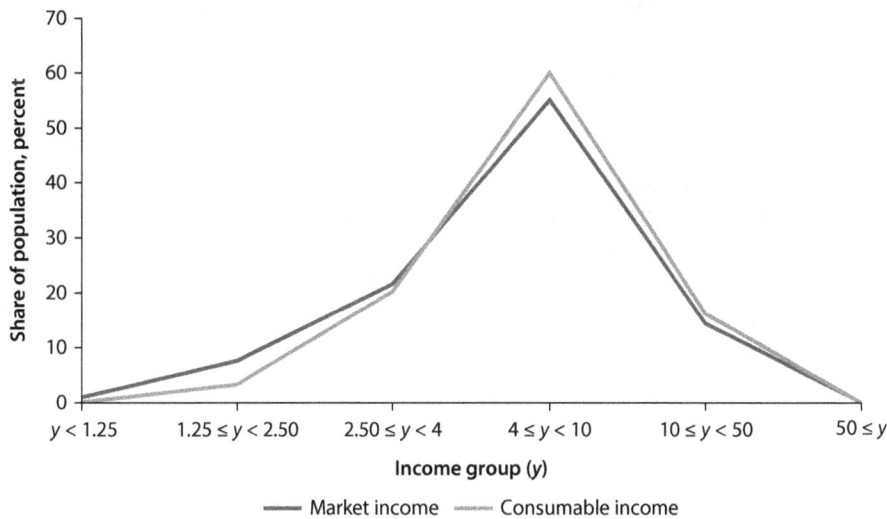

Source: 2010 Household Expenditure and Income Survey (HEIS) data and Jordan Department of Statistics national accounts database, http://web.dos.gov.jo/sectors/national-account/?lang=en.
Note: Income groups are defined by income per capita per day in U.S. dollars in 2005 purchasing power parity (PPP) terms. "Market income" comprises pretax wages, salaries, income earned from capital assets (rent, interest, or dividends), and private transfers. "Consumable income" is constructed by (a) subtracting from market income the payments for personal income taxes, social security contributions, and sales taxes; and (b) adding direct cash transfers.

according to their market income. Instead, a significantly greater percentage of people are in the middle income range (of US$4–US$10 and US$10–US$50) according to their consumable income than according to their market income. This result strongly suggests that people who were below the poverty line according to their market income rise above the poverty line in their consumable income through the government's fiscal interventions.

Poverty and Inequality Incidence

Next, we analyze the incidence results related to poverty and inequality. The results are presented in table 6.3. The poverty headcount indexes suggest that the Jordanian government's fiscal interventions have been quite successful in reducing poverty. At the level of US$4 a day (2005 PPP), the percentage of people below the poverty line decreases by 6.7 percentage points when we move from market income to consumable income. Similarly, at Jordan's official national poverty line, the poverty headcount decreases by 6.8 percentage points when we move from market income to consumable income.[11]

When we examine the overall impact of Jordan's fiscal policy on inequality, we find that the Gini coefficient decreases from 0.35 to 0.32 when we move from the initial market income to the final income (table 6.3). This indicates that, overall, Jordan's fiscal policies reduced inequality in the country. Additionally, the Gini

Table 6.3 Poverty and Inequality Incidence in Jordan, by Income Concept, 2010

Indicator	Market incomeª	Market income + contributory pensions	Disposable incomeᵇ	Consumable incomeᶜ	Final incomeᵈ
Gini	0.350	0.342	0.328	0.325	0.319
US$1.25 per day PPP					
Headcount index (%)	1.0	0.5	0.1	0.1	n.a.
Poverty gap (%)	0.3	0.2	0.0	0.0	n.a.
Fiscal impoverishment headcount (%)	n.a.	n.a.	0	0	0
US$2.50 per day PPP					
Headcount index (%)	8.6	5.2	4.0	3.4	n.a.
Poverty gap (%)	2.0	1.1	0.7	0.6	n.a.
Fiscal impoverishment headcount (%)	n.a.	n.a.	0.0	2.6	1.6
US$4 PPP					
Headcount index (%)	30.3	25.8	24.6	23.6	n.a.
Poverty gap (%)	8.3	6.2	5.4	5.1	n.a.
Fiscal impoverishment headcount (%)	n.a.	n.a.	0.5	13.2	3.1
National poverty lineᵉ					
Headcount index (%)	20.5	15.8	14.3	13.7	n.a.
Poverty gap (%)	5.1	3.5	2.8	2.5	n.a.

Source: Based on 2010 Household Expenditure and Income Survey (HEIS) data.
Note: The Gini coefficient measures the relative inequality of income distribution, ranging from 0 (full equality) to 1 (maximum inequality). The "poverty headcount" is the percentage of the population living in poverty below a specified poverty line. The "poverty gap" is the average percentage by which poor individuals fall below a given poverty line. The "fiscal impoverishment headcount" measures the percentage of the poor adversely affected (that is, whose incomes decrease) as a result of fiscal policies (Higgins and Lustig 2015). It is based on the percentages of postfiscal poor (that is, according to disposable, consumable, and final income). PPP = purchasing power parity; n.a. = not applicable.
a. "Market income" comprises pretax wages, salaries, income earned from capital assets (rent, interest, or dividends), and private transfers.
b. "Disposable income" (a) subtracts from market income the payments for personal income taxes and social security contributions, and (b) adds direct cash transfers.
c. "Consumable income" adds to disposable income the impact of sales taxes.
d. "Final income" adds to consumable income the effects of in-kind transfers for health care and education.
e. The national poverty line in Jordan is determined from the "cost of basic needs," based on the consumption and expenditure patterns of the bottom 30 percent of the population (poor or near-poor) in the 2010 HEIS data (Jolliffe and Serajuddin 2015). The estimated poverty line to meet basic needs was set at JD 813.7 per person per day in 2010 (US$3.42 per day at 2005 PPP).

coefficient decreases as we move from each income concept to the next, showing that each set of fiscal interventions being measured decreases inequality.

This reduction in poverty numbers across income groups is also reflected in figure 6.3, which shows the percentage of cumulative income in Jordan earned by the poorest income groups across the different income concepts.

To understand the fairness of these fiscal interventions, we next employ a measure called "fiscal impoverishment," as proposed by Higgins and Lustig (2015). This measure allows us to examine the proportion of the poor adversely affected (that is, whose incomes decrease) by fiscal policies.

At both the US$2.50-a-day and US$4-a-day poverty lines (2005 PPP), fiscal impoverishment increases significantly (by 2.6 points and 12.7 points, respectively) when we move from disposable income to consumable income, as shown in table 6.3. This suggests that indirect taxes may be making some of the poor

Figure 6.3 Percentage of Cumulative Income Earned by the Poor in Jordan, by Income Concept, 2010

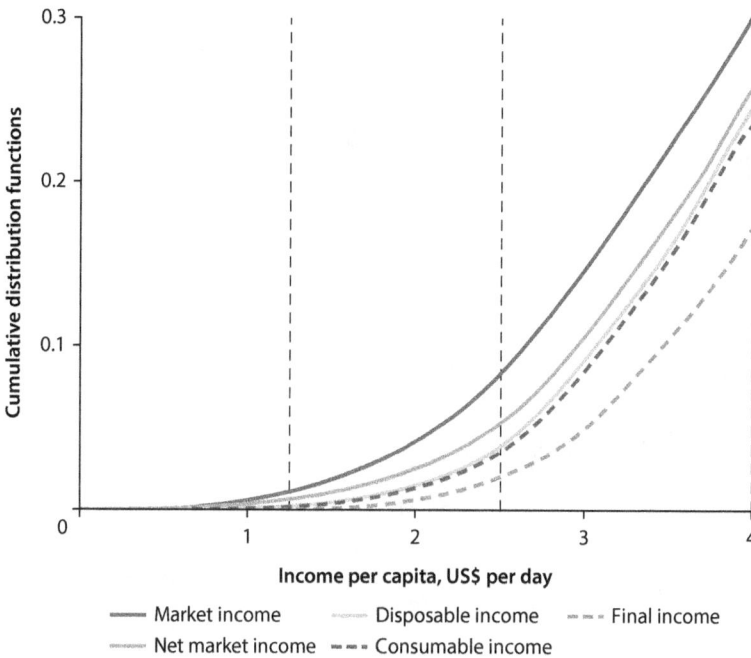

Source: 2010 Household Expenditure and Income Survey (HEIS) data and Jordan Department of Statistics national accounts database http://web.dos.gov.jo/sectors/national-account/?lang=en.
Note: Vertical dotted lines designate three poverty lines (in 2005 PPP terms): US$1.25, US$2.50, and US$4. "Market income" comprises pretax wages, salaries, income earned from capital assets (rent, interest, or dividends), and private transfers. "Net market income" subtracts direct (income) taxes from market income. "Disposable income" is constructed by adding direct cash transfers to net market income. "Consumable income" subtracts from disposable income the impact of sales taxes paid. "Final income" adds to consumable income the effects of in-kind transfers for health care and education. PPP = purchasing power parity.

even poorer. However, it is important to note that indirect taxes would have different effects on different individuals depending on their spending patterns. We do not see such large fiscal impoverishment for movements between any of the other income concepts. We will further detail the impact of each of these interventions later in this chapter.

Progressivity of Fiscal Interventions

Our next task is to determine whether the fiscal system in Jordan is progressive or regressive. To illustrate whether policies are having a progressive or regressive impact, we show the cumulative proportion of taxes and transfers for the population by income percentile in figure 6.4.

The figure clearly shows that direct taxes and direct transfers are very progressive, whereas the indirect taxes appear to be slightly regressive. The curve for direct taxes shows a high concentration at the highest end of the income distribution, and the curve for direct transfers shows the highest concentration at the lowest end of the distribution.

Figure 6.4 Progressivity of Taxes and Transfers in Jordan, 2010

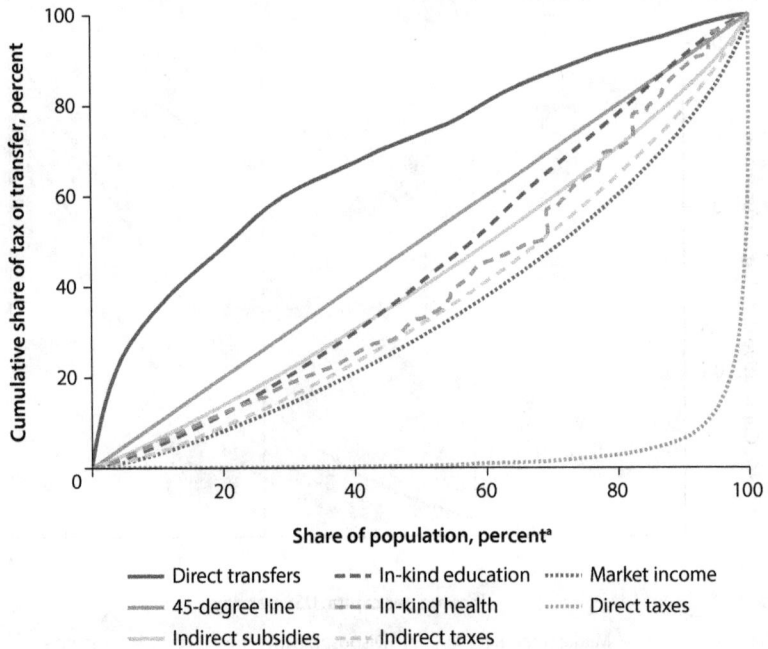

Source: Based on 2010 Household Expenditure and Income Survey (HEIS) data.
Note: Figure shows concentration curves for taxes and transfers and a Lorenz curve representing the distribution of "market income," which comprises pretax wages, salaries, and income earned from capital assets (rent, interest, or dividends) and private transfers. "Direct taxes" include income, capital gains, and property taxes. "Indirect taxes" include general sales taxes.
a. The cumulative share of the population is ordered by market income.

Furthermore, the Kakwani coefficients suggest that direct taxes, direct transfers, indirect subsidies, and in-kind education are strongly progressive (table 6.4). In-kind health benefits have close to a proportional effect on income. However, as suggested by the Gini index results, indirect taxes (GST) have a slightly regressive effect.[12]

To get a more methodical understanding of the progressivity of each of these fiscal interventions, we rely on the marginal contributions of these interventions to the changes in the Gini coefficient.[13] In Jordan, direct taxes and direct transfers are equalizing (table 6.4). Indirect subsidies are equalizing, too, but indirect taxes are nonequalizing. Education spending is quite equalizing, but health spending is slightly nonequalizing. The equalizing effect of education dominates; hence, in-kind spending overall is equalizing.

It is also important to understand whether the redistributive effect that we have seen in the figures and tables result from vertical equity (VE) between the rich and poor households rather than from simple reranking (RR) of households. VE tells us the amount of inequality reduction that would be possible if the tax and transfer system treated equals (that is, two households with the same level of income) equally (Duclos 2008). In contrast, RR is a measure of inequity, which shows whether a poorer household becomes wealthier than a comparatively

Table 6.4 Kakwani Coefficients for, and Marginal Contributions to Redistribution of, Taxes and Social Spending in Jordan, 2010

Fiscal intervention	Kakwani coefficient[a]	Marginal contribution, by income concept[b] (change in Gini index)		
		Market to disposable income	Market to consumable income	Market to final income
All direct taxes and contributions	0.203	0.007	0.007	0.006
Direct taxes	0.594	0.008	0.008	n.a.
Direct transfers	0.550	0.006	0.005	0.005
Indirect taxes: GST	−0.066	n.a.	−0.002	−0.001
Indirect subsidies	0.151	n.a.	0.005	0.004
All taxes	0.126	n.a.	0.006	n.a.
In-kind health	0.056	n.a.	n.a.	−0.009
In-kind education	0.478	n.a.	n.a.	0.015
Kindergarten	0.666	n.a.	n.a.	0.000
Primary	0.581	n.a.	n.a.	0.013
Secondary	0.403	n.a.	n.a.	0.002
Tertiary	0.006	n.a.	n.a.	0.000
All in-kind	0.344	n.a.	n.a.	0.025

Source: Based on 2010 Household Expenditure and Income Survey (HEIS) data.
Note: The Gini coefficient measures the relative inequality of income distribution, ranging from 0 (full equality) to 1 (maximum inequality). GST = general sales tax; n.a. = not applicable.
a. Kakwani coefficients measure whether a fiscal intervention exercises an equalizing or unequalizing force; progressive interventions have positive Kakwani coefficients, and regressive ones have negative coefficients.
b. The "marginal contribution" is the difference between the Gini coefficients with and without the designated row's tax or expenditure. Income concepts are as follows: "Market income" comprises pretax wages, salaries, and income earned from capital assets (rent, interest, or dividends) and private transfers. "Disposable income" is constructed by adding direct cash transfers to net market income. "Consumable income" adds to disposable income the impact of indirect taxes, including value added taxes; import duties; and excises on petroleum products, alcoholic beverages, and tobacco products. "Final income" adds (to consumable income) the value of in-kind transfers including health care and education.

richer household after a government transfer or tax intervention (Duclos, Jalbert, and Araar 2003).

The redistributive effect in Jordan is mostly occurring through VE (table 6.5). We find that RR represents somewhere between 2 percent and 34 percent of the magnitude of VE, depending on the income concept, which shows that horizontal inequity in the form of RR is relatively low. This suggests that most of the redistributive effect from fiscal interventions occurred through VE.[14]

Income Mobility

Finally, it is important to examine the income mobility of the poor. Figure 6.2 earlier provided evidence of upward income mobility in the transition from market income to final income. To further understand the details of the transition, we have created a mobility matrix that shows the fractions of individuals in certain income groups who transition to other income groups (table 6.6). This will help us calculate the percentage of people living beneath a certain poverty line who transition out of poverty. To conduct this analysis, we have

Table 6.5 Redistributive, Vertical Equity, and Reranking Effects of Fiscal Policy in Jordan, 2010

Indicator	Market income[a] to net market income[b]	Market income to disposable income[c]	Market income to consumable income[d]	Market income to final income[e]
Redistributive effect (change in Gini)[f]	0.0076	0.0132	0.0161	0.0230
Vertical equity (VE) (change in Gini)[g]	0.0077	0.0149	0.0180	0.0348
Reranking (RR) (change in Gini)[h]	0.0001	0.0017	0.0019	0.0118
Horizontal inequity (RR as % of VE)	2	11	11	34

Source: Based on 2010 Household Expenditure and Income Survey (HEIS) data.
Note: The Gini coefficient measures the inequality of income distribution, ranging from 0 (full equality) to 1 (maximum inequality).
a. "Market income" comprises pretax wages, salaries, income earned from capital assets (rent, interest, or dividends), and private transfers.
b. "Net market income" is market income minus direct taxes.
c. "Disposable income" is constructed by adding direct cash transfers to net market income.
d. "Consumable income" adds to disposable income the impact of indirect taxes, including value added taxes; import duties; and excises on petroleum products, alcoholic beverages, and tobacco products.
e. "Final income" adds to consumable income the effects of in-kind transfers for health care and education.
f. The "redistributive effect" refers to the change in inequality associated with direct and indirect taxes as well as direct transfers and subsidies, calculated in terms of the change in Gini coefficient.
g. "Vertical equity" (VE) tells us the amount of inequality reduction that would be possible if the tax and transfer system treated equals equally.
h. The "reranking" (RR) effect is a measure of inequity, which shows whether a poorer household becomes wealthier than a comparatively richer household after a government transfer or tax intervention.

Table 6.6 Mobility of Jordanian Households across Income Concepts, by Income Group, 2010
Percentage

Market income[a] + pensions group (y)	Disposable income[b] group (y)						Share of population (%)
	y < 1.25	1.25 ≤ y < 2.50	2.50 ≤ y < 4.00	4.00 ≤ y < 10.00	10.00 ≤ y < 50.00	50.00 ≤ y	
y < 1.25	13	58	18	11	0	0	0.9
1.25 ≤ y < 2.50	0	65	30	6	0	0	5.5
2.50 ≤ y < 4.00	0	0	92	8	0	0	20.9
4.00 ≤ y < 10.00	0	0	0	99	1	0	57.0
10.00 ≤ y < 50.00	0	0	0	1	99	0	15.6
50.00 ≤ y	0	0	0	0	62	38	0.1
Market income + pensions group (y)	Consumable income[c] group (y)						Share of population (%)
	y < 1.25	1.25 ≤ y < 2.50	2.50 ≤ y < 4.00	4.00 ≤ y < 10.00	10.00 ≤ y < 50.00	50.00 ≤ y	
y < 1.25	9	54	25	11	0	0	0.9
1.25 ≤ y < 2.50	0	46	47	8	0	0	5.5
2.50 ≤ y < 4.00	0	0	81	19	0	0	20.9
4.00 ≤ y < 10.00	0	0	0	98	2	0	57.0
10.00 ≤ y < 50.00	0	0	0	1	99	0	15.6
50.00 ≤ y	0	0	0	0	53	47	0.1

Source: Based on 2010 Household Expenditure and Income Survey (HEIS) data.
Note: All income groups stated in terms of U.S. dollars per person per day (in 2005 PPP terms). Shaded cells designate same income group across two income concepts. PPP = purchasing power parity.
a. "Market income" comprises pretax wages, salaries, income earned from capital assets (rent, interest, or dividends), and private transfers.
b. "Disposable income" is constructed by adding direct cash transfers to net market income.
c. "Consumable income" adds to disposable income the impact of indirect taxes, including value added taxes; import duties; and excises on petroleum products, alcoholic beverages, and tobacco products.

created two mobility matrixes, showing the transition from market income (including pension) to (a) disposable income and (b) consumable income.

The results show that the fiscal interventions had contributed toward a clear upward mobility for the people below various poverty lines across income concepts, for example, as follows:

- Of those with market incomes of US$1.25–US$2.50 PPP per day, 30 percent moved to a higher income bracket of US$2.50–US$4.00 PPP per day for their disposable income, and 47 percent moved to the higher bracket for their consumable income. Interestingly, a small percentage of households moved to an even higher income bracket of US$4–US$10 PPP per day. Six percent moved to this higher bracket for their disposable income, and 8 percent moved to the higher bracket for their consumable income.
- Of those with market incomes of US$2.50–US$4.00 a day (that is, under the poverty line of US$4 PPP a day), 8 percent improved to US$4–US$10 a day for their disposable income, and 19 percent for their consumable income.

In addition to these improvements, it is also important to note that none of the households with market income below the poverty line suffered from any deteriorations that forced their disposable, consumable, or final income to deteriorate into a lower income group. Overall, these results suggest that the poor benefited strongly from the Jordanian government's fiscal policies.

Conclusion

This chapter analyzed the impact of the Jordanian government's fiscal policies on poverty and inequality in the country. We use data from Jordan's 2010 HEIS and records from administrative accounts, applying the CEQ methodology in our analysis. We cover all the key fiscal policies employed by the government, such as direct taxes (personal income taxes); indirect taxes (sales taxes); direct transfers; indirect subsidies (subsidies for food, oil, electricity, and water); and in-kind benefits (benefits for education and health).

Our results indicate that the Jordan's policies are mostly progressive and equalizing, primarily through direct taxes, direct transfers, indirect subsidies, and in-kind benefits. Moreover, the results show that the combination of tax and expenditure policies is poverty reducing. However, the indirect tax system, in its current form, is slightly regressive and inequality increasing, as the poor are paying a greater fraction of their income than the rich as sales tax.

Notes

1. For a thorough description of the CEQ project and its methodologies, see chapter 1.
2. For a detailed list of tax-exempt items and items with different tax rates, see the U.S. Agency for International Development report, "Evaluating Tax Expenditures in Jordan" (Heredia-Ortiz 2013).

3. For more information about the NAF, see "Jordan: Schemes—National Aid Fund" on the International Labour Organization website, accessed February 1, 2016, http://www.ilo .org/dyn/ilossi/ssimain.viewScheme?p_lang=en&p_geoaid=400&p_scheme_id=1665.

4. For more information about the Zakat Fund, see "Jordan: Schemes—National Zakat Fund" on the International Labour Organization website, accessed May 19, 2017. http://www.ilo.org/dyn/ilossi/ssimain.viewScheme?p_lang=en&p_geoaid=400&p _scheme_id=3233.

5. For more information about these social assistance programs, see "Jordan: Schemes— Ministry of Social Development" on the International Labour Organization website, accessed February 1, 2016, http://www.ilo.org/dyn/ilossi/ssimain.viewScheme? p_lang=en&p_scheme_id=3234&p_geoaid=400.

6. Although government accounts indicate that government spending on subsidies in Jordan is equivalent to 1 percent of GDP, indirect subsidies in fact amounted to about 3 percent of GDP in 2010. The disparity occurs because calculations in the government accounts exclude electricity and water expenditures. For example, electricity losses incurred by the National Electricity Production Company have been financed not from the government's budget but from debt raised and guaranteed by the government on behalf of NEPCO (World Bank 2012b). For consistency, table 6.2 includes only the numbers from the government accounts.

7. For more information about the national pension system managed by the Social Security Corporation, see "Jordan: Schemes—Social Security Corporation SSC [Old Age, Disability and Death Insurance and Work Injury]" on the International Labour Organization website, accessed May 24, 2016, http://www.ilo.org/dyn/ilossi/ssimain .viewScheme?p_lang=en&p_scheme_id=532&p_geoaid=400.

8. For more information about the Civil Pension System and Military Pension System, see "Jordan: Schemes—Government Pension Fund (Civil Servants and Military)" on the International Labour Organization website, accessed May 24, 2016, http://www .ilo.org/dyn/ilossi/ssimain.viewScheme?p_lang=en&p_scheme_id=2632& p_geoaid=400.

9. Chapter 1 provides a detailed explanation of how the CEQ income concepts are constructed.

10. For a discussion of the rationale and methodology for scaling up or scaling down certain transfers in the calculation of the income aggregates, see chapter 1.

11. The national poverty line in Jordan is determined from the "cost of basic needs," based on a national caloric requirement of 2,347 calories per capita per day and a common food and nonfood basket for all households. The poverty line is based on the consumption and expenditure patterns of the bottom 30 percent of the population (poor or near-poor) as reflected in the 2010 HEIS (Jolliffe and Serajuddin 2015). The estimated poverty line to meet basic needs was set at JD 813.7 per person per day in 2010 (US$3.42 per day 2005 PPP).

12. See chapter 1 for detailed discussions of how Kakwani coefficients, marginal contributions, and other methodologies are used in the assessments of the progressivity, regressivity, and pro-poorness of the fiscal interventions examined in this volume.

13. For a discussion of the properties of the marginal contribution, see Enami, Lustig, and Aranda (2017).

14. For more about how vertical equity, reranking, and horizontal inequity are defined and used in the analyses throughout this volume, see chapter 1.

References

Al Jabery, M., and M. Zumberg. 2008. "General and Special Education Systems in Jordan: Present and Future Perspectives." *International Journal of Special Education* 23 (1): 115–22.

Atamanov, A., J. Jellema, and U. Serajuddin. 2015. "Energy Subsidy Reform in Jordan: Welfare Implications of Different Scenarios." Policy Research Working Paper 7313, World Bank, Washington, DC.

Atkinson, A., and A. Brandolini. 2001. "Promise and Pitfalls in the Use of 'Secondary' Data-Sets: Income Inequality in OECD Countries as a Case Study." *Journal of Economic Literature* 39 (3): 771–99.

Deaton, A. 1997. *The Analysis of Household Surveys: A Microeconometric Approach to Development Policy.* Washington, DC: World Bank.

DOS (Department of Statistics, Jordan). 2012. *Statistical Yearbook 2012.* Annual statistical report, DOS, Amman. http://www.dos.gov.jo/dos_home_a/main/yearbook _2012.pdf.

DOS (Department of Statistics, Jordan) and World Bank. 2009. *Hashemite Kingdom of Jordan: Poverty Update—Volume 1: Main Report.* Report 47951-JO, World Bank, Washington, DC.

Duclos, Jean-Yves. 2008. "Horizontal and Vertical Equity." In *The New Palgrave Dictionary of Economics,* edited by Steven N. Durlauf and Lawrence E. Blume. 2nd ed. Basingstoke, U.K.: Palgrave Macmillan.

Duclos, Jean-Yves, Vincent Jalbert, and Abdelkrim Araar. 2003. "Classical Horizontal Inequity and Reranking: An Integrating Approach." In *Fiscal Policy, Inequality, and Welfare* (Research on Economic Inequality Series, Book 10), edited by Yoram Amiel and John A. Bishop, 65–100. Bingley, U.K.: Emerald Group Publishing Ltd.

Enami, Ali, Nora Lustig, and Rodrigo Aranda. 2017. "Analytical Foundations: Measuring the Redistributive Impact of Taxes and Transfers." In *Commitment to Equity Handbook: Estimating the Impact of Fiscal Policy on Inequality and Poverty,* edited by Nora Lustig, chapter 2. Washington, DC: Brookings Institution Press and CEQ Institute, Tulane University. Advance online version; available at http://www.commitmentoequity.org /publications/handbook.php.

Government of Jordan. 2015. "Jordan 2025: A National Vision and Strategy." Economic blueprint document, Hashemite Kingdom of Jordan, Amman.

Heredia-Ortiz, E. 2013. "Evaluating Tax Expenditures in Jordan: Jordan Fiscal Reform II Project." Publication prepared for the Jordan Economic Growth Office of the U.S. Agency for International Development (USAID), Amman.

Higgins, Sean, and Nora Lustig. 2015. "Can a Poverty-Reducing and Progressive Tax and Transfer System Hurt the Poor?" Commitment to Equity Working Paper 33, Center for Inter-American Policy and Research; the Inter-American Dialogue; and Department of Economics, Tulane University, New Orleans, LA.

IMF (International Monetary Fund). 2012. *Jordan: 2012 Article IV Consultation—Staff Report and Public Information Notice.* Country Report 12/119, IMF, Washington, DC.

Inchauste, G., Y. Mansur, and U. Serajuddin. 2017. "Jordan: Reform amid Turmoil." In *The Political Economy of Subsidy Reform,* edited by G. Inchauste and D. G. Victor, chapter 5. Directions in Development Series. Washington, DC: World Bank.

Jolliffe, Dean Mitchell, and Umar Serajuddin. 2015. "Estimating Poverty with Panel Data, Comparably: An Example from Jordan." Policy Research Working Paper 7373, World Bank, Washington, DC.

Lustig, Nora, ed. Forthcoming. *Commitment to Equity Handbook: Estimating the Impact of Fiscal Policy on Inequality and Poverty*. Washington, DC: Brookings Institution Press and CEQ Institute, Tulane University. Advance online version available at http://www .commitmentoequity.org/publications/handbook.php.

Mansour, Wael. 2012. "The Patterns and Determinants of Household Welfare Growth in Jordan 2002–2010." Policy Research Working Paper 6249, World Bank, Washington, DC.

MoF (Ministry of Finance, Jordan). 2013. *Jordan General Government Finance Bulletin—July 2013*. Monthly report, Studies and Economic Policies Directorate, MoF, Hashemite Kingdom of Jordan, Amman.

MoH (Ministry of Health, Jordan). 2012. *Ministry of Health Annual Statistical Book 2012*. Annual report, MoH, Hashemite Kingdom of Jordan, Amman.

Ravallion, M. 2003. "The Debate on Globalization, Poverty and Inequality: Why Measurement Matters." *International Affairs* 79 (4): 739–53.

Silva, J., V. Levin, and M. Morgandi. 2013. *Inclusion and Resilience: The Way Forward for Social Safety Nets in the Middle East and North Africa*. Washington, DC: World Bank.

Thomas, D., J. Strauss, and M. Henriques. 1991. "How Does Mother's Education Affect Child Height?" *The Journal of Human Resources* 26 (2): 183–211.

WHO (World Health Organization). 2006. *Health System Profile—Jordan*. Country health system report, Regional Health Systems Observatory, Regional Office for the Eastern Mediterranean (EMRO), WHO, Cairo.

World Bank. 2012a. "The Hashemite Kingdom of Jordan: A Note on Updating Poverty Measurement Methodology." Background paper for the Jordan Poverty Reduction Strategy, World Bank, Washington, DC.

———. 2012b. "Hashemite Kingdom of Jordan: Options for Immediate Fiscal Adjustment and Longer Term Consolidation." Report 71979-JO, World Bank, Washington, DC.

CHAPTER 7

Who Benefits from Fiscal Redistribution in the Russian Federation?

Luis F. López-Calva, Nora Lustig, Mikhail Matytsin, and Daria Popova

Introduction

The Russian Federation finished the first decade of 2000s as a high-income country, with a per capita gross national income of US$15,177 per year (2005 purchasing power parity [PPP])—comparable to that of Chile, Estonia, Hungary, or Poland—and a population of 142.8 million people. Indeed, Russia enjoyed sustained, significant economic growth during the 2005–15 decade, growth that was accompanied by high rates of income mobility for all population groups.

Between 2000 and 2012, increases in gross domestic product (GDP) averaged 5.16 percent a year, above the regional mean for Europe and Central Asia (4.82 percent).[1] Throughout this period, the positive trend was interrupted only by the 2008–09 global financial crisis (when GDP declined by around 7.8 percent), after which growth quickly resumed. Indeed, by 2012, GDP per capita had nearly doubled from its 2000 level (from US$8,613 to US$15,177 2005 PPP), and Russia was ranked the eighth-largest country by nominal GDP and the fifth-largest by PPP.[2]

The positive outcomes in economic growth were accompanied by economic mobility for most households, reflected in substantial poverty reduction (Cancho et al. 2015). The share of people living in poverty declined steadily for more than a decade, from around 30 percent of the population in 2000 to about 11 percent in 2014, based on the national poverty line.[3] The overall positive trend, however,

The authors are grateful to Irina Denisova (New Economic School, Moscow), Vladimir Gimpelson (National Research University Higher School of Economics, Moscow), and participants in the Higher School of Economics XVI International Academic Conference on Economic and Social Development in April 2015. Daria Popova gratefully acknowledges support from the Basic Research Programme of the National Research University Higher School of Economics.

masks the stagnation in poverty reduction in 2013–14. (After reaching a record low of 10.7 percent in 2012, the poverty rate remained at 10.8 percent in 2013 and increased to 11.2 percent in 2014.)

Russia's poverty rates are lower when measured using the international per capita poverty lines instead of the national poverty line: based on the US$5-a-day poverty line (real 2005 PPP), the poverty rate was 7.3 percent in 2012 (figure 7.1). On the other hand, extreme poverty is nearly nonexistent in Russia; using the international line of US$1.25 a day, the extreme poverty rate is close to zero (0.03 percent in 2012). Even using a higher international poverty line (US$2.50 a day, roughly equivalent to Rub 41.7), extreme poverty was well below 1 percent (0.77 percent) in 2012.

Income inequality in Russia, on the other hand, increased significantly after the market transition in the 1990s and only stabilized toward the second decade of the 21st century. Income inequality in Russia exceeds the world's average: the Gini coefficient for an average of 78 advanced and low- and middle-income countries circa 2010 was 0.38 (Lustig 2016), whereas it was 0.42 in Russia.[4] It must be recalled that in the late 1980s, Russia and the Scandinavian nations were among the countries with the lowest income inequality (OECD 2008). However, inequality in Russia sharply increased at the beginning of the transition from the state socialist economy to a market economy: between 1991 and 1994, the country's Gini coefficient grew from 0.260 to 0.409 (Milanovic 1999).

Figure 7.1 Poverty Headcount Ratio in the Russian Federation, 2000–12

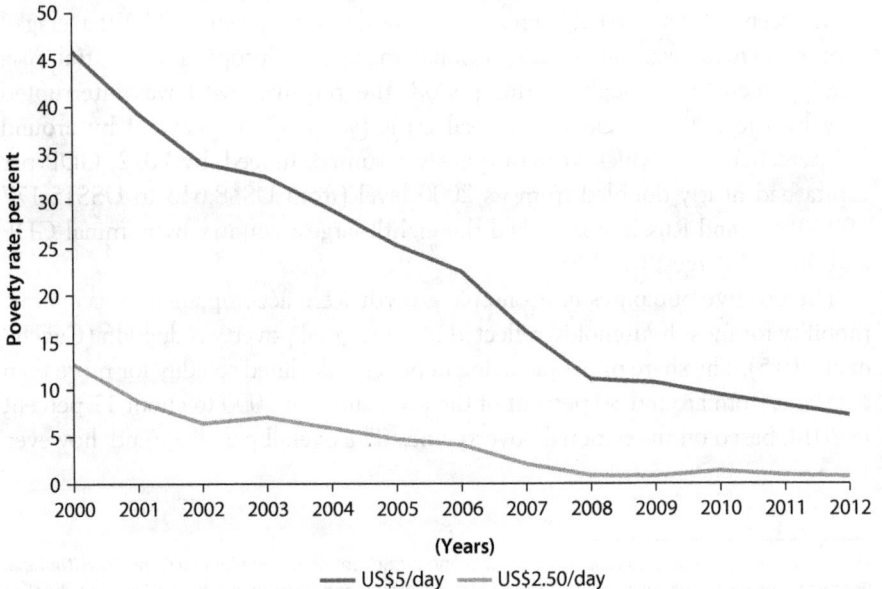

Source: World Bank Europe and Central Asia Team for Statistical Development (ECATSD), using the Europe and Central Asia Poverty (ECAPOV) Database.
Note: Figure shows the poverty headcount ratio using two international per capita poverty lines: US$5 and US$2.50 per day in purchasing power parity (PPP) 2005 terms.

Though the trend in overall inequality during the first decade of this century varied depending on the indicators used (income or consumption), it is well-established that income inequality remained basically flat (with slight fluctuations around the 0.42 level), whereas wage inequality decreased (Calvo, López-Calva, and Posadas 2015).

Some important questions arise after putting all these facts together: Particularly, what role does nonlabor income play in overall inequality? And, in turn, how sustainable are the observed trends in poverty, given that the poorest segments depend more heavily on nonlabor income sources? Indeed, after a period of profound reforms and retrenchment in the 1990s and early 2000s, the Russian welfare system began to expand again in the mid-2000s because of the greater fiscal space associated with the commodity boom. In spite of the introduction of means-tested programs, the social protection system continues to be dominated by categorical benefits, with two particular groups being the main beneficiaries: pensioners and families with children under age 1.5 years (Ovcharova, Popova, and Pishniak 2007; UNICEF 2011).

Objectives and Contributions of This Chapter

This chapter assesses the distributional impact of Russia's main tax and social spending programs by applying a state-of-the-art fiscal incidence analysis (Lustig 2017; Lustig and Higgins 2013). In particular, it quantifies the impact of direct and indirect taxes as well as cash and in-kind transfers on inequality and poverty. Second, the chapter assesses which sociodemographic categories of the population (defined by income, age, and household composition and size) are net payers or net beneficiaries of the fiscal system. It also examines the extent to which spending on education and health is not only equalizing but also pro-poor (meaning the average transfer declines with income).

For the analysis, we use data from the 2010 Russian Longitudinal Monitoring Survey of the Higher School of Economics (RLMS-HSE). Given the overwhelming weight of the pension system, both as a source of revenue (social insurance contributions [SICs] representing 17 percent of total government revenues) and as a component of social spending (contributory pensions representing 38.7 percent of total social spending), this chapter analyzes the redistributive and poverty-reducing effect of the fiscal system under two extreme assumptions: contributory pensions as deferred income and contributory pensions as pure government transfers. In reality, the distinction between contributory and noncontributory pensions in Russia is quite arbitrary because a large share of the budget of the Pension Fund (41 percent in 2010) is covered by transfers from the federal budget. Hence, these two scenarios can be considered as an upper and a lower bound of a true estimate of the impact of the pension system.

Our analysis has three unique features:

- It is the first comprehensive fiscal incidence study for Russia that estimates the cumulative impact of both direct and indirect taxes as well as both cash transfers and in-kind transfers (public education and health care). The previous fiscal

incidence studies for Russia assessed the impact of separate policy instruments, such as child and maternity benefits (Denisova, Kolenikov, and Yudaeva 2000; Notten and Gassmann 2008; Ovcharova and Popova 2005; Ovcharova, Popova, and Pishniak 2007; Popova 2013, 2016); in-kind privileges (Volchkova et al. 2006); direct taxes (Duncan 2014); or indirect taxes (Decoster 2003).
- The methodology applied in this study enables us to explore the redistributive capacity of the welfare system under two scenarios for the treatment of contributory pensions: as deferred income (benchmark scenario) and as government transfers (sensitivity analysis scenario).
- Because this chapter applies the Commitment to Equity (CEQ) approach (Lustig 2017; Lustig and Higgins 2013), the results for Russia are comparable with those for a number of middle-income countries for which the framework has been applied previously.

Summary of Results
The main results from the study concern the dominant fiscal impact of pensions on overall income redistribution, on poverty reduction, and on which demographic groups are net payers and net beneficiaries under this fiscal system. These results can be summarized as follows:

Redistributive Impact of Pensions
In terms of the redistributive capacity of fiscal policy, the defining role belongs to pensions—and when they are considered to be transfers instead of deferred income, the overall redistributive impact is dramatically larger. Specifically, when pensions are considered deferred income (under the benchmark scenario), the redistributive effect of the fiscal system equals 0.028 Gini points, or a 7 percent reduction in the Gini, for consumable income relative to market income.[5] In contrast, if contributory pensions are considered to be transfers (under the sensitivity analysis scenario), the reduction in the Gini for consumable income relative to market income equals 0.129 Gini points, or 26.2 percent Gini reduction.

When pensions are considered deferred income, Russia's reduction of the Gini through direct taxes and transfers (0.031 Gini points) is comparable to that of Brazil and Chile (0.035 and 0.037 Gini points, respectively). However, if pensions are considered transfers, the redistribution (a Gini reduction of 0.132 points) is larger than in the United States (a Gini reduction of 0.109 points).

Net direct taxes (such as income taxes) are always equalizing, but net indirect taxes (such as sales and excise taxes) are unequalizing in both the benchmark and the sensitivity analysis scenarios. In addition, if contributory pensions are treated as deferred income, in-kind transfers (public education and health care) are the largest redistributive fiscal component. In-kind transfers are always equalizing.

Poverty impact of pensions. If contributory pensions are considered deferred (market) income, we observe a 0.7 percent reduction in the poverty headcount using the national poverty threshold after net direct taxes (for disposable income) and a 2.6 percent increase after net indirect taxes (for consumable income).

However, if pensions are treated as transfers, the Russian system achieves a 13.5 percent reduction in poverty for disposable income and an 8.9 percent reduction for consumable income. This is quite a modest outcome given the amount of spending on social benefits in Russia.

Net indirect taxes increase the poverty rate (above the rate based on market income alone) by a nontrivial amount if contributory pensions are treated as market income. If contributory pensions are treated as transfers, in contrast, consumable-income poverty is lower than market-income poverty for any of the poverty lines considered. These results indicate that, in Russia, the poor who are not pensioners are not protected from poverty to the same extent as the poor who are pensioners.

Fiscal policy impact by demographic group. It appears that the households of working-age people with and without underage children are net payers, whereas only pensioners' households benefit from the fiscal redistribution in Russia under both the pensions-as-market-income and pensions-as-transfers scenarios. The biggest losers under both scenarios are one- and two-child couples. Among age groups, adults younger than age 30 are penalized the most.

Overall, the Russian system of taxes and transfers has a limited redistributive capacity vertically (among different income groups), but it does achieve considerable horizontal redistribution (among different sociodemographic groups). There seems to be room to reconsider the targeting of some programs to enhance the fiscal system's distributional impact.

The chapter is organized as follows: "The Russian Fiscal System" briefly describes the country's tax and transfer system. "The Fiscal System's Distributive Capacity: Data and Assumptions" discusses methodology and data. "The Impact of Fiscal Policy on Inequality and Poverty" presents the main results. The final section summarizes "Conclusions and Policy Implications."

The Russian Fiscal System

Taxes

The Russian tax system is largely a unified, national system with few regional and local taxes. The major federal taxes are SICs, personal income tax (PIT), value added tax (VAT), tax on mineral resource extraction, corporate profit tax, and excises.[6] All regional and local taxes—property tax, vehicle tax, and land tax—are asset related. Some federal taxes such as the PIT may be forwarded to regional budgets through intrabudgetary transfers. Meanwhile, the corporate profit tax is split into federal and regional shares defined by the tax code. The structure of tax revenues in Russia is shown in table 7.1.

Social Insurance Contributions

SICs are the largest source of tax revenues, accounting for 5.3 percent of GDP in 2010. They represent a financial obligation imposed on employers (employees do not pay separate contributions) and the self-employed to obtain revenues

Table 7.1 Tax Revenues in the Russian Federation, 2010

Revenue component	Rubles, billions	Share of GDP (%)	Included in analysis?	Ratio of survey total to external statistics (%)[a]
Social insurance contributions				
Social Insurance Fund contributions	243.4	0.5	Yes	120.2
Health care funds contributions	280.8	0.6	Yes	113.8
Direct taxes				
Personal income tax	1,790.5	3.9	Yes	86.4
Vehicle tax	—	—	Yes	n.a.
Indirect taxes				
Value added tax	2,498.6	5.4	Yes	62.3
Excise taxes	471.5	1.0	Yes	45.5
Other taxes				
Corporate profit tax	1,774.6	3.8	No	n.a.
Property taxes	628.2	1.4	No	n.a.
Taxes on natural resource extraction	1,440.8	3.1	No	n.a.
Taxes on total income	207.7	0.4	No	n.a.
Arrears and overpayment on canceled taxes	56.1	0.1	No	n.a.
Total taxes and contributions analyzed (benchmark)[b]	5,284.8	11.4	n.a.	74.4
Total taxes and contributions (benchmark)[b]	9,392.2	20.3	n.a.	41.8
Pension Fund contributions	1,929.0	4.2	Yes	106.8
Total taxes and contributions analyzed (sensitivity analysis)[c]	7,213.8	15.6	n.a.	83.0
Total taxes and contributions (sensitivity analysis)[c]	11,321.2	24.4	n.a.	52.9

Source: "Social Status and Standard of Living of the Russian Population," statistical digest, Russian Federal State Statistics Service (Rosstat): http://www.gks.ru/wps/wcm/connect/rosstat_main/rosstat/ru/statistics/publications/catalog/doc _1138698314188.
Note: GDP = gross domestic product; n.a. = not applicable; — = not available.
a. The "ratio of survey total to external statistics" is the ratio of the amount computed using the survey data used for analysis (the Russian Longitudinal Monitoring Survey of the Higher School of Economics, or RLMS-HSE) and the amount from the external data source (Rosstat).
b. Under the "benchmark" scenario, contributory pensions are treated as part of market income, and pension social insurance contributions as lifetime savings (that is, not included in direct taxes).
c. Under the "sensitivity analysis" scenario, contributory pensions are treated as government transfers, and pension insurance contributions as taxes.

required for providing pensions; social insurance allowances (including maternity, temporary incapacity, and unemployment benefits);[7] and health care.

Employers contribute a specified percentage of employees' gross annual earnings. Self-employed individuals, who contribute a specified percentage of the minimum wage, are only required to pay pension and health insurance contributions; participation in other social insurance programs is voluntary. The same tax rates apply for both employers and the self-employed. In 2010, an overall tax rate of

26 percent was applied to individuals' gross annual earnings below Rub 415,000, whereas earnings exceeding this amount were exempt.[8]

Personal Income Tax
PIT revenues accounted for 3.9 percent of GDP in 2010. Individuals' main income (from work for pay, contractor's agreements, or housing rents) is taxed at a 13 percent rate. Capital gains from asset sales are taxable only if the seller owned the asset for less than three years. A higher tax rate of 35 percent applies to some sources of income (for example, bank interest that exceeds the upper limit computed using a refinancing rate). However, interest rates are usually below the threshold, making interest generally tax free. For nonresidents, all types of income received on Russian territory are taxed at a 30 percent rate. Dividends received by shareholders are subject to a 9 percent tax rate.

For taxpayers whose only taxable income comes from employment, the PIT is withheld by the employer, and there is no need to file a tax return. There are small tax deductions for parents with low earnings in addition to tax deductions for expenses related to charity, education, and health care as well as the purchase and sale of housing.

Value Added Tax
VAT is the second-largest source of federal revenue, accounting for 5.4 percent of GDP in 2010. From 2004 on, the standard VAT rate has been 18 percent. However, a reduced rate of 10 percent is applicable to sales of basic foodstuffs such as bread, potatoes, vegetables, meat, fish, dairy, fats, sugar, and eggs; sales of some goods for children, including clothes; sales of periodical printed publications, except for those of advertising or of an erotic nature; and sales of some important medical goods manufactured both in and outside of Russia.

VAT-exempt transactions include, among other things, export sales, international transportation services, and supplies exported from Russia. Some types of activities, under certain conditions, are also exempt from VAT, such as the sale of specifically listed medical goods and services; funeral services; warranty repair services; license-based educational services rendered by nonprofit institutions; services provided by organizations carrying out activities in the areas of culture and art; and banking and insurance services.

Excise Taxes
Excise taxes account for 1 percent of GDP and are mainly imposed on the sale or import of manufactured excisable goods. Excisable goods include raw and refined alcohol; alcoholic drinks with more than 0.5 percent alcohol by volume, including beer; tobacco products; gasoline, diesel fuel, and motor oils; passenger cars and motorcycles with engines exceeding 90 horsepower; and, since 2013, home heating oil. In contrast to VAT, excise duties are typically expressed as a fixed amount of rubles per quantity bought by the consumer. Since 2007, cigarettes have been additionally taxed based on a percentage of the manufacturers' suggested retail price.

Other Taxes

The analysis takes all of the abovementioned taxes into account. Other taxes not included in the analysis include the corporate profit tax (3.8 percent of GDP); the natural resource extraction tax (3.1 percent of GDP); property taxes (1.4 percent of GDP); and the unified taxes on total income (0.4 percent of GDP), paid by taxpayers who have switched to a simplified taxation scheme. In 2009, the revenues from taxes on labor (PIT and total contributions toward pensions, health care, and social insurance) began to exceed the revenues from the natural resource extraction and corporate taxes.

Social Spending

Social spending in Russia without considering pensions accounted for 13.1 percent of GDP in 2010 (table 7.2). This figure comprises spending on direct cash and

Table 7.2 Social Spending in the Russian Federation, 2010

Spending component	Rubles, billions	Share of GDP (%)	Included in analysis?	Ratio of survey total to external statistics (%)
Direct transfers (cash and near-cash)	2,443.8	5.3	n.a.	42.1
Noncontributory (social) pensions[a]	230.4	0.5	Yes	125.1
Unemployment benefit and ALMPs (quasi-insurance)	183.9	0.4	n.a.	n.a.
Unemployment benefit and material aid to unemployed[b]	52.8	0.1	Yes	54.0
Employment promotion and ALMPs[c]	128.4	0.3	No	n.a.
Social insurance benefits	473.4	1.0	n.a.	n.a.
Maternity leave allowance[d]	67.3	0.1	Yes	74.4
Lump-sum birth or family placement grant[d]	18.7	0.0	Yes	103.5
Childcare allowance up to age 1.5[d]	121.8	0.3	Yes	72.2
Temporary incapacity benefit[d]	185.2	0.4	No	n.a.
Other	80.4	0.2	No	n.a.
Noncontributory (social assistance) benefits	1,316.6	2.8	n.a.	n.a.
Non–means-tested benefits	1,078.4	2.3	n.a.	n.a.
Monthly and lump-sum cash payments (monetized privileges)[e]	419.3	0.9	Yes	33.8
Other privileges (cash and in-kind)[f]	362.4	0.8	Yes	45.2
Maternity capital[g]	97.6	0.2	Yes	47.1
Compensation for childcare fees[h]	9.9	0.0	Yes	139.9
Special forms of support for families with children[i]	16.4	0.0	No	n.a.
Other benefits (scholarships and others)[j]	172.7	0.4	Yes	29.9
Means-tested benefits	238.3	0.5	n.a.	n.a.
Child allowance up to age 16 (or 18)[b]	43.1	0.1	Yes	160.8
Housing subsidy[b]	55.7	0.1	Yes	96.3
State social assistance[h]	8.3	0.0	Yes	178.4
Social supplement to pension[g]	130.6	0.3	No	n.a.
Social care (not direct transfers)	239.5	0.6	n.a.	n.a.
Social care[k]	168.3	0.4	No	n.a.
Other social programs[l]	71.2	0.2	No	n.a.

table continues next page

Table 7.2 Social Spending in the Russian Federation, 2010 (continued)

Spending component	Rubles, billions	Share of GDP (%)	Included in analysis?	Ratio of survey total to external statistics (%)
Education	1,893.9	4.1	n.a.	51.7
Childcare and preschool[m]	321.3	0.7	Yes	57.9
Primary and secondary[m]	827.4	1.8	Yes	57.9
Vocational[m]	163.8	0.4	Yes	57.9
Tertiary[m]	377.8	0.8	Yes	57.9
Other[m]	203.6	0.4	No	n.a.
Health care	1,708.8	3.7	n.a.	50.4
Primary (outpatient) care and inpatient care[m]	1,592.9	3.4	Yes	54.1
Physical culture and sports[m]	115.9	0.3	No	n.a.
Social spending analyzed (benchmark)[m]	4,943.3	10.7	n.a.	58.0
Total social spending (benchmark)	6,046.5	13.1	n.a.	47.5
Contributory pensions[n]	3,819.5	8.2	Yes	99.6
Social spending analyzed (sensitivity analysis)[o]	8,762.9	18.9	n.a.	76.2
Total social spending (sensitivity analysis)	9,866.1	21.3	n.a.	67.6

Sources: Federal Treasury data (http://www.roskazna.ru/); laws on implementation of the federal and regional budgets; "Social Status and Standard of Living of the Russian Population," statistical digest, Russian Federal State Statistics Service (Rosstat): http://www.gks.ru/wps/wcm/connect/rosstat_main /rosstat/ru/statistics/publications/catalog/doc_1138698314188; Federal Service for Labour and Employment (Rostrud) data (http://www.rostrud.ru/).

Note: The "ratio of survey total to external statistics" is the ratio of the amount computed using the survey data used for analysis (the Russian Longitudinal Monitoring Survey of the Higher School of Economics, or RLMS-HSE) and the amount from the external data source (Rosstat). Under the "benchmark" scenario, contributory pensions are treated as part of market income and pension social insurance contributions as lifetime savings (that is, not treated as taxes). Under the "sensitivity analysis" scenario, contributory pensions are treated as government transfers and pension insurance contributions as taxes. GDP = gross domestic product; ALMP = active labor market program; n.a. = not applicable; — = not available.

a. Total spending on pensions is the sum of spending of the federal and regional budgets (excluding expenditures on the regional social supplement to pension) and spending of the Pension Fund (excluding expenditures on privileges, maternity capital, and other social transfers). Spending on noncontributory pensions is approximated as total expenditures on state social pensions. Spending on contributory pensions is equal to total spending on pensions minus spending on noncontributory pensions.

b. Spending on the unemployment benefit and material aid to unemployed, the child allowance up to age 16 (age 18 if the child is in full-time education), and the housing subsidy come from Rosstat data on expenditures on some social benefits.

c. Employment promotion and ALMP spending is provided through subventions to the regional budgets for implementation of the federal ALMPs.

d. Spending on the maternity leave allowance, lump-sum birth or family placement grant, the childcare allowance (for up to age 1.5 years), and the temporary incapacity benefit are provided through the Social Insurance Fund budget implementation. (See budget line [budget category] "Social Policy" [excluding expenditures on benefits for the victims of nuclear accidents, in-kind benefits for the disabled, recreation and vouchers to sanatoriums and transportation to the place of recreation, the guaranteed list of social services, and funeral benefit].)

e. "Monthly and lump-sum cash payments (monetized privileges)" refers to expenditures on the unified monthly payment and other regular and lump-sum cash payments for the privileged categories, such as the disabled, veterans of wars and labor, and so on. It is estimated as the sum of expenditures on payments from the federal budget (including interbudgetary transfers) and the regional budgets.

f. "Other privileges (cash and in-kind)" equals the sum of expenditures on social support for payment of rent and utilities for all categories of the population, provision of the set of social services for federal beneficiaries, provision of the technical means of rehabilitation for the disabled, transportation of pensioners to and from the place of recreation, and all other types of social support provided by the regional budgets.

g. Spending on the maternity capital and the social supplement to pension come from Pension Fund budget implementation data. The social supplement to pension is reported by the survey respondents together with pensions, hence it is accounted for in pension benefits.

h. Spending on compensation of childcare fees and state social assistance are provided for in the regional budget implementation laws.

i. "Special forms of support for families with children" equals the sum of expenditures on the lump-sum and monthly child allowance for the enlisted military, benefits related to the family placement of orphans, and the child allowance for the victims of radiation because of accidents.

j. "Other benefits (scholarships and others)" equals the sum of expenditures on compensations for material damage to the victims of political repressions, aid to refugees and internally displaced people, and other types of benefits (including noncontributory scholarships).

k. Social care expenditures of the consolidated budget. (See budget line [budget category] "Social Care" [excluding expenditures on the social supplement to pension in Moscow].)

l. Other social program expenditures of the federal budget. (See budget line 1005, "Applied Scientific Research in the Area of Social Policy"; article 1006, "Other Social Policy Issues" and expenditures of regional budgets; article 1003, "Social Welfare of the Population"; and article 1004, "Support to Families and Children" [excluding social welfare expenditures].)

m. Education and health care spending from treasury data on implementation of the consolidated budget.

n. Under the "benchmark" scenario, contributory pensions are treated as part of market income, and pension social insurance contributions as lifetime savings (that is, not included in direct taxes).

o. Under the "sensitivity analysis" scenario, contributory pensions are treated as government transfers, and pension insurance contributions as taxes.

near-cash transfers, social care services, education, and health-related spending at all levels of administration (federal, regional, and municipal). If spending on contributory pensions is taken into account, the total social spending in Russia amounts to 21.3 percent of the GDP. Direct transfers include a quasi-insurance unemployment benefit, insurance-based benefits, noncontributory (social) pensions, and other social assistance benefits, some of which are means tested. In-kind transfers are benefits derived from the universal public education and health care systems.

Pensions

Public pensions—including both contributory and noncontributory pensions account for the major part of social spending in Russia: 8.7 percent of GDP in 2010. Since 2002, Russia has maintained a three-pillar pension system:

1. A pay-as-you-go benefit, financed by contributions to the extrabudgetary Pension Fund paid by employers and the self-employed
2. A funded system (for those born after 1966), also financed by the Pension Fund
3. Contributory mechanisms whereby individuals can save additional money toward a better pension on a voluntary basis

In addition, Russia has a "zero" pillar that provides "social pensions," which are general revenue–financed benefits for uninsured pensioners (the disabled, orphans, and others). In 2010, out of 44.14 million pensioners, 2.6 million received social pensions accounting for 0.5 percent of GDP. The average social pension benefit in 2010 (Rub 4,731) was slightly more than half the average old-age labor pension benefit (Rub 8,166).[9]

Since the mid-2000s, the Pension Fund has been running a permanently growing deficit, which reached 41 percent in 2010. The distinction between contributory and noncontributory pensions in Russia is therefore quite arbitrary. As noted earlier, under our benchmark scenario, social pensions are treated as government transfers whereas contributory pensions are treated as a part of market income. In the sensitivity analysis, contributory pensions are treated as government transfers along with social pensions.

The statutory retirement age in Russia is one of the lowest in the world: age 55 for women and age 60 for men. Both early retirement and postponement are possible, and various occupational pensions also exist. All state pensions are untaxable, and people are allowed to work while receiving pension benefits; about 30 percent of pensioners continue to work. Contributory pensions are indexed to inflation and average wage growth rates. Social pensions are indexed to inflation rates and changes in the cost of a pensioner's minimum consumer basket. Additional ad hoc increases have been common in recent years. Therefore, the poverty risk of pensioners in Russia is the lowest relative to all other social groups. The replacement ratio, however—the ratio of the average pension to average earnings in the economy—amounted to 35.7 percent in 2010, well below its 1980s level (40 percent).

Unemployment Benefits and Programs

Total spending on unemployment-related programs accounted for 0.4 percent of GDP in 2010. Russia's unemployment benefit can be considered a quasi-insurance program, because it is financed by general revenues and weakly related to an employee's earnings and length of service.[10] The benefit is paid monthly, conditional on the applicant's registration with the State Employment Service (SES) every two weeks. Registered unemployment rates in Russia are substantially lower than survey-based unemployment rates (by the International Labour Organization's definition),[11] predominantly because of the limited incentives for registration. Only about one-third of the unemployed are registered with the SES. The unemployment benefit is paid to nearly 90 percent of the registered unemployed. The total number of recipients in 2010 was 1.36 million, which is less than 1 percent of the population. The maximum unemployment benefit was set at Rub 4,900 per month, and the minimum at Rub 850 per month.

Until 2009, few workers benefited from the active labor market programs (ALMPs) in Russia. This changed when, in response to the global economic crisis of 2008–09, the government launched additional measures to decrease tension in the regional labor markets. In 2010, ALMPs covered 1.85 million unemployed people.[12]

Social Insurance Benefits

Spending on social insurance–based transfers accounted for 1 percent of GDP in 2010. These benefits are part of the contributory social security system. The most expensive of these benefits include (a) a temporary incapacity benefit (0.4 percent of GDP), paid during an absence from work because of sickness or to care for a sick family member, and (b) a (partly noncontributory) child allowance for children up to age 1.5 years (0.3 percent of GDP).

The child allowance has become one of the main child-related cash transfers after the implementation of the pro-natalist package resulting from the 2007 reforms. It is provided to socially insured mothers upon the completion of a 140-day maternity leave (during which they are entitled to a benefit equal to 100 percent of their average earnings for the 12 months preceding the leave, subject to an upper limit). The child allowance equals 40 percent of the mother's average monthly earnings, subject to both upper and lower limits.[13] Mothers whose contribution record is less than six months are entitled to the minimum size of the allowance. As of 2010, the allowance was paid to 3.63 million people (of whom 44 percent were uninsured), or 2.5 percent of the population.

Noncontributory Social Assistance

Noncontributory social assistance accounted for 2.8 percent of GDP in 2010, with most of the resources being spent on categorical programs (2.3 percent of GDP) rather than means-tested programs (0.5 percent of GDP).

Privileges. The most expensive of the categorical (non-means-tested) programs is the "privileges" program (representing approximately 1.7 percent of GDP), which was inherited from the former Soviet social protection system. Privileges are free or discounted services provided to vulnerable categories of the population, such as people with disabilities, war veterans, dependents of war victims, victims of the Chernobyl accident, and so on.[14] They also cover numerous privileges for groups based on specific merits before the state (mainly military) and based on their occupational status. Since 2005, the responsibility to finance privileges has been divided between the federal and the regional governments.

By 2005, almost all federally funded privileges (apart from discounts on housing or utility payments) had been monetized (replaced by cash). As of 2010, a few regions (including Moscow) still provided in-kind benefits to the population along with regular and lump-sum cash payments. The complex structure of the system of privileges—the possibility of being entitled to several types of benefits at the same time, manifold forms of provision (cash and in-kind benefits), and the different sources of financing (federal and regional)— make it almost impossible to assess the full scope and scale of the program based on official statistics.

In 2010, 16.69 million people received a monthly cash payment for federal beneficiaries. The size of the benefit ranged from Rub 436 for blood donors to Rub 10,851 for holders of certain military decorations. At the same time, at least 11.01 million people received regular cash payments from the regional authorities, ranging from Rub 467 for labor veterans[15] to Rub 605 for citizens with honorary degrees or special merits recognized by the region. Hence, by a conservative estimate, at least 27.7 million people, or 19.4 percent of Russia's population, were entitled to one or another type of privilege in 2010. However, given that the privileged citizens are mainly elderly people, their number has been decreasing.

Maternity Capital. The maternity capital is Russia's second-most expensive non-means-tested social program (amounting to 0.2 percent of GDP). Another element of the pro-natalist 2007 policy package, this lump-sum grant is paid to any woman who gives birth to, or adopts, a second (or third or subsequent) child. In total, 2.6 million people (1.8 percent of the population) were issued certificates for maternity capital between 2007 and 2010. Among those, 346,000 people (13.3 percent of all recipients) redeemed the capital (or a part of it). The size of the transfer is annually indexed for inflation; in 2010 it amounted to Rub 343,278.

The assets can be used once the child is age 3 in three ways only: to purchase new housing or pay for a mortgage credit; to pay for any type of children's education; or to add to the funded element of the mother's pension. So far, 99 percent of families have chosen to spend these assets to improve their housing. Therefore, the program can be treated as either a direct transfer or an in-kind housing benefit. For the purpose of this analysis, we chose the first option, assuming that the maternity capital is a cash transfer that is disposed of in the same year as it is granted. A random non-take-up was assumed when the benefit was simulated, in order to account for the fact that only 13.3 percent of beneficiaries had redeemed the assets by 2010.

Means-Tested Benefits. There is no such thing in Russia as a solely antipoverty benefit, but the country does have four assistance programs that combine poverty and other eligibility criteria:

- A social supplement to pensions
- A child allowance up to age 16 (or up to age 18 if the child is in full-time education)
- A housing subsidy
- State social assistance

Altogether, the means-tested benefits of these programs account for 0.5 percent of GDP. Eligibility for means-tested benefits is derived from comparing family or household disposable income with the national poverty line. The poverty line is referred to as the minimum subsistence level (MSL) and equals the cost of a minimum basket of goods and services. The composition of the basket is defined for three demographic groups (children under age 16 years, men and women of active working age, and men and women of state pension age) and estimated quarterly for each region and for the country as a whole. In 2010, the average national MSL amounted to Rub 5,688 (about US$261 2005 PPP) per capita per month.

The social supplement to pensions is funded by both federal and regional budgets. Regional budgets provide the other three means-tested benefits, although the federal budget cofinances housing subsidies and child allowances through intrabudgetary transfers. Their generosity and coverage therefore varies from region to region.

Social supplement to pensions. The most expensive means-tested benefit is the social supplement to pensions, which accounts for more than half of all means-tested social spending. This benefit is provided to all nonworking pensioners whose total income is below the cost of a pensioner's poverty line in a given region. The size of the benefit is equal to the gap between the pensioner's poverty line and the pension benefit. In 2010, 4.94 million people (12 percent of pensioners) received the supplement. In our analysis, this benefit is considered as part of the pension, as it is paid together with it and cannot be separated from pensions in the survey.

Child allowances. These allowances are provided to families with children up to age 16 (age 18 if in full-time education) whose per capita income is below the regional poverty line, constituting the classic example of an antipoverty program. Nevertheless, the targeting accuracy of the program is low. As a result, the allowance fails to provide adequate support to participating families, while spreading its budget to 9.94 million children (about 40 percent of children under age 16), of whom 65 percent are not poor. Regional authorities set the size of this benefit; as a result, a basic monthly payment in 2010 varied from Rub 70 to Rub 1,000 per child, with a median monthly payment of Rub 150.

The Distributional Impact of Taxes and Transfers • http://dx.doi.org/10.1596/978-1-4648-1091-6

Housing subsidies. In contrast, Russia's housing subsidies have a more complex objective. One of the major reforms of the 2000s in Russia was the transition to full cost recovery (no subsidies) for the population. This implied a cancellation of the program of cross-subsidies, whereby enterprises and companies paid for utilities at inflated rates, which helped to recoup a part of the cost of utilities for the population.

Housing subsidies were designed to protect people from spending a high share of their income on rent and utilities.[16] A household whose housing costs exceed the regional threshold (not more than 22 percent of household income) qualifies for a subsidy that brings the share of housing costs down to the threshold. However, eligibility and benefit formulas allow nonpoor households to qualify as beneficiaries. Regional authorities have little control over the program design, which is set by the federal legislation. In 2010, the average size of the monthly benefit was Rub 896 per household-beneficiary; the benefit was paid to 3.76 million households (or 7.3 percent of all Russian households).

State social assistance. The program of state social assistance provides relief to poor or in-need households. The program design and the decision as to whether to target any benefits solely to the poor, however, have been fully left with regional authorities. Most often, the rules mix the notion of targeting with categorical assistance, defining certain groups (such as pensioners, families with three or more children, students, and others) who are eligible for the benefits. In addition, targeted assistance is often confused with one-time emergency assistance (for example, for loss of the breadwinner, severe illness, or natural disaster).

The interregional variation in spending on this program is the highest among the means-tested assistance programs. In 2010, the average monthly cash payment was Rub 306 per family member, and the average lump-sum payment was Rub 1,789. A total of 1.39 million people received a regular cash benefit, and 1.1 million people received a lump-sum payment, which altogether was less than 2 percent of the population.

Social Care Programs

The system of social care institutions provides services for orphans or children left without parental care, elderly and disabled people, and the homeless. In 2010, 126,000 children lived in state care institutions, and inpatient-care institutions for disabled and elderly people accommodated 269,000. Larger groups of the population were attended in centers of temporary or day care for disabled and elderly people (573,000) or were clients of the home-based care program (1.089 million). Thus, the most generous estimate of the number of clients of care institutions is 1.5 percent of the population, although spending for these purposes amounted to 0.4 percent of GDP.

Education Spending

Education-related spending in Russia accounted for 4.1 percent of GDP in 2010. The Russian constitution guarantees equal access to education free of charge at the preschool, primary, and secondary school levels as well as for primary vocational school and secondary vocational and tertiary education (on a competitive basis) at state and municipal educational institutions.

The current system of preschool education, inherited from the Soviet era, formally guarantees full-time day care for all children under the minimum school age (7 years). About 55–60 percent of preschool-age children attended preschool institutions during the 2000s.[17] Childcare is mostly public. Parents contribute in the form of fees, covering part of the actual cost. The supply-side subsidies for childcare constitute at least 80 percent of the cost of childcare services.[18]

Primary and secondary general education (for children age 7–16 years) is compulsory. After that, children may either (a) proceed to secondary school for two more years to obtain a secondary education certificate, which allows them to start four to six years of tertiary education or (b) follow the vocational education track to obtain a primary vocational degree (in one and a half years) or a secondary vocational degree (in three to four years). The secondary vocational degree also allows students to continue with tertiary education after completing their vocational education.

Most of the students attending primary and secondary general school (13.57 million) and primary vocational school (1.01 million) are enrolled in the public system; the share of private schools at this level of education is negligible. Among the students enrolled in secondary vocational education (2.13 million), 95 percent attend public institutions. Close to 83 percent of all students in the tertiary education system (7.05 million in the 2010/2011 academic year) were enrolled in public colleges and universities, and only one-third of them occupied budgetary slots (that is, did not pay fees).

Health Care Spending

Health care is free at the point of demand for Russian citizens.[19] In 2010, health care spending amounted to 3.7 percent of GDP (including spending on physical culture and sports at 0.3 percent of GDP).[20] As for other services, there is a high disparity in health care spending among different regions.

The state guarantees of free health care include inpatient and outpatient treatment as well as rehabilitation or nursing care and provision of medicines and medical appliances for specific patient categories. In practice, however, free provision is quite limited, which results in the growth of private spending on health care services, including "additional" services provided by public medical institutions. The share of out-of-pocket spending by the population in total health care spending increased from 10 percent in the mid-1990s to 40–45 percent in the mid-2000s (UNICEF 2011).[21]

Public health care for working people is funded through contributions paid by employers and the self-employed to the Federal and Territorial Mandatory Health Insurance Funds. The cost of health insurance for nonworking citizens is covered from the regional budgets; the share of health care spending subsidized by the regional budgets is 56 percent.

The Fiscal System's Distributive Capacity: Data and Assumptions

Data

Although a number of national household surveys were considered for the analysis, the one that fulfilled all the essential conditions was the Russian Longitudinal Monitoring Survey of the Higher School of Economics (RLMS-HSE).[22] The survey collects individual-level information on demographic characteristics, within-family relationships, labor market status, primary income by source, and social benefits as well as expenditure and other relevant characteristics that may affect tax liabilities or benefit entitlements. The survey also satisfies international standards in terms of sampling and quality of data collection.[23]

The sample includes both cross-sectional and panel components and is large enough to support the analysis of small groups at the national level. The analysis in this chapter uses the 2010 cross-sectional sample, which consists of 6,323 households and 16,867 individuals. In geographical terms, the survey covers 32 (of 83) regions and is not representative at the regional level, which is the main limitation of the survey.

The data set (further described in table 7.3) contains weights that adjust the cross-sectional sample not only for design factors (sampling probabilities and nonresponse) but also for deviations from the census characteristics. For our purposes, we have additionally computed the *grossing weights*. In other words, the weights provided with the original data were scaled up to the overall population. They were calculated as the ratio of population to sample counts for

Table 7.3 Description of Data and Sampling for Fiscal Incidence Analysis, the Russian Federation, 2010

Characteristic	Description
Source survey name	Russian Longitudinal Monitoring Survey of the Higher School of Economics (RLMS-HSE)
Provider	National Research University Higher School of Economics
Year of collection	2010
Period of collection	October–December 2010
Income reference period	Typically income and expenditure for the month preceding the survey; for some types of expenditures, three months preceding the survey
Sampling	A three-stage stratified clustered probability sample of dwellings
Unit of assessment	Household (people living together and sharing income and expenses)
Coverage	Permanent residents, excluding people living in institutions
Sample size	21,343 individuals; 7,923 households (total sample including the panel element)
Response rate for household grid	80 percent (60 percent in Moscow and St. Petersburg)
Final sample used in the analysis	16,867 individuals; 6,323 households
Weighting	The weights must be used to adjust the sample for design factors (sampling probabilities and nonresponse) and deviations from the census characteristics. In addition, the weights provided with the original data were scaled up to the overall population

subgroups defined by household size (1, 2, 3, 4, and 5+ members) and location of residence (urban or rural). Population totals are taken from the 2010 census. Applying weights to gross the numbers up to the population figure gives about 54.4 million households and about 137.8 million individuals.[24]

Another major data adjustment was the imputation of user-missing data on earnings, income or expenditure, and other important variables. "Don't know" or "Refuse to answer" responses were imputed whenever reasonable using median values. (Median values at the regional level were used if the sample was big enough.) Some households reported zero income or expenditure (the reference period in the survey is one month); however, there was no justification for omitting or imputing those observations.

Methodological Approach and Assumptions

To construct the four CEQ income concepts (market, disposable, consumable, and final income) used in the analysis, it is necessary to "map" the taxes and transfers from Russia's national accounts and administrative fiscal data to individual household members. This approach, however, differs from that followed by other initiatives with similar objectives such as EUROMOD, the tax-benefit microsimulation model for the European Union.[25] EUROMOD attempts to fully simulate as many fiscal interventions as possible and validates them against external statistics (including administrative data, national accounts, Eurostat data). The instruments that are simulated in all countries are cash transfers, direct taxes, and SICs. Noncash transfers, imputed rent, and indirect taxes are beyond the scope of the model, although they can be potentially accounted for within the EUROMOD framework.

The CEQ analysis, on the other hand, mainly relies on the data reported by survey participants. However, if the survey does not include questions on certain items, the values are either simulated or imputed following the methodologies described in Lustig (2017) and Lustig and Higgins (2013). The specific method followed for each fiscal intervention is presented in table 7A.1.

The welfare indicator used in the fiscal incidence analysis is income per capita. No calibration has been done toward external income aggregates for the reasons described below. Therefore, income distribution estimates do not match perfectly between the RLMS-HSE and the income distribution and poverty statistics published by the Russian Federal State Statistics Service (Rosstat).

Unfortunately, none of the current external sources generates fully reliable quantitative estimates of inequality in income distribution in Russia. The source of original data for assessing income distribution is the Household Budget Survey (HBS), which is administered by Rosstat. Since 1997, the HBS has collected data on consumption only, because income data are considered a priori unreliable. According to various estimates, the HBS sample does not cover about 5–10 percent of the Russian population, including the poorest, and—especially—the richest households.

To deal with unit nonresponse, the welfare aggregate derived from the HBS is statistically manipulated to match macrolevel estimates of income using a two-parameter lognormal model. One of the parameters of this model, a root mean square deviation of logarithms, is derived from the HBS; another parameter, the mean per capita income, is taken from national accounts. Because of the adjustment for unreported earnings, the mean income in national accounts is considerably higher than the expenditure aggregate in HBS. Rosstat estimates the share of unreported earnings to be 30–40 percent of the official (declared) earnings, ranging from less than 15 percent in the bottom income decile to over 50 percent in the top income decile. These unreported earnings are imputed and included as an element of total population income in macroeconomic statistics.[26] As a result, poverty and inequality estimates in the macroeconomic statistics are lower than those derived from the original HBS data, and mean income is higher.

As for the quality of the RLMS-HSE income data and our simulations, as shown earlier in table 7.1 (in the "ratio of survey total to external statistics" column), the survey appears to provide reliable estimates of formal earnings, direct taxes, and SICs, which are simulated based on formal earnings. The total amount of simulated VAT is 37 percent lower than the one in external statistics, which is the result of our approach whereby we do not use actual amounts of indirect taxes paid but apply the percentage of consumption paid in indirect taxes to income to calculate indirect taxes. This method allows us to correctly estimate the progressivity of indirect taxes, since for many households—especially for those at the bottom—the reported consumption is higher than income. Excises, on the other hand, are underestimated to a greater extent because of the lack of more precise survey data on consumed quantities of excisable goods.

Also, as shown earlier in table 7.2 (in the "ratio of survey total to external statistics" column), our survey is accurate in predicting the total amount of contributory pensions whereas it overestimates the amount of noncontributory pensions by approximately 25 percent—probably because pensioners do not distinguish pensions from other benefits paid from the Pension Fund (such as the social supplement to pension). Other social benefits that are also reported or simulated with a high degree of precision are the birth grant and housing subsidies. Conversely, social benefits that are underreported include unemployment benefits, the maternity leave allowance, the child care allowance up to age 1.5 years, the maternity capital, and privileges provided in cash and in-kind. The programs that are the responsibility of regions—such as the child allowance up to age 16 (or 18), state social assistance, and compensation of childcare fees—are overreported in the survey. The imputed amounts of publicly provided education and health care were scaled down on purpose to reflect a lower mean income in the survey.

Table 7.4 shows that the income distribution characteristics in our analysis diverge from the Rosstat figures to varying degrees. The mean disposable income in RLMS-HSE is 33–40 percent lower than in national accounts (Rosstat), whereas the poverty headcount is 60–95 percent higher.

A large share of the earnings of both informal and formal sector workers is likely to remain unaccounted for by the RLMS-HSE survey because of the

Table 7.4 Comparison of Disposable-Income Distribution Indicators by Statistical Source and Method, the Russian Federation, 2010

Indicator	Source and method		
	Rosstat, disposable income (macro statistics)	RLMS-HSE, disposable income (benchmark)[a]	RLMS-HSE, disposable income (sensitivity analysis)[b]
Mean income (rubles per month)	18,958.40	12,628.30	11,382.05
Income distribution, 1st quintile (%)	2.0	6.0	6.1
Income distribution, 2nd quintile (%)	9.8	11.9	12.1
Income distribution, 3rd quintile (%)	14.8	16.6	16.8
Income distribution, 4th quintile (%)	22.5	22.8	22.7
Income distribution, 5th quintile (%)	47.7	42.6	42.3
Gini index[c]	0.421	0.362	0.359
Funds ratio[d]	16.6	13.6	13.3
National poverty rate[e] (%)	12.5	20.1	23.8

Source: Based on 2010 Russian Longitudinal Monitoring Survey of the Higher School of Economics (RLMS-HSE) data.
Note: "Disposable income" = "market income" (pretax salaries, wages, income from capital assets, and private transfers) – direct taxes and social security contributions + direct cash transfers. Rosstat = Russian Federal State Statistics Service. Income distribution quintiles range from poorest (1st quintile) to richest (5th quintile).
a. The benchmark analysis treats contributory pensions as part of market income and pension social insurance contributions as lifetime savings (that is, not included in direct taxes).
b. The sensitivity analysis treats contributory pensions as government transfers and social insurance contributions as taxable income.
c. The Gini index measures the equality of income distribution, ranging from 0 (perfect equality) to one (maximal inequality).
d. The funds ratio is the ratio of total income of the top decile to the total income of the bottom decile.
e. The national poverty rate is calculated using the official regionally adjusted poverty line. National poverty lines for the 4th quarter of 2010 in local currency are as follows: children under age 16 = Rub 5,709 per month; adults = Rub 6,367 per months; pensioners = Rub 4,683 per month. The mean per capita poverty line = Rub 195.2 per day, US$9 per day in 2005 purchasing power parity (PPP) terms.

atypical composition of earnings in Russia (which have a large variable part)[27] or because of the nonresponse or underreporting by respondents. The greatest disparity on poverty measures is in the estimates for working-age population and children, whereas the estimates of pensioners' poverty are very close to external statistics. This reflects the fact that the survey reports public pensions much better than income from employment and capital incomes and that the latter are concentrated in the households of working-age people.

Inequality measures are affected to a lesser extent. The survey appears to overestimate the share of the bottom quintile and to underestimate the share of the top quintile, which results in a 15 percent lower value of Gini index and a 20 percent lower value of the ratios of mean incomes of the top and bottom deciles (funds ratio) than the one reported by Rosstat.

It would be unrealistic to expect to achieve completely identical results for all income distribution indicators, because of the additional statistical adjustments of Rosstat data (such as the lognormality assumption) to account for the HBS sample bias. The appropriateness of using the lognormality assumption for modeling income distribution in Russia has been a subject of criticism in the Russian academic community for quite a while. The development of a more accurate method of accounting for unit nonresponse in Russian survey data is beyond the scope of this study, but it is a highly relevant area for future research.

Other limitations of fiscal incidence analysis apply here as well. This study uses point-in-time analysis and does not incorporate behavioral or general equilibrium effects. It is a first-order approximation that measures the average incidence of fiscal interventions. However, our estimates take into account economic rather than statutory tax incidence. For example, it is assumed that PIT and contributions by employees and employers are borne by labor in the formal sector. Individuals who are not contributing to social security are assumed to pay neither direct taxes nor contributions. Consumption taxes are fully shifted forward to consumers. The analysis takes into account the lower consumption tax incidence associated with own consumption.

The Impact of Fiscal Policy on Inequality and Poverty

Table 7.5 shows the change in the Gini coefficient induced by fiscal policy for each of the four income concepts (market, disposable, consumable, and final) for the two scenarios: pensions as deferred income (the benchmark) and pensions as government transfers (sensitivity analysis).

The first result to note is the striking difference in the redistributive effect of net direct taxes—that is, from "market income" to "disposable income," depending on whether pensions are treated as deferred income (and contributions to social security as mandatory savings) or treated as government transfers (and social security contributions as taxable income). When pensions are considered deferred income, the overall redistributive effect of the fiscal system is −0.028 Gini points, or a 7 percent Gini reduction with respect to market income. In contrast, if contributory pensions are considered government transfers, the effect amounts to −0.129 Gini points, or a 26.2 percent reduction in inequality.

Table 7.5 Changes in Gini Index, by Income Concept, in the Russian Federation, 2010

Indicator	Market income[a]	Disposable income[b]	Consumable income[c]	Final income[d]
Benchmark analysis (contributory pensions are market income)				
Gini index	0.394	0.362	0.366	0.331
Absolute change wrt market income (Gini points)	n.a.	−0.031	−0.028	−0.063
Change wrt market income (%)	n.a.	−7.9	−7.0	−16.0
Sensitivity analysis (contributory pensions are government transfers)				
Gini index	0.491	0.359	0.363	0.324
Absolute change wrt market income (Gini points)	n.a.	−0.132	−0.129	−0.168
Change wrt market income (%)	n.a.	−26.9	−26.2	−34.2

Source: Based on 2010 Russian Longitudinal Monitoring Survey of the Higher School of Economics (RLMS-HSE) data.
Note: The Gini index measures the equality of income distribution, ranging from zero (perfect equality) to one (maximal inequality). wrt = with respect to; n.a. = not applicable.
a. Market income comprises pretax wages, salaries, income earned from capital assets (rent, interest, or dividends), and private transfers.
b. Disposable income = market income − personal income taxes and social security contributions + direct cash transfers.
c. Consumable income = disposable income − indirect (sales and excise) taxes + indirect subsidies.
d. Final income = consumable income + in-kind transfers for education and health care.

The next element to note is that net direct taxes (reflected in disposable income) are equalizing but net indirect taxes (reflected in consumable income) are unequalizing in both scenarios. The latter is observed by calculating the change from the disposable to consumable income Gini. In-kind education and health transfers (reflected in final income) are always equalizing. If pensions are transfers, the marginal contribution to the reduction in inequality from net direct taxes is large—almost as large as the marginal contribution of in-kind transfers. This is observable when comparing the change from the market to disposable income Gini with the change from the consumable to final income Gini.

The importance of the assumption regarding pensions also applies to changes in poverty (table 7.6). If pensions are considered market income, we observe a 0.7 percent reduction in the poverty headcount using the national poverty threshold after net direct taxes and a 2.6 percent increase after net indirect taxes. However, if pensions are treated as a transfer, there is a 13.5 percent reduction in poverty for disposable income and an 8.9 percent reduction for consumable income. In any case, net indirect taxes increase poverty above the market-income poverty rate by a nontrivial amount if pensioners are excluded from the poor

Table 7.6 Poverty Headcount, and Changes by Income Concept, in the Russian Federation, 2010

Percentage change

Poverty line	Market income[a]	Disposable income[b]	Consumable income[c]
Benchmark analysis (contributory pensions are market income)			
US$1.25 PPP	2.6	1.4	1.6
Absolute change wrt market income	n.a.	−1.2	−1.0
US$2.5 PPP	4.0	2.6	2.8
Absolute change wrt market income	n.a.	−1.4	−1.2
US$4 PPP	6.3	4.6	5.5
Absolute change wrt market income	n.a.	−1.7	−0.8
National poverty line (US$9 PPP)	18.9	18.2	21.5
Absolute change wrt market income	n.a.	−0.7	2.6
Sensitivity analysis (contributory pensions are government transfers)			
US$1.25 PPP	12.2	1.5	1.7
Absolute change wrt market income	n.a.	−10.8	−10.5
US$2.5 PPP	15.8	2.5	3.0
Absolute change wrt market income	n.a.	−13.1	−12.7
US$4 PPP	19.8	5.3	6.6
Absolute change wrt market income	n.a.	−14.5	−13.3
National poverty line (US$9 PPP)	35.2	21.8	26.4
Absolute change wrt market income	n.a.	−13.5	−8.9

Source: Based on 2010 Russian Longitudinal Monitoring Survey of the Higher School of Economics (RLMS-HSE) data.
Note: PPP = purchasing power parity; wrt = with respect to; n.a. = not applicable.
a. "Market income" comprises pretax wages, salaries, income earned from capital assets (rent, interest, or dividends), and private transfers.
b. "Disposable income" = market income − personal income taxes and social security contributions + direct cash transfers.
c. "Consumable income" = disposable income − indirect (sales and excise) taxes + indirect subsidies.

The Distributional Impact of Taxes and Transfers • http://dx.doi.org/10.1596/978-1-4648-1091-6

(for example, under the benchmark scenario in which pensions are part of market income). If pensions are treated as pure transfers, in contrast, consumable-income poverty is lower than market-income poverty for each one of the considered poverty lines.

How does Russia compare with middle-income countries, the EU-27, and the United States?[28] Again, depending on the assumption about pensions (whether treated as deferred income or as transfers), Russia can look as redistributive as Brazil and Chile or even more redistributive than the United States (figure 7.2).

Figure 7.2 Redistributive Effect of the Fiscal System in the Russian Federation versus the United States and Selected Middle-Income and European Union Countries, circa 2010

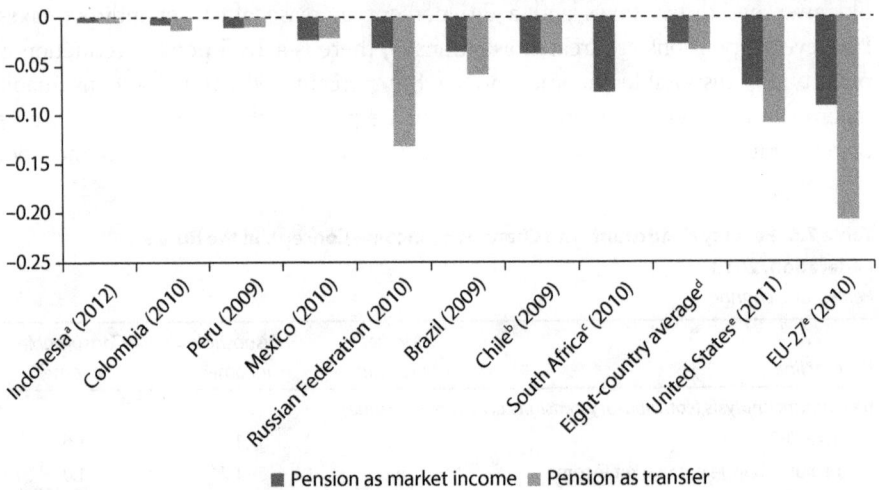

■ Pension as market income   ■ Pension as transfer

Sources: Higgins and Pereira 2014 (Brazil); Higgins et al. 2016 (United States); Inchauste et al. 2015 (South Africa); Jaramillo 2014 (Peru); Lustig 2016; Melendez 2014 (Colombia); Ruiz-Tagle and Contreras 2014 (Chile); Scott 2014 (Mexico). Indonesia data from chapter 5 of this volume. European Union data from EUROMOD Statistics on Distribution and Decomposition of Disposable Income (version G2.0), http://www.iser.essex.ac.uk/euromod/statistics/. Russian data from 2010 Russian Longitudinal Monitoring Survey of the Higher School of Economics (RLMS-HSE).
Note: The "redistributive effect" is here defined as the difference in income inequality (as measured by change in the Gini index) between "market income" (pretax wages, salaries, income from capital assets, and private transfers) and "disposable income" (market income − direct taxes and social security contributions + direct cash transfers). The Gini index measures the equality of income distribution, ranging from zero (perfect equality) to one (maximal inequality). The year of each country's (or country group's) household survey shown within parentheses.
a. For Indonesia, the fiscal incidence analysis was carried out adjusting for spatial price differences.
b. Chile only has a pay-as-you-go system for older workers and a fully funded system running since 1980 based on individual accounts. The contributions to the old system (the ones that may persist) are not available as a separate item in national accounts.
c. The scenario for South Africa assumed that free basic services (such as power, sanitation, water, and refuse removal) are direct transfers. The only contributory pensions in South Africa are for public servants, who must belong to the Government Employees Pension Fund (GEPF). Since the government made no transfers to the GEPF in 2010/11, there is no scenario in which contributory pensions are treated as transfers. Therefore, the fiscal incidence analysis for South Africa does not include a scenario with contributory pensions as transfers; hence it is not shown in the figure.
d. "Eight-country average" refers to the average of the eight leftmost countries shown (left to right): Indonesia, Colombia, Peru, Mexico, Russian Federation, Brazil, Chile, and South Africa.
e. The Gini coefficients for the United States and the EU-27 countries are for equalized income (household income divided by the number of equivalent adults). The EU-27 are the following European Union member states: Austria, Belgium, Bulgaria, Cyprus, the Czech Republic, Denmark, Estonia, Finland, France, Germany, Greece, Hungary, Ireland, Italy, Latvia, Lithuania, Luxembourg, Malta, the Netherlands, Poland, Portugal, Romania, the Slovak Republic, Slovenia, Spain, Sweden, and the United Kingdom.

When pensions are considered deferred income, Russia's inequality reduction (by 0.031 Gini points) because of direct taxes and benefits is comparable to Brazil's (0.035 Gini points) and Chile's (0.037 Gini points). However, if pensions are considered transfers, Russia's inequality reduction (by 0.132 Gini points) is larger than that of the United States (0.109 Gini points).

What is important to note is that the difference in outcomes between the two pension-treatment scenarios, while smaller than that observed for the EU-27, is the largest relative to all other countries. This reinforces the conclusion that Russia's redistributive machinery at the level of direct taxes and transfers is very modest unless pensions are considered as transfers.

Given that all public pensions are treated as transfers, the reduction in poverty induced by cash transfers net of direct taxes (as reflected in disposable income) is large as compared with other middle-income countries. Under that scenario, Russia achieves an 81 percent reduction in the poverty headcount based on the international poverty line of US$2.50 per person per day (figure 7.3). If pensions

Figure 7.3 Effect of the Fiscal System on Poverty Reduction in the Russian Federation versus Selected Middle-Income Countries, circa 2010

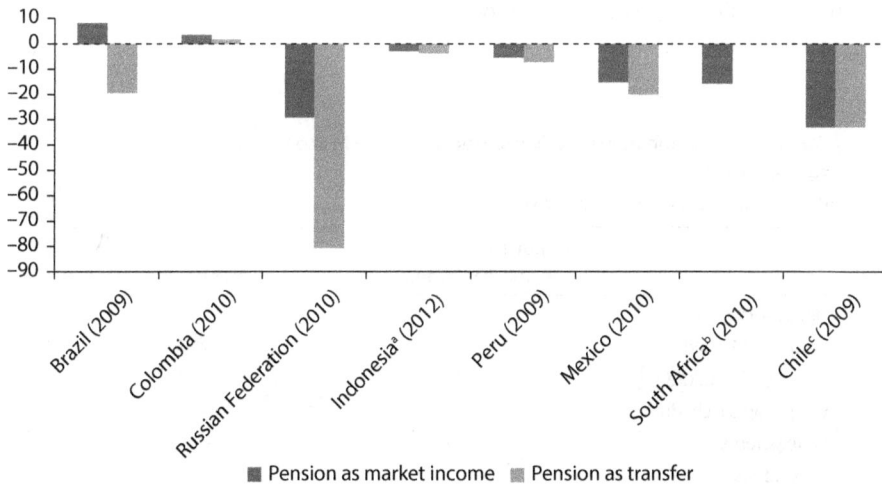

Pension as market income   Pension as transfer

Sources: Based on Higgins and Pereira 2014 (Brazil); Inchauste et al. 2015 (South Africa); Jaramillo 2014 (Peru); Melendez 2014 (Colombia); Ruiz-Tagle and Contreras 2014 (Chile); Scott 2014 (Mexico). Indonesian data from chapter 5 of this volume. Russian data from the 2010 Russian Longitudinal Monitoring Survey of the Higher School of Economics (RLMS-HSE).
Note: Poverty is measured using the international per capita poverty line of US$2.50 per day in 2005 PPP (purchasing power parity). "Market income" comprises pretax wages, salaries, income earned from capital assets (rent, interest, or dividends), and private transfers. "Consumable income" = market income – direct and indirect taxes and social security contributions + direct cash transfers and indirect subsidies.
a. For Indonesia, the fiscal incidence analysis was carried out adjusting for spatial price differences. Data are consumption based for Indonesia and income based for the rest of countries.
b. The scenario for South Africa assumed that free basic services (such as power, sanitation, water, and refuse removal) are direct transfers. The only contributory pensions in South Africa are for public servants, who must belong to the Government Employees Pension Fund (GEPF). Since the government made no transfers to the GEPF in 2010/11, there is no scenario in which contributory pensions are treated as transfers; hence, it is not shown in the figure.
c. Chile only has a pay-as-you-go system for older workers and a fully funded system running since 1980 based on individual accounts. The contributions to the old system (the ones that may persist) are not available as a separate item in national accounts.

are considered as market income, however, the poverty reduction in Russia drops to 29 percent, which is comparable to the reduction in Chile (33 percent).

Looking at the impact of the fiscal system by demographic group (table 7.7), it appears that the households of working-age people with and without children are net payers, while only pensioners' households benefit from the fiscal redistribution in Russia if contributory pensions are considered as market income. Once pensions are treated as transfers, the group of beneficiaries grows to include mixed households with working-age people and pensioners. The biggest losers under both scenarios are one- and two-child families and households with working-age adults only. Among the age groups, young adults under age 30 years are penalized the most.

The national poverty profile presented in table 7.8 shows that children under 18 years are in the most vulnerable position. In 2010, under both pension-treatment scenarios, the poverty headcount of this group was 1.7 times as high as the national poverty headcount using disposable income and 1.65 times as high using consumable income. The poverty headcount for young people (age 16–30) is slightly higher than the overall poverty measure. The probability of falling into poverty for working-age adults over age 30 years is approximately 10 percent higher than the average figures. People age 65+ years appear to be in the most privileged position: their poverty headcount is two-thirds lower than the national average.

Table 7.7 Fiscal Incidence by Demographic Group in the Russian Federation, 2010

Percentage change from market to consumable income

Group	Net payers (–), pensions as market income	Net payers (–), pensions as transfers
Household type		
Couple w/ 1 child	−16.4	−22.5
Couple w/ 2 children	−12.3	−18.2
Couple w/ 3+ children	−4.5	−7.2
Lone parents	−8.4	−3.0
Only adults	−16.2	−16.1
Only pensioners	5.1	365.0
Mixed	−11.5	24.3
Age group		
0–17 years	−13.0	−18.1
18–29 years	−15.9	−22.0
30–64 years	−14.9	−12.3
65+ years	−1.3	136.3
Total population	−13.1	−6.3

Source: Based on 2010 Russian Longitudinal Monitoring Survey of the Higher School of Economics (RLMS-HSE).

Note: Market income comprises pretax wages, salaries, income earned from capital assets (rent, interest, or dividends), and private transfers. Consumable income = market income − direct and indirect taxes and social security contributions + direct cash transfers and indirect subsidies.

Table 7.8 Poverty Headcount by Demographic Group in the Russian Federation, 2010
Percentage by income concept

Group	Market incomeᵃ	Net Market incomeᵇ	Disposable incomeᶜ	Consumable incomeᵈ
a. Benchmark analysis (contributory pensions are market income)				
Household type				
Couple w/ 1 child	16.8	19.7	17.5	20.7
Couple w/ 2 children	28.5	34.0	29.1	34.4
Couple w/ 3+ children	51.1	59.5	49.2	55.2
Single parents	39.1	42.0	37.6	41.2
Only adults	12.8	16.0	13.6	16.6
Only pensioners	5.9	6.0	2.0	2.5
Mixed	10.5	11.4	8.7	12.3
Age group				
0–17 years	31.4	35.7	31.4	35.7
18–29 years	19.6	22.6	19.4	23.2
30–64 years	18.6	22.0	19.1	22.5
65+ years	9.5	10.0	6.2	8.0
Total population	18.9	21.7	18.2	21.5
b. Sensitivity analysis (contributory pensions are government transfers)				
Household type				
Couple w/ 1 child	21.2	32.8	22.1	29.0
Couple w/ 2 children	31.8	45.4	36.6	44.3
Couple w/ 3+ children	56.8	67.1	55.5	59.9
Single parents	51.2	61.7	41.4	45.3
Only adults	15.6	24.1	17.2	20.6
Only pensioners	73.6	75.5	2.0	2.6
Mixed	31.1	40.1	9.5	13.8
Age group				
0–17 years	36.5	48.3	37.2	43.5
18–29 years	23.6	33.6	23.0	28.1
30–64 years	25.3	35.7	23.4	28.5
65+ years	58.0	63.3	6.8	9.0
Total population	35.2	44.6	21.8	26.4

Source: Based on 2010 Russian Longitudinal Monitoring Survey of the Higher School of Economics (RLMS-HSE).
Note: Poverty headcounts use the national poverty line, which in 2010 was approximately Rub 195.2 per person per day (US$9 2005, purchasing power parity.)
a. "Market income" comprises pretax wages, salaries, income earned from capital assets (rent, interest, or dividends), and private transfers.
b. "Disposable income" = market income − personal income taxes and social security contributions + direct cash transfers.
c. "Consumable income" = disposable income − indirect taxes (value added and excises) + indirect subsidies.
d. "Final income" = consumable income + in-kind transfers for education and health care.

These results show that there seems to be room to reconsider the targeting of some programs in order to enhance the distributional impact of the system. The existing redistributive impact (horizontal) may reflect political economy considerations, the efficiency implications of which have not been analyzed but could be non-negligible.

Conclusions and Policy Implications

This chapter shows that the system of taxes and transfers in Russia has a limited redistributive capacity vertically (among different income groups)—particularly when pensions are assumed to be deferred income—though it does achieve significant horizontal redistribution (among sociodemographic groups).

The analysis of the sources of redistribution in Russia is particularly important, given the large increase in inequality that took place after the market transition in the 1990s. Moreover, the tax-benefit system has been questioned given its risk of fiscal unsustainability. Changes may require a revision of the retirement age with pension rights—given also the demographic dynamics. The system could also benefit from a review and potential elimination or enhanced targeting of myriad transfer programs, which, as a net effect, redistribute relatively little.

The main results of the analysis, as summarized below, concern the Russian fiscal system's limited redistributive effect, low effectiveness in poverty reduction, and relatively poor net financial impact on all demographic groups except pensioners.

Impact on Redistribution

Benchmarking shows that the Russian system of direct taxes and transfers does not compare well with countries that achieve larger redistribution, in particular European Union countries. When pensions are considered deferred income, Russia's reduction of the Gini through direct taxes and transfers (a reduction of 0.031 Gini points between market income and disposable income) is comparable to Brazil's and Chile's (by 0.035 and 0.037 points, respectively). However, if pensions are considered transfers, the redistribution (an inequality reduction of 0.132 Gini points) is larger than that of the United States (0.109 Gini points).

Net direct taxes (incorporated into disposable income) are always equalizing, but net indirect taxes (incorporated into consumable income) are unequalizing in both the benchmark and the sensitivity analysis scenarios. When pensions are considered deferred income, the redistributive effect of the fiscal system equals 0.028 Gini points, or a 7 percent reduction in the consumable-income Gini with respect to the market-income Gini. In contrast, if contributory pensions are considered transfers, the reduction in the Gini for consumable income with respect to market income equals 0.129 Gini points, or 26.2 percent.

Impact on Poverty Reduction

Under the benchmark scenario, the net effect of the fiscal system is actually poverty increasing. If pensions are considered market income, we observe a 0.7 percent reduction in the poverty headcount using the national poverty threshold after net direct taxes (disposable income) and a 2.6 percent increase after net indirect taxes (consumable income).

If pensions are treated as transfers, the Russian system achieves a 13.5 percent reduction in poverty for disposable income and an 8.9 percent reduction for consumable income. Given the level of spending, the effectiveness is quite low. Poor people who are not pensioners are actually not protected by the tax-benefit system.

Impact by demographic group

It appears that all households of working-age people with and without children are net payers under the Russian fiscal system, while only pensioners' households benefit from the fiscal redistribution in Russia under both scenarios. The biggest losers under both scenarios are one- and two-child couples. Among the age groups, young adults under age 30 years are the most penalized group.

Overall, then, the Russian fiscal system has a weak capacity to redistribute and is basically taxing effectively the most productive population groups. Although the CEQ analysis does not take into account behavioral responses, these effects could be potentially negative for labor participation and efficiency in general. The main conclusion that emerges from this analysis is that there are both equity and efficiency reasons to review the tax and social spending structure. Such an exercise may require, however, a good understanding of the political economy of a potential reform.

Annex 7A. Construction of Income Concepts

Table 7A.1 Construction of Income Concepts: Definitions, Assumptions, and Sources

Income or taxation type, by income concept	Construction of income concepts	Benchmark	Sensitivity analysis
Market income			
Earned and unearned incomes from all possible sources, excluding government transfers	Included	Included	Included
Contributory pensions	*Direct identification method:* All labor and occupational pensions. Note that contributory pensions in Russia are not fully social-insurance based, as the Pension Fund deficit is covered from the federal budget.	Included	Not included
Gifts, proceeds from sale of durables	Included	Included	Included
Autoconsumption	Included	Included	Included
Imputed rent for owner-occupied housing	Not computed because of the lack of data in the survey. Also, few households in Russia rent housing at market prices.	Not included	Not included
Net market income = market income – direct taxes and employee contributions to social security (in benchmark except for contributions to pensions)			
Direct taxes	*Simulation method:* The data on income tax were not collected in the survey, and income measures reported were net (after-tax) incomes. Therefore, income tax was imputed using the inversion of rules for workers in the formal sector and added to net income to arrive at gross (before income tax) market income.	Included	Included
	Direct identification method: Vehicle and property taxes, stamp duties, and so on, apart from land tax.	Included	Included

table continues next page

Table 7A.1 Construction of Income Concepts: Definitions, Assumptions, and Sources *(continued)*

Income or taxation type, by income concept	Construction of income concepts	Benchmark	Sensitivity analysis
Employee contributions to social security	*Simulation method:* Social insurance contributions (SICs) were not reported in the survey and were simulated using the existing tax rates for formal sector workers and added to the income tax base to arrive at gross market income (before SICs and income tax).	Only contributions to the Social Insurance Fund and Health Insurance Funds were deducted from market income, whereas contributions to the Pension Fund were not deducted because they are treated as a form of lifetime earnings.	Contributions to the Pension Fund, Social Insurance Fund, and Health Insurance Funds were deducted from market income.

Disposable income = Net market income (including contributory pensions in benchmark scenario) + direct government transfers (including contributory pensions in sensitivity analysis)

Noncontributory pensions	*Direct identification method:* All social pensions and state provision pensions.	Included	Included
Targeted monetary transfers	*Direct identification method:* Child allowance up to age 16 (or age 18 if in full-time education); state social assistance; and housing subsidy. The fourth means-tested transfer is a supplement for nonworking pensioners, whose pensions are below the minimum subsistence level. This one is paid together with the state pension and cannot be separated.	Included	Included
Other direct transfers	*Direct identification method:* Unemployment benefit, unified monthly payment (monetized privileges), childcare allowance up to 1.5 years, scholarships.	Included	Included
	Simulation method: Maternity allowance, lump-sum birth grant, the maternity capital, and compensation of childcare fees.	Included	Included
	Imputation method: Other privileges in cash and in kind, including various irregular cash transfers; free or discounted public transportation for pensioners, pupils and students, disabled people, and families with many children in some regions; and vouchers to summer camps or sanatoriums for children and pensioners, the disabled, and so on. We imputed the estimated average cost of these transfers (Rub 13,082.2 per year) to those who received a unified monthly payment (monetized privileges).	Included	Included
Food transfers	All in-kind transfers are accounted for within the category "other privileges" (see above).	Included	Included
Contributory pensions	*Direct identification method:* All labor and occupational pensions. Note that contributory pensions in Russia are not fully social-insurance based, as the Pension Fund deficit is covered from the federal budget.	Not included	Included

table continues next page

Table 7A.1 Construction of Income Concepts: Definitions, Assumptions, and Sources *(continued)*

Income or taxation type, by income concept	*Construction of income concepts*	*Benchmark*	*Sensitivity analysis*
Consumable income = disposable income + indirect subsidies − indirect taxes			
Indirect subsidies	*Imputation method:* Subsidized tariffs for utilities for the population. Subsidies vary from region to region, although on average the price subsidy amounted to 5–7 percent of the total cost of utilities.	Included	Included
Indirect taxes	*Simulation method:* Value added tax (VAT) is simulated using the data on expenditures available in the same survey. Tax evasion is unlikely, so it was not considered. Excises on alcohol, tobacco, and car fuel are simulated using consumed quantities. Indirect effects are not accounted for, because an input-output matrix is not available.	Included	Included
Final income = consumable income + government in-kind transfers			
Education	*Imputation method:* The survey reports whether the individual attends kindergarten or preschool; general secondary school; vocational school; or is in tertiary education. We assumed that all kindergartens or preschools and secondary schools are public (private education at these levels is rare) and excluded students who reported paying fees at secondary vocational schools and higher education institutions. The education benefit is based on the estimated average cost per student by level, as follows: (a) childcare: Rub 59,641.5 per year; (b) secondary general school: Rub 60,978 per year; (c) vocational school: Rub 53,975.8 per year; and (d) tertiary education: Rub 64,591.2 per year. The amounts were scaled down using the ratio of income in national accounts and income from sensitivity analysis scenario.	Included	Included
Health care	*Imputation method:* Basic health care coverage is universal, although there are user fees for services beyond the basic coverage and informal payments are still quite widespread. Imputations are based on average cost of public health care per one citizen (Rub 11,952.9 rubles per year), which was imputed to those who reported using public services. The survey reports whether the individual visited a doctor or had tests in the past month and stayed in a hospital during the past three months (36 percent of the respondents). Those who reported having private health insurance (4 percent) were excluded, because we assumed that that they are unlikely to use public health care at the same time, although theoretically they are eligible. The amounts were scaled down using the ratio of income in national accounts and income from sensitivity analysis scenario.	Included	Included

Note: The shaded rows indicate the income components that are treated differently in the benchmark and sensitivity scenarios. Under the benchmark scenario, contributory pensions are treated as part of market income, and pension social insurance contributions are treated as lifetime savings (that is, not included in direct taxes). Under the sensitivity analysis scenario, contributory pensions are treated as government transfers, and pension social insurance contributions are taxable.

The Distributional Impact of Taxes and Transfers • http://dx.doi.org/10.1596/978-1-4648-1091-6

Notes

1. GDP data from the World Development Indicators database: http://databank.worldbank .org/data/reports.aspx?source=world-development-indicators.

2. Economic rankings from the World Bank's International Comparison Program (ICP) database: http://data.worldbank.org/. For more information, see the ICP website: http://siteresources.worldbank.org/ICPEXT/Resources/ICP_2011.html.

3. In 2010, the national poverty line was approximately Rub 195.2 per person per day (US$9 2005 PPP) (Rosstat database, Federal State Statistics Service of the Russian Federation, http://www.gks.ru/wps/wcm/connect/rosstat_main/rosstat/ru/statistics /population/poverty/).

4. Here and thereafter, unless indicated otherwise, inequality is measured using *per capita disposable income*: the household market income plus direct transfers minus direct taxes divided by the household size. Moreover, unless indicated otherwise, the statistics for Russia, including all poverty figures, refer to data from the Federal State Statistics Service of the Russian Federation (Rosstat): http://www.gks.ru/.

5. In the CEQ framework, "consumable income" (also sometimes called postfiscal income) takes into account all market income (also referred to in this chapter as "benchmark income"), direct and indirect taxes, direct cash transfers, and indirect subsidies. For a more detailed discussion of the CEQ income concepts used throughout the volume, see chapter 1.

6. Other federal taxes prescribed by the tax code include a tax on animal and water wildlife (levied upon licensed hunters and fisheries) and a document tax (for example, the ad valorem duty required to start civil litigation in state courts).

7. Note that the workplace accident insurance is not part of the social insurance contributions. Each employer must contribute to group accident insurance. The rate varies between 0.2 percent and 8.5 percent, depending on the type of business.

8. Since 2010, there have been several increases in the tax rates and changes in the tax schedule aimed at reducing the deficit of the Pension Fund.

9. The 2005 PPP conversion factor used throughout the paper is Rub 21.79 per US$1 (World Development Indicators Database).

10. In addition to this benefit, the State Employment Service provides early-retirement pensions to the recipients of unemployment benefits and material aid to those unemployed who exhausted their eligibility for the benefit.

11. The International Labour Organization (ILO) unemployment rate assesses the number of persons in the given group who are unemployed (including jobless people who want to work, are available to work, and are actively seeking employment) in relation to the total of employed and unemployed persons in the group. See "Main statistics (annual)—Unemployment," LABORSTA database, ILO, http://laborsta.ilo .org/applv8/data/c3e.html.

12. The ALMP measures ranged from public works to subsidies for unemployed people interested in starting up a new business.

13. In 2010, the lower limit was set at Rub 2,060 per month for the period of leave with the first child and at Rub 4,121 per month for the period of leave with the second and subsequent children.

14. These programs have a broad range, including free or discounted access to a wide span of services and goods such as exemptions from or discounts for rent or utility

payments; telephone services; medicines, medical appliances, and health care services; municipal, commuter, or long-distance transport; and vouchers for sanatoriums, spas, childcare facilities, or summer camps. Some categories of citizens are exempted from or discounted for real-estate taxes, may receive substantial financial support for house repairs or may receive a land plot.

15. "Labor veterans" are holders of the civilian labor award of the former Soviet Union to honor workers for many years of hard work in the national economy, education, health care, government agencies, and so on.

16. By 2010, some regions, however, had not switched completely to 100 percent utility costs for the population. The cost of the discounted utility tariffs can be approximated by subtracting the gross amount of the utility costs actually covered by the population from the gross amount of accrued utility costs in each region. In Russia as a whole, the population covered approximately 93–95 percent of utility costs in 2005–12.

17. Currently, the offer of such services, both in quantity and quality, does not satisfy the growing demand. During the economic recession of the 1990s, which was accompanied by a fall in fertility rates, many preschool institutions closed. In the 2000s, the demand for childcare services started to grow again because of demographic and economic factors: an increasing number of preschool-age children and increasing economic activity in the population. These factors, in combination with the uneven distribution of these institutions across regions and municipalities, have led to a tenfold increase in the number of children waiting for a place in a preschool institution (from 200,000 in 1999 to over 2.2 million children in 2010–11). The problem is aggravated by the fact that the system of care services for the elderly is also weak, and the supply of these services is lower than the demand (UNICEF 2011).

18. Starting in 2013, the percentage of the total costs covered by parents is to be defined by regions.

19. People without citizenship have a right to free emergency care.

20. Relative to the level of public expenditure recommended by the World Health Organization (WHO)—6 percent of GDP—the health care system in Russia is underfunded. It is also inefficient. Russia ranked 75th among 191 countries in per capita health care spending and only 127th in the health of its population (WHO 2000). The same level of population health could be achieved at 60 percent of the actual health care expenditure (WHO 2000).

21. The total figure includes expenditures of the public system and expenditures of the population on additional health care services in the public system or the private sector.

22. For more about the RLMS-HSE, see the survey website: http://www.hse.ru/en/rlms/. Other potential sources of data were the Household Budget Survey (HBS) and the Survey of Income and Social Programmes (SISP). The HBS is conducted on a sample of 50,000 households but only collects consumption data. The SISP is designed for income distribution analysis but does not collect consumption data. Moreover, only the data of the 2012 pilot survey of 10,000 households are currently available.

23. RLMS-HSE uses a three-stage probability sample drawn from the population of dwellings. Persons living in institutional households (such as children's homes, social care institutions, and convents) are excluded. On average, the household response rate exceeds 80 percent, but it is lower in Moscow and St. Petersburg (less than 60 percent).

24. The census figures are 54.56 million households and 142.87 million individuals.

25. See the EUROMOD Statistics on Distribution and Decomposition of Disposable Income, EUROMOD version G2.0, https://www.iser.essex.ac.uk/euromod.

26. The unreported earnings refer to something other than "hidden" or illegal economies (such as related to tax fraud or evasion or to other illegal activities). The nonobserved economy also comprises activities not related to criminality or tax evasion but that still remain unobserved because the traditional survey tools are not perfect (nonresponse, underreporting, short income reference period, and so on) and because business registers are not always complete and up-to-date.

27. The variable part of earnings comprises premiums and bonuses that can fluctuate contingent upon general economic conditions and firm performance. In case of economic slowdown, the variable part of earnings shrinks, while in the upturn the employees are likely to enjoy an additional premium. For the majority of Russian firms both in the public and private sector, more than a third of total earnings are variable and not fixed in labor contracts (Gimpelson and Kapeliushnikov 2011).

28. The EU-27 member states are Austria, Belgium, Bulgaria, Cyprus, the Czech Republic, Denmark, Estonia, Finland, France, Germany, Greece, Hungary, Ireland, Italy, Latvia, Lithuania, Luxembourg, Malta, the Netherlands, Poland, Portugal, Romania, the Slovak Republic, Slovenia, Spain, Sweden, and the United Kingdom.

References

Calvo, P., Luis-F. López-Calva, and J. Posadas. 2015. "A Decade of Declining Earnings Inequality in the Russian Federation." Policy Research Working Paper 7392, World Bank, Washington, DC.

Cancho, C., M. Davalos, G. Demarchi, M. Meyer, and C. Sanchez-Paramo. 2015. "Economic Mobility in Europe and Central Asia: Exploring Patterns and Uncovering Puzzles." Policy Research Working Paper 7173, World Bank, Washington, DC.

Decoster, A. 2003. "How Progressive Are Indirect Taxes in Russia?" *Economics of Transition* 13 (4): 705–29.

Denisova, I., S. Kolenikov, and K. Yudaeva. 2000. "Child Benefit and Child Poverty." Working Paper WP/00/03, Center for Economic and Financial Research, Moscow.

Duncan, D. 2014. "Behavioral Responses and the Distributional Effects of the Russian 'Flat' Tax." *Journal of Policy Modeling* 36 (2): 226–40.

Gimpelson, V., and R. Kapeliushnikov. 2011. "Labour Market Adjustment: Is Russia Different?" Discussion Paper 5588, Institute of Labor Economics, Bonn.

Higgins, Sean, Nora Lustig, Whitney Ruble, and Timothy M. Smeeding. 2016. "Comparing the Incidence of Taxes and Social Spending in Brazil and the United States." *The Review of Income and Wealth* 62 (S1): S22–46.

Higgins, Sean, and Claudiney Pereira. 2014. "The Effects of Brazil's Taxation and Social Spending on the Distribution of Household Income." *Public Finance Review* 42 (3): 346–67.

Inchauste, G., N. Lustig, M. Maboshe, C. Purfield, and I. Wollard. 2015. "The Distributional Impact of Fiscal Policy in South Africa." Policy Research Working Paper 7194, World Bank, Washington, DC.

Jaramillo, Miguel. 2014. "The Incidence of Social Spending and Taxes in Peru." *Public Finance Review* 42 (3): 391–412.

Lustig, Nora. Lustig, N., ed. 2017. *Commitment to Equity Handbook: Estimating the Impact of Fiscal Policy on Inequality and Poverty*. Washington, DC: Brookings Institution Press and CEQ Institute, Tulane University. Advance online version available at http://www.commitmentoequity.org/publications/handbook.php.

Lustig, N., and S. Higgins. 2013. "Commitment to Equity Assessment (CEQ): Estimating the Incidence of Social Spending, Subsidies and Taxes. Handbook." Commitment to Equity Working Paper 1 (revised), Center for Inter-American Policy and Research; the Inter-American Dialogue; and Department of Economics, Tulane University, New Orleans, LA.

Melendez, M. 2014. "CEQ Master Workbook: Colombia. Version: November 21, 2014." Workbook, Commitment to Equity (CEQ) Data Center, CEQ Institute, Tulane University, New Orleans, LA.

Milanovic, B. 1999. "Explaining the Increase in Inequality during Transition." *Economics of Transition* 7 (2): 299–341.

Notten, G., and F. Gassmann. 2008. "Size Matters: Targeting Efficiency and Poverty Reduction Effects of Means-Tested and Universal Child Benefits in Russia." *Journal of European Social Policy* 18 (3): 260–74.

OECD (Organisation for Economic Co-operation and Development). 2008. *Growing Unequal? Income Distribution and Poverty in OECD Countries.* Paris: OECD Publishing.

Ovcharova, L., and D. Popova. 2005. *Child Poverty in Russia: Alarming Trends and Policy Options.* United Nations Children's Fund (UNICEF) report, Moscow.

Ovcharova, L., D. Popova, and A. Pishniak. 2007. "New Measures Supporting Families with Children: Improving Living Standards and Raising Birthrates?" United Nations Children's Fund (UNICEF), Moscow.

Popova, D. 2013. "Impact Assessment of Alternative Reforms of Child Allowances Using RUSMOD—The Static Tax-Benefit Microsimulation Model for Russia." *International Journal of Microsimulation* 6 (1): 122–56.

———. 2016. "Distributional Impacts of Cash Allowances for Children: A Microsimulation Analysis for Russia and Europe." *Journal of European Social Policy* 26 (3): 248–67.

Ruiz-Tagle, J., and D. Contreras. 2014. "CEQ Master Workbook: Chile. Version: August 27, 2014." Workbook, Commitment to Equity (CEQ) Data Center, CEQ Institute, Tulane University, New Orleans, LA.

Scott, J. 2014. "Redistributive Impact and Efficiency of Mexico's Fiscal System." *Public Finance Review* 42 (3): 368–90.

UNICEF (United Nations Children's Fund). 2011. *The Situation Analysis of Children in the Russian Federation: The Road to Equity.* Assessment report, UNICEF, Moscow.

Volchkova, N., E. Gorshkova, S. Lobanov, N. Turdyeva, J. Khaleeva, and K. Yudaeva. 2006. "Microsimulation Analysis of the Consequences of Monetization of Social Benefits in Russia." Working Paper WP/2006/063, New Economic School, Moscow.

WHO (World Health Organization). 2000. *The World Health Report 2000: Health Systems: Improving Performance.* Geneva: WHO.

CHAPTER 8

The Distributional Impact of Fiscal Policy in South Africa

Gabriela Inchauste, Nora Lustig, Mashekwa Maboshe, Catriona Purfield, and Ingrid Woolard

Introduction

Since the end of apartheid in the early 1990s, South Africa has made progress toward establishing a more equitable society. In particular, advances in areas such as electrification and access to education have increased equality of opportunities (World Bank 2012). In recent years, poverty has decreased significantly. Between 2006 and 2011, the proportion of the population living below the national poverty line fell from 57.2 percent to 45.5 percent.[1] Inequality of per capita household consumption also declined during this period: the Gini coefficient fell from 0.67 in 2006 to 0.65 in 2011.[2]

In spite of this progress, South Africa continues to be one of the most unequal countries in the world. In 2011, the top 20 percent of the population accounted for 61.3 percent of national consumption, whereas the bottom 20 percent accounted for 4.3 percent (Stats SA 2014). South Africa also has higher poverty rates than other middle-income countries with similar per capita gross domestic product (GDP). For example, using the international poverty line of US$2.50 per person per day, South Africa's poverty head-count ratio was 34 percent in 2011, whereas it was 11.7 percent in Brazil and 5 percent in Costa Rica the same year.[3]

In large part, progress toward greater income equality has proven elusive because of the enduring legacy of the apartheid system. This is true even though South Africa's government has tried to attack the inequality inertia on several fronts, most prominently through taxation and social spending. The 1996 Constitution's Bill of Rights established citizens' rights to health care, food, water, social security, and social assistance. It required the state to fulfill these rights progressively and to the best of its ability. Since the end of apartheid, the government has expanded social assistance programs and spends sizable resources (by the standards of middle-income countries) on health and education services. By 2013/14, total government spending amounted to 33.2 percent of GDP, more than half of which was devoted to social spending (Stats SA 2014).

Indeed, largely owing to the expansion of the social grant system, disposable income in the lower part of the distribution grew between 1995 and 2005; without the grants, two-fifths of the population would have seen its income decline in the first decade after apartheid (Van der Berg 2009). Indeed, Van der Berg (2009) found that social spending had become increasingly progressive. More recently, Leibbrandt et al. (2010) estimated that redistributive spending policies have undone about 40 percent of the increase over the 1993–2008 period in market income inequality (measured by the Gini coefficient), with the expansion of social cash transfers being particularly important. Meanwhile, the tax system generated considerable resources for redistribution, with total general government revenue collections amounting to 29.2 percent of GDP in 2008.

The government's commitment to greater equality remains strong. The *National Development Plan 2030* sets the ambitious goal of eliminating poverty and reducing inequality. It aims to (a) cut the Gini coefficient to 0.60 by 2030 by raising employment and (b) increase the share of income of the bottom 40 percent from 6 percent to 10 percent (NPC 2011). In 2014, with an overall fiscal deficit at about 4 percent of GDP and debt burden close to 40 percent of GDP, fiscal space has become more limited. In such an environment, the question becomes whether the government is using fiscal policy adequately to achieve its goals of reducing poverty and inequality.

In this context, this chapter assesses the distributional impact of the main taxes and social spending programs in South Africa by applying a state-of-the-art fiscal incidence analysis based on the methodological framework described by Lustig and Higgins (2013) and Lustig (2017). In particular, the chapter first quantifies the impact of taxes and social spending on inequality and poverty. Second, it examines the extent to which spending on education and health is not only equalizing but also pro-poor. Given the differences across provinces in the country, we calculate education benefits by province and level to impute the monetary value of these benefits. Finally, the chapter estimates the contribution of the different components of fiscal policy to the changes in inequality and poverty. We carry out this fiscal incidence analysis using the Income and Expenditure Survey (IES) from 2010/11 (Stats SA 2012b), which contains data on household income, expenditures, cash transfers, and use of educational services collected from 25,328 households covering more than 95,000 individuals.

As described in chapter 1, one important drawback in the methodology is that we are unable to account for the distribution of spending on infrastructure, defense, state-owned enterprises, and other public goods, as the information available in household surveys does not enable us to assign the benefits of this spending to individual households. Similarly, corporate taxes are not included in the analysis, as assigning the burden of these taxes across the distribution is not straighforward because corporations are likely to shift at least a portion of the tax burden to workers (through lower wages or lower employment) and to their consumers. These issues are not unique to the methodology employed here; they are common to microlevel analysis of this kind.[4]

Our analysis makes three main contributions:

- Existing studies are more than a decade old. In contrast, this chapter uses a household survey collected more than 15 years after the end of apartheid; thus, the information on employment, consumption, and use of services in this survey must have captured the behavioral changes induced by fiscal policy reforms in the postapartheid period.
- The chapter applies methodological innovations in fiscal incidence analysis to estimate both (a) the combined effect of the most important fiscal interventions on income redistribution and poverty reduction and (b) the marginal contribution to income redistribution associated with each component.
- By applying the common methodological framework of the Commitment to Equity (CEQ) project, the chapter can compare the results for South Africa with those of other middle-income countries to which the framework has also been applied.[5]

The main results are the following:

- Fiscal policy in South Africa achieves significant reductions in income inequality and poverty—the largest among the emerging-market countries so far included in the CEQ project. Yet despite fiscal policy being both equalizing and poverty reducing, the country's inequality and poverty levels remain very high, as previously noted, ranking as some of the highest in middle-income countries.
- Except for tertiary education, spending on education is well targeted at the poor and so is spending on health, although concerns remain about the quality and effectiveness of such spending.
- Except for excise taxes, all the components of fiscal policy are equalizing, including the value added tax (VAT).

The next section provides an overview of the key fiscal tools used by the South African government to tackle poverty and inequality. The "Data and Assumptions" section describes the data used in the analysis as well as the fiscal incidence assumptions. "Impact of Taxes and Government Spending on Inequality and Poverty" analyzes how taxation and social spending have affected inequality, poverty, and horizontal equity and examines the marginal contribution of individual components to the redistributive effect. The final section summarizes the chapter's findings and conclusions.

General Government's Fiscal Instruments to Tackle Poverty and Inequality

Tax Revenue

On the revenue side, the tax system in South Africa generates considerable resources for potential redistribution by middle-income country standards.[6] Just over half of South Africa's general government tax collections (totaling 27.1 percent of GDP in 2010/11) came from direct taxes: the personal income tax (PIT), corporate income tax, and payroll taxes in the form of unemployment insurance and the skills development levy (table 8.1). South Africa relies relatively more on PIT and less on indirect or consumption taxes than other CEQ countries (figure 8.1)—a welcome feature of its tax system (in terms of equity, that is) because PIT tends to be more progressive than consumption taxes, as further discussed in this chapter.[7]

The analysis presented next focuses on the major tax items, namely PIT, payroll taxes, VAT, specific excise duties on alcohol and tobacco, and the general fuel levy. These items made up about 64.5 percent of all general government tax revenue in 2010/11 (Stats SA 2012a).[8]

Direct Taxes

PIT is levied on individual taxable income (gross income less exemptions and allowable deductions), including capital gains. Individuals generally receive their income as salary or wages, pension or annuity payments, and investment income (interest and dividends). Filing is done individually, and the system does not

Table 8.1 South Africa General Government Revenue Collections, 2010/11
Percentage of GDP

Revenue source	2010/11	Incidence analysis
Total general government revenue	30.9	17.5
Tax revenue	27.1	17.5
Direct taxes	15.0	8.5
Personal income tax	8.5	8.5
Corporate income tax	5.6	n.a.
Skills development levy	0.3	0.3
Other direct taxes	0.5	n.a.
Indirect taxes	10.4	9.0
Value added tax	6.9	6.9
Specific excise duties	0.9	0.8
General fuel levy	1.3	1.3
International trade taxes	1.0	n.a.
Other indirect taxes	0.3	n.a.
Other taxes	1.8	n.a.
Nontax revenue	3.8	n.a.
Memo: UIF contributions	0.4	0.4

Sources: Stats SA 2012a (for totals); National Treasury 2013 Budget Review (for line items under direct and indirect taxes).
Note: GDP = gross domestic product; n.a. = not applicable; UIF = Unemployment Insurance Fund.

Figure 8.1 Composition of Taxes as Share of GDP, Ranked by GNI per Capita, Selected Countries

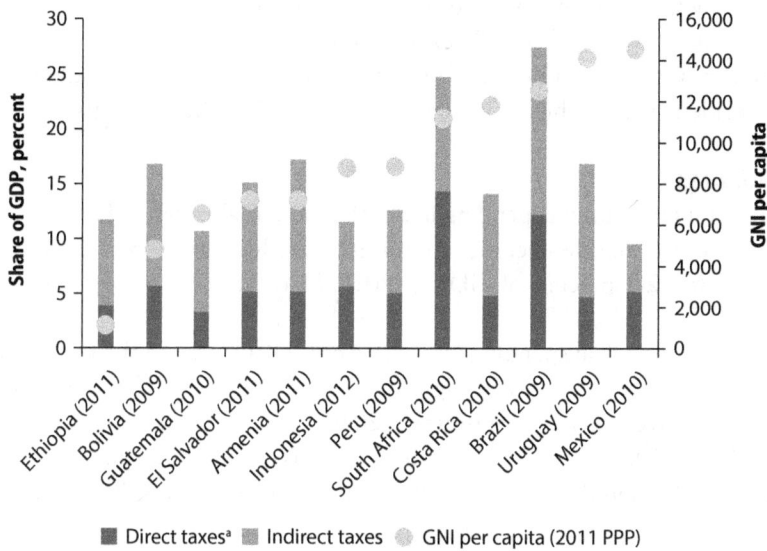

Direct taxes[a] Indirect taxes GNI per capita (2011 PPP)

Sources: Beneke, Lustig, and Oliva 2015 (El Salvador); Bucheli et al. 2014 (Uruguay); Higgins and Pereira 2014 (Brazil); Jaramillo 2014 (Peru); Lustig 2017, based on Cabrera, Lustig, and Morán 2014 (Guatemala); Paz Arauco et al. 2014 (Bolivia); Sauma and Trejos 2014 (Costa Rica); Scott 2014 (Mexico); World Bank estimates based on Stats SA 2012b (South Africa); Armenia, Ethiopia, and Indonesia data from chapters 2, 3, and 5 of this volume, respectively.
Note: GDP = gross domestic product; GNI = gross national income; PPP = purchasing power parity. Parentheses indicate year of survey.
a. Direct taxes include both corporate and personal income tax collections.

provide deductions for married persons or children. All formal sector employees must be registered by their employers for PIT, and the employer is responsible for calculating and withholding the PIT payable.[9] Limited deductions are permitted for travel expenses, contributions to pension funds, and medical aid (health insurance) schemes. There are no social security taxes because there is no contributory social security in South Africa.

Two earmarked payroll taxes exist. The first is the skills development levy, under which employers contribute 1 percent of total payroll toward a levy used to fund training facilitated through the Sector Education and Training Authorities.[10] The second is the Unemployment Insurance Fund (UIF), under which employers and employees each contribute 1 percent of earnings (up to a cap, currently set at R 14,872, or US$1,487 per month) toward a fund that provides income protection for up to 236 days in the event of unemployment.

Indirect Taxes

The South African VAT system is an example of a "modern" VAT in the sense that most goods and services are subject to a uniform standard rate of 14 percent. Certain foodstuffs are zero rated, and educational and financial services as well as certain forms of passenger transport are exempt.[11]

Specific excise duties are levied on tobacco products, alcohol products (malt and traditional beer, wine and other fermented beverages, and spirits), and petroleum products (gasoline, distillate fuel, residual fuel, and base oil). Fuel levies include general levies and specific excise duties on gasoline, diesel, and illuminating paraffin. Gasoline and diesel fuel are also levied with a contribution to the Road Accident Fund, which compensates victims of traffic accidents.

Expenditures

Total general government spending in South Africa is also somewhat higher than the average for middle-income countries.[12] Excluding interest payments, it amounted to 32.2 percent of GDP in 2010/11 (Stats SA 2012b), as shown in table 8.2.

South Africa's social spending (as a share of GDP) is among the highest in our sample of comparable countries (figure 8.2). Just over one-half of South Africa's total general government expenditure in 2010/11 was devoted to social spending (Stats SA 2012b). Some 3.3 percent of GDP was dedicated to direct cash transfers to individuals in 2010/11, including items such as noncontributory pensions

Table 8.2 South Africa General Government Expenditure, 2010/11
Percentage of GDP

Expenditure type	2010/11	Incidence analysis
Total general government expenditure[a]	34.8	14.9
Primary government spending[b]	32.2	14.9
Social spending	17.6	14.9
Cash transfers	3.8	3.8
Child support grant	1.1	1.1
Old-age grant (noncontributory)	1.3	1.3
Disability grant	0.6	0.6
Foster care grant	0.2	0.2
Other grants	0.1	0.1
Free basic services[c]	0.5	0.5
In-kind transfers	12.6	11.1
Education	7.0	7.0
Health	4.1	4.1
Housing and urban development[d]	1.5	—
Other social spending[e]	1.1	—
Nonsocial spending (incl. public sector pensions)	14.6	—

Sources: Stats SA 2012b (totals); National Treasury 2013 Budget Review (line items).
Note: — = not available; GDP = gross domestic product.
a. Total government spending = primary government spending + interest payments on debt.
b. Primary government spending = social spending + nonsocial spending.
c. For free basic services, the data represent the amount transferred under the equitable share formula for 2010/11 to municipalities to compensate them for providing basic services (such as power, sanitation, water, and refuse removal) to poor households. Data were provided by the Financial and Fiscal Commission of South Africa.
d. In-kind transfers for housing and urban development include expenditure for the Integrated Residential Development Program (IRDP), which was not included formally in the incidence analysis for lack of detailed administrative data on housing values.
e. Data limitations preclude an incidence analysis of the remaining items of social spending.

Figure 8.2 Social Spending and Subsidies as a Share of GDP in Relation to GNI per Capita, Selected Countries

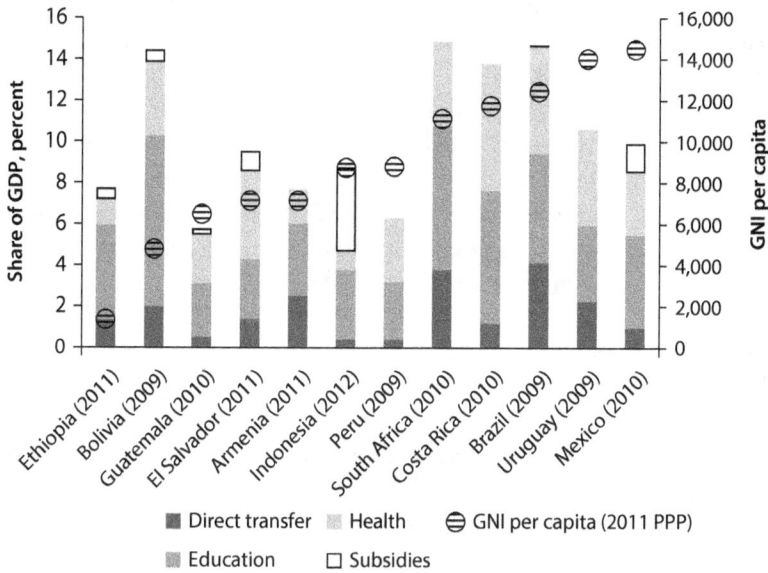

Sources: Beneke, Lustig, and Oliva 2015 (El Salvador); Bucheli et al. 2014 (Uruguay); Higgins and Pereira 2014 (Brazil); Jaramillo 2014 (Peru); Lustig 2017, based on Cabrera, Lustig, and Morán 2014 (Guatemala); Paz Arauco et al. 2014 (Bolivia); Sauma and Trejos 2014 (Costa Rica); Scott 2014 (Mexico); World Bank estimates based on Stats SA 2012b (South Africa); Armenia, Ethiopia, and Indonesia data from chapters 2, 3, and 5 of this volume, respectively.
Note: Social spending does not include contributory old-age pensions. GDP = gross domestic product; GNI = gross national income; PPP = purchasing power parity. Parenthesis indicate year of survey.

and child grants (table 8.2). Transfers amounting to an additional 0.5 percent of GDP covered "free basic services" such as power, sanitation, water supply, and refuse removal, which the government provides free to low-income households (Stats SA 2012b). Because these are sometimes provided in the form of cash transfers, the expenditure on free basic services can be thought of as a cash transfer under a benchmark scenario (as further discussed below).

South Africa's total social expenditures are more than twice the median level among low- and middle-income countries (World Bank 2009). Over the past decade, the number of beneficiaries receiving social grants doubled— from almost 8 million in 2003/04 to 15.8 million in 2013/14—mainly reflect- ing the expansion of direct cash transfers to children and the elderly. The child support grant (CSG) was introduced in 1998 and initially targeted children ages 0–7 years, with the age limit progressively raised to 18 years. The age of eligibility for the old-age grant for men was also lowered from 65 to 60 years to match the eligibility age for women.

In addition, 12.6 percent of GDP in 2010/11 was spent on in-kind transfers through health (4.1 percent of GDP) and education (7 percent of GDP) outlays, and 1.5 percent of GDP was devoted to housing and urban development in-kind

transfers, including Integrated Residential Development Program (IRDP) housing (table 8.2).[13] Compared with other relatively big social spenders such as
Bolivia and Brazil, South Africa spends somewhat more on education and less on
health and direct cash transfers than Brazil does, but more on direct cash transfers
than Bolivia does (figure 8.2).

The components of social spending included in this study are direct cash transfers, free municipal basic services, and in-kind transfers in the form of health and
education spending. Together, these items account for 43 percent of total spending
and 85 percent of social spending (table 8.2). Data limitations made it impossible
to include the remaining items of social spending. The text below further describes
the main features of each of these social spending programs in South Africa.

Cash Transfer Programs

Social assistance is prioritized in the national budget in line with section 27(1) of
the Constitution, which states, "[E]veryone has the right to have access to ... social
security, including, if they are unable to support themselves and their dependents, appropriate social assistance." Social grants target categories of individuals
who are unlikely to be able to provide for their own needs, namely the elderly,
the disabled, and children. Not including free basic services, the social grant system comprises the following programs, on which government spending amounted
to 3.3 percent of GDP in 2010/11, as further described below (Stats SA 2012a):
the old-age grant (1.3 percent of GDP), the disability grant (0.6 percent of
GDP), the CSG (1.1 percent of GDP), the care dependency grant (CDG)
(0.1 percent of GDP), and the foster care grant (FCG) (0.2 percent of GDP).
In addition, spending on the grant-in-aid (for social grant beneficiaries who need
to pay a full-time caregiver) amounted to 0.01 percent of GDP, and the war
veterans pension to 0.001 percent of GDP.

Old-Age Grant. This noncontributory pension transfers cash to eligible people
ages 60 years or above. It is means-tested, reaching over 80 percent of age-eligible
individuals, totaling 2.65 million beneficiaries in fiscal year 2010/11 (Woolard
and Leibbrandt 2010). The value of the old-age grant in 2010 was R 1,080 per
month, which increased to R 1,410 (US$127.5) per month by 2015, having kept
pace with inflation in recent years.

Disability Grant. This grant (which has the same monetary value as the old-age
grant) is paid to about 1.1 million working-age people who cannot work because
of chronic illness or disability. The number of beneficiaries is slightly down from
2010/11, when 1.2 million people collected this grant (Stats SA 2012a).

Child Grants. The social grant system also includes three child grants:[14]

- *The* CSG is the main poverty-oriented child grant available to all primary
  caregivers who pass a means test. In fiscal year 2014/15, a CSG of R 330
  (US$29) per month was paid for 11.6 million children.

- *The* CDG is provided to caregivers of severely disabled children with intensive care needs. In fiscal year 2014/15, a CDG of R 1,410 (US$127) per month was paid for 138,000 children.
- *The* FCG is available to foster parents of children found by the courts to need "care and protection" under the Children's Act. In fiscal year 2014/15, an FCG of R 860 (US$78) per month was paid for 478,000 children.

The number of FCG and CDG beneficiaries has remained steady over the past few years, whereas the number of CSG beneficiaries has risen by 1 million children between 2010/11 and 2014/15.

Education

Education spending amounted to 7 percent of GDP in 2010/11 (Stats SA 2012b). Schooling is compulsory for all children ages 7–15 years. The vast majority (96 percent) of schoolchildren attend public schools. The government provides all public schools with a grant to finance their operational costs and teacher salaries. Schools in poorer neighborhoods are designated "no fee" schools, which receive a slightly higher state subsidy to compensate for the absence of school fees. In 2011, 78 percent of students attended no-fee schools (DBE 2012).

Other public schools charge fees that vary enormously, from about R 100 to about R 30,000 per year. Even at fee-paying schools, however, parents can apply for a full or partial reduction of fees, and schools may not refuse admission to students living in the immediate vicinity. On application, beneficiaries of the CSG should automatically be exempted from the payment of school fees. Tertiary education is not free but is subsidized.

Health

The health care system in South Africa is divided into public care (serving more than 80 percent of the population) and private care (serving only those who can afford the high fees). Public health spending amounted to 4.1 percent of GDP in 2010/11 (Stats SA 2012b).

Primary health care is available free of charge to everyone, whereas hospital services are provided at relatively low cost, with a sliding tariff scale calculated according to income level. Individuals living in households with an income of less than R 6,000 (US$566) per month in 2010/11, children under age 6, pregnant women, and social grant beneficiaries were automatically exempt from paying for any public health services.

Free Basic Services

The Municipal Property Rates Act explicitly requires municipalities to provide relief for the poor from charges for municipal services (including water, electricity, and sanitation and refuse removal), which are referred to as "free basic services." Drawing on international benchmarks, South Africa has adopted a minimum provision of 50 kilowatt-hours of free electricity and 6 kiloliters of free water per household per month, although the minimum requirement for sanitation is a ventilated pit latrine. In 2010, 97 percent of households had access to water supply infrastructure (although this includes communal taps) and 79 percent had access to adequate sanitation.[15] More than three-quarters of households are connected to the electricity grid.

The national government funds about half of total municipal spending through an "equitable share formula." This transfer amounted to about 1 percent of GDP in 2010/11 (SALGA 2012). About three-quarters of the equitable share transfer reflects that part of the formula used to cover the operating costs of providing basic services to poor households in each municipality, using an estimated number of poor households in each area. However, at the local level, some municipalities also use a block tariff system, which makes it possible for municipalities to cross-subsidize free basic service allocations to the poor, using revenue from service fees paid by the nonpoor.

The availability of free basic services is variable, in that municipalities determine their own eligibility criteria or "indigence" levels. Larger municipalities provide a certain amount of free water and electricity by not charging for the first few units and then applying rising block tariffs for consumption over that amount. Other municipalities provide a rebate to households that apply on grounds of indigence (typically defined as a monthly income below twice the amount of the old-age grant). An important limitation of the free basic services safety net is that households in areas without service infrastructure cannot benefit from the free services.

Data and Assumptions

Data

This chapter uses the 2010/11 IES conducted by Statistics South Africa, which contains data on household income, expenditures, cash transfers, and use of educational services collected from 25,328 households across the country over a 12-month period (Stats SA 2012b).[16] The allocation or "mapping" to individuals is obtained by dividing the total tax paid or transfer received by each household by the total number of household members (excluding lodgers and domestic workers).

In addition, we use national accounts, administrative, and fiscal account information for 2010 and 2011, coinciding with the years of the household survey. Finally, we use the 2009 input-output table provided by the National Treasury (the closest one available to the year of the survey) to estimate second-round effects of indirect taxes and subsidies.

Assumptions

In some cases, information on the incidence of a particular component of fiscal policy can be obtained directly from the IES. When the direct identification method is not feasible, one can use other methods to allocate taxes or transfers, as described in detail by Lustig and Higgins (2013) and Lustig (2017).

The methods used for each category of taxes and transfers in our study are summarized subsequently, with details in annex 8A.

Tax Estimation

On the tax side, the IES does not provide information on PITs or payroll taxes such as the skills development levy and contributions to the UIF. Thus, the burden of these payments had to be simulated. Consistent with other conventional tax incidence analyses, we assume that the economic burden of direct PITs is borne by the income recipient. The burden of payroll taxes is assumed to fall entirely on workers.

In contrast, for indirect taxes, the IES provides detailed consumption data that allow us to estimate the burdens of the VAT, the fuel levy, and specific excise duties on alcohol and tobacco. Consumption taxes are assumed to be shifted forward to consumers (see annex 8A for details). Evasion of consumption taxes was taken into account implicitly by using "effective" rates (that is, collected tax as a share of total consumption of that good according to national accounts) rather than statutory rates. As for excise taxes on alcohol and tobacco, the survey severely underestimates actual consumption relative to what is recorded in the national accounts. To correct for this, we assume that the extent of underreporting is proportional across the income distribution. In other words, we assume that the survey provides the correct *distribution* of spending on alcohol and tobacco but that the *levels* of spending are too low.[17]

Finally, we use the National Treasury's 2009 input-output matrix and a price-shifting model to estimate the second-round effects of indirect taxes, whereby these taxes result in higher costs in sectors that use these goods as inputs.[18] For the VAT, the indirect effects are only considered in the case of exempt items because VAT refunds ensure that there is no cascading of nonexempt items.

Public Spending Estimation

On the spending side, the IES provides detailed information on the receipt of cash transfers. The numbers of old-age, child, disability, and foster care grant beneficiaries represented in the survey align well with the figures provided by administrative fiscal data from the National Treasury 2014 Budget Review. As for consumption subsidies, note that these are relatively small except for the free basic services provided by municipal governments. However, many municipalities essentially give these services for free to nearly the entire population instead of in the form of reduced rates targeted to the poor, and thus they are similar to a direct transfer to households. In most of this chapter, these municipal services are considered a transfer in our baseline scenario. Under an alternative scenario, we treat these services as an indirect subsidy; these results are available upon request.

To estimate the incidence of public spending on education and health, we follow the "government cost" approach, which measures the input costs per beneficiary obtained from administrative fiscal data (disaggregated by province and type of service) and assigns it to households using those services as identified in the household survey. This approach, also known as the "classic" or "nonbehavioral" approach, amounts to asking the following question: how much would the income of a household have to be increased if it had to pay for the free or subsidized public service at the full cost to the government?

The IES provides information on educational enrollment by level and type (that is, public vs. private institutions). Education benefits at the preschool, primary, and secondary school levels as well as for vocational training were imputed as total government education expenditure (by province) divided by total enrollment (also by province). Given that university education falls under the mandate of the national government, university education benefits were imputed as total national government spending on university education divided by total university enrollment.

As for health spending, data on the use of public health services come from the 2008 National Income Dynamics Study (SALDRU 2014). Details on the assumptions used for the health incidence are included in annex 8A.

Household Income Estimation

Once we allocate taxes and transfers to households, we construct the CEQ income concepts:

- *Market income* comprises pretax wages, salaries, income earned from capital assets (rent, interest, or dividends), and private transfers.[19] It also includes imputed rent for owner-occupied housing but does not include self-consumption because this concept is ambiguous in the survey.
- *Disposable income* is constructed by subtracting direct taxes (PIT and employee and employer contributions to the UIF and skills development levy) from market income and adding direct cash transfers. In South Africa, direct cash transfers include the old-age, child, disability, and foster grants.
- *Consumable income* adds the impact of indirect taxes and subsidies to disposable income. In South Africa, indirect taxes included in this analysis include VAT, excises on alcohol and tobacco, and the fuel levy.
- *Final income* adds in-kind benefits such as health and education to consumable income.

Limitations

Bear in mind the following important caveats about what the fiscal incidence analysis applied here does *not* address:

- It does not take into account behavioral, life-cycle, or general equilibrium effects, and it focuses on average incidence rather than incidence at the margin. Our tax-shifting and labor supply response assumptions are strong because they imply that both consumer demand and labor supply are perfectly inelastic. In practice, they provide a reasonable approximation, and they are commonly used.

- It does not take into account intrahousehold distribution of consumption.
- It does not take into account the differences in the quality of services delivered by the government across income groups.
- We cannot include some important taxes and spending that are in the general government budget. Revenues such as corporate income, international trade, or property taxes and spending categories such as infrastructure investments (including urban services and rural roads) are excluded even though they affect income distribution and poverty; these exclusions reflect a combination of data and methodological constraints.[20]

Note, too, that by considering the poverty and redistributive effects of the fiscal instruments examined in this chapter, we do not offer a full analysis of whether specific taxes or expenditures are *desirable*. When one tax or expenditure is found to be more redistributive to the poor than another, the temptation is to conclude that it is preferable. However, redistribution is only one of many criteria that matter when making public policy. Good tax policy will aim to be sufficient, efficient, and simple in addition to being equitable. Moreover, public spending will aim (among other goals) to provide the minimal functions of a state (such as security) and invest in the essential public goods (such as infrastructure) that are necessary to ensure prosperity in addition to improving equity. The assessments of the equity of specific taxes and spending programs presented in this chapter are just one type of input to public policy making—one that should be weighed with other evidence before deciding whether a tax or expenditure is desirable.

To try to control for possible shortcomings and biases, we conduct various robustness tests. In particular, although we treat free basic services as targeted cash transfers in most of the chapter, some municipalities provide these services as untargeted indirect subsidies. Because we cannot differentiate across municipalities, one robustness check is to treat free basic services as an indirect subsidy in all municipalities. We also construct all income concepts beginning with reported household consumption from the survey (as is done in other chapters in this volume) instead of starting from income as reported in the survey. These robustness test results corroborate the main findings and are available upon request.

Impact of Taxes and Government Spending on Inequality and Poverty

From theory, one knows that a tax or expenditure instrument could be progressive but not have large impacts on equity if it is too small (Duclos and Tabi 1996). Moreover, a tax could be regressive but still equalizing if analyzed in conjunction with other taxes and, especially, transfers.[21] Furthermore, taxes and transfers could be equalizing and yet poverty increasing, because inequality is measured on the basis of *relative* incomes, whereas poverty is affected by *absolute* incomes: that is, a tax system could be progressive and equalizing but hurt the poor if they pay more in taxes than they receive in transfers (Lustig 2017).

Finally, taxes and transfers could introduce horizontal inequity. One typical form of horizontal inequity occurs when the ranking of individuals (that is, the ordering of individuals in the income distribution before taxes and transfers) gets changed (swapping some individuals' positions) by the fiscal system.[22]

In what follows, we show that taxes and transfers in South Africa are designed such that the combination of their size, progressivity, and interaction among fiscal components results in a fiscal system with several desirable characteristics from the equity point of view:

- Taxes and transfers in South Africa reduce inequality *and* poverty.
- The system produces relatively little horizontal inequity in the form of reranking.
- Except for tertiary education, spending on education is pro-poor (that is, the share of spending devoted to the poorest deciles exceeds what is spent on the richer deciles), and so is spending on health.
- Except for excise taxes, all the components of fiscal policy are equalizing, including the VAT.

Impact on Inequality

Fiscal policy contributes substantially to reducing market income inequality in South Africa (table 8.3). Using income per capita as the welfare indicator, fiscal policy reduced the market income Gini coefficient from 0.771 to a disposable income Gini of 0.694 once direct taxes (PIT and payroll taxes) and transfers (cash transfer and free basic services) are taken into account, in line with what is typically reported by Statistics South Africa,[23] representing a drop of some 7.7 Gini points. If indirect taxes (VAT, excise taxes, and the fuel levy) are included, the Gini remains more or less the same. However, if one wanted to take an extra step and monetize the value of health and education spending—bearing in mind potential differences in the quality of services, as described below—the final income Gini coefficient would be 0.596, a decline of 17.5 Gini points.

In terms of fiscal redistribution, South Africa performs quite well when compared with other middle-income countries, although its inequality is still much higher than other countries even after well-targeted transfers. The reduction in the Gini coefficient for consumable income (income after direct transfers and both direct and indirect taxes and subsidies) relative to the Gini for full market income (all pretax wages, salaries, capital earnings, and private transfers) is larger in South Africa than in the other countries included in our sample (table 8.3).

Nonetheless, South Africa's Gini of 0.596 on final income (or 0.695 on consumable income, which excludes the monetized value of education and health services)—reflecting the full impact of redistribution through the fiscal instruments that we examined—is still higher than the market income Gini of Brazil, the second-most-unequal country shown in table 8.3. In other words, before

Table 8.3 Overall Redistributive Effect of Taxes, Transfers, and Subsidies in South Africa Relative to Other Selected Middle-Income Countries

Indicator	South Africa (2010)	Bolivia (2009)	Brazil (2009)	Indonesia (2012)
Gini (market income[a])	0.771	0.503	0.579	0.394
Gini (consumable income[b])	0.695	0.503	0.546	0.391
Redistributive effect[c]	0.077	0.000	0.033	0.003
Vertical equity (VE)[d]	0.083	0.003	0.048	0.006
Reranking effect (RR)[e]	0.006	0.003	0.014	0.003
RR/VE[f]	0.075	1.000	0.300	0.451

Sources: Lustig 2017, based on Higgins and Pereira 2014 (Brazil); Paz Arauco et al. 2014 (Bolivia); World Bank estimates based on Stats SA 2012b (South Africa); Indonesia data from chapter 5, this volume.
Note: Gini coefficients are calculated starting from income-based data in the cases of Bolivia, Brazil, and South Africa and from consumption-based data in the case of Indonesia.
a. "Market income" comprises pretax wages, salaries, and income earned from capital assets (rent, interest, or dividends) and private transfers. It also includes contributory pensions in all cases as well as imputed rent for owner-occupied housing but not self-consumption. (For more information about how market income is calculated for South Africa, see endnote 19 of this chapter.)
b. "Consumable income" = market income − direct and indirect taxes + direct cash transfers, social security contributions, and consumption subsidies and taxes.
c. The "redistributive effect" refers to the change in inequality associated with fiscal policy (direct and indirect taxes, direct transfers, and subsidies). It is calculated as the difference between the market income and consumable income Gini coefficients. Declines in the consumable income Gini relative to the market income Gini indicate a positive redistributive effect.
d. "Vertical equity" (VE) is equal to the difference between the Gini coefficient for incomes *before* taxes and transfers and the concentration coefficient for incomes *after* taxes and transfers.
e. The "reranking (RR) effect" refers to a form of horizontal inequity that occurs when the fiscal system changes the ordering of individuals in the income distribution. RR is equal to the difference between the Gini coefficient for incomes *after* taxes and transfers and the concentration coefficient for incomes *after* taxes and transfers (where households are ranked by their incomes before taxes and transfers. See chapter 1).
f. "Horizontal inequity" is calculated as the RR effect as a proportion of the VE effect, or RR/VE.

Brazil even begins to implement redistribution through its fiscal system, it starts off with market income that is already less unequal than what South Africa can achieve *after* using all the fiscal policy instruments at its disposal.

Analyzing the equity dimension of a fiscal system should also assess how much horizontal inequity is generated by fiscal policy (Duclos and Araar 2006). Table 8.3 shows the redistributive effect (RE), vertical equity (VE) effect, and reranking (RR) effect for four middle-income countries with comparable data. Here the RE is measured by subtracting the Gini coefficient for consumable income from the Gini for market income; in other words, it is the change in inequality associated with direct and indirect taxes as well as direct transfers and subsidies. As table 8.3 also shows, South Africa is the country with both the highest RE and the lowest horizontal inequity. Reranking as a proportion of the VE effect (or RR/VE) is significantly lower in South Africa (7.5 percent) than, for example, in Brazil (30 percent), the country with the second-lowest RR/VE ratio.[24] An extreme case of horizontal inequity induced by fiscal policy is Bolivia, where reranking completely wipes out the reduction in vertical inequity.

Impact on Poverty
Tax and expenditure instruments in South Africa reduced the incidence of extreme poverty (measured as US$1.25 per person per day at 2005 purchasing

power parity [PPP]) from 39.2 percent (based on market income) to 25.9 percent (based on consumable income) in 2010, as shown in table 8.4. As previously noted, consumable income includes the combined effect of all taxes, cash transfers, and free basic services.[25]

It is also more common to see the incidence of poverty calculated on the basis of disposable income (subtracting direct taxes from market income and adding direct cash transfers but excluding the effects of indirect taxes and subsidies). By this calculation, direct taxes and transfers cut extreme poverty in 2010 almost in half: from 39.2 percent (market income) to 20.2 percent (disposable income).[26]

In this regard, South Africa also stands out relative to comparator countries (table 8.5). It shows the largest percentage-point poverty reduction of the "CEQ countries" (countries to which the same methodological approach was applied, as described by Lustig and Higgins 2013). Most notably, indirect taxes on consumption do not reverse the poverty reduction associated with direct transfers; thus South Africa's consumable-income poverty (column 3) is still lower than its market-income poverty (column 1), in contrast to what happens in several of the other countries, including Brazil.

By how much does social spending in South Africa boost the incomes of the poor? Our analysis finds that households in the poorest decile receive transfers

Table 8.4 Inequality and Poverty Indicators in South Africa, by Income Concept, 2010

Indicator	Market income[a]	Disposable income[b]	Consumable income[c]	Final income[d]
Inequality indicators				
Gini coefficient	0.771	0.694	0.695	0.597
Theil index[e]	1.222	0.971	0.971	0.723
90/10[f]	198.9	32.7	33.2	12.2
Headcount poverty indicators				
National food poverty line (%)	40.8	23.4	29.0	—
Official consumption-based food poverty line (%)	—	20.2	—	—
National lower-bound poverty line (%)	46.5	34.2	39.6	—
Official consumption-based poverty line (lower bound) (%)	—	32.2	—	—
National upper-bound poverty line (%)	52.3	45.1	50.1	—
US$1.25 per day at 2005 PPP (%)	39.2	20.2	25.9	—
US$2.50 per day at 2005 PPP (%)	44.1	29.6	35.2	—
US$4.00 per day at 2005 PPP (%)	52.3	44.9	49.9	—

Source: World Bank estimates based on 2010/11 Income and Expenditure Survey (IES) data.
Notes: These results correspond to the scenario in which free basic services are treated as a direct transfer. PPP = purchasing power parity; — = not available.
a. "Market income" comprises pretax wages, salaries, and income earned from capital assets (rent, interest, or dividends) and private transfers. It also includes contributory pensions in all cases as well as imputed rent for owner-occupied housing but not self-consumption. (For more information about how market income is calculated for South Africa, see endnote 19 of this chapter.)
b. "Disposable income" = market income − direct taxes and contributions + cash transfers.
c. "Consumable income" = disposable income − indirect taxes + consumption subsidies.
d. "Final income" = consumable income + in-kind transfers (such as public health and education expenditure).
e. Although less commonly used than the Gini coefficient, the Theil index is another inequality indicator (Theil 1967).
f. 90/10 is the ratio of the 90th income percentile to the 10th income percentile.

Table 8.5 Poverty Headcount of CEQ Countries, by Income Concept

Percentage earning US$2.50 (PPP 2005) per person per day

Country (year of data)	Market income[a]	Disposable income[b]	Consumable income[c]
Armenia (2011)	31.3	28.9	34.9
Bolivia (2009)	19.6	17.6	20.2
Brazil (2009)	15.1	11.2	16.3
Costa Rica (2010)	5.4	3.9	4.2
El Salvador (2011)	14.7	12.9	14.4
Guatemala (2010)	35.9	34.6	36.5
Indonesia (2012)	56.4	55.9	54.9
Mexico (2010)	12.6	10.7	10.7
Peru (2009)	15.2	14.0	14.5
South Africa (2010)	44.1	29.6	35.2
Uruguay (2009)	5.1	1.5	2.3

Sources: Beneke, Lustig, and Oliva 2015 (El Salvador); Bucheli et al. 2014 (Uruguay); Cabrera, Lustig, and Morán 2014 (Guatemala); Higgins and Pereira 2014 (Brazil); Jaramillo 2014 (Peru); Lustig 2017, based on Sauma and Trejos 2014 (Costa Rica); Paz Arauco et al. 2014 (Bolivia); Scott 2014 (Mexico); World Bank estimates based on Stats SA 2012b (South Africa); Armenia and Indonesia data from chapters 2 and 5 of this volume, respectively.

Note: "CEQ countries" are those assessed using the same methodological approach in the Commitment to Equity (CEQ) initiative (Lustig and Higgins 2013). PPP = purchasing power parity.

a. "Market income" comprises pretax wages, salaries, and income earned from capital assets (rent, interest, or dividends) and private transfers. It also includes contributory pensions in all cases as well as imputed rent for owner-occupied housing but not self-consumption. (For more information about how market income is calculated for South Africa, see endnote 19 of this chapter.)

b. "Disposable income" = market income − direct taxes and contributions + cash transfers.

c. "Consumable income" = disposable income − indirect taxes + consumption subsidies.

and indirect subsidies that are worth 11 times the household's market income. (The benefits would be 32 times their market income if the monetized value of in-kind benefits such as health and education were added to the cash transfers.) Households' tax burden, in contrast, amounted to twice their market income. Households in the bottom half of the income distribution overall receive far more in direct transfers and free basic municipal services than they pay in taxes. The net cash position of the household after taxes and transfers is positive for the bottom 60 percent of the population, a far larger share of the population than in other middle-income countries.

Furthermore, once the monetized value of in-kind spending on education and health are also included in benefits, the bottom decile received R 6,900 (or US$945) per capita in 2010/11 from the government, compared with R 724 (US$99) paid in taxes. Only the top three deciles of the market income distribution pay more in taxes than they receive in all forms of cash and in-kind benefits.

Education and Health Spending: How Pro-Poor?

As shown earlier in table 8.4, adding the monetized value of spending on education and health results in an additional reduction of the Gini coefficient (from consumable income to final income) of 10 percentage points. Apart from this decrease in inequality, how *pro-poor* is the government's spending on education and health? ("Pro-poor" means spending that is progressive in absolute terms; that is, per capita spending that decreases with income.)

In assessing how education and health spending benefit the poor, we have to caution that our analysis does not address the *quality* of such spending. We use government expenditure data on the various forms of education and health services to estimate unit costs of these programs. The analysis thus assumes that the actual benefit received by individuals is equal to the amount spent per capita. A clear limitation of the analysis is the variation in quality of school infrastructure, teachers, and health clinics and hospitals across the country.

Education Spending

Spending in South Africa on preschool, primary, and secondary education is pro-poor (figure 8.3), reflecting both relatively high spending and high enrollment rates (over 97 percent participation for children ages 7 to 15 and 83 percent for those ages 16 to 18 [NPC 2011]). Spending on adult education is also pro-poor: about half of the spending on adult training centers benefits households with incomes of less than US$4 a day in 2005 PPP. However, although postsecondary

Figure 8.3 Distribution of Benefits from Government Education Spending in South Africa, by Educational and Household Income Level, 2010/11

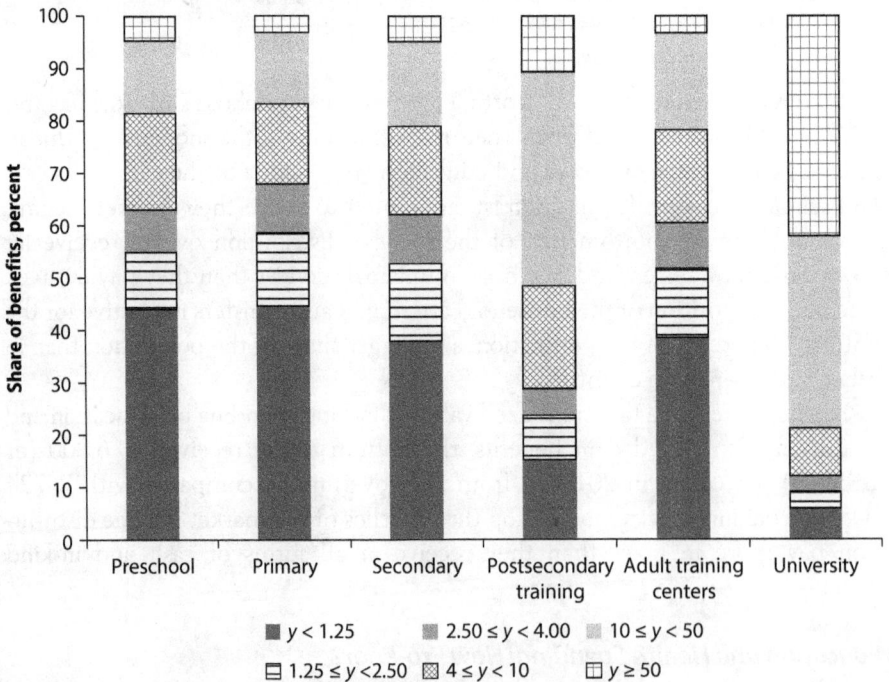

Legend:
- $y < 1.25$
- $1.25 \leq y < 2.50$
- $2.50 \leq y < 4.00$
- $4 \leq y < 10$
- $10 \leq y < 50$
- $y \geq 50$

Source: World Bank estimates based on 2010/11 Income and Expenditure Survey (IES) data.
Note: Figure shows the share of education benefits going to households (y) within ranges of per capita income per day (in U.S. dollars at 2005 purchasing power parity [PPP]).

school is still equalizing, it is not pro-poor because the poor have lower rates of attendance at colleges and universities. Spending on college education and university education is progressive only in relative terms, with spending on college education being more progressive than spending on university education.[27]

Health Spending

Health spending is pro-poor to a (roughly) similar extent as education spending. The monetized value of health spending per patient makes up a larger share of the market incomes of those at the bottom of the income distribution than of those at the top of the distribution, amounting to nine times the market incomes of the poorest market-income decile. Public spending on health is relatively well targeted, not because poorer people have higher utilization rates but because high-income households choose not to use the public health care system.

The public sector, whose health expenditure in 2010/11 equaled 4 percent of GDP, serves roughly 83 percent (41.7 million) of the South African population (NPC 2011). The remaining 17 percent (8.3 million) of the population have private health insurance (termed "medical aid" in South Africa) and mostly use private facilities, with total private sector health-related spending amounting to about 4.3 percent of GDP in 2010 (NPC 2011). Many households use both private and public health care systems, with even quite poor households often choosing to see private general practitioners (GPs) rather than attend public clinics, where waiting times are long, and where a GP can only be seen after a referral from a nurse.

Education and Health Performance and Outcomes

Given the limitations of the analysis mentioned earlier, a few words of caution are warranted to explain how our findings on targeting may not translate into a commensurate actual impact on the poor. Despite good policy and relatively high spending on education and health in relation to GDP, actual performance and outcomes in these sectors have been disappointing.

Education. South Africa achieves sixth-grade test scores in reading and mathematics that are below the regional averages for South and East Africa, even though many of these comparator countries spend the same or less on education per capita (Presidency, Republic of South Africa 2014; SACMEQ 2011). The 2011 Trends in International Mathematics and Science Study (TIMSS) showed large improvements in ninth-grade scores relative to 2002, but South African students are still ranked in the bottom 5 out of 42 economies. Moreover, the TIMSS results showed that the average math and science scores for South Africa's best-performing students (those in the 95th percentile) were below the average scores of students in Finland; Japan; the Republic of Korea; the Russian Federation; Singapore; Slovenia; and Taiwan, China (Presidency, Republic of South Africa 2014).

Another important consideration is how education spending per student varies by population group. One of the major features of social spending under apartheid was the large gap in spending per schoolchild: per capita funding for white students was 10 times that of black students. However, race-based allocations became unconstitutional under the postapartheid rules. As expected, the gap in public financing based on a student's race has been eliminated: although in the early 1990s the average white child still received a spending subsidy for education that was 4.5 times that of a black child, the disparity was eliminated by 2006 (Van der Berg 2009).

Any remaining gap in spending per pupil is caused by the fact that more highly qualified teachers tend to be concentrated in richer schools, implying a slight bias in salary expenditure per student to these schools. But this disparity is virtually balanced by the higher allocations of spending to meet national norms and standards in poorer schools. Although schools in more-affluent neighborhoods can supplement state resources by charging school fees, the public financing of schools is more or less equal. As a result, public spending per student averaged R 11,000 in 2011, and about 78 percent of students (more than 8 million) in 80 percent of public schools (almost 20,000) benefited from no-fee schools (Presidency, Republic of South Africa 2014).

Health. Despite steady improvements, South Africa still has comparatively high maternal and infant mortality by middle-income country standards even though its health spending (public and private) of just over 8 percent of GDP is comparatively high (DPME 2013).

Contribution of Taxes and Transfers to Income Redistribution

As shown above, the *combined* effects of taxes and social spending in South Africa are quite redistributive. Next we turn to this question: which components of the fiscal system are equalizing, which ones are unequalizing, and to what extent?

As discussed by Lustig (2017) and summarized in chapter 1, in a world where multiple fiscal interventions exist, one cannot rely on the standard progressivity measures (such as the Kakwani coefficients) to determine whether an intervention exercises an equalizing or unequalizing force, because of path dependency. To measure the contribution of a particular fiscal intervention (or combinations of them), we have opted to use the "marginal contribution." Recall that the marginal contribution to the redistributive effect of a particular fiscal intervention is measured as the difference in the Gini for the income concept without that intervention and the Gini with the intervention. For example, to calculate the marginal contribution of the VAT to the observed change from the market income Gini to the consumable income Gini, one must take the difference between the Gini coefficient of consumable income *without* the VAT and the Gini coefficient of consumable income *with* the VAT. If the VAT is equalizing, this difference will be positive; if unequalizing, the difference will be negative.

Table 8.6 shows the marginal contributions of each individual fiscal intervention analyzed here as well as those of the conventional broad categories such as direct taxes, direct transfers, indirect taxes, and in-kind transfers for education and health. Hence, the marginal contributions are shown for the cash portion of the fiscal system (cash transfers, direct taxes, and indirect taxes) as well as for the fiscal system, including noncash benefits in education and health.

As mentioned above, the redistributive effect of the cash portion of the fiscal system is measured as the difference in the market-income Gini minus the consumable-income Gini. As indicated earlier (and shown again in table 8.6), this redistributive effect equals 7.7 Gini points. As one can observe, direct transfers are equalizing and have the largest marginal contribution to the reduction in inequality (6.7 Gini points), followed by direct taxes and contributions (3.3 Gini points). Indirect taxes are neutral.

The specific interventions with the largest equalizing marginal contributions are PIT (3.2 Gini points); the CSG (2 Gini points); the old-age grant (2 Gini

Table 8.6 Marginal Contribution of Taxes and Transfers in South Africa, 2010/11

Fiscal intervention	Size[a] (%)	Concentration coefficient	Kakwani coefficient[b]	Marginal contribution[c] Redistributive effect (Gini points)	Poverty reduction effect (pp)
Total from market income to consumable income[d]	n.a.	n.a.	n.a.	0.0766	0.1054
Direct taxes and contributions	13.58	0.8966	0.1254	0.0327	−0.0018
Personal income tax	13.58	0.9093	0.1381	0.0321	−0.0002
Payroll taxes (UIF and SDL)	—	0.7711	−0.0001	0.0013	−0.0018
Direct transfers	5.38	−0.2709	1.0421	0.0672	0.0881
Old-age pension	1.93	−0.1744	0.9456	0.0198	0.0384
Child support grant	1.47	−0.3352	1.1065	0.0204	0.0281
Disability grant	0.93	−0.2545	1.0257	0.0103	0.0217
Child care dependency grant	0.07	−0.3729	1.1441	0.0008	0.0024
Child foster care	0.11	−0.3203	1.0915	0.0013	0.0039
Grant-in-aid	0.03	−0.1538	0.9250	0.0003	0.0007
War veterans grant	0.00	−0.1009	0.8721	0.0000	0.0000
Other grants	0.02	0.0112	0.7600	0.0001	0.0004
Free basic services (treated as direct transfers)[e]	0.84	−0.3890	1.1602	0.0117	0.0197
Indirect taxes	14.09	0.6885	−0.0828	−0.0002	−0.0534
Value added tax	10.05	0.7098	−0.0614	0.0025	−0.0364
Excise taxes on alcohol and tobacco	1.07	0.4062	−0.3650	−0.0040	−0.0107
Fuel levy	2.97	0.7179	−0.0533	0.0010	−0.0112
Total from market income to final income[d]	n.a.	n.a.	n.a.	0.1758	0.3689
Direct taxes and contributions	13.58	0.8966	0.1254	0.0430	−0.0003
Direct transfers	5.38	−0.2709	1.0421	0.0517	0.1762
Indirect taxes	14.09	0.6885	−0.0828	0.0127	−0.0258
In-kind transfers	12.45	−0.0505	0.8217	0.0992	0.3169
Education spending	6.93	−0.0457	0.8169	0.0490	0.1944
Preschool	0.05	−0.1140	0.8852	0.0004	0.0010

table continues next page

The Distributional Impact of Taxes and Transfers • http://dx.doi.org/10.1596/978-1-4648-1091-6

Table 8.6 Marginal Contribution of Taxes and Transfers in South Africa, 2010/11 *(continued)*

Fiscal intervention	Size[a] (%)	Concentration coefficient	Kakwani coefficient[b]	Marginal contribution[c]	
				Redistributive effect (Gini points)	Poverty reduction effect (pp)
Primary school	3.45	−0.1898	0.9611	0.0298	0.1090
Secondary school	2.20	−0.1226	0.8938	0.0166	0.0511
College education	0.27	0.2952	0.4760	0.0008	0.0014
Adult education	0.08	−0.0779	0.8491	0.0005	0.0012
University education	0.88	0.6150	0.1562	−0.0007	0.0011
Health spending	5.52	−0.0563	0.8275	0.0433	0.1283

Source: World Bank estimates based on 2010/11 Income and Expenditure Survey (IES) and 2010 National Income Dynamics Study (NIDS) data.
Note: n.a. = not applicable; — = not available; pp = percentage points; SDL = skills development levy; UIF = Unemployment Insurance Fund.
a. Size equals the ratio of the amount collected or spent divided by total market income.
b. The Kakwani coefficient, a measure of progressivity, is computed as the difference between the market-income Gini coefficient and the concentration coefficient for each fiscal intervention; those with positive Kakwani coefficients are progressive. The Gini coefficient measures inequality of income distribution, from 0 (full equality) to 1 (maximum inequality).
c. The "marginal contribution" columns show the difference between (a) the Gini coefficient, or the headcount poverty rate, of the relevant income concept *without* the specified fiscal intervention and (b) the Gini coefficient, or headcount poverty rate, of the relevant income concept *including* that intervention. By definition, the sum of the marginal contributions does not fulfill the adding-up principle, so it will not be equal to the redistributive effect unless by coincidence.
d. "Market income" comprises pretax wages, salaries, and income earned from capital assets (rent, interest, or dividends) and private transfers. It also includes contributory pensions in all cases as well as imputed rent for owner-occupied housing but not self-consumption. (For more information about how market income is calculated for South Africa, see endnote 19 of this chapter.) "Consumable income" = market income − direct and indirect taxes and contributions + cash transfers + consumption subsidies. "Final income" = consumable income + in-kind transfers (such as public health and education expenditure).
e. In this analysis, the "free basic services" (municipal provision of free power, sanitation, water supply, and refuse removal to low-income households) are considered to be a direct transfer because these services are sometimes provided in the form of cash transfers.

points); free basic services, which although not cash transfers, are treated here as cash transfers (1.2 Gini points); and the disability grant (1 Gini point).

Notably, despite the fact that the UIF and indirect taxes are regressive as measured by the Kakwani coefficient, their marginal contributions are equalizing (that is, the Gini coefficient for consumable income would be higher if the fiscal system did not include these taxes). The VAT in particular has an equalizing effect that is not negligible. This counterintuitive result—that a regressive tax can be equalizing—results from the fact that although these three taxes are regressive in relation to market income, they are progressive in relation to the income concept that includes all the other interventions except the one analyzed.[28] In the case of the VAT, the equalizing effect stems from the fact that although the VAT is regressive in relation to market income, this tax is no longer regressive when measured against post-cash-transfer income. In contrast, based on their marginal contribution, excise taxes increase the Gini by 0.4 points when they are included in the analysis. That is, even after cash transfers, these taxes are regressive.

The redistributive effect of the whole fiscal system—cash and in-kind portions—equals 17.6 Gini points (table 8.6). Direct taxes, direct transfers, education spending, and health spending are all strongly equalizing, and their marginal contributions are similar (reducing the Gini by 4.3, 5.2, 4.9, and 4.3 points, respectively). Interestingly, when the income definition includes the in-kind transfers (final income) and not just net cash transfers, we see that net indirect taxes (consumable income) turn from neutral (no change in the Gini if we take them into account in the analysis) to equalizing (subtracting 1.2 Gini points). The order of magnitude, as expected, is much smaller than the equalizing marginal contributions of the other categories.

Conclusions

This chapter estimated the distributional impact of the main elements of general government taxation and spending in South Africa, applying fiscal incidence analysis to the 2010/11 IES (Stats SA 2012b). On the tax side, it analyzed the incidence of 64.5 percent of total tax revenue, including PIT, VAT, excise taxes on alcohol and tobacco, and the general fuel levy. On the expenditure side, it analyzed the incidence of 43 percent of general government expenditures, focused on social spending including direct cash transfers, free basic services, and health and education spending.

The results show that South Africa uses its fiscal instruments to significantly reduce market income inequality and poverty through a progressive tax system and highly progressive social spending. The rich in South Africa bear the brunt of taxes that we examined, and the government redirects these resources to the poorest in society to raise their incomes. Only the top three deciles of the income distribution pay more in taxes than they receive in transfers. As a result, the fiscal system lifts some 3.6 million individuals out of poverty (measured as those living on less than US$2.50 per day in 2005 PPP adjusted). It also reduces inequality from a situation where, without these progressive fiscal instruments, the incomes of the richest decile would be over 1,000 times higher than the poorest to one where they are about 66 times higher. The Gini coefficient falls from 0.77 before taxes and social spending programs to 0.59 after their application (or 0.695 when the monetized value of health and education spending are excluded). Despite the large fiscal redistribution, however, South Africa remains one of the most unequal countries in the world.

On the tax side, the only unequalizing component in the analysis consisted of excise taxes. Apart from those, fiscal policy relies on a mix of equalizing direct taxes (such as PIT) and neutral or equalizing indirect and consumption taxes. In combination, they generate an equalizing tax system as follows:

- *Direct taxes* (PIT and payroll taxes) are progressive and equalizing. Because they make up a relatively high share of GDP, their contribution to reducing the gap in incomes between the rich and poor is high. Among the direct taxes, all three (PIT, skills development levy, and UIF) are equalizing.
- *Indirect taxes* are neutral when measured against consumable income (the income concept excluding education and health spending) and slightly equalizing when their contribution is measured against final income (the income concept including education and health spending). Among the indirect taxes, both the VAT and the fuel levy are equalizing.

On the spending side of fiscal policy, social spending is not only progressive but also contributes to large reductions in inequality and poverty (which, as stated earlier, nonetheless remain very high), as follows:

- *Direct transfers* are strongly equalizing, with the CSG and the old-age grant showing the largest marginal contributions to the redistributive effect.
- *In-kind transfers* through education spending (both in the aggregate and for each level), as well as through health spending, are equalizing. Total spending on education and health makes a high marginal contribution to the reduction in inequality. Except for tertiary education, spending on education is pro-poor (per capita spending declines with increasing income), and so is spending on health.

Relative to other middle-income countries, South Africa performs well: it achieves the most income redistribution of the comparator middle-income countries, but its inequality and poverty remain far higher than in other countries (Lustig 2015). In fact, inequality in South Africa *after* taxes and spending is still higher than that of other middle-income countries *before* they begin to use fiscal policy interventions.

Our analysis suggests that although South Africa has some scope to improve the targeting of certain social programs like free basic services, cash transfer programs are already well targeted and substantive. Education and health spending also benefit the poorer parts of the income distribution relatively more than the rich. However, given concerns about the quality of such spending, South Africa could do more to maximize the potential of education and health spending in reducing poverty and inequality. Excise taxes clearly deserve attention from the equity point of view because they are unequalizing and may be too onerous on the poor.

In sum, fiscal policy already goes a long way toward achieving redistribution. Nevertheless, the levels of inequality and poverty in South Africa after taxes and spending remain unacceptably high. More can and should be done to improve the quality of education and health service delivery. But South Africa's fiscal deficit and debt indicators show that the fiscal space to do so is extremely limited, and little room remains on the macro front to spend more to achieve even greater redistribution. Addressing the twin challenges of poverty and inequality in a fiscally sustainable way requires higher and more-inclusive economic growth to support fiscal policy. Such growth would be particularly important in addressing the need for more jobs and higher incomes, especially at the lower end of the income distribution—thus helping narrow the gap in incomes between rich and poor and reinforcing the effectiveness of fiscal policy.

Annex 8A. Fiscal Incidence Assumptions

Personal Income Taxes

Labor incomes reported in the household survey were assumed to reflect labor incomes net of taxes. As a result, PIT was imputed based on the 2010 PIT rules specified in the National Treasury Budget Review. Similarly, employee contributions to social security, including the Unemployment Insurance Fund (UIF) and skills development levy, were imputed based on reported net incomes. Given imputed direct taxes and contributions, we construct a measure of market income for each individual whereby market income is the imputed income before taxes and contributions.

Indirect Taxes
Value Added Tax

First, to find the incidence of VAT, we applied the statutory rate of 14 percent to all goods consumed by households in the survey except for exempt items and the 19 food items and petroleum products that are zero rated. In general, because retailers can claim VAT refunds for the inputs they used in production, the final burden on the consumer is simply the VAT rate at the final point of sale. For exempt goods, a final consumer pays no VAT *directly*; in exempt sectors, VAT works exclusively *indirectly* when the final consumption price of a good in an exempt sector is higher by the amount of VAT paid on inputs (which a producer in an exempt sector cannot reclaim). To capture this effect, we used the 2009 social accounting matrix (SAM) for exempt goods and find that the indirect effect is 5 percent of the total incidence, given that exemptions are narrowly defined.

Excise Taxes

For excise taxes, we found that the total weighted value of expenditure on excisable alcohol and tobacco products in the household survey is far below estimates from administrative data. For instance, the ratio of the value of IES consumption on alcohol is only 17 percent of total sales, according to South African Reserve Bank records. This is because a very large number of households indicated purchasing zero amounts of alcohol or tobacco. To correct for this underreporting, the analysis

1. Rescaled verified excise tax collections from administrative data by the ratio of private consumption in the household survey to what is observed in national accounts;
2. Calculated each (market income) decile's share of alcohol and tobacco expenditure in total alcohol and tobacco expenditure recorded in the household survey; and
3. Multiplied the shares calculated in step 1 by the total calculated in step 2 and distributed that amount uniformly to every household in the market income decile.

The allocation of excise collections in step 3 is, in essence, an estimate of the expected burden. Because excises are primarily a tax to deter consumption, the burden on the income of those who consume these goods can be sizable. Alcohol and tobacco outlays comprise about 1 percent of total expenditure in the bottom decile, and thus, as a share of those households' relatively low market income, the excise on these goods is high.

Fuel Levy

Finally, the fuel levy has a non-negligible impact across the income distribution, reflecting not only direct taxes paid on fuel consumed but also the indirect impact where the levy increases input costs for other sectors that use fuel. More specifically, the fuel levy was taken as a weighted average of the statutory rates on diesel and gasoline, which average 31.75 percent.

To calculate the direct incidence, this average rate was applied to the household purchases of these fuels observed in the IES. The indirect effects were calculated using a "price-shifting" model (Coady 2008) and the 2009 SAM to assess the price changes for goods and services in sectors that use fuel as an input and assuming that the fuel tax was passed on to the consumer in the form of higher prices. The price-shifting model is static and assumes that exogenously generated price changes are either "pushed forward" to output prices or "pushed backward" onto factor payments. We therefore take results generated as an upper-bound or "overnight" estimate of the impact of any change in government-administered price policy on household welfare.

The percentage price changes derived from the SAM (in all sectors other than fuel) are multiplied by the household budget shares of those sectors to produce a total price change for each household's consumption basket. Because fuel is used as an input in so many sectors, the indirect effects are sizable, accounting for 58 percent of the total fuel tax incidence in South Africa.

Direct Transfers

Households receiving cash transfers are directly identified in the household survey. Direct transfers overwhelmingly benefit the poor in relative terms, regardless of whether we use market incomes or consumption as the welfare measure.

Health Spending

We used the National Income Dynamics Study (NIDS) Wave 1 data (SALDRU 2014) to look at health facility use. We chose the NIDS Wave 1 data (from 2008) rather than the Wave 2 data (from 2010) because of concerns about the quality of the expenditure data in Wave 2 and selective attrition rates (as higher-income households were much more likely to attrite) between Wave 1 and Wave 2.

A limitation of the data is that different questions were asked of adults and children. For individuals ages 15 years and over ("adults" in the NIDS methodology), we have information about how long ago the last health visit occurred and the type of facility visited. For children (individuals ages 14 years and under), we know whether the child had any routine health checks (when not ill) in the previous year and whether the child had been ill and saw a health care practitioner in the previous 30 days. In cases where the child consulted a health worker, we do not know whether the consultation occurred at a public or private clinic, hospital, or private doctor's office.

Medical Aid

The NIDS data suggest that 16 percent of adults and 12 percent of children (under the age of 15 years) in the NIDS sample were covered by medical aid (private health insurance) (SALDRU 2014). Reassuringly, 17 percent of adults and 12 percent of children in the 2010/11 IES data also reported that they were covered by medical aid. Taking adults and children together, this implies that 15 percent of the population was insured in 2010.

Type of Facility Visited

As shown in table 8A.1, adults without medical aid typically use public clinics (49 percent) or public hospitals (21 percent), although large numbers go to private doctors (25 percent) (SALDRU 2014). As one would expect, adults with medical aid rarely use public facilities.

User Fees

Primary health care user fees were abolished in 1996. Whereas Burger and Grobler (2007), using 2003 General Household Survey data, find that 7–10 percent of public clinic users in the bottom 60 percent of the distribution reported paying a fee for service, the NIDS data show this percentage was less than 2 percent. The median fee reported among the 60 respondents who did report a fee was R 35. Given this, we assume that copayments are zero.

Fee-for-payment in public hospitals was more common, with almost a quarter (24 percent) of those who used public hospitals reporting that they had been charged a fee. In the cases where there was a charge, the fees were very low, with the median fee being R 20 and the mean R 51. Across all hospital visits, the mean copayment was R 12. Relative to the cost of a hospital visit (R 2,782), these copayments are so small that they can safely be disregarded.

Table 8A.1 Adult Use of Health Facilities in South Africa, by Medical Aid Status, 2008

percentage

Last health consultation was at a...?	Adult has medical aid?		Total
	Yes	No	
Public hospital	3.4	20.8	17.0
Private hospital	11.1	1.7	3.8
Public health clinic	5.8	48.9	39.5
Private clinic	3.6	2.6	2.8
Private doctor	74.5	25.0	35.7
Nurse or chemist	1.5	0.5	0.7
Traditional healer	0.1	0.3	0.2
Do not remember	0.0	0.3	0.2
Total	100	100	100

Source: Estimates based on 2010 National Income Dynamics Study Wave 1 data.
Note: "Medical aid" refers to private health insurance.

Number of Visits

For adults, the NIDS data indicate whether the last visit to a health facility was in the past 30 days, 1–5 months, 6–12 months, and so on. From this, we estimate that the median number of adult visits per year is 1.33.

For children, we know very little. We know whether the child went for a checkup (when not ill) once, more than once, or not at all in the past 12 months. We also know whether the child was ill for more than three days in the past month and whether the ill child was taken to a health care provider.

These data indicate that almost one-tenth (9.6 percent) of children were reported to have been ill for more than three days in the past 30 days. Of these, more than three-quarters (78 percent) sought medical attention. Of those who did not seek medical attention, almost half (48 percent) were regarded by their caregivers as "not sick enough" to need attention. Just over one-quarter (27 percent) of caregivers said that they did not take the child to a health facility because they "did not have the money."

Children covered by medical aid were much more likely to have been "ill" in the past 30 days (13 percent vs. 9 percent overall). This disparity may simply reflect varying caregiver perceptions of what "ill" means. In addition, children with medical aid were more likely to have been taken to a health care provider when ill (84 percent vs. 76 percent overall).

Overall, 7 percent of children sought medical attention for illness in the 30 days preceding the survey. Among those with medical aid, this percentage was 10 percent versus 7 percent for the uninsured.

Assumptions

For children, the NIDS survey does not indicate what type of health facility the child visited. However, for routine health checks (when the child is not sick), we assume that all these health checks occur at clinics. We assume that uninsured children use public clinics for health checks and that insured children only use private clinics. If more than one routine health checkup (when the child was not ill) occurred in the past year, we assume that there were two visits.

When children are sick, we assume that their patterns of health facility use are similar to those of the adults in the same households. We thus assign facility use to children in proportion to the usage patterns (for public clinic, public hospital, or private facility) of all the adults in the household. Among the 406 cases in which no adults in the household reported ever having made a health visit, we assume that insured children go to private doctors and uninsured children go to public clinics.

Ranking of Households

We rank households according to per capita expenditure to later merge these data into our primary survey. To make expenditure broadly comparable between the NIDS and IES data, we exclude income tax payments and "lumpy" expenditures such as the purchase of jewelry and durables, bride payments, and expenditures on ceremonies such as weddings, and funerals.

We create expenditure ventiles (5 percent shares), each one containing equal numbers of individuals, ranked by per capita expenditure. We played around with creating more groups such as percentiles, but the small sample size (28,226 individuals in 7,296 households) made the results very sensitive to variations in the data.

Value of a Health Visit

The total health budget in 2010/11 was R 98 billion. Of this, R 54 billion was for hospitals and about R 17 billion was for primary health care. These line items are assigned to respondents in the survey that report using public hospitals and clinics, respectively. An additional R 7 billion went toward medicines and R 5 billion toward medical supplies. These are assigned equally across all visits to public hospitals and clinics. The residual of R 14 billion is assumed to benefit all individuals who make contact with the health system, regardless of whether they are insured or uninsured and whether they use private or public facilities.

Notes

1. The 2010/11 national poverty headcount is calculated on the basis of the 2011 national upper-bound poverty line of R 620 per month (Stats SA 2014). (The upper-bound poverty line represents the level of consumption at which individuals can obtain both adequate food and nonfood items.) On February 3, 2015, Statistics South Africa released a methodological report on the rebasing (updating) of national poverty lines and development of pilot provincial poverty lines. That report estimated the upper-bound poverty line to be R 779 per capita per month in February–March 2011 prices, representing a 25.6 percent increase from R 620 when the 2000 line was consumer price index–adjusted to 2011. As a result, the new poverty rate using the national upper-bound poverty line was 53.8 percent in 2011 (Stats SA 2015).

2. The Gini coefficients are calculated on the basis of expenditure (rather than income) per capita excluding taxes (Stats SA 2014).

3. Country-specific poverty headcount data come from the World Bank's PovcalNet online analysis tool, http://iresearch.worldbank.org/PovcalNet. The US$2.50 poverty line is measured in purchasing power parity (PPP) using private consumption conversion factors for 2005. The headcount ratios are based on disposable income.

4. See, for example, the European Union's microsimulation model, EUROMOD (https://www.euromod.ac.uk/), or models developed by the Institute for Fiscal Studies (https://www.ifs.org.uk/).

5. Led by Nora Lustig since 2008, the Commitment to Equity (CEQ) is joint project of the Center for Inter-American Policy, the Department of Economics at Tulane University, and the Inter-American Dialogue. For more details, see http://www .commitmentoequity.org.

6. The ratios reported throughout this section are calculated from the revenue and expenditure levels reported at the time of writing by the National Treasury, the various line ministries, and the Financial and Fiscal Commission; they do not capture the 2015 revision to nominal GDP series.

7. Of course, equity is not the only criterion by which a tax system should be evaluated. Direct taxes can constrain economic growth, which in turn limits the ability of the fiscal system to reduce inequality in the future.

8. The largest omitted item is corporate income tax, which accounts for about 21 percent of tax revenue. The analysis only assesses items included in South Africa's general government budget and therefore excludes revenues collected or activities undertaken by state-owned enterprises.

9. In 2010/11, individuals with an annual income of less than R 120,000 (US$16,438, calculated at the average 2010/11 exchange rate of R 7.3 per US$1)—comprising more than half of all taxpayers—were not required to file tax returns. In 2010/11, the tax threshold (the taxable income below which no PIT was payable) was R 54,200 (US$7,424) for individuals below age 65 and R 84,200 (US$11,534) for individuals over age 65. The top marginal tax rate was 40 percent and kicked in at R 525,000 ($71,917) per year. A certain level of interest income (R 22,300 or US$3,054 per year in 2010/11) is tax-exempt to promote saving.

10. Under the Skills Development Act No. 97 of 1998, employers pay a monthly skills development levy (determined by the employer's salary bill) to the South African Revenue Service for skills development of employees. If employees undergo training, the employer can reclaim this amount from the relevant Sector Education and Training Authority.

11. The following foodstuffs are currently zero rated: brown bread, maize meal, samp, maize rice, dried maize, dried beans, lentils, tinned pilchards or sardines, milk powder, dairy powder blend, rice, vegetables, fruit, vegetable oil, milk, cultured milk, brown wheaten meal, eggs, and legumes or pulses. Other goods such as diesel and gasoline are zero rated because they are instead subject to excise duties, and municipal taxes are zero rated to avoid cascading taxes.

12. "General government" excludes state-owned enterprises.

13. In-kind transfer data come from the National Treasury 2013 Budget Review. The Integrated Residential Development Program (IRDP) focuses on the development of integrated housing projects. It provides for land acquisition; servicing of stands for a variety of land uses including commercial, recreational, schools, and clinics; and residential stands for low-, middle-, and high-income groups. The IRDP land use and income group mix are based on local planning and needs assessment, but the program is not explicitly targeted to the poor. IRDP expenditure was not included formally in the incidence analysis because of the lack of detailed administrative data on housing values.

14. Data on the child grants come from the National Treasury 2015 Budget Review.

15. Data on access to services come from the National Treasury 2011 Budget Review.

16. The methodology for IES data collection is an internationally accepted best practice, and the quality of the survey's income and consumption data is generally considered to be good. However, because the reported share of food consumption of the extreme poor in South Africa is much lower than one would expect, there is concern about potential underreporting at the bottom of the distribution. The survey combines the diary and recall methods to calculate total household consumption, and surveys using these methods over extended periods often risk underestimation of income and consumption. In addition, the IES does not separately identify own-produced goods, which also could lead to underreporting of consumption at the bottom of the distribution and could account for at least part of the gap in the

share of food in the consumption basket of the poor relative to what surveys report in other countries. Finally, as in other countries, there are questions about the ability of this type of survey to collect adequate information on households at the top of the distribution. One area for further research would be to try alternative methods to simulate the top of the distribution to try to correct for this.

17. The IES value of alcohol consumption is only 17 percent of total sales reported by the Reserve Bank of South Africa, because many households report zero alcohol or tobacco consumption. Although previous fiscal incidence analysis for South Africa used scaling assumptions similar to the ones used here, the results were mixed, with excise duties found to be quite regressive in 1995 but almost neutral in 2000 (Woolard et al. 2005). Although we could be overestimating the incidence of excises at the bottom of the distribution because of this scaling, we apply the same excise tax regardless of the quality of the alcoholic beverage or tobacco product, which could underestimate excises at the top of the distribution. See annex 8A for details.

18. See Coady (2008) for a description of the price-shifting model and annex 8A for a description of the approach.

19. In South Africa, we take net market income reported by each household in the IES and impute each direct tax paid to arrive at market income. This figure is then divided by the number of members in each household to arrive at per capita market income. We did not include the value of own production (sometimes called auto-consumption). Statistics South Africa did not measure autoconsumption in the conventional way; instead its variable captured both home production and business inventories, and we had no way of separating out the autoconsumption component. Market income does include the imputed value of an owner's occupied housing, though.

20. The incidence of international customs tariffs can be estimated in the same way as the incidence of other indirect taxes. However, this chapter does not do so because of time constraints. For property taxes, the cadastral value of property would be required, and this value was not available for this study. Moreover, the empirical tools necessary to undertake incidence analysis of corporate taxes and investment spending are not well established in the literature and were beyond the scope of what could be done in this chapter.

21. As soon as there is more than one intervention, assessing the progressivity of fiscal interventions individually is not sufficient to determine whether they are equalizing (see, for example, Lambert 2002).

22. For more about how vertical equity, reranking, and horizontal inequity are defined and used in the analyses throughout this volume, see chapter 1 as well the work by Enami, Lustig, and Aranda (2017).

23. The Gini coefficient, including all forms of income and social grants but *excluding* free basic services, was 0.69 in 2011 (Stats SA 2014).

24. One element that causes reranking in Brazil is the country's large program of special circumstances pensions, a social safety net designed to help households cope with adverse shocks (such as unemployment, illness, death, and disability). The program is available regardless of household poverty level, and because the size of compensation is determined by the previous labor income of the household, it can lead to larger transfers to nonpoor families.

25. In line with international practice, we exclude the monetary value of education and health services in calculating the impact of fiscal policy on poverty rates

because households are unlikely to be willing to pay as much as the government spends on these services and consequently do not view these services as part of their income.

26. A caveat is in order. For reasons explained in Bibi and Duclos (2010), care should be taken not to attribute effects to individual interventions on the sole basis of the difference between consecutive pairs of indicators. For example, the difference between the Gini coefficients for consumable and disposable income *is not equal to* the contribution of indirect subsidies and indirect taxes to the decline of inequality from market to consumable income. This is simply because the contribution of each intervention is path dependent, and what we are showing is just one of the paths. We *can* compare, however, the impact of interventions on any indicator with respect to market income, which is what we do in this section.

27. Note that students are captured in surveys wherever they find themselves when studying, which sometimes are not the same places as their households of origin. As a result, it may be that some students from very poor households are not actually appearing in the survey as poor.

28. As discussed in chapter 1, this counterintuitive result has been dubbed "Lambert's conundrum" to acknowledge the author's discovery of such a phenomenon (Lambert 2002).

References

Beneke, Margarita, Nora Lustig, and José Andrés Oliva. 2015. "El impacto de los impuestos y el gasto social en la desigualdad y la pobreza en El Salvador." Commitment to Equity Working Paper 26, Center for Inter-American Policy and Research; the Inter-American Dialogue; and Department of Economics, Tulane University, New Orleans, LA.

Bibi, Sami, and Jean-Yves Duclos. 2010. "A Comparison of the Poverty Impact of Transfers, Taxes and Market Income across Five OECD Countries." *Bulletin of Economic Research* 62 (4): 387–406.

Bucheli, Marisa, Nora Lustig, Máximo Rossi, and Florencia Amábile. 2014. "Social Spending, Taxes, and Income Redistribution in Uruguay." *Public Finance Review* 42 (3): 413–33.

Burger, Ronelle, and Christelle Grobler. 2007. "Have Pro-Poor Health Policies Improved the Targeting of Spending and the Effective Delivery of Health Care in South Africa?" Development Policy Research Unit Working Paper 07/122, School of Economics, University of Cape Town, South Africa.

Cabrera, Maynor, Nora Lustig, and Hilcías Morán. 2014. "Fiscal Policy, Inequality, and the Ethnic Divide in Guatemala." Commitment to Equity Working Paper 20, Center for Inter-American Policy and Research; the Inter-American Dialogue; and Department of Economics, Tulane University, New Orleans, LA.

Coady, David. 2008. "The Distributional Impacts of Indirect Tax and Public Pricing Reforms: A Review of Methods and Empirical Evidence." In *Poverty and Social Impact Analysis by the IMF: Review of Methodology and Selected Evidence*, edited by Robert Gillingham, 33–72. Washington DC: International Monetary Fund.

DBE (Department of Basic Education). 2012. *Education Statistics in South Africa 2010.* Pretoria: DBE.

DPME (Department of Planning, Monitoring, and Evaluation). 2013. *Development Indicators 2012.* Statistical report. Pretoria: Presidency of the Republic of South Africa.

Duclos, Jean-Yves, and Abdelkrim Araar. 2006. *Poverty and Equity: Measurement, Policy, and Estimation with DAD.* New York: Springer and International Development Research Centre.

Duclos, Jean-Yves, and Martin Tabi. 1996. "The Measurement of Progressivity, with an Application to Canada." *The Canadian Journal of Economics* 1 (S1): 165–70.

Enami, Ali, Nora Lustig, and Rodrigo Aranda. 2017. "Analytical Foundations: Measuring the Redistributive Impact of Taxes and Transfers." In *The Commitment to Equity Handbook: Estimating the Impact of Fiscal Policy on Inequality and Poverty,* edited by Nora Lustig, chapter 2. Washington, DC: Brookings Institution Press and CEQ Institute, Tulane University. Advance online edition available at http://www.commit mentoequity.org/publications/handbook.php.

Higgins, Sean, and Claudiney Pereira. 2014. "The Effects of Brazil's Taxation and Social Spending on the Distribution of Household Income." *Public Finance Review* 42 (3): 346–67.

Jaramillo, Miguel. 2014. "The Incidence of Social Spending and Taxes in Peru." *Public Finance Review* 42 (3): 391–412.

Lambert, Peter. 2002. *The Distribution and Redistribution of Income.* 3rd ed. Manchester, U.K.: Manchester University Press.

Leibbrandt, Murray, Ingrid Woolard, Arden Finn, and Jonathan Argent. 2010. "Trends in South African Income Distribution and Poverty since the Fall of Apartheid." Organisation for Economic Co-operation and Development (OECD) Social, Employment and Migration Working Paper 101, OECD Publishing, Paris. doi: 10.1787/5kmms0t7p1ms-en.

Lustig, Nora. 2015. "Inequality and Fiscal Redistribution in Middle Income Countries: Brazil, Chile, Colombia, Indonesia, Mexico, Peru and South Africa. Evidence from the Commitment to Equity Project (CEQ)." Commitment to Equity (CEQ) Working Paper 31, CEQ Institute, Tulane University, New Orleans, LA.

———, ed. 2017. *The Commitment to Equity Handbook: Estimating the Impact of Fiscal Policy on Inequality and Poverty.* Washington, DC: Brookings Institution Press and CEQ Institute, Tulane University. Advance online version; available at http://www .commitmentoequity.org/publications/handbook.php.

Lustig, Nora, and Sean Higgins. 2013. "Commitment to Equity Assessment (CEQ): Estimating the Incidence of Social Spending, Subsidies and Taxes." CEQ Working Paper. 1, Center for Inter-American Policy and Research; the Inter-American Dialogue; and Department of Economics, Tulane University, New Orleans, LA.

NPC (National Planning Commission). 2011. "National Development Plan 2030: Our Future—Make It Work." Final NDP document. Pretoria: NPC, Republic of South Africa.

Paz Arauco, Verónica, George Gray Molina, Wilson Jiménez Pozo, and Ernesto Yáñez Aguilar. 2014. "Explaining Low Redistributive Impact in Bolivia." *Public Finance Review* 42 (3): 326–45.

Presidency, Republic of South Africa. 2014. "Twenty-Year Review: South Africa, 1994–2014." Retrospective report, Presidency of the Republic of South Africa, Pretoria.

SACMEQ (Southern and Eastern Africa Consortium for Monitoring Educational Quality). 2011. "Trends in Achievement Levels of Grade 6 Pupils in South Africa." Policy Brief 1, SACMEQ, Paris.

SALDRU (Southern Africa Labour and Development Research Unit). 2014. "National Income Dynamics Study 2008, Wave 1. Version 5.2." Dataset, SALDRU, University of Cape Town School of Economics, Cape Town.

SALGA (South African Local Government Association). 2012. "Analysis of the Current Local Government Equitable Share Formula." Discussion Paper 2, Local Government Equitable Share Formula Review conducted by SALGA, National Treasury of the Republic of South Africa, and the Cooperative Governance Department of the Republic of South Africa, Pretoria.

Sauma, Pablo, and Juan Diego Trejos. 2014. "Social Public Spending, Taxes, Redistribution of Income, and Poverty in Costa Rica." Commitment to Equity Working Paper 18, Center for Inter-American Policy and Research; the Inter-American Dialogue; and Department of Economics, Tulane University, New Orleans, LA.

Scott, John. 2014. "Redistributive Impact and Efficiency of Mexico's Fiscal System." *Public Finance Review* 42 (3): 368–90.

Stats SA (Statistics South Africa). 2012a. "Financial Statistics of Consolidated General Government." Annual statistical release, Stats SA, Pretoria.

———. 2012b. "Income and Expenditure Survey of Households 2010/11." Statistical release P0100, Statistics South Africa, Pretoria.

———. 2014. *Poverty Trends in South Africa: An Examination of Absolute Poverty between 2006 and 2011*. Report 03-10-06. Pretoria: Statistics South Africa.

———. 2015. *Methodological Report on Rebasing of National Poverty Lines and Development of Pilot Provincial Poverty Lines*. Report 03-10-11. Pretoria: Statistics South Africa.

Theil, H. 1967. *Economics and Information Theory*. Chicago: Rand McNally and Company.

Van der Berg, S. 2009. "Fiscal Incidence of Social Spending in South Africa, 2006." Stellenbosch Economic Working Paper 10/09, Department of Economics, Stellenbosch University, South Africa.

Woolard, Ingrid, and Murray Leibbrandt. 2010. "The Evolution and Impact of Unconditional Cash Transfers in South Africa." Working Paper 51, Southern Africa Labour and Development Research Unit, University of Cape Town, South Africa.

Woolard, Ingrid, Charles Simkins, Morné Oosthuizen, and Christopher Woolard. 2005. "Final Report: Tax Incidence Analysis for the Fiscal Incidence Study Being Conducted for National Treasury." Report to National Treasury, Republic of South Africa, Pretoria.

World Bank. 2009. "Levels and Patterns of Safety Net Spending in Developing and Transition Countries." Safety Nets Primer 30, World Bank, Washington, DC.

———. 2012. "South Africa Economic Update: Focus on Inequality of Opportunity." Working Paper 71553, World Bank, Washington, DC.

CHAPTER 9

The Incidence of Taxes and Spending in Sri Lanka

Nisha Arunatilake, Gabriela Inchauste, and Nora Lustig

Introduction

During a surge of economic growth between 2002 and 2012—as Sri Lanka's gross domestic product (GDP) increased by an average of 6.2 percent per year—poverty in the country also declined dramatically. Between 2002 and 2012/13, the headcount poverty rate fell from 22.7 percent to 6.7 percent using national poverty lines (World Bank 2015).

Despite these gains, important development challenges remain, and the country has limited fiscal resources to address them. Although public spending, at 20–25 percent of GDP, is similar to other middle-income countries, this level of spending may not be fiscally sustainable because revenues have been systematically lower than spending and were decreasing. Sustained fiscal deficits of 7–8 percent annually during 2002–12 were driven by increases in public spending that have outpaced revenue growth, leading to significant accumulation of public debt. The government became committed to fiscal consolidation and managed to reduce public spending from 25 percent of GDP in 2009 to 19 percent by 2015, while reducing the budget deficit from 9.9 percent of GDP to 6.5 percent over the same period (World Bank 2015). Given the limited fiscal space, efficiency in spending is critical.

In this context, it is important to evaluate the effectiveness and efficiency of fiscal policy in addressing Sri Lanka's development challenges and accelerating poverty reduction. Specifically, we seek to answer three questions:

• How much redistribution and poverty reduction is accomplished through taxes, social transfers, and subsidies?

We want to thank Neluka Gunasekera, Nipuni Perera, Kaushalya Attygalle, and Jayamini Hewawasam, for excellent research assistance on Sri Lanka, Sean Higgins for useful advice and technical coordination throughout the project, Sandra Martinez for coordination and assistance at the World Bank, and Ali Enami, Nicole Florack, David Roberts, and Xinghao Gong at Tulane for their excellent help in the process of checking the results.

- How progressive are revenue collection and government spending?
- What individual impacts do taxes and transfer policies have on inequality and poverty, given the fiscal resources used?

The main contribution of this analysis is to provide systematic empirical evidence on the progressivity of the fiscal interventions. Although similar studies exist for other countries in the world, this study is the first comprehensive examination of Sri Lanka's fiscal instruments and their ability to redistribute income and reduce poverty. By using a harmonized methodology, this approach allows for comparative analytics with other countries in the region and the world.[1]

The analysis finds that, overall, taxes and social spending were redistributive and poverty-reducing in Sri Lanka in 2009/10, the latest year for which a household survey was available at the time of this analysis. In particular, we find that direct taxes provide a very small contribution to redistributive efforts, while indirect taxes are regressive and unequalizing. On the spending side, direct transfers are absolutely progressive, making their marginal contribution both equalizing and poverty-reducing. However, given the country's relatively low revenue and limited fiscal space, overall social spending was small, leading to limited impacts. Although indirect subsidies are equalizing, they are not an efficient redistributive mechanism, because they benefit higher-income groups more than the bottom of the distribution. Among the in-kind transfers, education spending has the largest redistributive impact, in line with other country studies in low- and middle-income countries (LMICs). This is partly due to high enrollment rates in primary and secondary education.

The rest of the chapter is organized as follows: The next section provides an overview of tax and social spending systems that were implemented by the government of Sri Lanka as of 2009. The chapter then describes the data and assumptions used for each fiscal intervention in the analysis. This is followed by presentation of the redistributive and poverty impacts of Sri Lanka's tax and transfer system as a whole. The chapter then discusses the impact of each of the fiscal interventions analyzed, including their progressivity and the marginal contributions to poverty and inequality reduction. The final section summarizes the findings and their policy implications.

Patterns of Taxes and Social Spending

Tables 9.1 and 9.2 show the breakdown of the major government tax revenue and public spending in 2009 and identify which taxes and transfers were included in the incidence analysis. The country generated total tax revenues amounting to about 12.8 percent of GDP in 2009, which continued to decline to 10.7 percent of GDP in 2014. Sri Lanka now has one of the lowest tax revenue-to-GDP ratios in the world (World Bank 2015).

Total general government spending in Sri Lanka (amounting to about 25 percent of GDP in 2009) is also lower than the average for economies

Table 9.1 Composition of Taxes and Inclusion in Incidence Analysis, Sri Lanka, 2009

Share of GDP, percent

Revenue source	Total	Incidence analysis
Total revenue	14.5	6.1
Taxes	12.8	6.1
Direct taxes	2.9	0.6
Personal income tax	0.6	0.6
Corporate income tax[a]	1.4	n.a.
Tax on interest	0.9	n.a.
Indirect taxes	7.2	5.6
Value added tax	3.5	3.5
Excise taxes	2.0	2.0
Import duties	1.7	n.a.
Other taxes and fees	2.7	n.a.
Nontax revenues	1.7	n.a.

Sources: Column 1: CBSL 2011; Column 2: Based on 2009/10 Household Income and Expenditure Survey (HIES) data.

Note: Total and incidence analysis percentages based on fiscal data. The difference between the second and third columns arises because the numerators in public accounts may differ from those obtained in the survey. The methodology does not necessarily force the two to be equal. GDP = gross domestic product; n.a. = not applicable (not included in incidence analysis).

a. Excludes the withholding tax on Treasury Bill holdings of the Central Bank.

Table 9.2 Composition of Government Spending and Inclusion in Incidence Analysis, Sri Lanka, 2009

Share of GDP, percent

Spending category	Total	Incidence analysis
Total government spending[a]	24.86	5.57
Primary government spending[b]	18.45	5.26
Social spending[c]	6.49	5.26
Total direct transfers	2.00	1.92
Cash transfers (excluding all pensions)	0.55	0.47
Samurdhi[d]	0.19	0.19
Assistance to Disabled Soldiers	0.20	0.20
Free textbooks[e]	0.05	0.05
Nutrition program[e]	0.05	n.a.
School uniforms[e]	0.03	0.03
Other cash transfers	0.04	n.a.
Noncontributory pensions (PSPS)[f]	1.45	1.45
Total in-kind transfers	3.44	3.34
Education	1.94	1.87
Health	1.48	1.48
Flood and drought relief	0.02	n.a.
Other social spending	1.06	n.a.
Contributory pensions[g]	0.35	0.31
Nonsocial spending	11.61	n.a.
Indirect subsidies	1.27	0.74

table continues next page

The Incidence of Taxes and Spending in Sri Lanka

Table 9.2 Composition of Government Spending and Inclusion in Incidence Analysis, Sri Lanka, 2009 (continued)

Spending category	Total	Incidence analysis
Fuel subsidies	0.16	n.a.
Fertilizer subsidy	0.56	0.56
Domestic water	0.03	0.03
Domestic electricity	0.15	0.15
Transport	0.33	n.a.
Other	0.05	n.a.
Other nonsocial spending	10.34	n.a.
Debt servicing	17.08	n.a.
Interest payments (foreign and domestic)	6.40	n.a.
Amortization payments	10.67	n.a.

Source: Column 1: CBSL 2011; Column 2: Based on 2009/10 Household Income and Expenditure Survey (HIES) data.
Note: The difference between second and third columns arises because not all of the expenditure elements in government accounts can be analyzed given the household survey data at hand. GDP = gross domestic product; n.a. = not applicable (not included in the incidence analysis).
a. Total government spending = primary government spending+ interest payments. Amortization payments are accounted for separately (below the "interest payments" line), in line with standard government accounts.
b. Primary government spending = social spending with contributory pensions + nonsocial spending.
c. Social spending = current and capital expenditure on social services, including total cash transfers, total noncontributory pensions, total in-kind transfers, and other social spending. It excludes contributory pensions. "Other social spending" includes small social assistance programs not included in the household survey so were not included in the analysis.
d. The Samurdhi Poverty Alleviation Program is Sri Lanka's flagship cash transfer program, including eight subprograms.
e. Free textbooks and school uniforms are not included in education spending, which has been reduced by a corresponding amount to avoid double counting. Similarly, nutrition programs are not included in health spending.
f. PSPS = Public Service Pension Scheme. This figure also includes gratuity.
g. Contributory pensions include the Social Pension and Social Benefit scheme, the widows/widowers and orphans pension scheme, the public service provident fund, and the farmer's and fisherman's pension scheme.

in LMICs (30 percent of GDP in 2009).[2] The overall fiscal deficit in 2009 amounted to 10 percent of GDP but has since been declining in an effort toward fiscal consolidation. Nonetheless, that revenues have not kept pace with economic growth and have barely kept pace with inflation in absolute terms is a continuing constraint on the budget.

Taxes and Fees
Tax collections in 2009 amounted to 12.8 percent of GDP, of which about 7.2 percent were indirect taxes and fees and the remaining 2.9 percent, direct taxes (table 9.1). The incidence analysis includes personal income, value added, and excise taxes, covering roughly half of tax revenue collection.

Personal Income Tax
Direct taxes include personal income taxes (PIT), corporate income tax, and tax on interest. Personal income is taxed on an incremental basis, with the first SL Rs 500,000 of taxable income being taxed at 4 percent and progressively increasing to a maximum of 35 percent. All taxpayers are required to pay their taxes by self-assessment on a current year basis in quarterly installments.

A pay-as-you-earn (PAYE) scheme applies to employment income: employers deduct taxes at the source. PAYE withholdings are calculated according to tables provided by the revenue authorities. Spouses are taxed separately and taxes are withheld by their respective employers. Income received by one spouse for services rendered in any trade, business, profession, or vocation carried on or exercised by the other spouse, or by a partnership of which that spouse is a partner, is deemed to be income of that other spouse. In the past, contributions to approved provident or pension funds and donations to approved charities were tax-deductible up to either one-third of the individual's assessable income or SL Rs 75,000, whichever was lower. However, this relief was withdrawn in April 2011 such that neither charitable donations nor provident or pension fund contributions are tax-deductible.

Although this analysis includes PIT, it does not include the corporate income tax and taxes on interest because methods are not well developed enough to apportion the burden of these taxes across the relevant households.

Indirect Taxes

Among indirect taxes, the most important is the value added tax (VAT), making up about one-third of total revenue collection. The standard VAT in 2009 was 12 percent on goods and services. All goods and services are subject to VAT except for telecommunication services, educational services, locally manufactured briquettes and pallets using biomass wastes, locally developed software, and goods and services provided to foreign-funded infrastructure.

In addition, selective sales (or excise) taxes, including taxes on cigarettes, liquor, and motor vehicles, amounted to 2 percent of GDP in 2009. The tax rates vary by the type of product and were increased in 2012 (Sri Lanka, Ministry of Finance and Planning 2012). For purposes of this analysis using 2009 data, however, the 2009 tax rates were as follows:

- *Alcohol:* SL Rs 85 per bulk liter for malt, SL Rs 778 per proof liter for wine or liquor made out of any cereal, and SL Rs 1,063 per proof liter for foreign spirits
- *Tobacco:* SL Rs 4,000 per kilogram net weight for cigars and SL Rs 16,400 per 1,000 for cigarettes exceeding 84 millimeters in length
- *Motor vehicles:* 8 percent for hybrid motor vehicles with a vehicle cylinder capacity below 2,000 and 138 percent for diesel cars with a vehicle cylinder capacity above 2,500
- *Petroleum:* SL Rs 2.50 per liter of diesel and SL Rs 25 per liter of gasoline (Sri Lanka, Ministry of Finance and Planning 2010)

Gasoline and diesel prices have been set administratively since at least 1990—in the case of diesel, usually below the global benchmark diesel price.[3] The impact of fixing the price exceeded the impact of the excise, which means that there was a net subsidy of approximately SL Rs 3 per liter. Although the implicit subsidy is not an explicit fiscal expenditure, it has led to losses at the state-owned petroleum importer and thus to capital infusions by the government, making it an effective fiscal burden (Sri Lanka, Ministry of Finance 2016, 172). However, the analysis of the impact of taxes and spending only focuses on the incidence of the petroleum excise by the central government and does not take into account the impact of the implicit subsidy conferred by the gasoline importer.

In addition to VAT and excise taxes, Sri Lanka charges import duties and fees at the border on imported goods. These amounted to 1.7 percent of GDP in 2009. Finally, other smaller taxes and levies jointly contributed less than 3 percent of GDP.[4]

Government Spending

Total government spending in 2009 amounted to about 25 percent of GDP in 2009 (table 9.2). Interest payments were 6.4 percent of GDP, highlighting the heavy debt burden that Sri Lanka carried at the time. Total primary spending was 18.5 percent of GDP, making up about one-third of primary spending, (6.5 percent of GDP) of which 3.4 percent of GDP was dedicated to in-kind transfers including health and education, and about 2 percent of GDP was spent on direct cash transfers. In addition, there were relatively large outlays for Public Service Pension Scheme (PSPS), amounting to about 1.5 percent of GDP, while spending on contributory pensions amounted to 0.4 percent of GDP.

Direct Transfers and Noncontributory Pensions

Direct transfers include the flagship program, Samurdhi, and several smaller transfer programs as well as the noncontributory pension program, the PSPS. Total spending on direct transfers amounts to 2 percent of GDP, as detailed below.

Noncontributory Pensions. The noncontributory PSPS is the largest pension scheme in operation for permanent public sector employees who have completed at least 10 years of service. The pension received by each employee depends on his or her last drawn salary and years of service. Employees in service for 10 years receive 40 percent of their final salary, while employees in service for more than 10 years receive 90 percent of their salary. Civil servants are eligible for a pension at the age of 55 (men) or 50 (women) or, at the latest, by the age of 60. Transfers are not adjusted for inflation over time.

Samurdhi Poverty Alleviation Program. The flagship cash transfer program in Sri Lanka is the Samurdhi Poverty Alleviation Program is a means-tested program, which revolves around poverty cushioning through eight subprograms including an income support scheme, an insurance scheme, and social development programs—collectively amounting to spending of about

0.2 percent of GDP in 2009. The Samurdhi subprograms include the following:

- *Income support:* an unconditional monthly cash transfer to women with children[5]
- *Social security fund:* cash transfers at important events, including the death of any household member, the birth of the first or second child, and during illness[6]
- *Nutrition food package program:* a monthly voucher that can be used for food purchases for a period of 20 months to both pregnant and lactating mothers
- *Nutrition allowance program:* a monthly voucher to lactating mothers of beneficiary families during the period of 12 months following birth[7]
- *Kerosene subsidy:* a monthly payment of SL Rs 100 to Samurdhi beneficiaries who lack electricity in their homes
- *Dry ration stamp:* stamps to purchase goods, issued to families displaced because of the Sri Lankan civil war that ended in 2009 in the north and east
- *Glass of Milk Program*: a stamp to provide a glass of milk per day for children aged 2–5 years of beneficiary households
- *Sipdora scholarship program*: SL Rs 500 per month to the children of Samurdhi beneficiaries (20 from each divisional secretariat) with the highest scores in the General Certificate of Education (Ordinary Level) examination.

A recent evaluation of Samurdhi found the program has a positive and significant impact on both short-run and long-run welfare of households, especially in the areas of consumption, education, and income (Thibbotuwawa et al. 2012). As for nutrition, however, the Samurdhi grants cover only about 10 percent of household expenditure and hence are unlikely to be effective in raising the nutrition standards of beneficiary households (Gunatilaka et al. 1997).

Other Direct Transfers
Other direct transfer programs include the following:

- *Assistance to Disabled Soldiers:* cash transfers to disabled soldiers and to the families of soldiers who passed away during the Sri Lankan Civil War
- *Transfers to schoolchildren:* cash transfers in the form of bursary and scholarship allowances to needy children, provision of free textbooks and uniforms, and spending on nutritional programs for children in underprivileged areas
- *Transfers to university students:* bursary payments to needy students
- *Poshana Manpetha Program:* fresh milk to children aged 2–5 years[8]
- *Transfers to internally displaced persons:* cash transfers to households displaced because of the Sri Lankan Civil War or the 2004 Indian Ocean tsunami disaster
- *Additional transfers:* cash and in-kind transfers, usually targeting vulnerable groups of the poorer sections of society (including expectant mothers, disabled people, handicapped students, and the elderly), and assistance programs provided through provincial councils

In-Kind Transfers

Spending on in-kind transfers, amounting to 3.5 percent of GDP in 2009, include spending on health, education, and flood and drought relief. Incidence analysis was undertaken for both health and education—the areas that cover the largest share of in-kind spending.

Education Spending. Sri Lanka provides free public education through the 13th grade.[9] Shortly after gaining independence from British rule in 1948, the government took extensive measures to make this provision accessible and compulsory for as many children as possible, regardless of income. As a result of this decades-long commitment to education, primary education attendance is essentially universal; secondary school attendance is also high by middle-income standards; and secondary completion rates saw a major increase between 2002 and 2013, reaching about 60 percent of the target population.

Education is provided mainly by the state, but private schools and privenas (religious institutions where monks receive general education) also provide education in Sri Lanka. All local schools in Sri Lanka prepare students for the Ordinary Level examination, which then qualifies them to sit for the Advanced Level examination. Obtaining the required z-score (calculated using test results of students for that particular year) on this examination ensures that students are eligible to apply for free tertiary education at a Sri Lankan university (for which students are required to pay a small registration fee of about SL Rs 500 per semester).

In the tertiary education sphere, all universities in operation are state-held establishments, including one Open University run by the state. In addition, a few institutions not bearing the title "university" offer degrees for a fee; almost all of these institutions are affiliated with foreign universities. Sri Lanka has 14 conventional universities (excluding the Open University of Sri Lanka). Nearly 63 percent of students who sit for the Advanced Level examination are deemed eligible to enter these universities, but only around 16 percent of these students are admitted.

The government of Sri Lanka is the sole funder of education in public schools and universities in Sri Lanka. Although public education up to the first-degree level (college up through a bachelor's degree) has been state-funded for decades, public spending on education has amounted to less than 3 percent of the country's GDP between 2000 and 2010 and even less than 2 percent between 2010 and 2014. Despite public demand to increase public expenditure on education, these levels continue to be constrained in part by relatively low revenue collections.

Health Spending. Health care services in Sri Lanka are provided by both the public and private sectors. Public health care is provided to everyone free of charge, and citizens can access free medicine and health services at government hospitals and dispensaries around the country. The Killinochchi, Mannar, Vavauniya, and Mullativu districts in the Northern Province had the fewest government hospitals in 2007 compared with other provinces in the country.

Public health care services are managed by the Ministry of Health, Nutrition & Indigenous Medicine, which is the central body in control. The provincial Ministries of Health control health care services within the limits of each province. Beginning in the early 2000s, however, the Ministry of Health assumed centralized control of several provincial and district hospitals.

General government spending on health fell from 2 percent to 1.4 percent of GDP between 2006 and 2013. In 2009, government expenditure on health amounted to 1.5 percent of GDP, or 5.9 percent of total public expenditure. This is low relative to other middle-income countries, particularly given the rising costs of health care associated with the aging population in Sri Lanka (World Bank 2015). As a result, private expenditure on health care is very high, amounting to 56 percent of total expenditure on health in 2008. Almost 90 percent of private spending on health care is out-of-pocket spending, while only 10 percent comes from insurance schemes and other private sources.

Flood and Drought Relief. Finally, flood and drought relief includes assistance in the form of dry rations and financial assistance for flood and drought victims. Spending on this assistance constitutes a relatively small share of all social spending, amounting to only 0.02 percent of GDP in 2009.

Contributory Pensions

Contributory pension schemes have low coverage and are relatively small. These pensions, which are nontaxable, are the following:

- *Social Pension and Social Security Benefit Scheme:* Any person not entitled to a noncontributory government pension is eligible to enroll for this pension scheme. The monthly pension received by an individual depends on the age at enrollment. Members are required to make monthly contributions for a minimum number of years that vary according to the age of enrollment. The monthly pension upon retirement ranges from SL Rs 1,000 to SL Rs 8,000. Formerly known as the Pension Scheme for the Self-Employed (now expanded to cover all those who do not receive a government pension), this scheme has lower coverage than others because workers' reluctance to enroll (also seen in other pension schemes) due to their inability to pay a combined worker and employer contribution.
- *Widows/Widowers and Orphans Pension Scheme (W&OPS):* This scheme ensures that if government employees have been contributing to the W&OPS (4–7 percent of employee's wages) during their time of employment, upon their demise, the pension benefits from the PSPS will be received by their dependents.
- *Public Service Provident Fund:* This fund was set up for the benefit of public sector employees who receive a monthly income but are not eligible for a noncontributory pension. Employees contribute 8 percent of their salary, while the government contributes 12 percent each month. The employee is entitled to withdraw the accumulated funds upon retirement.

- *Farmer's Pension Scheme and Fisherman's Pension Scheme:* In both schemes, the contributions are fixed according to the age at enrollment and range from SL Rs 260 (enrolled at age 18) to SL Rs 1,380 (enrolled at age 59). Depending on the enrollment age, retired farmers and fishermen receive a monthly pension between SL Rs 1,000 and SL Rs 4,167. The farming community makes up 25–30 percent of the workforce, and the fishing community comprises of 1 percent of the workforce.

One of the main problems arising in these pension schemes is low, ineffective coverage. However, the schemes set up for the informal sector collectively cover approximately 80 percent of the sector, which is high for South Asia (Gaminiratne 2004).

Indirect Subsidies

The government of Sri Lanka provides price subsidies on key commodities to targeted households to reduce the cost of living. The following subsidies were provided in 2011/12:

- *Fertilizer:* Subsidized rates for fertilizer have been available since 1962 intermittently. The subsidy was not given during 1990–94 but was reintroduced in 1995 for all three types of fertilizer (nitrogen, phosphorus, and potassium). From 1997 to 2005, the subsidy was limited to urea. Since 2005, the subsidy was again extended to cover all three main types of fertilizer according to a fixed price scheme: it started with subsidies to paddy cultivation and tea plantations in 2005 but has extended to all crops since 2011. The government has borne an increasing share of fertilizer cost in the form of subsidies. In 2011, the government subsidies for urea, triple superphosphate, and muriate of potash were 85 percent, 86 percent, and 90 percent of total fertilizer cost per 50 kilograms, respectively.

- *Petroleum:* The government provides fuel subsidies to households that lack access to electricity as well as for fishing boats. In 2009, fuel subsidy expenditures amounted to 0.16 percent of GDP.

- *Electricity:* Consumers pay subsidized prices for electricity according to their level of consumption. The gross electricity subsidy is spread out among household consumption, industries, hotels, street lighting, government hospitals, schools, and religious places. Of these, household consumption and industries received the largest share of subsidies, amounting to 50 percent and 42 percent of total electricity subsidies, respectively. Domestic electricity subsidies amounted to 0.15 percent of GDP in 2009.

- *Water:* Households can receive a subsidized rate for water depending on their consumption level. Of the households with access to pipe-borne water and consumption of 25 units, 89 percent receive water at subsidized prices. Domestic water subsidies amounted to 0.03 percent of GDP in 2009.

- *Transport:* The government provides reduced railway fares and bus transport facilities through season tickets for schoolchildren. In 2009, the Ceylon Transport Board (CTB) and the Ceylon Government Railway (CGR) incurred operational losses that translated into a subsidy amounting to 0.33 percent of GDP (SL Rs 15.6 per kilometer for CTB and SL Rs 0.54 per kilometer for CGR) (Sri Lanka, Ministry of Finance and Planning 2009, 58).

Data and Assumptions

Data

The main data source used throughout this analysis is the Household Income and Expenditure Survey (HIES), produced by the Department of Census Statistics between July 2009 and June 2010. The survey has national coverage and is representative at the provincial level, collecting data on all household members as well as on household assets, including cultivated land.

The survey contains information on consumption and self-consumption, fringe benefits, imputed rents, remittances, direct taxes, and contributions to social security. Although it also includes data on pensions, it does not differentiate between the contributory and noncontributory programs. It also identifies households benefiting from the Samurdhi program, disability relief payments, food transfers, and the use of public education. Finally, although HIES provides information on the use of health facilities, it does not differentiate between public and private facilities.

Assumptions

To carry out the incidence analysis, we construct the income concepts described in chapter 1, starting from the official aggregate of households' per capita consumption in the 2009/10 HIES. We count as "disposable income" a household's total reported consumption.

Market Income

To create "market income," we subtract from "disposable income" direct monetary transfers and near-cash transfers and add direct taxes. Regarding the transfers, the 2009/10 HIES directly identifies Samurdhi beneficiary households and reports disability or relief payments to disabled soldiers, assistance to internally displaced persons, flood and drought relief, and public assistance through provincial councils. We also impute the value of free textbooks and school uniforms.

The Commitment to Equity (CEQ) framework (Lustig and Higgins 2013b; Lustig 2017) distinguishes between contributory and noncontributory pensions because, in some countries, contributory pensions are funded by the household's own (prior) savings in the form of social security contributions rather than by general government revenues. Separating these concepts out in the case of Sri Lanka was challenging because the HIES questionnaire does not explicitly identify beneficiaries as having contributory pensions as opposed to noncontributory pensions.

However, the questionnaire gathers detailed information about "social groups" to which individual household members belong that would entitle them to certain benefits. Among these is a set of "pensioner" individual characteristics to impute the likely beneficiaries of each type of pension.

Given the characteristics of the pension system in Sri Lanka, we assume that both the PSPS and contributory pensions come closest to being a savings plan in which a share of income is accumulated during active years.[10] Therefore, pensions are treated as part of lifetime earnings and included as part of market income (the pretax, pretransfer income on which the incidence analysis is based).

As for direct taxes, the HIES does not ask about taxes paid, so we must simulate these values. We assume that formal sector employees and self-employed workers pay statutory PIT rates and mandatory retirement savings in the social security system where appropriate. We do not distinguish between formal and informal employment.

Consumable Income

To calculate "consumable income," we return to our "disposable income" measure, subtract indirect taxes paid, and add indirect subsidies.

The VAT system in Sri Lanka has three rates: some goods and services have a zero tax rate, others a standard tax rate (12 percent), and some a luxury tax rate (20 percent). However, the goods belonging to each category can be directly identified in the 2009/10 HIES. Although there is likely some informality (e.g., purchases in rural areas and informal markets are more likely not to pay VAT), it is impossible to know from the HIES whether a household bought something from a firm that pays VAT. Further, in a standard competitive model, prices at firms that do not pay VAT would be the same as those at VAT-paying firms, with the benefits of nonpayment going to the firms' owners rather than the customers. Households suffer the incidence of the tax regardless of the tax status of the seller, though not all the benefits go to the fisc; some are captured by small-business owners. As such, we use an effective tax rate (rather than the statutory tax rate), which is applied to all households.[11]

Excise duties are the most complicated of the indirect taxes in Sri Lanka, with different rates depending on the type of product. These values were imputed by proportionately dividing the petroleum, tobacco, and alcohol excise taxes collected by the government according to the percentage of petroleum, tobacco, and alcohol expenditure share by market income deciles from the survey.

For indirect subsidies, we can identify and estimate water, electricity, and fertilizer subsidies as follows:

- *Water subsidies:* Based on the domestic tariff structure, we estimate total units consumed by households in HIES because the HIES survey provides the total amount of the water bill, not units consumed. We then compare this to the total cost per unit of water produced to estimate the amount of water subsidies per household. We calculate water subsidies separately for Samurdhi recipients and non-Samurdhi recipients and then aggregate these to get a total value.

- *Electricity subsidies:* Similarly, based on the domestic tariff structure from the Ceylon Electricity Board, we estimate total units consumed by households in HIES because the HIES survey provides the total amount of the electricity bill, not units consumed. We then apply the total cost per unit of electricity produced and estimate the amount of electricity subsidies.
- *Fertilizer subsidies:* We first identified eligible households in the HIES, because the fertilizer subsidy is only given to paddy farmers not exceeding 4.942 acres. Using the total land area identified in the survey as the eligibility criterion for the subsidy, we worked out the unit cost of subsidy received by an acre of cultivated, subsidy-eligible land and distributed the total subsidy to eligible households accordingly.

Final Income

To calculate "final income," we add to "consumable income" the in-kind transfers associated with public provision of education and health care. We did not subtract copayments or fees from these values. Both schools and health care facilities manage their own budgets. The state supports these institutions with transfers based on the numbers of students and types of school, the numbers of patients and types of facilities and procedures, and so on.

For schooling, we use information from the Ministry of Education for each type of school and divide by the number of students in those schools, at a national level. For health, we distinguish between inpatient and outpatient services according to information in the survey. The total annualized health benefit received by an individual (unit cost) is estimated as the total public expenditure for a health care service divided by the total number of individuals receiving that service according to the HIES. Then the total annualized benefit of health care services for the population is estimated by summing over all individuals in the country.

Overall Impact of Fiscal Policy on Poverty and Inequality

In what follows, we report the results of this analysis. It is important to note that in the results presented here, both contributory pensions and the (noncontributory) pensions to longtime civil servants are included in market (prefiscal) income. Essentially, this implies that pensions are treated as deferred income.

The net impact of fiscal policy is equalizing and poverty-reducing, with the poorest deciles receiving more benefits relative to their market income than what they pay out (figure 9.1). This result occurs primarily from the impact of spending on in-kind transfers in the form of education, given that spending per pupil is a relatively large share of the market incomes of the poorest deciles. As a result, household income, once taxes and transfers have been taken into account ("final income"), is slightly better distributed than before the influence of fiscal policy.

Figure 9.1 Incidence of Taxes and Transfers, by Income Concept and Decile, in Sri Lanka, 2009/10

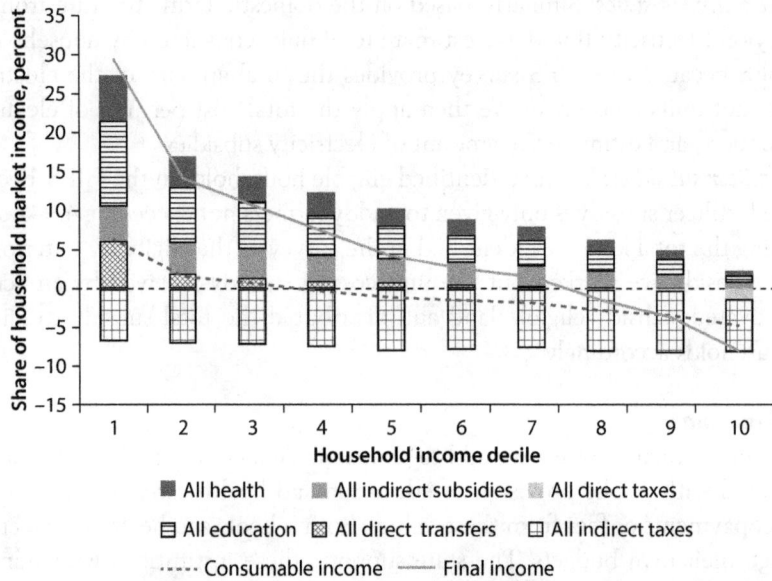

Source: Based on 2009/10 Household Income and Expenditure Survey (HIES) data.
Note: "Market income" comprises pretax wages, salaries, income earned from capital assets (rent, interest, or dividends), and private transfers. Here, both contributory and noncontributory pensions are included in market income. "Consumable income" = market income – direct and indirect taxes + direct cash transfers + indirect subsidies. "Final income" = consumable income + in-kind transfers.

When focusing on the net cash position of households (consumable income), the results show that all but the bottom 30 percent were net payers to the government.

Impact on Inequality

Fiscal policy makes a substantial contribution to reducing market-income inequality in Sri Lanka (table 9.3), reducing the market-income Gini coefficient from 0.372 to 0.344 when all taxes (PIT, payroll taxes, VAT, excise taxes, and the fuel levy) and transfers (cash transfers and the monetized value of education and health) are taken into account. If one excludes the monetized value of education and health services, the Gini coefficient still falls from the initial level of 0.372 for market income to 0.360 for consumable income (i.e., after taxes and cash transfers).

How did Sri Lanka compare in terms of fiscal redistribution relative to other middle-income countries at the end of 2010? As shown in table 9.3, the reduction in the consumable-income Gini relative to the market-income Gini was lower in Sri Lanka than in the other countries included in our sample that have similar GDP per capita. (For comparisons of all the CEQ sample countries in terms of fiscal redistribution, see chapter 1.) These relatively small changes in inequality are partly related to the smaller size of government in Sri Lanka than

Table 9.3 Inequality and Poverty Indicators in Sri Lanka, by Income Concept, 2010

Indicator type	Market income[a]	Disposable income[b]	Consumable income[c]	Final income[d]
Inequality indicators				
Gini coefficient[e]	0.3719	0.3646	0.3598	0.3435
Theil index[f]	0.2863	0.2743	0.2690	0.2473
90/10 ratio[g]	4.4892	4.3521	4.2414	3.9180
Headcount poverty indicators				
National poverty line (%)[h]	9.6	8.7	9.6	n.a.
Food poverty line (%)	2.3	1.9	2.0	n.a.
US$1.25 per day 2005 PPP (%)	0.7	0.3	0.4	n.a.
US$2.50 per day 2005 PPP (%)	9.8	8.5	8.9	n.a.
US$4.00 per day 2005 PPP (%)	35.9	34.6	35.7	n.a.

Source: Based on 2009/10 Household Income and Expenditure Survey (HIES) data.
Note: PPP = purchasing power parity; n.a. = not applicable (not included in the analysis).
a. "Market income" comprises pretax wages, salaries, income earned from capital assets (rent, interest, or dividends), and private transfers. Here, both contributory and noncontributory pensions are included in market income.
b. "Disposable income" = market income − personal income taxes and social security contributions + direct cash transfers.
c. "Consumable income" = disposable income − indirect (sales and excise) taxes + indirect subsidies.
d. "Final income" = consumable income + in-kind transfers for education and health care. Poverty rates are not calculated by final income because households may not be aware of the amounts spent on their behalf and may not value this spending as much as a direct cash transfer. Hence, the analysis does not assume that this spending improves their welfare by a corresponding amount.
e. The Gini coefficient measures the equality of income distribution, ranging from zero (perfect equality) to one (maximal inequality).
f. The Theil index, a measurement of economic inequality and other economic phenomena, is a member of the family of generalized entropy inequality measures (Theil 1967).
g. The 90/10 ratio measures how the relatively rich fare compare with the relatively poor. It is calculated as the average income of those in the 90th percentile divided by the average income of those in the 10th percentile (Lustig and Higgins 2013b).
h. The national poverty line in 2010 was defined by the value that affords consumption of a minimal nutritional intake (2,030 kilocalories) per day per adult.

in other middle-income countries. More important, however, is the fact that the kinds of taxes and transfers that could make the biggest difference were relatively small.

Impact on Poverty

When using the US$2.50-per-day international per capita poverty line, the incidence of poverty before taxes and transfers in Sri Lanka was 9.8 percent in 2010, but this rate declined to 8.9 percent after the impact of direct and indirect taxes and transfers (table 9.3).[12] Following convention, this analysis refrains from calculating poverty rates after in-kind transfers because households may not be aware of the actual amount spent on their behalf and may not value this spending as much as they would value a direct cash transfer. As a result, the analysis does not assume that this spending improves their welfare by a corresponding amount. Regardless of the poverty line being used, the analysis shows that taxes and transfers slightly reduce the incidence of poverty (table 9.3).

However, some people are made worse off by the fiscal system. The fiscal transition matrix (table 9.4) measures the share of households that have moved

Table 9.4 Fiscal Transitions in Sri Lanka, 2009/10

Percentage

Market income[a] group (y, US$)	Consumable income[b] group (y, US$)						Horizontal sum	Share of population
	y < 1.25	1.25 ≤ y < 2.50	2.50 ≤ y < 4.00	4.00 ≤ y < 10.00	10.00 ≤ y < 50.00	50.00 ≤ y		
y < 1.25	81	18	1	0	0	0	100	5
1.25 ≤ y < 2.50	2	95	3	0	0	0	100	34
2.50 ≤ y < 4.00	0	8	91	1	0	0	100	31
4.00 ≤ y < 10.00	0	0	9	90	0	0	100	26
10.00 ≤ y < 50.00	0	0	0	11	89	0	100	4
50.00 ≤ y	0	0	0	0	16	84	100	0

Source: Based on 2009/10 Household Income and Expenditure Survey (HIES) data.

Note: The transition matrix measures the share of households that moved into different income groups after taxes and direct transfers are taken into account (not including in-kind health and education). All income groups stated in terms of U.S. dollars per person per day (in 2005 PPP terms). Shaded cells show the percentage of each market-income group that remained in the same income category when defined by consumable income (after taxes, transfers, and subsidies).

a. "Market income" comprises pretax wages, salaries, income earned from capital assets (rent, interest, or dividends), and private transfers. In this analysis, both contributory and noncontributory pensions are included in market income.

b. "Consumable income" = market income − direct and indirect taxes + direct cash transfers + indirect subsidies.

into different income groups after taxes and direct transfers (not including in-kind health and education).[13] What is clear is that despite the improvement in the poverty headcount with the intervention of fiscal policy, as much as 8 percent of households that were above the US$2.50-a-day poverty line before fiscal intervention become poor in cash terms. This is because the benefits delivered through direct transfers and indirect subsidies are not enough to compensate for the indirect taxes being paid by these households.

Progressivity, Marginal Contributions, and Pro-Poorness of Taxes and Transfers

As shown above, the combined effect of taxes and social spending in Sri Lanka is equalizing and poverty-reducing. Still to be assessed, however, are *which* components of the fiscal system are equalizing, *which* ones are unequalizing, and to what extent?

As discussed in Lustig (2017) and summarized in the chapter 1, in a world with more than one fiscal intervention, standard progressivity measures (such as Kakwani coefficients)[14] are insufficient to determine whether a particular intervention exercises an equalizing or unequalizing force. As a result, to measure the contribution of a particular fiscal intervention (or combinations of them), we have opted to use the marginal contributions.

Recall that the marginal contribution to the redistributive effect of a particular fiscal intervention is measured as the difference in the Gini for the income concept without that intervention and the Gini with the intervention. For example, if one wants to calculate the marginal contribution of VAT to the observed change from the market-income Gini to the consumable-income Gini, one must take the difference between the Gini coefficient of consumable income with and without the VAT. If the VAT is equalizing (unequalizing), this difference shall be positive (negative).

The marginal contributions of each individual fiscal intervention are analyzed here within conventional broad categories such as direct taxes, direct transfers, indirect taxes, education, and health (table 9.5). The marginal contributions are shown for the "cash" portion of the fiscal system (cash transfers, direct taxes, and indirect taxes and subsidies) as well as for the noncash portion (in-kind education and health benefits). The results show that although direct taxes and transfers are progressive and equalizing, indirect taxes are unequalizing. As described in detail below, both indirect subsidies and in-kind transfers are also equalizing, with the relative impact of in-kind transfers in the form of education being most important.

Table 9.5 Marginal Contribution of Taxes and Transfers to Inequality and Poverty Reduction in Sri Lanka, 2009/10

Type of fiscal intervention	Size[a] (%)	Concentration coefficient[b]	Kakwani coefficient[c]	Redistributive effect[e] (change, Gini points)	Poverty reduction effect[f] (headcount change, pp)
				Marginal contribution[d]	
Total from market to consumable income				0.0074	0.0126
Direct taxes and contributions					
Personal income tax	0.45	0.9171	0.5458	0.0025	0.0000
Contributory pensions	0.55	0.6597	0.2884	0.0017	−0.0004
Direct transfers	0.63	−0.3859	0.7572	0.0044	0.0088
Samurdhi payment[g]	0.40	−0.4163	0.7876	0.0031	0.0062
Disability payment	0.11	−0.6061	0.9775	0.0008	0.0014
Free textbooks	0.07	−0.0801	0.4514	0.0003	0.0007
Free uniforms	0.04	−0.0801	0.4514	0.0002	0.0005
Indirect taxes and subsidies					
Indirect subsidies	2.03	0.0658	0.3056	0.0057	0.0127
Water subsidy	0.28	0.1873	0.1840	0.0005	0.0011
Electricity subsidy	0.89	0.0672	0.3041	0.0026	0.0053
Fertilizer subsidy	0.86	0.0245	0.3468	0.0025	0.0050
Indirect taxes	7.42	0.3650	−0.0063	−0.0003	−0.0220
VAT	4.40	0.3258	−0.0456	−0.0016	−0.0172
Tobacco excise	1.20	0.3438	−0.0275	−0.0008	−0.0029
Liquor excise	0.91	0.4094	0.0381	0.0000	−0.0022
Petroleum excise[h]	0.90	0.5391	0.1678	0.0016	−0.0009
Total from market to final income				0.0278	0.0278
Direct taxes	0.00	0.0000	0.5458	0.0025	0.0000
Direct transfers	0.63	−0.3859	0.7572	0.0041	0.0066
Indirect subsidies	2.03%	0.0658	0.3056	0.0051	0.0087

table continues next page

The Distributional Impact of Taxes and Transfers • http://dx.doi.org/10.1596/978-1-4648-1091-6

Table 9.5 Marginal Contribution of Taxes and Transfers to Inequality and Poverty Reduction in Sri Lanka, 2009/10 *(continued)*

Type of fiscal intervention	Size[a] (%)	Concentration coefficient[b]	Kakwani coefficient[c]	Marginal contribution[d]	
				Redistributive effect[e] (change, Gini points)	Poverty reduction effect[f] (headcount change, pp)
Indirect taxes	7.42	0.3650	−0.0063	0.0006	−0.0122
In-kind transfers	4.84	0.0480	0.3916	0.3916	0.0358
Education	3.18	−0.0179	0.3892	0.0105	0.0233
All except tertiary	2.65	−0.0801	0.4514	0.0108	0.0227
Tertiary	0.53	0.2937	0.0776	−0.0003	0.0003
Health	1.65	−0.0250	0.3963	0.0056	0.0112

Source: Based on 2009/10 Household Income and Expenditure Survey (HIES) data.

Note: "Market income" comprises pretax wages, salaries, income earned from capital assets (rent, interest, or dividends), and private transfers. Here, both contributory and noncontributory pensions are included in market income. "Consumable income" = market income − direct and indirect taxes + direct cash transfers + indirect subsidies. "Final income" = consumable income + in-kind transfers for education and health care. pp = percentage points; VAT = value added tax.

a. "Size" refers to the ratio of the amount collected or spent divided by total market income.

b. The concentration coefficient, also called a quasi-Gini, is a measure of the proportion of total program benefits (of a particular program or aggregate category) received by the poorest *p* percent of the population. Spending is considered regressive whenever the concentration coefficient is higher than the Gini for market income.

c. The Kakwani coefficient is calculated by subtracting the concentration coefficient from the market-income Gini; progressive interventions have positive Kakwani coefficients, and regressive ones have negative coefficients (Kakwani 1977).

d. The "marginal contribution" equals the difference between the Gini coefficient of the relevant ending income concept without the intervention in question and the Gini coefficient of the relevant ending income concept (which, of course, includes that intervention). By definition, the sum of the marginal contributions does not fulfill the adding-up principle, so it will not be equal to the redistributive effect unless by coincidence.

e. The "redistributive effect" equals the difference between the market-income Gini and the relevant ending income concept Gini. The change is measured in Gini points.

f. The "poverty reduction effect" is based on the poverty headcount index using the poverty line of US$2.50 per day in 2005 purchasing power parity (PPP).

g. The Samurdhi Poverty Alleviation Program is Sri Lanka's flagship cash transfer program and includes eight subprograms.

h. Estimates only take into account the impact of the petroleum excise tax. The impact on poverty and inequality of the implicit petroleum subsidy (from the fixing of retail prices below global market prices) likely had the opposite effect, given that the implicit subsidy exceeded the petroleum excise, from which richer households benefit disproportionately.

Taxes

Our findings show that direct taxes are progressive and equalizing. The PIT burden is highest for the top decile, while the bottom 50 percent of the income distribution pays little or nothing. As a result, the wealthiest 20 percent of households contribute 95 percent of all PIT, with the top income decile contributing 87 percent of the total alone. In contrast, the fifth through eighth deciles jointly contribute only 5 percent of the total. Although PIT is progressive (with a Kakwani coefficient of 0.546), total revenue collection was only 0.6 percent of GDP, and it makes up less than 0.5 percent of household market income (table 9.5), so that its redistributive effect is limited (having a marginal contribution to redistribution of 0.004).

In contrast, we find that indirect taxes are slightly regressive, unequalizing, and poverty-increasing. In particular, the VAT has a negative marginal contribution to the redistributive effort (table 9.5), implying that it is unequalizing, because it taxes a higher share of the pretax income of the poorest deciles. This is because VAT taxes everyone the same amount on the purchase of goods or services, regardless of household income. Moreover, on its own, VAT has a poverty-increasing effect, raising the US$2.50 per day PPP poverty headcount rate by 2 percentage points (table 9.5).

The same is true for excise taxes: excises on tobacco are slightly regressive and unequalizing, and all excises are poverty-increasing. Note that the purpose of alcohol and tobacco excise taxes is to reduce the consumption of these goods because, in the long run, poor households could end up being poorer due to poor health. As such, the short-term redistributive efforts need to be weighed against longer-term human development objectives.

By contrast, the petroleum excise by itself reduces inequality (as the richer households consume more gasoline) but still increases the burden on the poor. However, this does not take into account the fact that richer households also benefit disproportionately from the implicit subsidy on petroleum due to the fixing of retail prices below global market prices. In 2009, this implicit subsidy exceeded the petroleum excise. As noted before, this analysis does not take into account this implicit subsidy.

Government Spending

Ideally, the slightly progressive nature of taxes would be complemented by social spending that would magnify the progressivity of fiscal policy. However, given the very low revenue collections and the associated concerns for fiscal sustainability, there is little room for spending in general in Sri Lanka. Indeed, low revenue collection has led to continued efforts to reduce the deficit through spending cuts. Unfortunately, this has included cuts to social spending that is progressive and equalizing.

Direct Transfers

In particular, spending on direct transfers has fallen from 0.87 percent of GDP in 2001 to less than 0.5 percent of GDP in 2012. Total expenditures on Samurdhi—Sri Lanka's flagship antipoverty program—fell from 0.87 percent to 0.14 percent of GDP between 2001 and 2012 (figure 9.2). Indeed, if the size of the Samurdhi program had not declined but had instead remained unchanged from 2002 to 2009/10, poverty would have been 1.5 percentage points lower, leading to about a 10 percent greater reduction in poverty (Ceriani, Inchauste, and Olivieri 2015).

Consistent with this result, we find that Samurdhi is both progressive and pro-poor, benefiting the poorest deciles more than the top deciles in relation to their market income but also in per capita terms.[15] Indeed, 27 percent of all Samurdhi spending benefits the bottom decile, and up to 70 percent of total Samurdhi spending benefits the bottom 40 percent of the distribution. However, total spending on Samurdhi is small, amounting to only 3.5 percent of the poorest decile's market income. In addition, not only is spending on the transfer small, but its targeting could be much more effective to make it even more progressive

Figure 9.2 Share of GDP Spent on Samurdhi and Other Direct Transfers in Sri Lanka, 2000–12

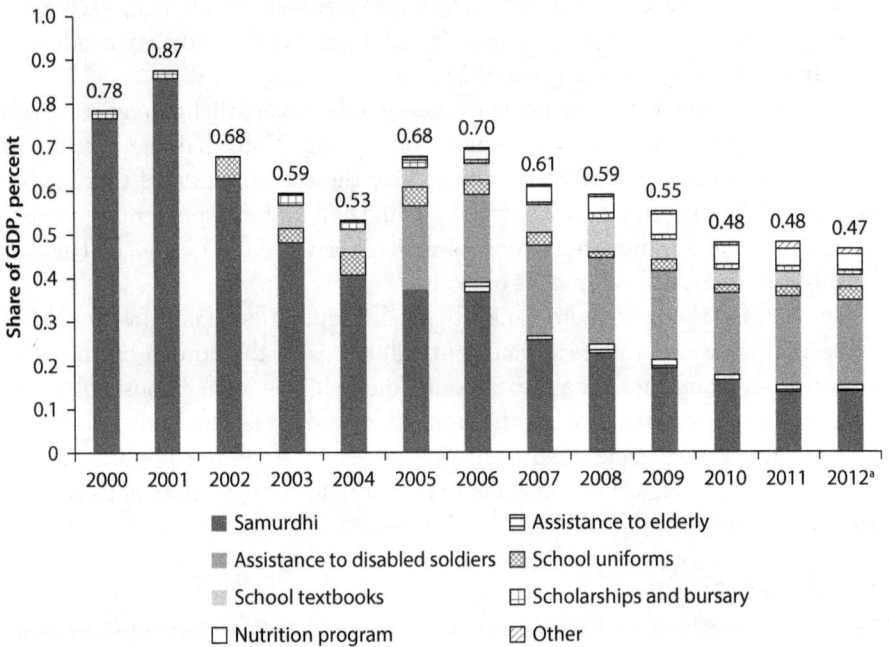

Source: CBSL 2013.
Note: The Samurdhi Poverty Alleviation Program is Sri Lanka's flagship cash transfer program and includes eight subprograms.
a. 2012 data are preliminary.

and have a much greater poverty impact. (Thirty percent of Samurdhi spending benefits households in the top 60 percent of the market income distribution, none of which are classified as poor.)

Other direct transfers—including assistance to disabled soldiers, free textbooks and school uniforms, and food assistance—are also progressive in absolute terms, equalizing, and poverty-reducing, with 57 percent of such spending benefiting the bottom 40 percent of the distribution. However, the amount of spending on these programs in 2009/10 was very small, amounting to 0.24 percent of GDP in 2009 and adding only 3 percent to market incomes of the poorest decile.

Indirect Subsidies

Spending on indirect subsidies (including fuel, fertilizer, water, and electricity subsidies) grew unpredictably over the 2000–10 decade, partly because fuel and electricity subsidies fluctuate with international prices. In 2009, indirect subsidies amounted to 1.27 percent of GDP, of which half was devoted to fertilizer subsidies (0.6 percent of GDP), representing more than six times the allocation for Samurdhi.

The results show that although these subsidies are progressive in relative terms and equalizing, they are not pro-poor (i.e., they are not progressive in absolute terms). This is because a large part of subsidies benefit nonpoor households. In particular, only about 35 percent of total spending on indirect subsidies for fertilizer, electricity, and water benefited the bottom 40 percent of the income distribution in 2009/10, and more than 20 percent benefited the top 20 percent[16]—partly because the poor lack access to land or piped water. Indeed, only 4.2 percent of paddy farmers with incomes of less than US$2.50 a day received fertilizer subsidies.[17] Access is one constraint, with 37 percent of individuals living on less than US$2.50 a day having access to electricity, and 34 percent having access to piped water. As a result, 65 percent of fertilizer subsidies, 73 percent of water subsidies, and 67 percent of electricity subsidies benefit households with incomes of more than US$2.50 a day.

Although indirect subsidies are not pro-poor, they represent an important benefit to the poor. If they are eliminated or reduced, the poor would have to be compensated so they are not made poorer by the change.

In-Kind Transfers

How much would a household's income need to increase if it were to pay for subsidized public services at the full cost to the government? To estimate the incidence of public spending on education and health, this subsection focuses on the so-called benefit or expenditure incidence—the government's cost approach. In essence, this question can be answered by using per beneficiary input costs obtained from administrative data as the measure of average benefits allocated to households. This approach is also known as the classic or nonbehavioral approach.

Taken together, spending on education and health is progressive and equalizing in Sri Lanka, but it was relatively low in 2009/10, with about 10 percent of spending captured by each decile. The analysis shows that spending on education up through secondary school is progressive and pro-poor. However, spending on tertiary education is progressive only in relative terms (as it is in other countries), given that students from poor households are less likely to attend.

Health spending is more pro-poor than education spending (figure 9.3). This is because the monetized value of health spending makes up a larger share of the market incomes of those at the bottom of the income distribution. Public spending on health is relatively well targeted not because poorer people have higher utilization rates, but more likely because high-income households choose not to use the public health care system.

Moreover, in assessing how education and health spending benefit the poor, we have to caution that our analysis does not address the quality of such spending. We use government expenditure data on the various forms of education and health services to estimate unit costs of these programs. The analysis thus assumes that the actual benefit received by individuals is equal to the amount spent per capita. Because the quality of school infrastructure, teachers, and

Figure 9.3 Share of In-Kind Education and Health Benefits, by Income Decile, in Sri Lanka, 2010

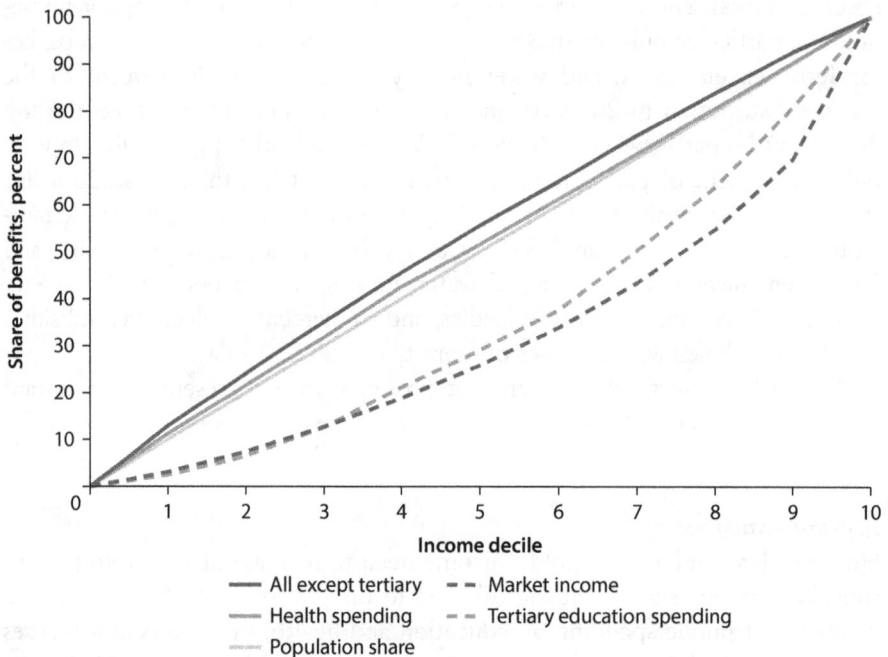

Source: Based on 2009/10 Household Income and Expenditure Survey (HIES) data.
Note: "Market income" comprises pretax wages, salaries, income earned from capital assets (rent, interest, or dividends), and private transfers. In this analysis, both contributory and noncontributory pensions are included in market income.

health clinics and hospitals vary across the country, this is a clear limitation of the analysis.

Although Sri Lanka has a net enrollment rate of almost 100 percent at the primary level, about 14 percent of households with school-aged children and per capita incomes of less than US$2.50 a day do not benefit from spending on education because the children do not attend school. This is partly because children in poor households are dropping out at the secondary level and therefore are not benefiting from spending on secondary or tertiary education. Even when we exclude tertiary education (of which only about 1.5 percent of enrollment comes from households with less than US$2.50 a day) we find that 32 percent of households with school-aged children and incomes of less than US$2.50 a day do not benefit from public spending on education below tertiary. This points to additional efforts required to improve enrollment and attendance rates among the poor.

More critically, the amount spent on education is low compared to other middle-income countries, not only in aggregate terms but also as a share of household incomes of the poor. As shown earlier (table 9.2), spending on education was less than 2 percent of GDP;[18] this level compares with 8.3 percent in Bolivia and 2.8 percent in Peru (see chapter 1).

Similarly, spending on health is woefully small relative to other middle-income countries, amounting to 1.5 percent of GDP, compared with 3.6 percent of GDP in Bolivia and 3.1 percent in Peru. Sri Lanka has a wide network of health care facilities throughout the country, and health is free of charge at public hospitals. Indeed, statistics show that access to institutional care and trained medical officers at birth is close to 100 percent in Sri Lanka. However, health care utilization rates for the bottom of the distribution are below the average for middle-income countries: 47 percent of households with incomes of less than US$2.50 a day do not use health services. This is high relative to Peru, where only 7 percent of similarly poor households do not use health care (see chapter 1).

Conclusions and Policy Implications

Sri Lanka has made substantial progress in reducing poverty over the past decade. However, important social and economic development needs persist at a time when revenue collections have been disappointing, reducing the government's ability to expand spending. In this context, this chapter has sought to evaluate the effectiveness of fiscal policy in addressing inequality and accelerating poverty reduction. The exercise consisted of undertaking incidence analysis of the major tax and transfer programs individually, and then combining them to evaluate the incidence of fiscal policy as a whole. Although we could not carry out incidence analysis of all budget items, we have analyzed the major tax and spending items for which individual tax and benefits can be assigned to households using microdata.

The analysis finds that taxes and social spending were redistributive and poverty-reducing overall. However, given the country's relatively low revenue and the limited fiscal space, overall social spending was small, leading to very limited impacts. Indeed, low revenue collection has recently led to reductions in spending to maintain macroeconomic stability. Those cuts have made it difficult to maintain funding for key social programs in real terms. The analysis has shown that although direct taxes provide a very small contribution to redistributive efforts, indirect taxes are regressive, unequalizing, and slightly poverty-increasing. Therefore, revenue mobilization efforts aimed at increasing or expanding the VAT system could have negative impacts on the poor unless the social protection system is expanded. These trade-offs need to be taken into account at the design stage, with careful distributional analysis accompanying any reform effort.

On the spending side, direct transfers are absolutely progressive, so that their marginal contribution is both equalizing and poverty-reducing. In terms of direct transfers, the analysis found that although the Samurdhi program was progressive, it was too small to truly make a significant dent in reducing poverty. Similarly, other direct transfers, including soldier disability payments, free schoolbooks, and uniforms are effective in reaching the poor but also make very small contributions to poor households. Given the expansion of the Samurdhi program beginning in 2015, it would be interesting to see whether the expansion has made a substantial difference.

In contrast, spending on indirect subsidies increased from being more than twice the amount spent on direct transfers in 2009 to being more than five times the amount spent on direct transfers in 2012, with a large part of the resources benefiting nonpoor households. Indirect subsidies are equalizing because these benefits are large relative to the incomes of the poor. However, they are quite an inefficient use of resources, because they benefit higher-income groups more than they benefit the bottom of the distribution.

Finally, the analysis found that in-kind transfers in the form of education and health are equalizing. Education spending has the largest redistributive impact, in line with other country studies in LMICs. This is partly due to high enrollment rates in primary and secondary education. Similarly, health expenditures are progressive and equalizing, but the amount of spending is woefully low.

Going forward, any efforts to reform taxes could usefully include distributional analysis. Should the government wish to consider a tax reform, a distributional analysis of alternative scenarios could shed light on the impacts of alternative ways to increase tax collection while protecting poorer groups.

Given the leakages to nonpoor households benefiting from indirect subsidies, their impact on poverty alleviation is limited. In contrast, social assistance spending through direct transfers to poorer groups has a greater impact on poverty. Investing a share of the spending on the larger indirect subsidy programs into direct transfer programs—with a focus on targeting vulnerable groups—could have important impacts on poverty and inequality.

Ideally, any reduction in indirect subsidies or increase in VAT would need to go hand in hand with the strengthening of benefit targeting through improved methodologies for determining eligibility and consistency in implementation. Direct transfer programs, if well targeted, are typically cost-effective and could substantially improve the effectiveness of direct transfers in reducing poverty and inequality. Ideally, the consolidation of existing fragmented programs and moving toward a consolidated, targeted, more-generous program could have a greater impact on poverty alleviation.

Notes

1. This analysis applies the framework developed by the Commitment to Equity Institute (Lustig and Higgins 2013a, Lustig 2017). For more information, see the CEQ Institute website: http://www.commitmentoequity.org/.

2. Spending data as a percentage of GDP from the World Economic Outlook database, International Monetary Fund, https://www.imf.org/external/pubs/ft/weo/2016/02/weodata/index.aspx.

3. Ceylon Petroleum Corporation, "Historical Prices," http://www.ceypetco.gov.lk/History.htm. Los Angeles spot price adjusted for transmission and distribution (T&D) cost. This analysis has been performed on diesel prices only.

4. "Other taxes and fees" include the Nation Building Tax (an ad valorem 2 percent tax on the price of goods and services at the point of sale), the Ports and Airport Development Levy, the Stamp Duty, the Special Commodity Levy, the Regional Development Levy, the Cess Levy, and the Social Responsibility Levy. Note that in November 2009, customs duty, port levy, nation building tax, social responsibility levy, and value added tax were replaced by a lower special commodity levy (Mukherji and Iyengar 2013).

5. Households earning a monthly income of less than SL Rs 1,500 qualified for the program. Eligible families with six or more members receive SL Rs 1,500 a month (US$13.05 at the 2009 average exchange rate); those with 3–5 members, 2 members, and 1 member receive SL Rs 900 (US$7.83), SL Rs 525 (US$4.57), and SL Rs 375 (US$3.26), respectively. Beneficiaries exit the program when household income increased to SL Rs 2,000 for a consecutive period of six months or when a household member found employment.

6. Transfers for life events are as follows: SL Rs 10,000 (US$87 at the 2009 average exchange rate) at the death of any household member; SL Rs 5,000 (US$43.50) at the birth of the first baby and SL Rs 2,500 (US$21.75) at the birth of the second baby; and SL Rs 3,000 (US$26.10) is provided for 30 days at a rate of SL Rs 100 (US$0.87) per day during illness.

7. The nutrition allowance is a monthly stamp aid of SL Rs 200 (US$1.74 at the 2009 average exchange rate), while the Nutrition Food Package is a monthly stamp (voucher) that can be used for food purchases of SL Rs 500 (US$4.35).

8. The program falls under the purview of Ministry of Child Development and women's affairs.

9. Note that in-kind education spending does not include uniforms, textbooks, and scholarships, all of which are considered part of direct transfers. The structure of the Sri Lankan education system consists of primary (grades 1–5), junior secondary (grades 6–9), senior secondary (grades 10–11), collegiate (grades 12–13), and tertiary education levels. It is legally mandatory for students to study until the senior secondary level.

10. Contributory pensions include the Social Pension and Social Benefit scheme; the Widows, Widowers, and Orphans Pension scheme, the Public Service Provident Fund, and the Farmer's and Fisherman's Pension scheme.

11. The effective tax rate is defined as total VAT collections divided by taxable consumption. In this case, the effective tax rate for luxuries is taken to be 20 percent and, for basic goods, 7 percent (based on the effective tax rate for manufactured goods).

12. Typically, Sri Lanka measures welfare using a household consumption aggregate. This welfare measure is what we describe as "disposable income," as it corresponds to household consumption on goods and services paid for from sources that include public transfers and are after direct tax payments. Thus, the headcount rate for disposable income using the national poverty line is 8.7 percent, coinciding with the official headcount rate for 2009/10.

13. The fiscal transition matrix, for analysis within the CEQ framework, was introduced in Higgins and Lustig (2016).

14. Kakwani coefficients are calculated by subtracting an intervention's concentration coefficient from the market-income Gini; progressive interventions have positive Kakwani coefficients, and regressive ones have negative coefficients (Kakwani 1977).

15. Spending is considered "progressive" whenever the concentration coefficient is lower than the Gini for market income—meaning that the benefits from that spending as a share of market income tend to fall with market income. Spending is "pro-poor" whenever the concentration coefficient is not only lower than the Gini but also negative. Pro-poor spending implies that the *per capita* government spending on the transfer *tends* to fall with market income. For further discussion of "progressive" and "pro-poor" spending, see chapter 1.

16. This analysis does not include analysis of fuel subsidies because of their relatively small size in 2009.

17. Of a total of 7.791 million paddy farmers who report receiving fertilizer subsidies (farmers with less than five acres of land), only 327,374 have market incomes of less than US$2.50 per person per day.

18. Spending on education excludes spending that is included as part of direct transfers, including expenditures on textbooks, uniforms, scholarships, and school feeding programs.

References

CBSL (Central Bank of Sri Lanka). 2011. *Annual Report 2010.* CBSL, Colombo.

———. 2013. *Annual Report 2012.* CBSL, Colombo.

Ceriani, Lidia, Gabriela Inchauste, and Sergio Olivieri. 2015. "Understanding Poverty Reduction in Sri Lanka: Evidence from 2002 to 2012/13." Policy Research Working Paper 7446, World Bank, Washington, DC.

Gaminiratne, Nirosha. 2004. "Population Ageing, Elderly Welfare, and Extending Retirement Cover: Case Study of Sri Lanka." ESAU Working Paper 3, Economics and Statistics Analysis Unit, Overseas Development Institute, London.

Gunatilaka, R., R. Salih, R. Perera, and C. De Silva. 1997. *Samurdhi Programme: A Preliminary Assessment.* Report on the National Poverty Alleviation Programme for the Ministry of Finance and Planning, Colombo, Sri Lanka.

Higgins, Sean, and Nora Lustig. 2016. "Can a Poverty-Reducing and Progressive Tax and Transfer System Hurt the Poor?" *Journal of Development Economics* 122 (September): 63–75.

Kakwani, Nanak C. 1977. "Measurement of Tax Progressivity: An International Comparison." *The Economic Journal* 87 (345): 71–80.

Lustig, Nora. 2017. *Commitment to Equity Handbook: Estimating the Impact of Fiscal Policy on Inequality and Poverty.* Washington, DC: Brookings Institution Press and CEQ Institute, Tulane University. Advance online version; available at http://www.com mitmentoequity.org/publications/handbook.php.

Lustig, Nora, and Sean Higgins. 2013a. "Commitment to Equity Assessment (CEQ): A Diagnostic Framework to Assess Governments' Fiscal Policies. Handbook." Working Paper 1119, Department of Economics, Tulane University, New Orleans, LA.

———. 2013b. "Commitment to Equity Assessment (CEQ): Estimating the Incidence of Social Spending, Subsidies and Taxes." Handbook and Commitment to Equity (CEQ) Working Paper 1, Center for Inter-American Policy and Research (CIPR); the Inter-American Dialogue; and Department of Economics, Tulane University, New Orleans, LA.

Mukherji, Indra Nath, and Kavita Iyengar, eds. 2013. *Deepening Economic Cooperation between India and Sri Lanka*. Manila: Asian Development Bank.

Sri Lanka, Ministry of Finance and Planning. 2012. "Revision of Customs Duties and Excise Taxes—31.03.2012." Press Release, March 31. http://203.94.72.22/depts/mofp/taxnews/vehicleTaxes20120402-en.pdf.

———. 2016. *Annual Report 2015*. May 31. http://www.treasury.gov.lk/documents/10181/12870/2015/68f51df3-5465-4805-ab6f-4a024ec672f6?version=1.1.

Sri Lanka, Ministry of Finance and Planning. 2009. *Annual Report 2009*. December 31. http://www.treasury.gov.lk/documents/10181/12870/2009/58021c57-e8c6-4d64-ad77-ce7d3978cec9?version=1.0.

———. 2010. *Fiscal Management Report—2010*. June 29. http://203.94.72.22/reports/fmr/fmr2010-eng.pdf.

———. 2012. "Revision of Customs Duties and Excise Taxes—31.03.2012." Press Release, March 31. http://203.94.72.22/depts/mofp/taxnews/vehicleTaxes20120402-en.pdf.

Theil, H. 1967. *Economics and Information Theory*. Chicago: Rand McNally and Company.

Thibbotuwawa, R., B. Printhika, U. Jayasinghe-Mudalige, and J. Udugama. 2012. "Impact of Microfinance on Household Welfare: Assessing the Case of Samurdhi Program in Sri Lanka." Paper presented at the 56th Annual Australian Agricultural and Resource Economics Society (AARES) National Conference, Fremantle, February 7–10. http://ageconsearch.umn.edu/bitstream/124320/2/2012AC%20Jayasinghe%20CP.pdf.

World Bank. 2015. "Sri Lanka: Ending Poverty and Promoting Shared Prosperity: A Systematic Country Diagnostic." Report 103246, World Bank, Washington, DC. http://documents.worldbank.org/curated/en/363391467995349383/pdf/103246-SCD-P152526-PUBLIC-NON-BOARD-VERSION-SriLankaCompleteFinal-122515lr-2.pdf.

Environmental Benefits Statement

The World Bank Group is committed to reducing its environmental footprint. In support of this commitment, we leverage electronic publishing options and print-on-demand technology, which is located in regional hubs worldwide. Together, these initiatives enable print runs to be lowered and shipping distances decreased, resulting in reduced paper consumption, chemical use, greenhouse gas emissions, and waste.

We follow the recommended standards for paper use set by the Green Press Initiative. The majority of our books are printed on Forest Stewardship Council (FSC)–certified paper, with nearly all containing 50–100 percent recycled content. The recycled fiber in our book paper is either unbleached or bleached using totally chlorine-free (TCF), processed chlorine–free (PCF), or enhanced elemental chlorine–free (EECF) processes.

More information about the Bank's environmental philosophy can be found at http://www.worldbank.org/corporateresponsibility.

green press INITIATIVE

www.ingramcontent.com/pod-product-compliance
Lightning Source LLC
Chambersburg PA
CBHW081429270326
41932CB00019B/3137